Politics Inc.

Politics Inc.

America's Troubled Democracy and How to Fix It

John Raidt

Foreword by
General James N. Mattis

ROWMAN & LITTLEFIELD
Lanham • Boulder • New York • London

Published by Rowman & Littlefield
An imprint of The Rowman & Littlefield Publishing Group, Inc.
4501 Forbes Boulevard, Suite 200, Lanham, Maryland 20706
www.rowman.com

86-90 Paul Street, London EC2A 4NE, United Kingdom

British Library Cataloguing in Publication Information Available

Library of Congress Cataloging-in-Publication Data

Names: Raidt, John, 1960- author.
Title: Politics Inc. : America's troubled democracy and how to fix it / John Raidt ; foreword by General James N. Mattis.
Other titles: Politics Incorporated

Description: Lanham : Rowman & Littlefield, [2021] | Includes bibliographical references and index. | Summary: "The book examines the dynamics driving the country's deeply troubled political culture and highlights reforms needed in the post-Trump era to strengthen US democracy. The author paints a clear and sobering portrait of a mercenary election industry and its support structure tailored to perpetuate and exploit America's social and political division"— Provided by publisher.
Identifiers: LCCN 2021032089 (print) | LCCN 2021032090 (ebook) | ISBN 9781538151259 (Cloth : acid-free paper) | ISBN 9781538151266 (ePub)
Subjects: LCSH: Democracy—United States. | Liberty—United States. | Political culture—United States. | Elections—Corrupt practices—United States. | Voting—United States. | United States—Politics and government.

Classification: LCC JK1726 .R35 2021 (print) | LCC JK1726 (ebook) | DDC 320.473—dc23
LC record available at https://lccn.loc.gov/2021032089
LC ebook record available at https://lccn.loc.gov/2021032090

Contents

Acknowledgments   vii

Foreword   ix
    General James N. Mattis

Preface   xi

 1   The System Is Blinking Red   1

 2   Politics Incorporated (Power Gear)   15

 3   Endless and Dirty Campaigns (Tactics Gear)   31

 4   Money Chase (Financial Gear)   45

 5   Running in Place (Structural Gear)   61

 6   Suffering Suffrage (Structural Gear)   75

 7   Laws and Sausages (Structural Gear)   91

 8   Mercenary Media (Media Gear)   107

 9   High Tech and Low Down (Technology Gear)   125

10   We the Problem (Cultural Gear)   143

11   The Casualty of Virtues   157

12   The American Evolution   175

Notes   187

Index   235

About the Author   247

Acknowledgments

The author wishes to express his deep gratitude to those whose inspiration, expertise, and assistance made this project possible. Foremost, to my family, W. T. and Joan Marie, Bill, Ellen, Judy, Doug, and Bob, thank you for your love and support, and to my friend and mentor General Jim Jones. To the Atlantic Council, whose early advocacy and input was instrumental to this project, including David Bray, Ian Brzezinski, Mat Burrows, Fred Kempe, Matthew Kroenig, Andrew Marshall, Barry Pavel, Ellen Riina, Mike Rossi, and Damon Wilson. Many thanks to the honored group of friends and colleagues, brought together so long ago by John McCain, who provided their insights and support, including Rick Davis, Joe Donoghue, Carla Eudy, Christian Ferry, Nancy Ives, Trevor Potter (and his associate Brendan Fischer), Sonya Sotak, Becky Tallent, and Craig Turk; and to Mark Salter for his special assistance.

With enormous appreciation for the outstanding help and support provided by Daria Boulos, Alice Falk, Romina Fincher, and Steve Smith; and to Doug Raidt for his vital contribution and encouragement from the beginning. Thank you as well for the input of Mike Barbero, Tom Eldridge, John Farmer, Mike Hurley, Ed Norton, Robert "Wheels" Wheeler, and Quinn Bottum. To the amazing people at Rowman & Littlefield, Jed Lyons, Jon Sisk, Benjamin Knepp, Brianna Westervelt, Elaine McGarraugh, Sarah Sachina, and Sally Rinehart, much gratitude for your superb guidance and professionalism and for giving me the opportunity to make the case, and to Bob Tyrer for his friendship and support. Finally, to the late Ellen Tauscher, who was an early advocate of this work. We miss you. To sweetest Romina.

Foreword

General James N. Mattis

Underlying the undeniably serious and complex problems we are facing as Americans—including the immediate and lasting effects of a pandemic, deepening evidence of a climate crisis, the return of great power competition, and ongoing terror threats around the world, to name but a few—is a much more urgent and existential question: how to stop the corrosive and cynical rot inside our political system that is making it increasingly difficult to find constructive solutions to the simplest problems, let alone the truly vexing issues that need our attention.

That citizens and leaders have robust and differing viewpoints on how problems should be solved is an elemental aspect of our democratic system. What has changed so dangerously is the increasing tone of contempt, suspicion, cynicism, and disrespect that has increasingly infected life and discourse in the public square.

The founders of our country had an unsentimental assessment of human nature and created institutions designed to withstand the frailties and shortcomings of the participants. But it was beyond question that everyone taking part in that grand experiment was united in a common cause to create and sustain this new nation.

Too often today, we appear to have lost sight of the principles that citizens of this or any democracy must live by and the shared responsibilities citizens must embrace, whatever our individual differences. The foundational virtue of democracy is trust in the capacity of collective deliberation to move us forward. Taking office as President in 1861 in a moment of national crisis, Abraham Lincoln said this to the deeply divided nation: "We are not enemies, but friends. We must not be enemies. Though passion may have strained, it must not break our bonds of affection."

It is getting harder and harder to recognize those "bonds of affection" between citizens who hold different viewpoints today. Too often, we snarl at each other in the harshest terms. We refuse to concede that a person we disagree with could be right. When we most need our leaders and citizens to display humility, patience, and determination, too often they are shrill, cynical, and unserious.

Instead of celebrating the enduring wisdom of the institutions created by our founders, we are living through a season of mindless populism, the belief that public passions should be translated directly into policy without being considered and refined through our representative institutions. Political leaders often seem frightened of their voters, and as a result don't respect them enough to speak with candor and wisdom. Increasingly elected officials are unwilling to seek thoughtful compromise, instead playing to the "base" and doing so without courage, conviction, or collegiality.

The consequences of this descent into national fracturing and disunity and the increasingly sclerotic nature of our system are dismally clear. In addition to our increasing difficulty solving complex problems at home, our internal discord reduces our ability to lead on the global stage, invites threats from malign actors, and results in allies and adversaries alike not respecting us as they once did.

In *Politics Inc.*, John Raidt has given us both a thoughtful and sober diagnosis of the many origins of our current situation as well as a powerful call to action on how we can reverse course and begin to reclaim our core values. He makes a careful and well-informed assessment of how current incentive structures in many parts of our system result in a distortion of the "common ground and common good" that a healthy system must have. This is an important book that should be read with care by any citizen who is rightly distraught about the worrisome state of our system of self-government and is looking for a hopeful and constructive road map to improvement.

Our wisest leaders knew that America can never be judged by our best or worst moments and be considered either a finished work or a failed project. We are an ongoing experiment, and a far more fragile one than is often imagined. As John Raidt argues eloquently in this book, we can no longer take for granted the freedoms we enjoy. This is a moment of crisis requiring the urgent attention of all citizens who wish to strengthen the country we love, and we must act.

Speaking in 1940 to the Harvard Class of 1910 at their 30th reunion as the darkening clouds of World War II were upon us, Walter Lippmann said these words that apply to us more than 80 years later:

> Upon the standard to which the wise and honest will now repair it is written: You have lived the easy way; henceforth, you will live the hard way. You came into a great heritage made by the insight and the sweat and the blood of inspired and devoted and courageous men; thoughtlessly and in utmost self-indulgence you have all but squandered this inheritance. Now only by the heroic virtues which made this inheritance can you restore it again. You took the good things for granted. Now you must earn them again. For every right that you cherish, you have a duty which you must fulfill. For every hope that you entertain, you have a task that you must perform. For every good that you wish to preserve, you will have to sacrifice your comfort and your ease. There is nothing for nothing any longer.

James N. Mattis
Richland, Washington
September 17, 2021

Preface

In 2007, the US-led multinational force in Iraq surged to quell insurgent and terrorist violence sowing chaos in the fledgling democracy. Alongside combat operations, the United States and its allies had undertaken a comprehensive training mission to strengthen free Iraq's ability to stand up a government and provide for its own security. Having worked for two national commissions reporting to the public and Congress on national security matters, I was asked by General James Jones, former commandant of the United States Marine Corps, to aid him as part of a Senate-mandated panel to independently assess the mission readiness of Iraq's security forces.

The team's early itinerary included a site visit for a briefing by US military personnel at a combat outpost located along the Tigris River in Baghdad in an area that had seen some of the heaviest fighting. In the headquarters' foyer was a large wall displaying the portraits of US service members who had lost their lives in that sector. This heartbreaking memorial resembled the yearbook pages of a typical American high school or college. The faces of the fallen kept flashing through my mind. I wondered about their hopes and dreams and about their families, friends, hometowns, and lost futures. Accompanying the sense of mourning, a strain of anger welled up as I contemplated a terrible truth manifest by their sacrifice—the jarring disparity between the devotion and professionalism that America's service members exhibit defending democracy abroad and how the country's political ranks and election industry had come to practice democracy at home.

The dishonor done to the former by the latter and the unforgettable faces on that wall were the impetus to write this book. It's a project that proved long past due on January 6, 2021, when a mob stormed the US Capitol to disrupt the democratic process that countless Americans have given all to preserve and protect.

The bulk of my career in public service was spent working on the staff of Senator John McCain. His love for America and understanding of what the country and democracy mean to the enduring cause of freedom and human rights inspired and informed this undertaking. I can't be certain he would agree with all the findings and recommendations set forth in the following pages about the forces afflicting America's political life and how to fix it, but I know he would be in sync with most. Above all, he would agree on the essentiality of a concerted reform movement to right American political culture and to restore the functionality of the nation's democratic institutions and processes if the United States is to remain a force for good in a needy world.

When I started on his staff in the 1980s, congressional ethos and the national political culture it reflected was far different than what the country has come to know. In a long and honored tradition, elected representatives came to the nation's capital from the four corners of the country bearing wide philosophical differences, all shades of opinion, and native interests befitting a pluralistic democracy. Though rivalrous, the people's branch operated with a sense of institutional pride and purpose and a commitment to fulfilling its constitutional responsibilities fairly and functionally.

House and Senate members would clash passionately over policy but at the end of the day shake hands, call one another friend, and mean it. Norms of collegiality and fairness were conscientiously observed by a largely respectful majority and reliably loyal opposition. A general reverence for shared national principles framed the day-to-day questions and controversies over national interest and precisely how Americanism should be expressed in law and policy. That's not to say that the national legislature and the hard work of policy making were harmonious and docile enterprises. Such was never meant to be in a true democracy. But elected representatives had decent opportunity to be heard and their ideas considered and to perform their constitutional duties through fair and participatory processes.

Over the ensuing years, the character and capacities of America's political culture and institutions sunk into decline under the sway of the discrete forces described in the forthcoming pages—catalyzed by a mercenary election industry and a stale party duopoly. The nation's policy debates and political campaigns grew ever more degrading. Permanent campaign mode overtook the people's branch of government, its processes corrupted and incapacitated by rivalry resorting to demonization and blame. As the cost of running for office skyrocketed, political fundraising became obsessive and distracting, fueled by rising levels of partisan animus—the nastier the better. Electioneers and their issue advocacy groups found defter ways to create and cash in on public disputes, stoking political division and twisting the nation's pluralism into factionalism. Meanwhile, the power to shape and govern the nation's two main political parties migrated from their members to hired campaign professionals and political consultants. The institutions of elective politics came to look and operate less like the hallowed apparatus of democratic government and more like an industry with a business model based on perpetuating and exploiting domestic conflict.

As American political culture became more fractured, the nation's leadership found it increasingly difficult to forge consensus on which problems demanded national attention, much less on practical ways to solve them. Many of the country's public institutions, most notably Congress, grew dangerously dysfunctional. Official proceedings took on an air of political performance art and partisan theater. When favored special interests came calling or partisan advantage was at risk, public interest became expendable.

This lesson was driven home to me while serving as lead staffer on the Senate Commerce Committee for major 1998 tobacco legislation. Sponsored by Senator McCain, the measure sought to address the costly public health crisis fostered by the tobacco industry's long-running campaign to market its addictive products to kids. After a record number of weeks of debate on the Senate floor, the bill neared its final fate. The parties met in their respective caucuses to discuss how the endgame would play out. In the Republican conference, a senior GOP leader announced that the tobacco companies had pledged to donate generously to the campaigns of members willing to vote against the measure. In the Democrats' caucus, a senior member warned his colleagues that passage of a strong Republican-sponsored public health bill over the tobacco companies' opposition would deliver a devastating blow to the Democratic Party's traditional advantage on the issue. That afternoon the bill went down to defeat on a procedural vote. The parties got precisely what they wanted. Public interest? Not so much.

Press releases gushed from the Hill with justifications bearing no mention of the tobacco companies' promised largesse or the bare-knuckle partisan calculus that sealed the measure's fate. For the warring political parties, winning the news cycle had become the supreme objective, granting power to words over deeds and perception over reality. All the better for maintaining partisan tensions at a steady boil to feed the election industry's need for dispute.

Among the most insightful observations I have heard about modern Washington is that delivered by former secretary of state Henry Kissinger. When asked how national leadership had changed over his long service, he replied without hesitation that in earlier times politicians "asked me what I think. Today when one meets politicians, they ask one what to say. Those are two different problems. And I don't blame the politicians for that. It's in the nature of our system."

Kissinger put his finger on the problem. The very nature of the American system has been altered in ways the founders never intended and that cannot sustain healthy democracy. The country's rational center has been outflanked and marginalized by the ideological fringes crippling the capacity for constructive compromise. Centrists who had long served as the bridgework between the Republican and Democratic bases have all but disappeared from office. Once regarded as statesmen, they have been defeated or chased away from public life by party hardliners and campaign professionals who benefit from conflict-oriented and winner-take-all approaches to American governance. Vanishing with them is the construction zone for functional democracy, endangering the nation's unity, prosperity, and security.

Hijacked and incapacitated by the election industry, America's troubled political culture has sparked a crisis in public confidence, government competence, and national political legitimacy. The handiwork of "Politics Inc." can be summed up in a simple, tweetable handle: *#alienation*. The parties have been alienated from one another, the citizenry from their government, the executive branch from Congress, Congress from its duties, many good people from elective service, and the political process from the virtues that sustain healthy democracy.

Most damagingly, the electorate has been alienated from the hope that our political culture is fixable or even that our system is preferable. Many young people have lost faith in democracy, disgusted by inadequate outcomes and convinced by the political class that Americans don't agree on much anymore. Nonsense! Despite the turmoil, America's unifying principles stand unimpeached, even if they are unappreciated and overlooked. Poll Americans of any generation, and one would be hard-pressed to locate a bona fide critic of the right to life, liberty, and the pursuit of happiness. The protection of human rights, equal justice under law, self-determination, and self-governance would show wildly popular across party lines. Though we may argue about where the line should be drawn, public approval for limits on the power and reach of government would likely register at near 100 percent. The desire for public-sector proficiency in its rightful roles and missions would rank as high, as would supporting entrepreneurship, encouraging and rewarding work and productivity, and helping those in need.

Contrary to the fringy advocates of anarchy at the noisy extremes, most Americans wouldn't abandon support for rule of law if given thoughtful study or a taste of life without it. Most certain of all is a widely shared faith in love over hate and a preference for national cooperation and consensus over antagonism and extremism, at least in the hearts of the muted political center and outshouted majority.

The truth is that America's core principles are not the source of America's troubles. They remain our strength and hope. Trouble has come when we have failed to respect and live by them. Unless America's public officials reconnect earnestly with our principles and democratic virtues and leverage them to make our politics and governance more cohesive and functional, we risk all.

Every four years the federal government produces a National Security Strategy to spotlight threats to the country and outline strategies for countering them. Conspicuously left unmentioned is our nation's political deterioration, though it is a clearer and more present danger than any martial threat from abroad. It imperils the nation's most precious asset—who we are and what we stand for as a people. And, ultimately, it undermines the country's ability to counter every other threat we face.

Chief among them are threats posed by autocratic powers looking to displace American leadership and shape a very different global future. Strategic competitors thrill at clear signs the United States is weakening from within, and they are working diligently to exploit our internal divisions. The outcome of the contest between democracy and autocracy will determine whether mankind lives in freedom protected by self-government, respect for human rights, and the rule of law or under arbitrary power and its familiar evils.

History tells us that American leadership—security, economic, technological, and political leadership—is indispensable if light is to prevail over darkness and mankind is to surmount the sweeping challenges that will define the future. Ensuring food, energy, and water security to meet the needs of a growing population while coping with a changing climate is an existential mission, as is confronting the unyielding menace of global pandemics. Science is poised to fully unleash powerful new technologies—artificial intelligence, machine learning, advanced robotics—that can either be harnessed to enhance human life or weaponized to destroy it. Solving each of these challenges the right way is a job for democracies requiring American democracy at its best just as we seem to have lost our sense of who we are, what we stand for, and how much we are counted on. Unless we right our political culture and processes, desperately needed American global leadership cannot be sustained, the many challenges we face cannot be overcome, and our ability to author a better future will not be possible.

The dynamics undermining American democracy and political culture are multifaceted and complex. Nevertheless, they are understandable. Most importantly, they are fixable. But only if we break the stale party duopoly and dismantle the infrastructure that Politics Inc. has erected to serve itself at the country's expense. This book unpacks the machinery driving the political division, official dysfunction, and steady deterioration of American democracy. It dissects the technological and cultural forces abetting the damage and lays out an agenda for comprehensive reform.

The stakes could not be higher or the urgency greater. Political modernization is the gateway to all we must accomplish in this century. On it depends the fate of liberty and progress of humanity—the indispensable mission for the indispensable nation. This duty is not imposed on government alone but is the responsibility of "we the people," owed to those who selflessly gave their all so we could live in a better world and to posterity to whom we owe the same. This book is dedicated to that mission.

1

The System Is Blinking Red

I'm very disappointed, and I hate leaving the world feeling this way.

—Private Jack Port, 97, June 6, 2019

On June 6, 1944, seventy-three thousand young Americans took part in the largest amphibious landing in history to end the evil of Nazism. Of those who stormed the beaches and dropped from the sky to overcome Hitler's Atlantic Wall, 6,603 would never come home. Each year, survivors of Operation Overlord assemble in northern France in the shadow of the US cemetery overlooking the North Atlantic to remember those who gave all to spare mankind an unthinkable fate. Ninety-seven-year-old Private Jack Port is among those who have returned regularly to honor their fallen comrades. While marking the seventy-fifth anniversary of D-Day in June 2019, he expressed sadness about the state of the American polity, speaking not only for his generation and their sacrifices but also for the nation and directly to it.[1]

Several months before the ceremony, amid partisan hostility that seemed to be deepening by the day, Pew Research Center had unveiled a public survey finding that 85 percent of Americans were worried or very worried about the way Washington works and "about the ability of political leaders to solve the nation's biggest problems."[2] A strong majority of respondents expected US political polarization to worsen. Most alarmingly, Americans found their leaders worse than misguided or incompetent: four out of five Americans expressed the belief that government can't be trusted most of the time, an all-time high.[3] The results were equivalent to a diagnosis of national cancer. In 1960, the question about "trust in government" yielded inverse findings: three-quarters of Americans said they trusted Washington all or most of the time. Pew has polled the question practically every year for the past six

1

decades.[4] The results chart a ski slope of decline, plummeting over the Obama and Trump administrations.

To most people the system seems better engineered for campaigning than governing, more apt to widen and exploit public divisions than reconcile them, and far more proficient at assigning blame for problems than solving them. Year after year, the country fails to perceive any semblance of bipartisan priority setting, collaboration, or comprehensive joint strategies to tackle big challenges.

Pew's findings on "polarization" were striking for another reason—their context. The poll was taken amid Congress's fiery hearings on foreign interference in US elections. At the time, ugly political Twitter fights and general partisan warfare were raging up and down Pennsylvania Avenue, across Capitol Hill, in the nation's chatrooms, and on the nightly cable opinion-casts. Given the withering crossfire, it seemed inconceivable that political polarization could intensify. Moreover, the United States was deep into a strong economic run, with historically high employment and a soaring stock market. The public's bleak view bucked the conventional wisdom about the linkage between economic prosperity and civic optimism. Most Americans, it seems, were deeply skeptical that the country could long maintain economic highs, much less meet other pressing national needs, when the leading political indicators kept tumbling to new lows.

DEGRADING POLITICAL CULTURE

Who can fault them? The preceding presidential campaign, Donald Trump versus Hillary Clinton, had been a national embarrassment. Big-time political campaigns are notorious for personal attacks, dirty pool, loose facts, low blows, and incendiary rhetoric, but this one added an alarming dose of a more lethal civic poison—partisan hostility descending into downright hatred. Gallup polls showed that a majority of Americans deeply disapproved of both candidates, whose election eve ratings were the worst of any major party presidential candidates since 1956.[5] In a March 2016 article titled "The Worst of All Worlds," Ron Fournier, author and former senior political columnist at *National Journal*, captured the low expectations for the campaign: "Today begins a process driven by their *aspersions* toward one candidate rather than their *aspirations* for another—the acceleration of a grim trend that political scientists call 'negative partisanship.'"[6] True to form, the high-intensity, low-substance contest featured a full complement of attack ads, personal insults, and verbal slap fights masquerading as debates.

The debasement of American political culture took its toll again in the 2018 midterm elections. A whopping fifty-two House members passed on running for reelection. The main reason given by departing members according to Issue One, a Washington-based political reform advocacy group including former members of Congress and former senior officials, was "the partisanship and dysfunction of Congress."[7]

The 2020 presidential election pitting incumbent Donald Trump against former vice president Joe Biden showed no improvement. The contest will go down among the nation's strangest elections. As public attention focused on the COVID-19 pandemic and racial unrest, presidential and congressional campaign activities and party primaries were relegated to a kind of sideshow. Worse, the crisis response was hampered by election-time posturing and finger-pointing and by the politicization of public health. Dr. Anthony Fauci, respected director of the US National Institute of Allergy and Infectious Diseases and a lead member of Trump's White House Coronavirus Task Force, believes that partisan politics contributed to the pandemic's massive US death toll.[8]

The candidates charged one another with mental unfitness for office. September polling in swing states showed their aspersions were sticking.[9] Political violence flared during and after the election. For the second consecutive presidential election, the losing political party charged that the election was stolen, but 2020 breached the limits. The January 6, 2021, siege on the Capitol triggered by bogus claims of election rigging brought American democracy to a previously unimaginable abyss, ending the unbroken tradition of peaceful transfer of power. Five Americans lost their lives, including a Capitol Hill police officer. Fifty officers were injured. Voting administrators and officials in both parties who authenticated the election came under threat.

Two months after the election, one-third of Americans still believed that voter fraud helped Biden win, even though Trump's own attorney general found no evidence of results-altering cheating.[10] Legal battles challenging the results still raged. NATO's secretary general publicly called on the country to respect the results of its democratic election, playing the role usually taken by the United States as the world's leading advocate of free elections and rule of law.[11]

The first Trump-Biden debate and the storming of the Capitol crystallized the accumulating fears of America's friends and allies about the perilous state of US political culture and its effects.[12] They look on our system's self-destructiveness and incapacity with growing alarm, knowing that gangrenous political culture is not the hallmark of a sustainable superpower. Fearing the implications for the future, the world asks the same head-shaking question that torments most Americans: What has become of the world's greatest democracy?

The answer resides in accreting forces long at work that no single election can reverse and no party or politician can wave away. Run charts covering many years and presidential administrations plot out steady declines in bipartisan cooperation, interparty confidence, Republican and Democratic Party favorability, and public faith in the political process. The drops are matched by steep rises in the length and cost of campaigns, the negativity of political ads, congressional gridlock, and defection from the Republican and Democratic Parties. Behind these gradients are systemic causes far deeper and more troubling than an electoral bump in the road or reflexive public grumbling about politicians and politics.

The following chapters describe the causes and implications behind toxic deficits in the qualities and virtues vital to healthy democracy—call it the software of self-governance. Respect for facts and truth is evaporating, impeding rational debate and the ability of the electorate and their political representative to make well-informed and wise decisions. Vital balances essential for maintaining the fairness and functionality of the political process are askew. Inclusiveness that gives the democratic process legitimacy and sustainability remains dangerously low. Civility and respect for norms are sliding, eroding trust and pushing principled compromise and consensus further out of reach. Lines of duty and responsibility are being erased, undermining the good order and discipline of the nation's public institutions and processes.

Whether the cause or an effect of a troubled political system at risk (or most likely both), serious thinkers, problem solvers, and leaders are disappearing from public office. Most dangerous of all, our political culture's poor vital signs are undercutting the public's faith in the civic processes and institutions designed to serve them and in democracy itself.

BROKEN GOVERNANCE

Spoiled political culture does more than wound the nation's spirit and character; it incapacitates governance, materially damaging the life of the nation and its citizens by allowing major national problems to fester and opportunities to better the future slip away.

General James Jones, former NATO commander and President Obama's first national security adviser, defined national decline to be "when a nation can no longer do what it knows it must for its own good." The list of monumental challenges the country knows must be overcome is growing longer and harder to fix as the warring political parties persist in endless campaign mode, wrestling one another into nationally debilitating stalemate.

Massive federal debt is a ticking time bomb. By 2030, not counting the colossal government spending on the COVID-19 pandemic, the United States will be in hock more than $36 trillion (nearing twice the nation's annual GDP, the equivalent of $110,000 for every American).[13] Each year a larger share of the federal budget is gobbled up to pay interest on the debt, leaving less money to fund pressing national priorities. By 2024, the country will spend as much on debt service as it does on national defense.[14]

Vital entitlement programs grow more insolvent by the day. Medicare will be unable to cover its costs by 2026 and Social Security by 2034. Our health and education systems remain deficient. The country vastly outspends every other country in health care but lags well behind advanced economies in access, cost control, and public health results. The nation's education system is producing an alarming number of dropouts and a student body unready for the jobs of the future and the responsibilities of self-government. Only about one-third of US eighth graders meet national proficiency standards in math and reading, and their science achievement is dismal.[15] In a candid interview about US elementary and secondary education, former secretary of education Arne Duncan lamented, "We're not top 10 in anything."[16]

Cyberinfrastructure touching every system supporting the national economy and American life remains a highly vulnerable target for adversaries. The volume and sophistication of cyberassaults on the country grow exponentially each year, as does their catastrophic potential.[17] Yet, in a comprehensive 2020 report, the US Cyberspace Solarium Commission found the country still has no clear national cybersecurity strategy and "is weighed down by an industrial-era bureaucracy and a labyrinth of outdated rules, laws, and regulations that limit America's ability to defend cyberspace."[18]

Practical efforts to confront climate change languish in partisan limbo despite stark warnings from three former secretaries of defense, two former secretaries of state, and forty senators, Republicans and Democrats, that the buildup of greenhouse gases in the atmosphere is "shaping a world that is more unstable, resource-constrained, violent, and disaster prone."[19]

The catalog of unmet national imperatives includes repairing a long-broken immigration system, overhauling byzantine tax and regulatory systems, upgrading crumbling physical infrastructure, equalizing opportunity, pulling families and communities out of generational poverty, and modernizing US global engagement. While the cost of Congress ($3 billion per year as of 2020) and the federal government (nearly $5 trillion per year, almost $1 trillion borrowed) grows, the public struggles to see the return on investment.

The country's long "to do" list languishes, employed mainly as talk fodder for endless congressional debates, recurring campaign promises, blue-ribbon panels, and torrents of pledges, bills, proposals, press releases, and official hearings. Elaborate as these activities may be, their noise is mainly Republicans and Democrats fighting one another to a draw. Progress stalls. Problems multiply. The nation weakens. Renowned constitutional law professor Samuel Issacharoff sees "a deep challenge to the core claim of democracy to be the superior form of political organization of civilized peoples," pointing to "the loss of a sense of social cohesion . . . and the decline in state competence."[20] These are exactly the outcomes the opponents of freedom and democracy seek to exploit by playing on the country's fractious political culture.

DEMOCRACY AT RISK

Perhaps most troubling of all, degrading American politics and declining US government competence contribute mightily to waning appreciation for democracy and a clear comprehension of its alternatives. Despite America's supreme sacrifices to preserve freedom and the horrors suffered by millions who lack it, one-quarter of US millennials—now the largest block of eligible voters and coming of age for national leadership—view democracy as a bad or very bad way to run a country. Reporting on the crisis of confidence in democracy, Freedom House observed, "Most worrisome for the future, young people, who have little memory of the long struggles against fascism and communism, may be losing faith and interest in the democratic project. The very idea of democracy and its promotion has been tarnished among many, contributing to a dangerous apathy."[21]

America was once the inspiration for young democracies, but political leaders around the world are thinking twice about whether ours is a worthy model to emulate. Many now look elsewhere for direction and partnership, including to freedom's adversaries, China and Russia. Consider Africa, whose vast human capital and resources position it to shape global affairs and security in the decades ahead.[22] One of the continent's most influential figures is Rwanda's president, Paul Kagame. Once Westward looking, he no longer believes that Africa's future lies with the US-European democratic model. In a wide-ranging interview in 2018, at the conclusion of his term as chairman of the African Union, Kagame observed that the West's system appeared to be "crumbling" and that developing nations were looking elsewhere for state templates. He saw the discord engulfing the United States and Europe and their key alliances, including NATO and the European Union.[23]

In 2020, Freedom House reported that democracy had suffered a fourteenth consecutive year of decline worldwide.[24] For the first time since 2000, most countries in the world were not democratic, and most people in the world did not live in democracies. Unsurprisingly, with autocracy and militant nationalism resurgent worldwide, indicators of freedom, rule of law, and the protection of human rights have plummeted. The American retreat from global leadership created a vacuum, and opponents of the rules and human rights–based global order are vigorously pressing the advantage: they push their model while seeking to destroy the US model from within. The nation seems yet to fully grasp the grim implications of their concerted campaigns.

On a raw Moscow winter day in 2019, while Pew was publicizing its latest poll results in Washington and Jack Port readied for the summer's D-Day observance in France, Vladimir Putin's top general strode briskly into the gray edifice housing the Russian Academy of Military Science. His address to the country's top military thinkers and strategists had been highly anticipated—and sent chills around the world.

General Valery Gerasimov spelled out Russia's vision for modern warfare. His call for modern high-tech weaponry to boost Russia's battlefield lethality—missiles that travel faster than sound, lasers that can vaporize a target at long range, and nuclear-tipped torpedoes—was not the surprise. More unnervingly, Gerasimov baldly described a comprehensive doctrine of weakening the Kremlin's adversaries by exerting influence on their internal workings through political subterfuge, obviating any need to unleash the country's kinetic arsenal.

The general was presenting the manifesto for an unofficially declared hybrid state of war—waged not just against young democracies on the Russian perimeter but also on the United States and its allies, as directed by his supreme commander in chief, Vladimir Putin. The Russian Federation's president began his career as a Cold Warrior in the Soviet secret police: NATO had long been his personal axis of evil and the United States the familiar geostrategic rival. When the doctrine of internally undermining Soviet adversaries began in the Cold War, it was branded "active measures"; the Kremlin's present-day enthusiasts call the program "controlled chaos."

Inside Russia, the program quashes political dissent and consolidates Putin's personal power. Outside the Motherland, "controlled chaos" weaponizes freedom, turning democracy's openness and pluralism against itself. By fueling domestic rivalries and sowing public distrust in the West's free institutions and alliances, Moscow calculated it could twist diversity into division. Division would give way to dysfunction. Dysfunction would produce disarray. Disarray would bring decline. Decline would yield geostrategic advantage. The World Wide Web and digital commons offered a battlespace tailor-made for hybrid warfare, enabling Russian spooks and their proxies to deliver the digital warheads from a safe distance under the veil of plausible deniability.

By blitzing foreign cyberspace with tweets, trolls, and disinformation from faked American sources, Russia's "web brigades" and "Putinbots" could turn terabytes of rumor, conspiracy theory, and falsehood into poison speeding throughout the American cyberscape. When opportune, bot attacks could be directed at strategic targets like key American voting blocs and influencers. The ability to electronically manipulate public opinion and fuel conflict and hatred would enable Russia to wreak destruction inside an adversary's borders without ever having to march a boot across them.

Well before Gerasimov read the Russian Academy into the future of warfare, "controlled chaos" had already struck at the crosshairs of its most coveted target. The US polity had been fighting over the circumstances and consequences of Russia's interference in the 2016 presidential race between Clinton and Trump and whether the Trump campaign abetted the intervention. Strategically, the discovery of Russia's digital fingerprints on the well-planned campaign made little difference to the Kremlin. Putin's cyberassault had achieved its aims. US political discord had been turbocharged. Washington was a political combat zone, further splintering the nation and distracting US leadership from attending to pressing matters of state. Bull's-eye! For Russia's primary foe to provide such a case study in controlled chaos must have been gratifying to the general as he delivered his remarks. The lesson could not have been lost on his attentive audience.

Just weeks after Gerasimov's speech in Moscow, the Senate Select Committee on Intelligence held a hearing examining Russia's use of digital bots and computer hacks to damage the United States. Among the witnesses was former FBI special agent Clint Watts, who in November 2016 had coauthored a comprehensive exposé on Putin's campaign to disrupt American democracy by harnessing "the force of politics" rather than the "politics of force."[25] Trending US social and political strife shows hybrid warfare to be enjoying frightening success in achieving the aims enumerated by Watts and his colleagues. "Undermine citizen confidence in democratic governance." Check. "Foment and exacerbate divisive political fractures." Check. "Erode trust between citizens and elected officials and democratic institutions." Check. "Create general distrust or confusion over information sources by blurring the lines between fact and fiction." Double check.[26]

"The long-run objective," Watts emphasized, "is to have democracy break down. To have so many internal divides and so many fights between elected officials that there is no policy—which is exactly where we're at in the United States right now."[27] The point was dead on. But it only told a fraction of the story. Russia is not the lone power targeting the United States using what US State Department calls weapons of mass distraction. "A growing number of states, in the pursuit of geopolitical ends," says its report, "are leveraging digital tools and social media networks to spread narratives, distortions, and falsehoods to shape public perceptions and undermine trust in the truth."[28] China, Iran, and North Korea and their proxies are among the perpetrators, but they are aided by forces much closer to home and far better positioned to threaten American democracy.

WE HAVE MET THE ENEMY

Two and a quarter centuries before General Gerasimov peeled back the curtain on controlled chaos, another commander predicted it. Nearing the end of his second term of office, four years shy of the new century, the general elected to serve as the first president of the United States rejected strong public appeals that he run again. Reasoning that a third term would be undemocratic, George Washington published a farewell address informing the nation of his decision to retire from public life.[29]

Washington's valedictory ranks among American democracy's most honored and important documents. In a tradition dating back to the Civil War, each February on the anniversary of the first president's birth, a US senator is appointed to recite the address aloud in the Senate chambers. In bidding goodbye to public life, President Washington reaffirmed the blessings of liberty, self-government, and national unity. He reminded fellow Americans of the virtues and passions that inspired the country's birth. Mindful of posterity, he warned future generations of the cardinal threat to constitutional republics and the democratic form of government—domestic political rivalries exploited by foreign powers.[30]

In Washington's words:

> The common and continual mischiefs of the spirit of party are sufficient to make it the interest and duty of a wise people to discourage and restrain it. It serves always to distract the public councils and enfeeble the public administration. It agitates the community with ill-founded jealousies and false alarms, kindles the animosity of one party against another, foments occasionally riot and insurrection. It opens the door to foreign influence and corruption, which finds a facilitated access to the government itself through the channels of party passions. Thus, the policy and the will of one country are subjected to the policy and will of another. . . . And there being constant danger of excess, the effort ought to be by force of public opinion to mitigate and assuage it. A fire not to be quenched, it demands a uniform vigilance to prevent its bursting into a flame, lest, instead of warming, it should consume.[31]

General Gerasimov's speech targeting "controlled chaos" at free societies would have come as no surprise to General Washington. Nor would Gerasimov find anything but prescience in President Washington's prophecy that reckless partisanship would be the most effective instrument for debilitating America's political antibodies to foreign subversion. One can imagine deep in Russia's intelligence files a memorandum with quotes from Washington's farewell warning underlined and bolded as a battle plan for undermining US strength and leadership with chilling implications worldwide.

Ronald Reagan famously called the United States "the shining city upon a hill." Two decades earlier, John F. Kennedy pronounced America's mission to help "build a world of peace where the weak are secure and the strong are just." The concept of American exceptionalism and leadership has been in existence at least since French diplomat and historian Alexis de Tocqueville penned his four-volume *Democracy in America* in 1831. The conviction that the United States has a special role in the world is not held by American politicians or nineteenth-century French diplomats alone. In a speech at Georgetown University, liberal-minded rock star and philanthropist Bono argued more powerfully than many officeholders the case for why the ideals that ennoble America are indispensable to human progress:

> Because America is an idea, isn't it? I mean, Ireland's a great country. . . . That's how we see you around the world, as one of the greatest ideas in human history. The idea is that you and me are created equal. . . . The idea that life is not meant to be endured, but enjoyed. The idea that if we have dignity, if we have justice, then leave it to us, we can do the rest. This country was the first to claw its way out of darkness and put that on paper. And God love you for it. Because these aren't just American ideas anymore. There's no copyright on them. You've brought them into the world. . . . These truths, your truths, they are self-evident in us.[32]

If the country's shining light and moral authority have dimmed, it is not because US values are invalid or democracy itself is passé. The justness of liberty, human rights, and rule of law is timeless, independent of the fate of any nation. If "active measures" work, we cannot blame foreign powers. Adversaries can exploit only the fissures we create. If the search for a culprit is on, cartoonist Walt Kelly has the answer. Riffing on a quip by Admiral Oliver Perry during the Battle of Lake Erie in 1813, his iconic character Pogo famously pronounced, "We have met the enemy and he is us."[33]

While perhaps comforting and even fashionable to pin the United States' deranged political environment on exceptionally polarizing political figures and their antagonisms, doing so would be wishful and deceptive. The destructive state of US politics is not the legacy of Donald Trump or Nancy Pelosi. The cast of characters striding the modern political stage are exemplars and products of a system gone awry, not its authors. Trust in government was plummeting well before they emerged on the scene. The problem will not disappear as they fade away. Something far deeper and more structural is at work.

What then is behind the nation's distracted councils and enfeebled public administration? Some look to the clash of diverging political convictions. Yet, American politics have always been of mixed opinion and contentious—rightly so. Democracy is meant to be a competitive marketplace of ideas, sometimes combative but also fair and functional. "Partisanship" is often named as the culprit, but that diagnosis is far too imprecise. Even organized partisanship in the form of political parties is no vice when exercised within the country's constitutional system designed to reconcile diverse views and interests and keep the ship of state moving forward. Something far deeper and more systemic and corrosive than partisanship is at work.

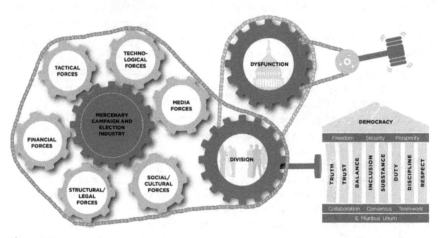

Figure 1.1.

POLITICS INC.

George Washington's fears and our adversaries' hopes are materializing by means of a stale party duopoly and booming election industry that has hacked American democracy to serve its own aims and livelihoods. The mercenary political cartel is much bigger than Republican and Democratic Parties and their franchised office-holders and candidates. It encompasses a vast partisan campaign support industry and ever-multiplying party-aligned special interest groups. For Politics Inc., public division and discord are big business. The enterprise's wildly successful revenue model centers on demonizing political foes, exploiting fear, turning America's pluralism into factionalism, and keeping the country in a permanent state of internal conflict—monetizable by the practitioners and exploitable by foreign adversaries.

The two parties need one another to play the moustache-twisting villain menacing each other's favored constituencies and pet issues, turning democracy from a process into warfare. In this way, they tap the pockets of donors in an escalating financial arms race whose sole winner is Politics Inc., which has devised an intricate network of laws, rules, and practices to keep its business model thriving. In return, the nation suffers unrestrained growth in rank partisanship, a decline in competitive congressional races, and the rise of ideological extremes who hold the balance of power in the parties' organizational apparatus and primary contests, squeezing out the rational center.

Politics Inc.'s communications strategy is enabled by digital-age tools perfect for propagandizing at scale and generating the social and political apartheid on which the system feeds. In this way it deftly exploits modern cultural dynamics, including the deep public anxiety and uncertainty wrought by globalization and jarring economic and social change. The wings of both parties have found their niche by targeting the forces responsible for society's ills—scapegoating that spreads distrust and national cognitive dissonance about our problems and the solutions.

In a great American irony that only the artistry of Politics Inc. could produce, the activist extremes share a deep antipathy for a national political culture they detest for completely opposite reasons. The left perceives an establishment that is reactionary, uncaring, too weak, and hijacked by corporatists. The right sees an establishment that is too big, intrusive, dependence fostering, and commandeered by bureaucrats and out of touch elites. As the political center weakens, so does the nation's capacity for responsible compromise and consensus—the keystones of democracy that works.

The media, both mainstream and alternative, are co-invested in the business model of perpetual conflict. They fuel and feed on animosities that the parties foment. The mushrooming number of cable stations and internet sites compete fiercely for partisan audiences, offering view-affirming opinion dressed up like news. As balkanized Americans belly up to their favorite information saloon for a shot of confirmation bias, media outlets convert ears, eyeballs, and computer clicks into advertising revenue. In the process, objectivity, balance, and fairness have become quaint professional relics—a big reason why the public finds the media almost as untrustworthy as politicians.

Most devastating of all, the political industry's handiwork is blinding Americans to the core principles and values that should unite us and that make the American system a model worth emulating. Americans are losing an appreciation for what's at stake. We have grown blind to the struggle of millions around the world to build what we have already constructed and deaf to their sacrifices in want of the rights, freedoms, and privileges we take for granted. The country faces a crisis of politics, governance, and democracy graver than any previously encountered because the threat is internal, rooted in the nation's structures and culture. Gerasimov himself could have designed this blueprint for national sabotage—but we are the architects.

George Tenet, former director of the Central Intelligence Agency, informed the commission investigating the September 11 terrorist attacks on the United States that in the summer of 2001 the warning signs of a major plot against the United States were "blinking red." The system is once again flashing urgently against a gathering threat—one emanating from within the United States and greater than any threat from abroad. How did we get here, and what do we do about it?

THE MISSION

How and why we got here is explored in the following chapters, which open the hood to examine Politics Inc. and each of its complementary gears—*tactics, finance, structures, media, technology,* and *culture*—that drive America's political division, civic dysfunction, and deteriorating democracy. The answer to what we do about it starts with defining a clear, overarching mission: to strengthen US democracy to meet the future-defining challenges and opportunities ahead. Achieving it requires a three-part strategy: First, reconnecting the country with the principles and stakes that unite us. Second, resuscitating the virtues that can make our system more cohesive, agile, and functional. And third, modernizing our political culture and its systems by breaking the party duopoly's stagnant hold on power and overhauling the machinery installed and exploited by Politics Inc.

The stakes couldn't be higher. Much is said about the reemergence of great power conflict between the United States and China. That is not precisely the tension. The struggle is between democracy and autocracy, determining whether the world order will be based on freedom rooted in self-government, human rights, and rule of law or yield the future to imposed power and state dominion over captive people.

It is no exaggeration to say that as much as preceding American generations have been tested, the most difficult challenges to the American idea remain ahead. New threats are emerging and old ones returning. Autocracy is on the march worldwide. China looks to replace the United States as the global standard setter and template for governance, claiming to offer the world a better model based on a modernized take on discredited concepts of state control. Advanced technology is arming authoritarians with new and powerful tools to propagandize, surveil, and control their populations. Weapons of mass destruction are possessed by a growing number of nation-states and becoming more accessible to rogue powers. Against this backdrop, the global population is set to double in the next fifty years, further stressing social, economic, and governmental systems. In a world of high-velocity change and scalable threats, stability has never been so fragile nor instability so dangerous.

America can't lead the world on the path of democracy if Americans no longer quite believe in it ourselves. Millennials who don't believe democracy is the preferable form of government should make a more careful study of its alternatives. Billions of human beings hunger for the basic rights and opportunities that many Americans casually regard and others have paid so dearly to preserve. We can only contemplate what the world would look like without the American idea and the sacrifices made to keep it alive. Imagine the darkness on earth if freedom had not prevailed over fascism in the last century. Or imagine if communism, responsible for murdering over one hundred million people under its dominion, had triumphed in the long struggle of the Cold War. Or if violent Islamic extremism had remained unchecked. Or if the United States does not remain strong and unified enough to face down mounting threats to liberty and the progress of human rights.

In a society taken with memes, on January 14, 2014, the world was given perhaps the most powerful geopolitical meme of our age. The International Space Station was gliding in low earth orbit 250 miles above east Asia, and from that lofty perch, the Expedition 38 crew snapped a nighttime photo of the Korean Peninsula. The iconic image said far more about differing political systems than geography and more about life on earth than adventures in space. Below the thirty-eighth parallel, South Korea, a liberal democracy and market economy, was illuminated brightly. Above it, North Korea, an autocracy, was shrouded in near total darkness, the border clearly marked by the light outside its margins. What the camera could not capture, except implicitly, was the grinding political and economic poverty imposed on the North Korean population below, where famine had claimed the lives of up to 3.5 million people owing largely to the autocracy's ineptitude and cruelty. The snapshot captured a profound if sometimes underappreciated truth. Systems matter. Government matters. Politics matter. They matter in ways that those who enjoy freedom from fear and deprivation cannot fathom. Those are the stakes—a reality that should shake the nation's political class from its focus on parochial fights and the nation from its partisan trance to see the bigger picture.

It is true that the American experiment was conceived in an era stained by the evil of slavery by men who did not uphold the country's ideals of freedom and equality under the law for all. But the human failure to live up to them does not taint the ideals themselves. "Democracy transformed from thin paper to thick action," observed Martin Luther King Jr., "is the greatest form of government on earth."[34] That ongoing mission must be informed by the reality that, from the country's inception, the threat to the American system of government has arisen not from any fault in the national principles of democracy but from the failure to abide by them.

Despite our shortcomings, the United States has earned admiration and gratitude in every corner of the globe. We have demonstrated the power of free people, free institutions, and free enterprise. We have been a bulwark against the excesses and evils of concentrated political power that have forever plagued mankind. Along the way, we built the largest economy ever known, nearly one-third larger than any other. Relying on the US model of economic freedom, one billion people have been lifted out of extreme poverty over the past twenty-five years. Through it all, the nation has thrived not primarily by dint of its wealth and military might but by the validity and resilience of what it stands for, the same reason people from every continent still aspire to call America home.

In an order transmitted on D-Day, General Dwight D. Eisenhower, the supreme commander of Operation Overlord, told the Allied troops that "the eyes of the world" were on them in their "great and noble undertaking."[35] About those like Jack Port on whose shoulders the fate of mankind fell, author and historian Stephen Ambrose wrote, "At the core, the American citizen soldiers knew the difference between right and wrong, and they didn't want to live in a world in which wrong prevailed. So they fought, and won, and we all of us, living and yet to be born, must be forever profoundly grateful."[36]

Today a great undertaking deeply rooted in June 6, 1944, awaits the nation—a mission to make the practice of democracy worthy of the service and sacrifices made to preserve it so that generations to come don't live in a world where wrong prevails. In that mission, the words of two other American leaders who guided the nation through perilous times ring clear. Abraham Lincoln invoked wisdom from the New Testament warning that: "A house divided against itself cannot stand." Franklin Delano Roosevelt, on the eve of World War II, avowed to the world, "In the face of great perils never before encountered, our strong purpose is to protect and to perpetuate the *integrity* [emphasis added] of democracy."[37]

This is our purpose today. Victory in protecting and perpetuating the unity of our nation and the integrity of our democracy will require the concerted effort of our whole people and our whole government—perhaps especially our states and cities, which continue to be innovative laboratories of policy and politics and have the power to effect many of the reforms required to break the grip of Politics Inc. and save our future.

2

Politics Incorporated (Power Gear)

It is difficult to get a man to understand something when his salary depends upon his not understanding it.

—Upton Sinclair

Deficits in the integrity of American democracy, real and perceived, feed the fertile imaginations among the large and growing confederation of right- and left-wing political conspiracists. They thrill to fantasies of "deep state" plots to destroy the American ideal as they define it. Imagine their disappointment if forced to acknowledge that powerful cabals from the opposite end of the political spectrum are not secretly manipulating the levers of government for nefarious ends. The forces of national derangement are far more prosaic. The internal threat to American democracy arises not from a clandestine deep state but from the sprawling election industry nominally headquartered at the Republican and Democratic National Committees.

Formal parties have been integral to American politics since they emerged in 1800, but politics as a massive, multitiered money-churning industry is a relatively recent and devastating phenomenon. The founders clearly foresaw the danger parties and factions would pose. "There is nothing I dread so much," wrote John Adams in 1780, "as a division of the republic into two great parties, each arranged under its leader, and concerting measures in opposition to each other."[1] George Washington warned that while factions and parties "may now and then answer popular ends, they are likely in the course of time and things, to become potent engines, by which cunning, ambitious, and unprincipled men will be enabled to subvert the power of the people and to usurp for themselves the reins of government, destroying afterwards the very engines which have lifted them to unjust dominion."[2] But Washington and Adams could never have dreamed how firmly modern, professionalized parties would

15

come to control the reins of government, or the extent of their concerted measures in opposition to one another yet their subversive financial codependence.

To be sure, there are many virtuous and altruistic people who labor in every dimension of elective politics seeking to do good as they see it. But the system created and maintained by the party duopoly has weakened their influence. W. Edward Deming's maxim holds true: "A bad system will beat a good person every time."[3] To some degree, the subtlety of the system's vices escapes the comprehension of practitioners preoccupied with the day-to-day political fray. To another, ideologues rationalize that the perceived righteousness of their ends justifies attaining them even by the most questionable and ultimately destructive means.

THE PARTIES

Despite the patriots' hopes for political cohesion, the ink had hardly dried on the Constitution before factional rivalry surfaced. Philosophical differences split the country's polity into competing camps. Federalists led by Washington and John Adams advocated stronger national government and stout executive authorities to promote national security and economic development—a platform favored by the North's industrial and financial interests. James Madison and Thomas Jefferson's Democratic-Republican Party that arose out of the anti-Federalist movement espoused greater state power and a stronger legislative branch as the bulwark of true representative democracy, policies supported predominantly by the South's agrarian interests. The 1800 presidential contest pitting Adams against Jefferson remains one of the nastiest campaigns in American history.

The Democratic Party emerged a quarter century later, formed by Andrew Jackson and Martin Van Buren on a populist platform from the remains of the defunct Democratic-Republicans that faded for lack of support following the War of 1812. Another twenty-five years would pass before the GOP was born in the lead-up to the Civil War on a platform of opposition to the expansion of slavery drawing in anti-slavery Democrats and the former Whig party that evaporated following the Mexican-American war that ended in 1848. Thus the two parties that still dominate US politics began their eventful and tortuous journey into modernity.

Since 1860, each of the country's thirty-one presidents has hailed from one of these parties (nineteen Republicans and twelve Democrats). In the eighty-two Congresses gaveled into session since that time, Republicans have held the majority in the House and Senate simultaneously thirty-two times; Democrats, thirty-four times. In fifteen Congresses, party control of the House and Senate was split.[4]

Of the many thousands of Americans elected to represent their states and districts in Congress since 1900, only twenty-two senators and 122 representatives have been aligned with "other" parties. The trend holds in the present. In the 117th Congress (2021–2023), only two of the 535 senators and House members who took the oath of office are neither Republican nor Democrat.[5]

The parties have a similarly firm grip on political power at the state level as well. Since 1900, only fifty-nine governors have been outside the Republican and Democratic Parties and only fifty-two of the 7,383 state legislators as of August 2020 (not including the forty-nine members of Nebraska's unicameral legislature, which per the state's constitution is nonpartisan).[6] Over their 160 years of rivalry, the Democratic and Republican Party brands have been molded and reshaped by relentless economic, social, cultural, and demographic change and by shifting public opinion and political opportunity. The lone constant has been the duo's reliable and codependent grip on the American political system.

In the twentieth century, despite stark philosophical differences and bare-knuckle partisan fights, the parties managed to forge traditions of a generally respectful majority, loyal opposition, and collegiality even in times of social and political upheaval. Until the 1970s, most registered voters affiliated with one of the two parties. The contemporary electorate, however, is not nearly so binary. In 1992, for the first time since polling on the question began in 1939, more Americans identified as Independents than as either Republicans or Democrats.[7] By 2021, 24 percent of the country's two hundred million voters identified with the Republican Party, 30 percent with the Democratic Party, and 45 percent as Independents.[8] Frustrated with the machinations of Politics Inc., unhappy with their choices at the ballot box, and weary of broken promises, a sizable majority of Americans say the two parties do such a poor job the country needs a third party.[9]

DECLARATION OF INDEPENDENCE

In an age boasting unlimited choice, fine customization, and sublime innovation driven by competition, binary options from failed providers of political services don't cut it. Most people no longer fit so neatly into the parties' ideological buckets. Not infrequently, the best answers to complex modern challenges reside somewhere outside of or between the ideological choices offered by the stale parties loath to compromise. Without a natural political home, good people and good ideas are frustrated by doctrinaire, conflict-centric party politics and their tired modalities. In their report for the Harvard Business School titled *Why Competition in the Politics Industry Is Failing America*, Katherine Gehl and Michael Porter note: "The real problem is that our political system is no longer designed to serve the public interest. . . . Free from regulation and oversight, the duopoly does exactly what one would fear: The rivals distort the rules of competition in their favor."[10] In the duopoly's unhealthy competition, "rivals win, but at the expense of customers overall."[11]

While demand for greater choice in the marketplace of political ideas and services is on the rise, the prospect of meaningful third-party competition and fundamental party reform appears distant. The twin mega brands of the American political industry have made themselves too big to fail, using their exclusive rule-setting power to block alternative parties and Independents from getting on ballots, onto the debate dais, and into the mix, and from having their votes count in any real way other than as spoilers. Like any good duopoly, say Gehl and Porter, the parties compete "in ways that reinforce their differentiation and separation from each other . . . [but] also depend on each other to take steps to enhance the attractiveness of the entire industry and avoid undermining it. . . . In unhealthy competition, entrenched rivals are dominant, protected from new competition and insulated from pressure by channels or suppliers to improve products and better serve customers. In unhealthy competition, customers lack the clout to pressure rivals to improve."[12] Most Americans want elected leaders and the parties to quit fighting so much and make politics and government perform better. Polling conducted in November 2020 by the *Economist* and YouGov found that four out of five registered voters said they want the two sides to work together to get more done.[13] But why should the parties change? While the customer isn't happy, the business is doing gangbusters—so the public's choice remains binary and unsatisfying.

THE REVENUE MODEL

Politics Inc. encompasses a vast network of campaign professionals, functionaries, franchisees, subcontractors, and branded affiliates whose livelihoods depend on perpetuating interparty conflict and the restraint of trade in the political industry. Fair enough, when money and livelihoods are organized to conduct politics in the public interest. Foul when the political system is organized to serve itself and its careerists. The hazards track with those arising from another complex, as President Dwight D. Eisenhower warned in his 1961 farewell address:

> This conjunction of an immense military establishment and a large arms industry is new in the American experience. The total influence—economic, political, even spiritual—is felt in every city, every State house, every office of the Federal government. . . . In the councils of government, we must guard against the acquisition of unwarranted influence, whether sought or unsought, by the military-industrial complex. The potential for the disastrous rise of misplaced power exists and will persist. We must never let the weight of this combination endanger our liberties or democratic processes.[14]

As prescient as he was about the nexus between the Pentagon and the defense industry, Eisenhower was perhaps unable to foresee the even more dangerous conjunction of an immense party establishment and a large campaign industry, what Gehl and Porter have termed the "political-industrial complex" and what I have labeled "Politics Inc."[15] Its total influence is felt in every city, every statehouse, every office of the federal government. The unwarranted influence it exerts on the counsels of government affects every aspect of the nation's economic, political, and spiritual life. The weight of its misplaced power continues to escalate disastrously.

The party establishments and their networks are predominantly giant fundraising operations organized and professionalized for partisan combat to facilitate their claim on resources. Together the Republican National Committee and Democratic National Committee operate six organizations created to raise cash. Four of them are located steps from Capitol Hill to service the House and Senate candidates, and ensure that elected members of Congress help the parties fundraise in return, as they raked in over $2.6 billion in 2019 and 2020.[16] Issue One, a bipartisan organization devoted to political reform, operates by the motto "fix Democracy first." In its blockbuster report *The Price of Power*, retired US representatives blew the whistle on the practice by both parties of selling House committee chairmanships to members who meet fundraising quotas not just for their own campaigns but to fill party coffers.[17]

In determining what House committees a member may sit on or chair, the party leadership gauges not just the candidate's experience, subject matter expertise, or popularity but rather their ability to raise money. The more prestigious the committee, the higher the "dues"—upward of seven figures. This has two effects, neither of which screams healthy democracy and sound governance. One, powerful committee leaders must spend an inordinate amount of time at party fundraisers or on the phone raising cash instead of doing the difficult and demanding job they were elected to do. Two, they must either schmooze or scare party money out of the industries and interests they are responsible for regulating.

Representative Niki Tsongas (D-MA) told Issue One and the R Street Institute that "the seriousness of your candidacy is often measured by your ability to raise funds."[18] Once elected, members both new and old are assigned an amount to raise for the party, and performance is carefully scrutinized. Imagine the disappointment of a newly elected member of Congress eager to roll up his or her sleeves to begin their constitutional duties only to find that their election certificate is more or less a contract to fundraise.

"They told us right off the bat as soon as we get here," says Representative Thomas Massie. "'These committees all have prices and don't pick an expensive one if you can't make the payments.'"[19] "Every time you walk into an NRCC [National Republican Congressional Committee] meeting," said former congressman Trey Radel, "a giant [expletive] tally sheet is on prominent display that lists your name and how much you've given—or haven't. It's a huge wall of shame."[20] According to Chris Shays, who represented Connecticut's 4th District in Congress for twenty-two years in Congress, "no such thing" existed when he was first elected.[21]

The money pays for a growing professional class of political operators and campaign service providers principally in the business of building contrast not consensus: fundraisers, pollsters, strategists, campaign administrators, political consultants, media consultants, media buyers, advertising agents, direct-mail managers, data analytics professionals, digital marketers, grassroots political organizers, petition collectors, election lawyers, and more.

THE PROFESSIONALS

If neither party is in sync with even a bare plurality of the American electorate, it is likely because, in another blow to the health of US democracy, the public no longer steers the political parties thanks to the campaign professionals who have commandeered them. Richard Harwood of the Brookings Institution puts it this way:

> The party machines that once provided the foot soldiers of politics have been replaced by a professional class of political consultants. . . . They create the propaganda, raise the money, train and market the candidates, define issues and election strategies, organize rallies, get out the vote, and write the script for party conventions. They perform virtually all the functions once performed by ordinary people who now sit on the sidelines viewing elections, as Peter Shapiro has written, either with indifferent detachment or as "shameful exercises in mudslinging, obfuscation and demagoguery."[22]

Adam Sheingate found that in the 2012 national elections, "consulting firms billed federal candidates, parties and super PACs [political action committees] more than $3.6 billion for products and services. Of this, more than 70 percent went to firms specializing in the production and placement of media advertising. Consultants earn lucrative commissions for every ad they place."[23] Their focus is not on issues or problem-solving but on creating and marketing differentiation—in particular, demonizing the competition to drive the dough. They get paid no matter what the election outcome or how damaging their tactics. A high-ranking staff member of an incumbent governor recalls with horror a phone conversation, midcampaign, between their top political consultant and his counterpart in the opposing camp: "They were negotiating what the two candidates could fight about in the coming week that would help both sides fundraise with their respective political bases."

The 2020 election continued the pattern of record-breaking fundraising and expenditures, topping $14 billion (nearly triple the amount spent in 2004), making the political profession among the nation's fastest-growing business sectors. Even when a campaign is over, a subsidiary of Politics Inc. is on the job. The 2020 presidential race set records for postelection litigation, with nearly fifty legal challenges to duly validated results. The law firms did much better than the country, which paid a hefty price in political strife and a delay in presidential transition.

After the election, the internet was afire with conspiracy theories and wild rumors. Fundraising kicked into high gear as text messages swept across the country for weeks, urgently fishing for donations to "stop the steal," promising "we have uncovered massive amounts of fraud." This despite the fact that the results were confirmed by recounts and by Republican election officials, secretaries of state, canvassing boards, and even top Trump administration officials. Postelection, the Trump Organization raised over $200 million to fight the results. That doesn't count the vast sums that other political actors and enterprises raised on the controversy to right a wrong that never occurred—a business case study not likely to be forgotten in coming elections, Trump or no Trump.[24]

The general counsel for John McCain's 2008 presidential campaign recalls being instructed on his postconvention visit to the Republican National Committee that a particular group of law firms would be handling election fraud–related legal issues for the campaign. A former federal elections commissioner, he asked somewhat skeptically whether significant fraud was truly a legitimate concern. His handler assured him, "We know they are cheating. We just haven't caught them yet"—and handed him the firm's business card.

THE SUBSIDIARIES

Politics Inc. has many such subsidiaries and franchisees orbiting the parties. Among them are organized issue advocacy and special interest organizations whose money and members heavily influence campaigns and policy. It bears emphasis that special interests are not inherently evil. On the contrary, each person is a unique agglomeration of them. A free society is obligated to protect the right of individuals and like-minded groups to politically advocate. Each "interest" is part of the raucous but beautiful symphony of democracy and has a right to be heard. Heard they are. Countless organized interests are active in the political process and maintain a presence in Washington and state capitals, not just large corporations, industries, labor unions, and professional associations but cities, states, universities, and charities.

Many operate federal and state government affairs offices, and hire law firms, lobbying shops, and PR companies that perform a wide variety of functions: monitoring and reporting federal activity to their constituencies, informing and lobbying the legislative and executive branches of government, contributing to campaigns through political action committees (PACs), engaging in express advocacy to influence elections and issue advocacy to inform or influence public opinion, policy, and decision-making. All these are legitimate and constitutionally envisioned functions of democracy and the political process—that is, unless access and influence is paid for in dollars instead of merit and when issue advocates themselves are improperly influenced by the priority of generating revenue for themselves. In this way, special interests, like partisan campaigns, are incentivized to manufacture and exaggerate crisis and conflict and to find financial advantage in partisan rivalry—the more heated the controversy, the better they do.

Among the most influential organizations in Washington are large 501(c) entities, including social welfare and issue advocacy groups like the National Rifle Association (NRA); the American Association of Retired Persons (AARP); and business, labor, and environmental groups. Many are far-flung enterprises with huge dues-paying memberships, highly paid executive teams, and enormous staffs. Some market merchandise and services. Whether they acknowledge it or not, many have a compelling financial interest in inflaming political problems and controversies. The greater the threat, the more money they make. The more members they have and dues they collect, and campaign contributions they can distribute, the greater their clout. Such organizations are in constant pursuit of members and fees. And nothing generates more revenue than identifying or manufacturing threats to their members' interests. Often the concerns are legitimate. Many times, they are exaggerated. Sometimes they are simply made up.

The National Rifle Association was formed in 1871 to promote "Firearms Safety Education, Marksmanship Training, Shooting for Recreation." In the 1920s and 1930s, the organization joined efforts to implement gun safety policies, including a gun sale waiting period, permits to carry concealed weapons, and registries of gun sales. In defending gun control, the NRA president told Congress, "I have never believed in the general practice of carrying weapons. I do not believe in the general promiscuous toting of guns. I think it should be sharply restricted and only under licenses."[25]

Today the NRA is a tax-exempt 501(c)4 "social welfare" organization and huge political player with a large and loyal membership. The organization collects membership dues from over five million people and spends over $30 million per year on political activity, including lobbying, directly donating to campaigns, and funding political super PACs.[26] The organization's chief executive makes over $2 million per year.[27] The NRA operates on the "camel's nose" principle—meaning that practically any legislation dealing with firearms must be opposed because even if it does not result in a material impediment to Second Amendment rights, the precedent could open the way to one. That standard justifies sending out urgent action alerts, proving the organization's worthiness and relevance. Noncontroversy, after all, is not a big seller. Over the past two decades, the NRA has weighed in heavily against measures such as waiting periods and bans on cop-killer bullets and high-capacity ammunition clips.[28]

Following the Sandy Hook school shooting in December 2012, bipartisan legislation was moving forward in the Senate to close the "gun-show loophole": the ability of private individuals to purchase firearms in side sales without the background check required in commercial sales to ensure that the would-be purchaser is not a convicted felon, mentally disabled, or in another prohibited class. Working closely with the NRA, the authors of the bill included provisions the organization had long sought, loosening various gun restrictions. Despite these concessions, the NRA withheld its support, and the measure died in the Senate as family members of the Sandy Hook victims looked on from the Senate gallery.[29] A Gallup poll in 2017 showed that 95 percent of gun owners support background checks for all gun purchases, including side sales.[30] Since 2019, the NRA has been grappling with reports of financial misdeeds by the organization and numerous board members.[31]

The American Association of Retired Persons (AARP) is a tax-exempt organization established to advocate for seniors. It rakes in nearly $1.6 billion in revenue each year. In addition to lobbying for people over the age of fifty-five, the enterprise sells a full range of products and services, including insurance, prescriptions, books, travel discounts, and more. During consideration of the Affordable Care Act in 2010, the AARP agreed to support significant spending cuts to Medicare despite the opposition of many seniors. Shortly thereafter, news reports surfaced that Medicare cuts would produce a jump in Medigap insurance sales, which would put an estimated $1 billion in AARP's pockets.[32] "AARP portrays itself as a classic membership organization, funded by dues in return for representation on a variety of issues," wrote Dr. Gerard Gianoli in a *Wall Street Journal* editorial. "Yet its public financial statements reveal that the group receives the bulk of its revenue from health insurers. In 2017 the group received $627 million from UnitedHealth Group, the nation's largest insurer, compared with $301 million in membership fees. . . . Out of its total $1.6 billion revenue in 2017, $908 million came from royalties [paid by UnitedHealth]."[33] In a 1996 editorial, "Can You Trust the A.A.R.P.?," the *New York Times* noted that "the policies that might be best for the elderly are not always the policies that are best for the bank account of the A.A.R.P."[34] In 2019, *Forbes* reported that "the AARP's for-profit financial juggernaut, AARP Services, Inc., has earned so many billions from big insurance companies that it stopped publishing its annual report on its web site in 2013. And it has expanded to other businesses that are too numerous to cite. Meanwhile, an unprecedented number of older Americans are being driven into bankruptcy due, in part, to astronomical health care costs."[35]

Organizations involved in practically every issue feed on the system. While serving as a Senate staffer, I worked closely with the director of a highly effective environmental organization, who stormed into my office one day carrying a stack of letters. We had been working together for many months on efforts to protect visibility and air quality at Grand Canyon National Park. Our efforts had yielded results, including the cleanup of a nearby power plant. The director slammed the letters on my desk with disgust. Authored by different environmental organizations, they were extraordinarily similar. Each grossly exaggerated the extent of the problem, in some cases depicting the canyon shrouded in a dark cloud of industrial smog. Each claimed to be working closely with our office and others in Congress to solve the problem, though none came from an organization I had ever heard of. And, of course, each appealed for an urgent donation to save the Grand Canyon. A cause that should have been an exercise in civil engagement suddenly seemed like garden-variety hucksterism. Such appeals take place everyday from every brand of professional special interest group and issue advocate who generate horror stories and hyperbole to generate income and support. There isn't a member of Congress, congressional staffer, or other Beltway dweller, past or present, who couldn't point to a chest full of examples where advocates exaggerated, twisted, exploited, and fundraised off of ginned-up controversy.

INDEPENDENT OPERATORS

Thousands of political action committees registered with the Federal Election Commission and permitted to donate directly to campaigns and parties under strict contribution limits and disclosure requirements. Among them is a far-flung network of outside operators that trade on partisan hostility.[36] Looking through Federal Election

Commission filings in 2014, *Politico* found thirty-three PACs targeting small donors by email and direct mail. Of the $43 million they hauled in, only $3 million was used for ads or contributed to campaigns. The bulk was spent on operating expenses, including $6 million to firms "owned or managed by the operatives who run the PACs."[37]

Super PACS, legally allowed to raise and spend unlimited sums of donations provided their electioneering doesn't coordinate directly with a campaign or party, have become the most powerful new subsidiary of Politics Inc., enabled by the Supreme Court's 2010 decision in *Citizens United v. Federal Election Commission*. During the 2020 presidential election, a group of Republican political consultants established the Lincoln Project to publicly oppose Donald Trump's reelection. The organizers were praised by elements of the press, Democrats, and disaffected Republicans for crossing the aisle on principle. The principal proved quite attractive as well. Federal Election Commission records show that the organization raised over $80 million and spent $49.7 million, including for campaign services provided by firms owned and operated by the founders.[38]

Worse are outright Scam PACs, feeding on partisan animosity and public fears. An exemplar is Kyle Prall, a grifter sentenced to three years for fraud. Of the $500,000 he raised for candidates on both sides of the aisle, he spent a total of $5,000 on political causes. The remainder, according to prosecutors, was spent on tropical vacations, "liquor, lap dances, room service, a deep-tissue massage and even a pet-cleaning fee."[39]

The Da Vinci of Scam PACs is Scott MacKenzie, the treasurer for dozens of political action committees. *Politico* estimated that between 2002 and 2018, MacKenzie's top twelve enterprises raked in $46 million from small contributors. Almost three-quarters of the take was used for "fundraising, wages, and administration"—including huge sums paid to companies owned by MacKenzie.[40] The Center for Public Integrity says that in 2003–2004, only about ten PACs hustled individuals for small donations and diverted the money to uses unintended by the contributor. By 2018, the number had grown to sixty.[41]

Like all mega industries, Politics Inc. has spawned downstream opportunities for a raft of other clever entrepreneurs and flimflam artists. Independent operators cash in on wild political propaganda, half-truths, and misinformation. The outrages they peddle are lapped up by a cynical public primed by Politics Inc. to believe the worst of the other and of the nation's civic institutions. The groups exploit every avenue to solicit money: mountains of targeted direct mail, never-ending robocalls, internet dunning, and text messages to fleece concerned citizens by fighting manufactured political outrages and threats to the country.

Jennifer Bell of California found her now-deceased mother, who suffered from dementia, living amid stacks of junk mail, much of it from political groups.[42] She had depleted her life savings by sending money to an assortment of shams and scams from groups promising to stop efforts to remove "In God We Trust" from US currency, block the UN from taxing American citizens, weed out the deep state, and stop an assortment of anti-American conspiracies. Outraged, Bell began a blog to publicize fundraising scams dressed up with misinformation, disinformation, and bogus crises.[43]

She broke down the common tactics used in the solicitations she collected from her mother's stockpile and other cons shared with her from across the country:

- Emphasis on a perceived crisis
- Threats to a way of life
- Idealistic revulsion against corruption
- Idealistic projections of a way of life
- A dedicated vanguard
- Self-identification as a movement
- A communications network
- And, the big objective—money to fund the revolution

The tactics neatly emulate the templates employed by political party and candidate fundraising letters. Creative means are used to bait people into opening the envelope, including making it look like official government correspondence or a legal summons. Once the recipient opens the envelope, he or she may be invited to take a bogus poll that is never tallied, cast a proxy vote for a nonexistent issue election, or be enrolled in an "exclusive" club for special patriots. The sponsor's feigned interest in the recipient's views is merely soft soap to encourage the requested donation. Whatever deception the solicitation is peddling to provoke a response drains its way into social networks where fakery becomes fact, spreading like town gossip at massive scale and speed.

Like any conglomerate, Politics Inc. has an all-important marketing arm—in this case the national media. The mutual dependence has created a high-margin, self-sustaining commercial arrangement that would earn the envy of CNBC's Shark Tankers. Campaign dollars pay for expensive political ad buys. The media use the revenue to finance 24/7 coverage of partisan theatrics. Spectacular political drama drives ratings that generate more income for the media and more political donations. The increased contributions are fed back into the system to finance additional media buys. Their profusion of opinion programming injects the media even more directly in political campaigns, keeping partisanship at a fever pitch and profitable.

HOSTILE TAKEOVER

One would think that duopoly powers would strengthen of the main political parties' national and state committees, but the irony is that even as negative partisanship solidifies party fealty, as indicated by the steady rise of straight ticket voting, the official party apparatuses are growing weaker and less influential. They are outspent and outdone by feral elements and free operators who fly the party flag but march to their own beat. Journalist and *New York Times* columnist Thomas Edsall sees the internet as only the latest influence weakening the parties, already affected by "the Civil Service undermining patronage, the rise of mass media altering communication, campaign finance law empowering donors independent of the parties, and the ascendance of direct primaries gutting the power of party bosses to pick nominees."[44]

New York University law professor Samuel Issacharoff describes the shift as "hostile takeovers" of "hollowed out political parties," noting that they "offered little organizational resistance to capture by outsiders. What was captured appeared little more than a brand, certainly not the vibrant organizations that are heralded as the indispensable glue of democratic politics."[45] The founders worried about the capture of government by factions and parties. The additional danger is in how the parties themselves are being co-opted, and overtaken by unaccountable elements.

To a certain extent, however, as Issacharoff suggests, the two national committees are franchisors of a brand they build but no longer control. They license, dole out money to franchisees to help them use it, aid candidate recruitment and strategy, and run the party convention every four years, but in almost every other respect, the parties are a shadow of their former selves. Much of their power and influence has been sapped by self-funding candidates and autonomous electioneers that, enabled by campaign finance laws, raise and direct more funds than they do but remain answerable and accountable only to themselves. Peter Levine of Tufts University observed that the "Koch brothers' political network . . . employs 3.5 times as many people as the Republican National Committee does."[46] Democratic patron George Soros funds a broad range of political causes and enterprises, including over $76 million in Democracy PAC contributions.[47] When leaders and forces behind Democratic politics are discussed, for most people he leaps to mind long before the chairman of the Democratic National Committee.

Donald Trump and his super PACs were able to raise more money for his campaign than did the Republican Party, helping him execute what some pundits described as a hostile takeover. Trump turned party messaging and branding on itself and used his ability to raise funds independently to make the party his own. If this sounds like a shot in the arm for political independence, it is not. The difference between independent and rogue is big and dangerous. The value of parties resides in their function as organizations directed and legitimized by the electorate, not the other way around.

Yet, as brands, the two political tribes have outdone the world. Taking a page from the commercial marketing domain, the Republican and Democratic Parties have become the consummate "lifestyle branders." Though the parties are organizationally weaker, party influence has never been stronger, helping create customer loyalty through "storytelling" that plays on people's emotions and embeds brand identity deep into the customer's sense of self, even helping shape it.

For party stalwarts, being a Democrat or a Republican is not just a personal political preference: it can be a personal brand signaling who you are, what you believe, and which side of the divide you occupy. For some it is a fashion statement, as a party's appeal is less to its performance than to how it makes you feel and the image it projects. Political marketing is reminiscent of the golden age of cigarette advertising, when a carcinogenic product was packaged and sold based on imagery and messaging that created customer fealty. A popular Tareyton cigarette ad campaign that began its two-decade run in 1963 featured smokers with a black eye promising they would "rather fight than switch."

On his way to gaining power, Trump harnessed interparty animosity to build a loyal base, making his administration seem like the most partisan ever despite many policies that defied party orthodoxy. What he understood best was how to appropriate the party brand and harness the force of negative partisanship—the emerging phenomenon of voters being motivated more by animus toward the other party than fealty to their own. Stanford political scientists Shanto Iyengar and Masha Krupenkin argue that "as animosity toward the opposing party has intensified, it has taken on a new role as the prime motivator in partisans' political lives. . . . The impact of feelings toward the out-party on both vote choice and the decision to participate has increased since 2000; today it is out-group animus rather than in-group favoritism that drives political behavior."[48]

NEGATIVE RETURNS

For many years, advocates of increasing government efficiency and accountability argued that public institutions should run more like a business. Instead, we have made politics run more like a business—one focused on its stockholders rather than its customers, on its marketing function rather than the quality of its product, and on its bottom line rather than customer service and satisfaction. That is why the customers are looking for alternatives to an industry granting them only two choices at the ballot box and why so many of America's best who should be embracing elective service are repelled by it or looking for the exits.

Upon the adjournment of the 114th Congress in 2017, a record number of House members decided to retire out of frustration with a system consumed by chasing money and prosecuting team rivalry. Elected officials interested in working across the parties to solve problems have been driven from office. John Adams said, "Public business my son, must always be done by somebody—it will be done by somebody or other—If wise men decline it others will not: if honest men refuse it, others will not."[49] As we lose good public servants, and Politics Inc. goes unchecked, and as the political parties become stronger brands but weaker, less accountable organizations, American democracy looks to plumb new incapacitating depths of polarization, balkanization, and immoderation.

Polarization

Negative partisanship and hatred for the other side will remain the dominant mode of modern political persuasion. The political consultants and communications element of Politics Inc. have outperformed when it comes to cementing brand loyalty by casting the other party as the greater evil. Using data from American National Election Studies (ANES), the *New York Times* showed that between 1968 and 2012, the "feeling thermometer" (100 being best and 0 being worst) measuring political party members' attitude toward the other party's candidate plummeted from 56.2 in 1968 and 25.1 in 2012 to 12.2 by 2016.[50]

Balkanization

Parties have always had liberal and conservative wings, but factions were tempered by organizationally strong parties who controlled sizable financial and administrative resources, enabling them to marshal their members. Party leaders no longer have the tools to herd the cats within their congressional caucus. Self-financed politicians beholden to their donors and the ideological base who elected them have no compelling incentive to compromise. Whatever the other side wants is bad, and whatever your own party leader might try to do in the way of compromise is simply not acceptable. In the world of political free agency and risk aversion, voting "no" in Congress is the best way to stay out of trouble and remain viable for reelection. Perpetual "no" disempowers Congress and leaves problems to the executive branch to figure out, adding new and exploitable fuel to the partisan bonfire. Ironically, the continued rise of factions and free agency will strengthen party brands as the increased gridlock they foster will help further sort the electorate into implacably hostile camps pointing fingers across the divide. But it will further weaken the parties' ability to build governing consensus within their own ranks, much less with the other side.

Immoderation

Polarization as a marketing strategy and balkanization as the consequence of dynamics outside the parties' control will continue to empower the factions dwelling at the ideological extremes, putting principled compromise and problem-solving further out of reach. Amid the Cold War showdown between John Kennedy and the Soviet leader Nikita Khrushchev, the US president lamented the difficulty of coming to terms on arms control because "the hard-liners in the Soviet Union and the United States feed on each other."[51] So it is with the parties in the Cold War of American politics. The Tea Party movement turned into the Freedom Caucus in Congress, becoming as much a thorn in the side of the Republican leader as the Democrats. Though it lacks a formal name, an emerging radical left wing is consolidating into a force much like the Tea Party. Both extremes have started PACs to rid their respective party caucuses of moderates. As centrists disappear, either because they are turned off by the process or turned out by the forces of party extremism, Congress looks to become even less representative of the broad electorate, less operationally functional, and less responsive to the national interest.

As each of these mutually reinforcing dynamics imbeds deeper into the political system, gridlock and unaddressed national problems can only worsen. Public dissatisfaction can only intensify. And the ranks of political Independents with no party to reflect their hopes, aspirations, and interests are likely to swell. Though the parties will endure, they will grow weaker and less cohesive, leaving them more vulnerable to hostile takeover by outliers and opportunists.

REAL COMPETITION

Democracy needs strong political parties. At their best, they bring organization and coherence to the democratic process—even if it is not always pretty or polite. All that counts for little, though, if parties are not in practical ways principled and responsible within a system that is fair, functional, and can produce governing consensus. To the political scientist E. E. Schattschneider, writing in 1942, modern democracy without parties was "unthinkable, because without competing parties, voters lack meaningful choices. Partisan conflict is necessary for democracy, because one-party politics is not democracy. It's totalitarianism."[52]

The country needs a party system that competes more over ideas and achievement than for money—a competition that reflects the nation's tremendous diversity can bring new thinking and greater innovation to the public sphere, and can push the two dominant parties to be more creative and responsive. Defenders of the two-party system and many in the media ridicule the idea of third parties as spoilers who steal votes and swing elections away from the major party most like them. Thus, Democrats frowned on Jill Stein of the Green Party for taking votes that likely would have gone to Hillary Clinton in 2016 and scolded Ralph Nader for taking votes from Al Gore in the close 2000 election. Republicans were unhappy with Ross Perot's role in George H. W. Bush's loss to Bill Clinton.[53]

Critics of more open and competitive multiparty politics maintain that long lists of candidates on election ballots can overwhelm and confuse voters. Moreover, they argue, plentiful choices increase the chance that elections produce winners who claim a bare plurality of votes—in other words, the largest minority. Congress watchers can't conceive of multiple caucuses, fearing they would impede legislative productivity.

But what good are two clear and cogent choices when neither is very appealing to most of the electorate? What could be more overwhelming to democracy than the election of unrepresentative representatives? What is more unsustainable than the broken status quo? Could congressional performance really get much worse? The plurality problem already infects the election system in party primaries, whose victors are often elevated to the general election ballot without winning the majority of even the small and unrepresentative segment of voters who participate in them.

The plurality problem can be and must be fixed in both primary and general elections to ensure winners enjoy majority support—a basic tenet of democracy—through reforms such as ranked-choice voting. This creative solution, described in chapter 6, would bring greater competition, inclusiveness, and election winners who are true majority vote getters to politics. The United States built the strongest economy in history by harnessing competition to drive quality and excellence. It is time to apply clean, honest, vigorous competition to the nation's political process. Politics Inc. wants no part of changes that might upset its operations by requiring internal reform or allowing third parties to compete. Given its way, however, the corporatization, professionalization, and monetization of the political system will continue to erode the nation's civic bonds, posing a gathering domestic threat. By weakening the nation's governance, it constitutes a national security threat. And, by tarnishing the US model and undermining democracy's reputation abroad, it becomes a danger to human rights and international development.

Whether the nation supports two parties, three, or ten, our system must be structured to ensure it reflects the hopes of the public, not a professional political class of electioneers; competes over ideas more than money; educates and informs the electorate with an eye to the nation's future, not their own; and advocates well-considered positions across the spectrum of public policy that builds coalitions rather than pits segments of society against one another by exploiting discord. If the status quo continues, Politics Inc. will continue powering the gears driving national division, public dysfunction, and democratic decay, including dirtier, never-ending campaigns.

3

Endless and Dirty Campaigns (Tactics Gear)

Passion and prejudice properly aroused and directed do about as well as principle and reason in any party contest.

—Thomas Elder, American politician

While a deadly pandemic was radiating from Asia, an ugly and divisive presidential election was running its course in the United States. Bitter accusations boomed back and forth in the campaign between a boorish populist and a more conventional "creature of Washington." The incumbent was a child of privilege. The challenger came from modest circumstances. One won fame outside politics, presenting himself to the electorate as a man of the people. The other was a trained lawyer with decades of government service, claiming the experience and temperament to handle the demands of the presidency.

The stinging charges and countercharges ran the gamut—corruption, misuse of office, financial misdeeds, sordid family affairs, Russian intrigues, racism, bad character, and unethical behavior. Each accused the other of being an extremist who would lead the nation to destruction. Powerful media outlets lined up behind their favored candidate like seconds in a duel. The incumbent was soundly defeated, expelled from office after a single term. Historians would cite the election as a pivot point in American party politics.

No, the election in question was not the 2020 US presidential contest. It was the 1828 rematch between John Quincy Adams and Andrew Jackson. Known as one of the dirtiest in presidential history, the campaign followed on the heels of the "era of good feelings"—a decade of single party politics under the Democratic-Republicans upon the demise of the Federalists. Convinced that corrupt maneuverings had cheated him of victory in the 1824 presidential race, when the absence of an Electoral College majority had thrown the vote to the House in Adams' favor, Jackson and a congressional coalition led by Martin Van Buren bolted to establish the Democratic Party. They thereby launched the modern two-party system, ushering in an era of increased public participation in politics and organized campaigning by candidates rather than surrogates.

The rancor of the rematch in 1828 was hardly a novelty. Mudslinging, sinister tactics, savage rhetoric, and cunning emotional appeals were already common in American elections. Every contest for national political office since has offered its own strain of muck and slander.

NONSTOP CAMPAIGNS

If manipulative campaign tactics are as old as politics, what makes contemporary campaigns so troublesome for US political culture? The answer resides in the Renaissance dictum *sola dosis facit venenum*, "only the dose makes the poison." Progressively longer and nastier national campaigns have toxified the political environment. The election industry's firm reliance on negativity and villainization to draw donations and votes increases the partisan venom in every election cycle. The extraordinary scale and speed with which modern digital communication and social networks circulate and target the poison supplies the killer dose.

Like other growth-focused industries, Politics Inc. has boosted its size and might by elongating its selling season and vertically integrating core business functions. Electioneering and governing were once quasi-discrete, sequential activities in the American political system with distinct seasons. Today, they are conjoined full-time operations.[1] Each election cycle, the date by which most major presidential candidates have declared their candidacy—triggering polling, media coverage, fundraising, and politicking—creeps up the calendar.[2] Dwight Eisenhower remained the NATO commander until June 1952 before announcing a run for president in the election held five months later. He kicked off his campaign at the Republican Convention in mid-July.[3] Kennedy, Nixon, and Johnson all announced their bids early in their respective election years. Reagan, Bush (41), Clinton, Bush (43), Obama, Trump, and Biden declared the year before. The last four announced over eighteen months before voting day.[4]

In a *New York Times* op-ed, Emma Roller put marathon US elections into global perspective. Over the many months between candidacy declarations and voting day, she observed, the United States could host "approximately four Mexican elections, seven Canadian elections, 14 British elections, 14 Australian elections or 41 French elections."[5]

Long campaigns are a relatively new phenomenon in US history, an outgrowth of the riotous 1968 Democratic Convention in Chicago. The presidential nomination process was then largely controlled by national and state party leaders; the big decision was made at the summer party conventions before the campaigns ramped up for the post–Labor Day sprint to the November general election.[6] That year the Democratic poohbahs tapped Hubert Humphrey to be the party's nominee, bypassing Minnesota's senior US senator Eugene McCarthy. An uproar over the choice by rank-and-file party members who shared McCarthy's opposition to the war in Vietnam flung the convention into turmoil, prompting the Democratic National Convention to empanel the McGovern-Fraser Commission to recommend reforms to the nomination process.[7] The panel urged that nominees be chosen by popular vote. Both major parties and most states promptly transitioned to secret ballot primary elections held sporadically by states over the year. It changed party politics forever.

Selection by plebiscite is surely more democratic than by the oft-caricatured backroom deals of cigar-sucking powerbrokers. Even so, some experts remain convinced that diminishing the role of experienced party leaders was a mistake, opening the door to candidates more skilled in campaigning than in leadership and governance.[8] Whether reform has improved the nomination process remains a matter of debate. Not in question is that primary elections have stretched the campaign season, as the throngs of office seekers hoping to catch fire with primary voters must be sorted out. More recently, as states have moved their primaries ever earlier, jockeying for greater influence on the national political stage, the march toward permanent campaign mode has accelerated.[9] With a term-limited Barack Obama ineligible to run for president again in 2016, twelve Republicans and six Democrats competed in the open race. During the 2020 elections, twenty-seven Democrats ran for the chance to unseat incumbent Donald Trump. The huge field compelled the Democrats to hold their first debate five months before the Iowa caucus, over a year before the November general election.

Dark horse candidates often enter particularly early, drawing inspiration from Jimmy Carter's example. As governor of Georgia, Carter was little known nationally. Looking to build name recognition and support in Iowa, the first test of voter sentiment, he announced his bid for the White House almost two years before his victory against Gerald Ford in the 1976 general election. Emulating Carter, John Delaney, a Democratic congressman from Maryland, threw his hat in the ring over three years before the 2020 election.[10] Trump formed his reelection committee immediately upon his inauguration in 2017—and not surprisingly started raising money immediately. He would ultimately spend a billion dollars before his uncontested convention. Mere weeks after the votes were counted in Joe Biden's victory, Trump advised supporters of his intention to run again in 2024. The year wasn't out before the press began floating the names of fourteen other likely GOP hopefuls. In January 2021 the Republican National Committee began planning to convene potential candidates for the race almost four years away. When asked at his first major press conference, Joe Biden announced he would run again in 2024.

Long leads are defended as helping voters learn more about the candidates and providing time to separate spin from truth, but the public clearly favors shorter contests.[11] Voters' pain from added months of election coverage, partisan propaganda, and TV punditry is not the only harm. Harvard professor and foreign policy expert

Stephen Walt noted that longer campaigns lengthen the time that policy is eclipsed by politics, giving foreign leaders a bigger window to take advantage of distracted US leadership.[12] Russian foreign policy experts point to Vladimir Putin's waiting for US officials to be engrossed in the campaign of 2016 to make a major move to strengthen Syria's Bashar al-Assad's barbarous regime.[13] President Bill Clinton has described never-ending presidential elections as a "constant four-year, peripatetic campaign" that damages the country by diverting leaders' focus from the nation's business.[14]

The earlier US national campaigns kick off and the longer they overlap congressional sessions, the more officialdom's focus shifts to politicking. When C-SPAN began televising congressional proceedings in the late 1970s during the intersection of the two seasons, a new era for electioneering was born as Congress became a grand stage for ongoing campaign theater.

Though hardly distinguishable today, electioneering and governing are incompatible elements of the political process having contradictory objectives and different skill sets. Electioneering is the art of partisanship and drawing contrasts with the opposition. "Political campaigns are designedly made into emotional orgies which endeavor to distract attention from the real issues involved," explains historian James Harvey Robinson, "and they actually paralyze what slight powers of cerebration man can normally muster."[15] Conversely, legislating and governing require peak cerebration: they demand leadership and consensus-building in pursuit of national interest, even contrary to political interests. Bridge-building—once a boost to the résumé of an aspiring politician—can now open them to career-ending attacks by hardcore partisans who dominate primary elections tend to view compromise as apostasy and consensus-building as appeasement.

Bipartisan cooperation and compromise are hard enough to achieve under the best of circumstances. By mixing it with campaign imperatives, the lawmaking process is more likely to be shunted to the side by partisan posturing, and government oversight is reduced to finger-pointing. Competitive zeal obliges both parties to force votes designed solely to embarrass the opposition and to block any accomplishment that might bolster the other side's prospects in the election. Above all, it encourages Congress to defer hard but urgent decisions and tough votes until after the next election. "The problem with that," observed Senator Lindsey Graham, "is that after every election comes another election." Still, gridlock can easily be blamed on the obstructive opposition, and there's always hope that a swing in the coming election might produce a majority strong enough to avoid the need for uncomfortable bipartisan compromises. But, of course, a new Congress begins a new campaign cycle. The system resets to chase larger and larger sums of cash so the parties, their candidates, and incumbents can out-holler one another over longer periods, keeping political tensions taut and distracting government from its duties.

Every national election has its unique spirit, character, and stakes, but they strike most people as painfully similar. The candidates at the top of the ticket reflexively profess it to be the most important in history, a choice between paradise and perdition filled with exaggerated promises and overwrought fears. In 2016,

Hillary Clinton told a reporter, "I'm the last thing standing between you and the apocalypse."[16] While Trump was intensely divisive and demonstrated few of the qualities associated with outstanding leadership, the national economy made demonstrable gains during his administration until the onslaught of COVID-19. In 2020, Donald Trump warned that Joe Biden's election would mean socialism and a plummeting stock market.[17] Following Biden's victory, the New York Stock Exchange and Nasdaq responded favorably.

NASTY AND NEGATIVE

Candidates insist they're "fighting for you" and they're "on your side." Of course, if someone is fighting for us, then someone must be fighting against us. This captures the theme of modern political communication—political salesmanship emphasizing threats, nightmares, and the dangers of one's opponent rather than opportunities, dreams, and one's own positive qualities. The political attack ad has become the defining meme of American elective politics.

That is not to say all "attack ads" are damaging to the political process. When accurate and fair, they provide valuable information: calling out hyperbole, hypocrisy, and bad policy is a service to the nation. However, when criticism is ad hominem, unfair, or inaccurate, and accompanied by requests for political donations, the service becomes a swindle.

Studies show that the public perception of negative campaign messaging as fair or unfair, civil or uncivil, and the sponsorship of the message, whether by a candidate or an "independent" group, influence the electorate's reaction to the content.[18] In general, the public looks more unfavorably on criticism of an opponent's character or motives than criticism of an opponent's policy positions or professional record. Typically, attacks sponsored by third parties are better received than those coming from the candidate's campaign. Nevertheless, political consultants love negativity, regardless of who sponsors it, because ads blasting the opposition are memorable. They usually outperform positive messaging at what matters most—grabbing attention and going viral.[19]

The ability to multiply the message for free through social media shares provides huge bang for the campaign buck. Investigation into whether negative ads and dirty campaign tactics play a significant role in the country's traditionally anemic voter turnout (2020 turnout excepted) and choices at the ballot box are largely inconclusive.[20] Such topics are worth examining, but other questions—who actually pays attention to attack ads, why, and what that attention means for campaign strategy and political culture—are perhaps not as closely scrutinized yet crucial.[21] Partisans, particularly Republicans, tend to tune in to negative ads launched by their favored candidate or preferred party while tuning out negative ads run by the opposition.[22] Viewer response, accordingly, is likelier to be a nod of the head and "That's right!" than "That's important and informative!" The point is that attacks do not look to inform voters, sway the undecided, or attract the center. Often, the principal objective of such ads is to inflame and motivate the sponsoring candidate's partisan base. Those who buy in to vitriolic charges experience mounting moral outrage at their political adversaries. For those who do not, disgust with the other party and disdain for the political arena is the likelier response. Neither emotion is conducive to a healthy political culture. Former Senate majority leader Tom Daschle calls negative ads "the crack cocaine of politics."[23] Colin Powell warned that the negativity of partisan politics is "running us into the ground."[24]

When Kennedy and Nixon faced off in the 1960 presidential election, about one in ten political advertisements on television were critical of the other candidate.[25] Even in 2000, only about 15 percent of broadcast and cable TV campaign commercials were explicitly negative, while 65 percent contrasted the two candidates and 20 percent were positive. The proportion of negative ads rose in each subsequent election, reaching 70 percent by 2012—when the total number of ads was vastly higher.[26] For instance, in the midterm elections of 2014 and 2018, television ads for governorships and congressional seats rose from 2.5 million to approximately 4 million.[27] By October 2020, the number aired in the presidential and congressional races was already double that for the entire 2016 national election season.[28] Three-quarters of Americans profess they wish campaigns would break their attack ad addiction.[29]

OUTSOURCING ATTACKS

Though barred from coordinating with an official campaign, super PACs (political action committees) can rake in unlimited contribution sums—which they use predominantly to run negative campaign attack ads. As they and other outside groups have taken on the attack dog role, candidate-sponsored commercials are trending positive. Andrew Mayersohn of the Center of Responsive Politics says, "That's to be expected because part of the value of outside spending is that the candidate can stay positive and keep their hands clean, while allied outside groups do the dirty work of tearing down the opponent."[30] Protected as political speech, such ads can make just about any charge, lodge any accusation, and tell any untruth. They have become the nuclear weaponry of American politics.

In 2012 and 2014, "independent" groups accounted for over one-quarter of the total campaign ads. All but 15 percent of them were negative. In 2014, a nonpresidential election year, political parties and outside groups spent almost $600 million on attack ads. In the midterm elections four years later, the figure had jumped to nearly $820 million. The 2020 national elections saw outside political spending surpass $1 billion.[31]

Political ads meant to provoke rather than inform and inflame instead of educate are the engine for negative partisanship. "In today's environment," say Alan Abramowitz and Steven Webster of Emory University, "rather than seeking to inspire voters around a cohesive and forward-looking vision, politicians need only incite fear and anger toward the opposing party to win and maintain power. Until that fundamental incentive goes away, expect politics to get even uglier."[32] As Harry Zahn of *PBS NewsHour* observed in 2016, the traditional question in a US election, "Who are you voting for?," has been replaced by "Who are you voting against?"[33] Stanford University political scientists Shanto Iyengar and Masha Krupenkin reached similar conclusions from the decline of ticket splitting (selecting candidates of different parties for different offices in a single ballot). According to their research, the practice doubled between 1950 and 1970, then gradually declined to a low mark by 2012.[34] Ticket splitting didn't rebound in the 2020 election. Even though the campaign featured a uniquely controversial incumbent whose poor character and abusive rhetoric alienated even members of his own party, voting a straight party line ballot still dominated.[35]

FEAR, ANGER, AND DISTRUST

The principal means of creating negative partisanship plays on powerful human emotions—fear, anger, and distrust—to build brand loyalty. Together they foster a sense of threat and victimhood that seeks scapegoats to blame, and, as is often now the case, to hate. "Fear and anger," admitted Trump political guru Steve Bannon, "is what gets people to the polls."[36] That was certainly the intent behind the infamous "Willie Horton" ad run by Republican George H. W. Bush's presidential campaign against Michael Dukakis, then governor of Massachusetts. Willie Horton, a Black man convicted of murder, committed rape and assault while on a weekend release from prison under a state furlough program instituted by a Republican predecessor; the ad blamed Dukakis for the policy.[37] Democrat Lyndon Johnson's dramatic "Daisy" ad, featuring a little girl picking daisy petals before being annihilated by an atomic bomb, suggested that challenger Barry Goldwater's election would lead to nuclear war. Johnson won the election and went on to commit the nation to the war in Vietnam that claimed the lives of almost fifty-nine thousand Americans. His predecessor, John Kennedy, helped himself to victory by fanning fear over what he knew was a fictitious US deficit in the nuclear missile balance with the Soviet Union.[38]

The spirit of Willie Horton, Daisy, and the threat of annihilation thrives in contemporary Republican appeals exploiting fear of violent crime by undocumented immigrants, blaming Democrats' policies, and in Democratic narratives about atmospheric warming that will burn up the world, thanks to Republican climate change deniers. Some people in the United States unlawfully commit violent crimes. Climate change is a scientifically proven threat. Rather than rally around facts to negotiate responses to the problem, the parties play to the fear and outrage of their bases, creating more heat than light. Three-quarters of the campaign ads in the 2012 presidential contest appealed to such emotions.[39] Though comparable figures for the 2016 and 2020 cycles aren't available, anyone with a TV set or internet connection knew negativity reigned supreme.

The appeals are hitting home. Approximately half the members of each party admit to having feelings of anger and fear about the opposition.[40] As these emotions intensify, so will the national culture of victimhood and finger-pointing. In politics, compulsive scapegoating has two benefits: exonerating oneself and providing voters a different object for their anger. Political scientist Matt Flinders finds that "politicians are primarily motivated by avoiding blame for failure rather than trying to claim credit for success for the simple reason that the public possess a strong 'negativity bias.' Politicians will use all sorts of tricks and tactics . . . to keep themselves blame free."[41] Blaming the other party—for inadequate COVID response, illegal immigration, rising health care costs, and racial strife, among other things—is an obvious tactic that played a central role in the 2020 campaign messaging.

Among the favored targets of blame is the working press. In a carnival of cognitive dissonance, both Republicans and Democrats decry the media as a tool of the other party, each side portraying a system stacked against it.[42] And outsiders, particularly those the opposition can be accused of coddling, can make excellent targets. During the 2020 presidential campaign, Republican National Committee documents leaked to *Politico* revealed that blaming China for the coronavirus would serve as a core Trump campaign strategy.[43] Indeed, Donald Trump implied that the Chinese intentionally caused the pandemic, asserting, "This is worse than Pearl Harbor, this is worse than the World Trade Center. There's never been an attack like this."[44] Near the election, Donald Trump Jr. tweeted a signature nastygram referring to "Beijing-Biden," hoping that the alliterative slander linking their opponent with Chinese bad actors would go viral and stick.[45] However implausible it was that China purposefully released the virus on its own population to attack the United States, the accusation served two purposes: One, it took the spotlight off the shortcomings of the Trump administration's COVID response. Two, pairing China's culpability with pre-COVID Biden soundbites playing down anti-China sentiment made Biden appear soft on a competitor and implicated him in the pandemic.

The Biden team fired its own broadsides. On a conference call with reporters, a longtime Biden adviser related the number of times Trump had praised China and President Xi in January and February 2020 when he was trying to keep the US-China trade deal on track purpotedly at the risk of public health and other American interests.[46] Democratic-aligned super PACs blanketed incumbent GOP senators with millions of dollars in ads fingering them for COVID-19 policy shortfalls.[47] Calling out the other side's mistakes is more than fair game in a democracy; it is essential. But when partisan finger-pointing is reflexive, exaggerated, and predictable over issues that both parties should be held accountable for, the system itself, not just the other party, is diminished.

VILLAINIZATION AND HATE

Fear, anger, distrust, and blame are all tools for the strategic objective of negative partisanship—villainization. Personalizing antipathy to your opponent has lasting power. We see it in all forms of political communication, especially fundraising appeals. Problems are not the enemy. The other team is. Villainization is honed to a sharp wedge in two steps. First is to delegitimize the opponent and their organization, creating a strong sense of distrust in their character and motives. During the 2004 national campaigns, *Los Angeles Times* reporter Janet Hook observed that "attacks on a candidate's character, patriotism, and fitness for office, which once seemed out of bounds, have become routine."[48] Indeed, a substantial portion of Republicans and Democrats find members of the opposing party morally and intellectually deficient.

Second is to cultivate a deep sense of antipathy for the other side. The strategy is perfectly logical for a political culture that has given up on building inclusive majorities as the road to electoral success in favor of firing up a loyal party base. Political scientist Lee Drutman observes, "Since partisans of each side are uninterested in compromise, each party's ability to win depends on casting the *other* party as too extreme, too terrible, too corrupt, too evil, too un-American—whatever parade of horribles resonates. This is why so much political communication is devoted to playing upon fear and anger. How better to divide? As a result, 'negative partisanship'—partisans hating the *other* party—is now the most consequential force in American politics."[49] In weaponizing cynicism, neither side perceives the extent to which it hurts the country and our system of government, tearing at the fabric of national unity.

Approximately half the members of each party see the other side as a threat to the country.[50] Drutman predicts that "the more the parties continue to unify their supporters by casting the other party as the enemy, the higher this number will rise."[51] In charting Republican and Democratic views of each other as measured in "favorability and warmth," Stanford economists Levi Boxell, Matthew Gentzkow, and Jesse Shapiro found a steep drop beginning in 1980.[52] Pew Research charted the decline as well, showing that in 1994, one-fifth of Republicans held a "very unfavorable" view of the Democratic Party.[53] That share jumped to one-third by 2008, reaching nearly 60 percent by 2016. Democrats' disdain for members of the Republican Party rose at almost precisely the same pace.[54]

Fostering animosity has other benefits. "When citizens' support for a candidate stems primarily from their strong dislike for the opposing candidate," says Thomas Edsall, "they are less subject to the logic of accountability. Their psychic satisfaction comes more from defeating and humiliating the out-group, and less from any performance or policy benefits that might accrue from the victory of the in-party. For this group of voters, candidates have every incentive to inflame partisan negativity, further entrenching affective polarization."[55]

Such animus is what frees politicians and their supporters to call opponents liars, traitors, crooks, deserters, racists—terms that now fly around Washington with appalling regularity. Hatred finds oxygen in virtual spaces, where political combatants don't have to look one another in the eye and outrageous statements are consequence-free. Political content on social media consists almost entirely of ridiculing the other party, typically with short blasts and ugly memes.

The long-term implications of partisan hatred are chilling. "It is not too much to say that a significant number of voters in both of America's major political parties see their adversaries as worthless," says Edsall. "And history teaches us that the logic of worthlessness has chilling implications."[56] In 2016, enraged to action by rumors propagated by Russian hackers and anti-Clinton bloggers, a North Carolina man fired shots at a Washington, DC, pizzeria. The restaurant had been randomly identified by a conspiracist blog as the headquarters of a child sex trafficking ring involving Hillary Clinton and political operative John Podesta. In 2020, ugly public clashes including violence erupted with regularity between Biden and Trump supporters. Foreign adversaries understand that partisan hatred divides and weakens the United States. After the election, a website appeared under the URL enemiesofthepeople.com. Traced to an Iranian cybergroup, the site depicted the election officials from both parties who had certified the legitimacy of election results in the crosshairs of a rifle scope and disclosed their personal information.[57] Something has gone terribly wrong in America when Iranian cyberterrorists and political partisans share a common interest in sowing antipathy.

At its worst, Politics Inc. foments hate and caters to it. During his 2020 debate with Joe Biden, Donald Trump was asked about his tolerance for white supremacists, specifically the Proud Boys. When pressed on the point, his response was to instruct the group to "stand back and stand by."[58] The unusual wording seemed intended to create an impression of opposition but also suggested that the group might be needed in the future. Several weeks after his statement, the FBI arrested members of a kindred group, the Boogaloo Bois, for firing semiautomatic rifles outside a Minneapolis police department in an attempt to provoke racial unrest and violence.[59]

In the 2000 presidential primaries, John McCain's victory in the New Hampshire primary made it imperative for his opponents to stop him in South Carolina—otherwise, his momentum would likely carry him to the nomination. Nearing the election, a phony push poll was discovered that asked Republican primary voters if they would be more or less likely to vote for McCain if they knew he had illegitimately fathered a Black child. At the time, the senator had been joined on the campaign trail by his family, including the daughter the McCains adopted from Bangladesh.[60]

DIRT AND NO HOLDS BARRED

The tactic used in the South Carolina case is no outlier. Push polls are a sordid and long-standing practice that plants negative information in the guise of conducting a survey. The American Association for Public Opinion Research defines a push poll as "an insidious form of negative campaigning disguised as a political poll."[61] They are designed to manipulate opinions, not measure them. A typical push poll would begin with some innocuous questions, giving the appearance of legitimacy, and then slide into questions about how knowledge that the candidate in question was guilty of some unflattering act—typically one never committed—would affect their vote.

Larry Sabato of the University of Virginia has studied the use of push polls extensively, finding them at all levels of elective politics. They were used widely by Democrats in 1986 to take back the Senate during the midterm elections in Ronald Reagan's second term by suggesting that the president was planning to cut Social Security. Their use ballooned beginning in 1994, including in state-level elections, and featured a cornucopia of "lies, rumors, half-truths, smears, and gross distortions."[62]

Push polling is far from the only dishonest campaign tactic prevalent today. FlackCheck.org, a program of the Annenberg Public Policy Center at the University of Pennsylvania, catalogues a broad set of categories and subcategories of deceptive practices common in political ads.[63] Most of them were used in recent national elections and over many congressional election cycles. Often, but not always, they include the following:

- Deceptive audio: manipulating the viewer's response, including by the strategic insertion of sounds.
- Deceptive dramatization: Annenberg defines this as "the use of inferential and misleading imagery that's harder than statements for truth checkers to call out as foul."
- Deceptive framing: the practice of presenting two pictures side by side to create a nonexistent negative relationship.
- Glass house attacks: ads slamming an opponent for "a behavior, position or vote that the attacker has made as well."
- Guilt by association: ads that pair pictures of the opponent with a photo of some unsavory character to establish an association in the mind of the voter.
- Hearing what's not said: the act of superimposing a derogatory word or term on the picture of an opponent to create a malicious association.
- Out of context: the act of "ignoring parts of a statement or the context in which a statement was made . . . to distort our sense of what an opponent said or meant."
- Photoshopping: altering a photo in some way that's favorable to the sponsoring candidate or unfavorable to the opponent.
- Restrictive definition: the selective use of language and employment of euphemisms or half-truths to deceive voters about the candidate's record, policies, or platform.
- Seeing what's not heard: using accurate words and false information in the visuals. Viewers draw false inferences because "when they conflict, pictures speak louder than words."
- Visual vilification: using an "unflattering photo of an opponent selected to underscore an attack."[64]

Employing these or more creative tactics, officially sponsored and freelance political mudslingers have never had it so good. Digital tools make it easy to create and distribute dirt and falsehoods. Elaine Kamarck of the Brookings Institution notes, "Every dirty trick that was possible before the Internet is possible today. The biggest difference is that they are cheaper, faster, and easier to hide."[65] Anyone with a laptop, a creative mind, and an agenda can play in the fakery using social networks to soak up and widely disseminate the outrageous, provocative, and salacious—the wilder and more emotional the better.

Whether dirty tactics are sponsored by candidate campaign committees, party committees, and independent electioneering groups or undertaken by foreign opera- tors and lone wolves, rationalizations abound. When the opponent is viewed as ille- gitimate, untrustworthy, and threatening, all manner of shady tactics and behaviors seem perfectly justified, whether they involve disseminating falsehoods, manipulat- ing public opinion, or interrupting House and Senate proceedings in protest.

Rising hostility, particularly among the hardcore political fringes, and the outra- geous rhetoric and tactics it begets can't be dismissed as the uncontrollable misbehav- ior of the unaccountable. The ethos has gone mainstream, creating a feedback loop between the public and the nation's elected leaders. Say Abramowitz and Webster, "Negative views of the opposing party among voters in turn, encourage political elites to adopt a confrontational approach to governing."[66] But many elected officials no longer want any part of undermining the nation's political culture and the efficacy of its governing institutions, as reflected in their exodus from Capitol Hill.[67] For the same reason, many of the nation's most promising leaders won't contemplate offering themselves for elective service.

Negative partisanship—manufactured, packaged, and delivered by Politics Inc.— is transforming American politics from a process to something closer to civil war. It's why we have shouting matches instead of debates and why election strategies center on inflaming the partisan base rather than attracting the political center.[68] While centrists have become the out-group, there is every indication that a frustrated, silent majority hungers for campaigns that are clean and substantive, understanding that they are the path to better governance and stronger democracy.

CLEANING IT UP

Fixing our destructive political campaigns should begin by shortening them. Restricting political ads until a reasonable time before the election and imposing other limits to abbreviate our increasingly long, alienating campaign seasons would help keep our elected officials focused on their duties, lower the cost of campaigns, and reduce fundraising pressures.

Ensuring the integrity of campaign communications and electioneering will require a multipronged approach focused on calling out deception, falsehood, and foul play for what it is, strengthening tools to expose and shut it down, and creating public and professional norms rejecting it. Proselytizing for cleaner campaigns, the Annenberg Public Policy Center's Kathleen Hall Jamieson notes that television and radio stations have no legal obligation to run deceptive political ads from third-party groups. Annenberg's FlackCheck.org calls deceptive political ads to the attention of station managers with recommendations that they refrain from airing the offending material.[69] Such efforts should be reinforced by broadcast industry norms rejecting deceptive political ads, as judged by criteria set by an independent, trusted third party. Badging protocols akin to a Good Housekeeping Seal of Approval could be utilized to demonstrate an outlet's adherence to best practices in filtering out bogus material.

Deceptive political ads online are trickier to remedy because internet service providers are legally classified as "content platforms," not publishers. As such, they are protected from liability for slander or libel. To avoid censorship or impinging free speech, the emphasis must be placed on empowering internet users to be better consumers of content through the following:

- A robust public information campaign helping people spot indicators and patterns of deception and foul tactics in ads and political communications
- An automated capability to filter out paid political ads from internet feeds
- Real-time access to software programs and linked services providing instant notification of material reviewed by trusted third-party fact-checkers like Flack-Check and PolitiFact[70]
- Basic transparency about who is paying for online political ads

Online political ads are presently not covered by Federal Election Commission rules requiring sponsor disclosure. People have a right to know who is behind the political messages they receive and how they were targeted. As the academics Matthew Crain and Anthony Nadler argue in their article "Political Manipulation and Internet Advertising Infrastructure," "the consumer of the ad should know as much about the sponsor as the sponsor knows about the target."[71]

The process would be well served by disclosing to the public and press all official campaign mass communication. Requiring political parties and campaigns to make all electioneering communications—including fundraising letters and campaign ads—available on their website would facilitate transparency and accountability. So would stipulating that outside expenditure groups that spend over certain amounts on mass communication for direct campaign advocacy have copies of the material posted by the Federal Election Commission. Greater transparency and access would help public interest watchdog groups curate and call out deceitful campaign activities.

While Congress resists passing anti–push polling legislation, states are stepping up to the task. Florida, Idaho, Iowa, Nevada, and Virginia require poll takers to disclose who is paying for the poll. Others require the sponsor to file the poll with the state. West Virginia bans any poll that is "deceptively designed or intentionally conducted in a manner calculated to advocate the election or defeat of any candidate or group of candidates or calculated to influence any person or persons so polled to vote for or against any candidate."[72] Such laws could be adopted nationwide and standardized to improve the integrity of federal elections as well as campaigns for state and local office.

Outlawing deception in political campaigns and electioneering communications is a fruitless undertaking, likelier to invite the abuse of democratic rights than to protect them. Reform centered on better informing "we the people" about deceptive speech and disreputable tactics, empowering us to evaluate the content we receive, is our best option. Responsible norms can be better enforced at the voting booth rather than in a courtroom or a censor's desk.

Absent such reforms, the degrading quality of never-ending, dirty political campaigns will continue to chip away at the quality of American democracy. Not the least of the effects will be ensuring that growing sums of money that finance modern elective politics will flow in stronger torrents for longer periods to their lowest and worst use.

4

Money Chase (Financial Gear)

> There are two things that are important in politics. The first is money and I can't
> remember what the second one is.
>
> —Senator Mark Hanna

Roger Tamraz was a wanted man. Law enforcement agencies in Europe and the Middle East sought him on criminal charges involving alleged financial fraud and embezzlement. Meanwhile, Politics Inc. was chasing him for campaign contributions, which suited him nicely because he wanted something in return. His story exemplifies why the country is so deeply cynical about the connection between money, politics, and public affairs.

Seeking to make his fortune in energy development, Tamraz looked to the oil- and gas-rich Caucasus region straddling Europe and Asia. Following the collapse of the Soviet Union, the region was independent and offering opportunities. Tamraz envisioned the construction of a pipeline to transport crude from Azerbaijan on the Caspian Sea to the Mediterranean. By his reckoning, bringing such an ambitious plan to fruition would require strong US political support.[1]

Upon coming to the United States in the 1980s, Tamraz had donated money to the Republican National Committee, seeking favor for his business interests from Republicans during a decade of leadership under GOP presidents Reagan and Bush. In 1995, with Democrat Bill Clinton at the helm, it was time to curry favor with a party newly in charge. A letter from the Democratic National Committee soliciting Tamraz for a donation provided the opening. Thus began a yearlong odyssey, turning campaign contributions into high-level political access, scandal, and a US Senate investigation.

Tamraz and his project had become well known to the National Security Council (NSC). Having examined both carefully, the NSC found no justification for granting official support either to Tamraz, given his shady past, or to the pipeline, given its commercial and strategic deficiencies. Notwithstanding the NSC's attempts to close the doors to US support, the force of campaign dollars kicked them open all the way to the White House.

As Tamraz showered various political organizations with donations totaling $300,000, party officials ushered him to dinners and other gatherings with President Clinton. A meeting with the president at the White House spurred a letter of thanks from Tamraz to Democratic National Convention officials for arranging it. The president in turn wrote Tamraz a note of appreciation "for being there when you are asked to help," while the White House chief of staff asked how to assist the project.[2] A couple of miles away at Democratic National Committee headquarters, party officials were seeking ways to overcome the NSC, cajoling political appointees at the Department of Energy to pressure NSC staff to change their position. Meanwhile, according to the party's top fundraiser, "All of us were continually asking him for money through the course of the year."[3]

Tamraz worked other US government agencies too, including the Overseas Project Investment Corporation (OPIC), which was created to financially assist US-sponsored commercial projects abroad. Seeking access, he made a $30,000 contribution to the Iowa Democratic Party. Not coincidentally, OPIC's director was the wife of a sitting US senator from that state. According to a witness in an ensuing Senate investigation of the affair, the director was "under enormous pressure" by party officials to meet with Tamraz.[4] A meeting eventually took place with midlevel OPIC personnel. The investigation report did not address whether the Iowa donation was an idea hatched by Tamraz or a political functionary. In the end, Tamraz did not realize his aspiration to become an oil baron. The episode, however, proved a case study in the never-ending struggle to right the relationship between money and politics and between politics and policy making.

The Senate's investigative report concluded with a note of admiration and gratitude to a lone "hero" at the NSC, Sheila Heslin, who stood her ground against political pressure.[5] Tamraz's conclusion was a little more cynical. He offered that he should have donated $600,000. In his own testimony before the Senate, he avowed that if someone blocks the door to access, then he would "come through the window."[6] The case may have been extraordinary for its publicity and perhaps the level of direct involvement of the West Wing. Quite common, however, is the general rule that when political donations are involved, doors and windows fly open all over Washington.

MOTHER'S MILK

Americans have every right to raise or donate money to support political parties, causes, and campaigns. Political organizations play an important role in democracy. Like any enterprise, they require financial resources to operate. But when enormous sums are raised from single sources and excessive time and effort is spent raising money, it has proven time and again to have a corrosive effect on the behavior of donors and recipients. At the very least, it gives the public the appearance that big donors pay for and receive special treatment.

The connection between money and politics has a long, scandal-stained history of worsening abuses followed by slow but eventual reform. Until Civil Service reform late in the nineteenth century, parties and politicians relied for money on kickbacks from government employees—the price of employment in jobs that depended on political patronage.[7] The next battle was to stop the flow of tainted campaign cash from corporations and unions, set limits on donations, and establish disclosure requirements. The cleanup took more than six decades of incremental reform beginning in 1907 and culminated with major overhaul in the early 1970s, including the long-awaited establishment of the Federal Elections Commission (FEC) to enforce campaign finance law. The last major campaign finance reform—the Bipartisan Campaign Reform Act, also known as McCain-Feingold—was passed in 2002. The measure closed loopholes created when corporations and unions evaded disclosure by spending millions on so-called issue ads. The ads attacked or promoted candidates but were not subject to reporting requirements because the ads stopped short of expressly advocating for or against a candidate's election, though their intent was clear. Beyond stopping scandal, the Bipartisan Campaign Reform Act and the modern campaign finance reform movement have sought to eliminate even the appearance of it—and not just the worst of it, outright bribery and extortion, but also the soft corruption of paid-for special access and undue influence. Doing so required eliminating unlimited donations and non-disclosure of donors.

Despite the legal, regulatory, and normative framework to help keep the system clean, political operators found ways to weaken and defeat it. Rather than directly attacking popular laws, they mobilize lawyers to find workarounds, lodge successful court challenges, and support the seating of judges unsympathetic to finance regulation and the appointment of regulators loath to enforce it. As a result, huge and rapidly growing sums now wash around the system, fueling a fevered race between the two parties to outraise and outspend one another.

When Ronald Reagan and Jimmy Carter squared off in the 1980 presidential race, their combined campaign expenditures fell short of $200 million (in 2020 dollars).[8] Climbing each cycle since, the cost of the presidential election in 2000 exceeded $2 billion and blew past the $5 billion mark in 2020.[9] Campaign spending for presidential and congressional races combined soared from $4.5 billion in 2000 to $7 billion in 2012 to an eye-popping $14 billion in 2020.[10] By comparison, between 2000 and 2020, the Consumer Price Index rose 50 percent.[11] Over that same period, what we could call the Political Price Index, campaign spending, rose 300 percent.[12]

Politics Inc. loves the escalating financial arms race, but practically no one else does. Most businesses, unions, and other interest groups are weary of being pestered but fear being ignored or punished for their failure to pony up. Many candidates detest shaking down people for donations and the perception that they are beholden to their beneficiaries. When asked their view of fundraising, colorful pejoratives fly from Republicans and Democrats alike—"painful," "miserable," "distasteful," and "embarrassing."[13] Congressman John Larson of Connecticut spoke for many colleagues when he attested, "You might as well be putting bamboo shoots under my fingernails."[14]

The overwhelming majority of Americans dislike the outsized role of money in elective politics and how it dominates the legislative branch.[15] Yet, political fundraising pervades the very architecture of the Capitol complex and unduly shapes congressional behavior. The party fundraising organizations—Democratic Senatorial Campaign Committee, Democratic Congressional Campaign Committee, Republican Senatorial Campaign Committee, and National Republican Congressional Committee—are within easy walking distance of the House and Senate chambers so members who endeavor to abide by the prohibition on fundraising in government quarters can call potential donors. Waiting for them are oversized tote boards depicting their progress toward filling fundraising quotas for the party as well as massive amounts raised for their own campaigns. Says Marcie Kaptur (D-OH), "It is clear that political party fundraising has been moved directly into Congress, at levels never imagined by the Founders."[16] The incessant push for cash consumes party rank and file down to the greenest freshman member.

The price tag party leaders place on committee chairs and top committee seats grows steeper every Congress, drawing the ire of Issue One's "reformers caucus"-- a group that knows from its experience on the inside how fundraising dominates officialdom's time, energy, and practices.[17] In *Extortion: How Politicians Extract Your Money, Buy Votes and Line Their Own Pockets*, Peter Schweitzer found that Republicans who chair the biggest committees had a quota of $990,000 in "party dues" and $750,000 for the second-tier panels. Documents obtained by Schweitzer and *Buzzfeed* revealed that in the 113th Congress (2013–2014), Democratic leadership of the A committees (the biggest and most influential) were on the hook to the party's congressional campaign committee for $1.5 million. Rank-and-file members are expected to produce half a million dollars.[18] The practice not only offends members just entering office; it encourages experienced members to leave. "I don't know of a single member that is leaving that does not include the pressures of raising money to advance and maintain your committee position as one of the contributing factors," says Zach Wamp (R-GA). "They all talk about it. It wears you out."[19]

DUN AND DONE

Where must the members who remain go for the funds to stay current with their party dues? To the industries and interests their committees are responsible for overseeing—creating what to even the most accommodating mind is a clear conflict of interest. Who can blame the public for thinking the worst? Barney Frank, a thirty-two-year Democratic member of Congress, said, "People say, 'Oh, it doesn't have any effect on me.' Well if that were the case, we'd be the only human beings in the history of the world who on a regular basis took significant amounts of money from perfect strangers and made sure that it had no effect on our behavior."[20] The pressures can and do alter the character of members' service. In the words of Representative Jim Jones, "Big money doesn't come in casually. It wants to have its point of view prevail, whether it's to block legislation or to promote legislation. Therefore, big money becomes more of the driving force in public policy than it should be."[21] According to one of Jones's former colleagues, "You won't ask tough questions in hearings that might displease potential contributors, won't support amendments that might anger them, will tend to vote the way contributors want you to vote."[22]

During a 1994 Senate run against Ted Kennedy and his enormous campaign war chest, Mitt Romney observed that "money plays a much more important role in what is done in Washington than we believe. . . . You've got to cozy up, as an incumbent, to all the special interest groups who can go out and raise money for you from their members, and that kind of a relationship has an influence on the way you're gonna vote."[23]

Over 90 percent of members of Congress seek reelection. They have to maintain a breakneck fundraising schedule, a daily rhythm of breakfasts, lunches, receptions, and dinners.[24] In between, they dial for dollars. Congressman David Jolly told *60 Minutes* about being instructed in that harsh reality by party strategists. "We sat behind closed doors at one of the party headquarter back rooms in front of a white board where the equation was drawn out," he said. "You have six months until the election. Break that down to having to raise $2 million in the next six months. And your job, new member of Congress, is to raise $18,000 a day. Your first responsibility is to make sure you hit $18,000 a day."[25] Congressman Steve Israel estimated that fundraising consumed 70 percent of his working time—approximately thirty hours per week. He chose to leave Congress rather than submit to the incessant demand to chase campaign cash at the expense of official duties.[26] Says Wamp, "There is more focus on that than solving the country's problems. For good people, that's a real bummer."[27]

Such a distracting grind makes it impossible for elected officials to devote their full energy toward the job they were elected to do—represent the interests of their constituencies, grapple with complex issues, and find solutions to pressing national challenges. An employee of any organization other than the United States Congress who spent most of their time preparing for their next job would be fired. But most members of Congress aren't fired. Though Congress's approval rating hovers just above food poisoning, incumbents enjoy a reelection rate of almost 95 percent.[28] Yet, the preoccupation with fundraising leaves vital business unattended and confers undue power and influence on congressional staff, lobbyists, and other unelected and unaccountable figures. In an interview with the *Huffington Post*, a member who asked to remain anonymous noted, "One thing that's always been striking to me is even the members playing a leading role on specific issues actually could not talk about the issues. They didn't have enough knowledge on their own issues to talk about them at length. I'm probably guilty of that."

He recalled a particular legislative negotiation where "staff members were all twitching at the discussion, because their principals were saying things that were just flat-wrong or uninformed. . . . The members were sitting around the table having a remarkably uninformed and unproductive discussion."[29] Disturbing, yes, but not terribly surprising in a congress of fundraisers. "It's not Republicans or Democrats," says Charles Lewis, founder of the Center for Public Integrity, "it's both. It's ugly, and it's getting uglier than ever."[30]

The time and energy drain is not a burden on the legislative branch alone. The commander in chief, dual-hatted as the party leader, is now the fundraiser in chief. In his third and fourth years in office, Ronald Reagan attended a total of eight fundraisers for the party and his reelection committee.[31] During the second half of their first terms, George H. W. Bush attended 25, Bill Clinton attended 80, George W. Bush attended 86, and Barack Obama attended 228.[32] Donald Trump attended 125 from late 2017 through 2020.[33]

THE BENEFACTORS

Super PACs have already received some attention above and will receive more below, but the venerable political action committee remains one of Washington's most reliable money conduits. PACs came into being when federal law prohibited corporations and unions from providing campaign contributions directly from their books. They enable collective interests to gather limited, voluntary personal contributions for political giving. The committees may then disburse the funds under set contribution limits to a federal campaign, other PACs (including those run by members of Congress), and political parties. PAC disbursements are typically directed by the organization's lobbyist or federal affairs personnel.

The dual-hatted fundraiser-lobbyist has become an important figure to the parties' fundraising committees, the 535 members of Congress, and their campaign treasuries, not only because they hook them up with PAC money; they also host Washington fundraisers attended by fellow lobbyists, typically from the same industry, who come bearing either PAC or personal contributions.

Lobbying suffers a poor public reputation, but the right to petition government is constitutionally protected, and lobbyists play a valuable role in educating lawmakers about the impact of their actions. The public interest is served so long as the process is open and accessible to all sides of an issue. Contributing money, likewise, is a legitimate form of civic engagement, provided contributions fall within sensible limits and the origins of the cash are fully disclosed. Combining the two roles, however—advising Congress and the executive branch while arranging large contributions to campaigns and parties—creates the foul.

As a young staffer, I observed an illuminating example of the system in action when I witnessed a lobbyist approach a United States senator just off the Capitol steps. The lobbyist enthusiastically reported to the senator the status of efforts to organize a major campaign fundraiser among his industry cohorts on the senator's behalf. When he finished the update, he said to the senator, "Now, let me take that hat off and put on another hat." Pantomiming the hat exchange, he proceeded to express the industry's wishes regarding the senator's position on an upcoming measure.

Who knows if the appeal had any impact on the senator's viewpoint. Perhaps the merits of the case were on the lobbyist's side. But it strains credulity to think that fundraising updates have no influence on policy appeals or that a system that encourages such two-hatted approaches should raise no concerns.

For many lobbyists, the ability to fundraise is inseparable from the need for access to be heard. Fundraising events at which PAC donations or personal contributions are delivered or pledged are treasured opportunities for the donors to give their inputs on politics and policy, which are often perspectives that officials should know to perform their duties properly—that is, provided the official seeks the views of those on the other side of an issue who may not be as well resourced. Not infrequently, there is another donor on the other side of the issue.

Sometimes, however, the largesse buys much more than access. A 2009 *New York Times* story revealed that twelve members of Congress who had received campaign contributions from a corporate PAC, along with individual donations from a number of the firm's employees, placed remarks into the congressional record written directly by the company.[34] One study found that when congressional staffers were aware that a group had donated to their respective congressman's campaigns, the group was three times more likely to get a meeting with a senior staffer and four times more likely to meet with the actual congressman.[35]

Much as many members of Congress dislike fundraising, many lobbyists tire of being bombarded by requests to donate and host fundraising events. In an interview with Public Radio International, a lobbyist for the real estate industry spoke for many of his colleagues. "You could look on your phone with these caller IDs and you would be like, really? I'm not taking that call," he said. "Every lobbyist does it."[36] The pressure to give and potential consequences of not donating are why many special interests do and must give to politicians, often to both parties—and not infrequently to both sides in the same race.

Sometimes, funds aren't just requested; they are demanded in ways that cross into outright extortion. A small anecdote tells the larger story. The president of a large company, accompanied by the company's lobbyist, was paying a visit to an important House member from his state. The visitors were ushered into the congressman's office. As the guests took their seats, the congressman kicked off the meeting by curtly observing that while his opponent in the upcoming election had received a full PAC donation from the company, he had not. As the congressman stared at him stone-faced, the executive was obliged to excuse himself so that he could place a phone call instructing the firm's PAC chairman to send a donation immediately to the member's campaign. The meeting was then allowed to resume. That kind of leverage over donors partly explains why incumbent members of Congress enjoy a twelve-to-one fundraising advantage over challengers.[37]

The obsessive race for money to foot skyrocketing campaigns costs creates other defects in the system. A growing share of congressional campaign funds come from donors who aren't even eligible to vote in the election they are seeking to influence. In the 115th Congress (2016–2017), four of five election winners received more than 50 percent of their contributions from outside their own congressional district.[38] A bare sliver of the donations to Paul Ryan, the Speaker of the House, came from within his district.[39] One study of the 2016 cycle found that over 77 percent of contributions (raised by candidates, PACs, super PACs, and party committees) to influence Senate races came from outside the state where the election was being held, and "in seven swing senate races highlighted in the report, a full 85 percent of election funding is coming from out-of-state."[40]

The Supreme Court's opinion in *Buckley v. Valeo* (1976) held that political finance and political speech are synonymous, a controversial and highly consequential legal theory.[41] If valid, could the framers have possibly intended for office seekers to "listen" more to parties they are not representing in Congress than those they are? It seems difficult to imagine the answer could be anything but a resounding "No!"

There is, however, a source of big money much closer to home on which politicians increasingly depend—themselves. Among the first questions party officials ask a prospective candidate are the extent of their personal wealth and their ability to tap a network of people who can write big checks. Craig Holman, government affairs lobbyist for the consumer advocacy organization Public Citizen, points out, "Wealthy candidates who try to buy office with their own money tend to lose, but in order to set up a campaign, you have to know a lot of wealthy people and wealthy special interests—and that's something that most of us are not privy to."[42] Two factors play a role. Campaigning is a full-time job. Candidates must have the personal wherewithal to afford a sustained effort. And, because the average cost of winning a Senate seat is well north of $10 million and a House seat almost $1.5 million, the parties have a strong interest in recruiting wealthy candidates to bring down the cost of their own contribution to financing the run.[43]

In the 2018 midterm elections, sixty-one candidates self-funded their congressional campaigns, the most ever. Forty-one spent at least $1 million out of their own pocket, totaling over $240 million.[44] In 2020, thirty-six spent at least $1 million out of their own pocket, totaling over $106 million.[45] Self-funders argue that their personal wealth insulates them from the need to rely on special interests for financing. (We must leave aside, at least for the moment, what that argument says about non-self-funders.) And wealthy individuals who are self-made often have prized talents and leadership skills. But it is decidedly undemocratic when wealth becomes a prerequisite for political service. Means-testing eligibility for elective service, de facto disenfranchises all but the tiniest sliver of the population, and bears the corrosive scent of plutocracy.

SUPER SPENDING

The force most responsible for driving up the cost and negativity of US politics is the astronomical amount of unlimited, and in some cases undisclosed, money flooding into the system. As mentioned in chapter 2, the US Supreme Court's 2010 opinion in *Citizens United v. FEC* paved the way for super PACs (also known as independent-expenditure-only political committees). While donors are limited in what they give directly to campaigns, a super PAC can collect unlimited amounts of money from corporations, unions, associations, and individual donors. The lone legal stipulation is that the PAC's spending must not be coordinated with the candidate's campaign or political party. The ruling also invalidated numerous state laws limiting independent expenditures.[46]

The court based its decision on the idea that if the "independent expenditure only committee" is not giving to or coordinating with a campaign, there can be no quid pro quo of money for favors and therefore no corruption. That sounds nice—but it is completely impractical. Republican senator John McCain called the fictional separation between benefiting candidate and the super PAC's contributors "the worst joke in Washington," saying, "it's an insult to anyone's intelligence to say they're not connected." Independent senator Angus King of Maine said the notion of an unaffiliated super PAC exists only in a "fevered imagination."[47] Chuck Schumer, the Senate's top Democrat, called the advent of super PACs a "disaster for our democracy."[48]

Super PACs reported total receipts of over $3 billion and total independent expenditures of over $2 billion in the 2020 federal elections cycle.[49] The big donors who fund them enjoy big access. Just ask Lev Parnas. A $325,000 donation made in the name of his "company," Global Energy Producers, to America First Action, an "independent" pro-Trump super PAC, led him to the Trump Hotel in Washington and a tony dinner with a select group of mega-donors and President Trump—before vaulting him into the news.[50]

Parnas was pursuing a natural gas project in Ukraine. He came to believe that the US ambassador to the country, Marie Yovanovitch, was an obstacle to his ambitions. Like Roger Tamraz, Parnas had a checkered past, but his campaign donations helped stamp his political passport. The black-tie dinner with Trump afforded him the opportunity to acquaint the president with his troubles and urge that Yovanovitch be fired. Rudy Giuliani, a longtime Parnas associate as well as Trump's personal lawyer, shared a commercial interest in Ukraine and a similar disdain for Yovanovitch.[51] He found the well-regarded career foreign service officer politically unhelpful in his quest to uncover dirt on Ukrainian business dealings of Hunter Biden, son of Joe Biden, then the presumptive Democratic nominee. Around the same time, Parnas made a campaign contribution to Representative Pete Sessions of Texas, who in a letter to Secretary of State Mike Pompeo echoed the call for Yovanovitch's ouster.

Yovanovitch was eventually removed, and Trump withheld US military aid to the Ukrainian government for snubbing his demand that Kiev publicly announce an investigation into Hunter Biden's activities. Trump's actions in the Ukraine were the cause of his first impeachment by the House of Representatives. In October 2019, Parnas and his associate Igor Fruman were arrested at Dulles Airport for US campaign finance law violations. Over a year earlier, well before the Ukraine scandal began to unfold, the Campaign Legal Center, a clean politics advocacy group in Washington, DC, alleged that the super PAC contribution that opened so many doors for Parnas—the $325,000 given in the name of "Global Energy Producers"— was illegal. Finding that the company was established shortly before the donation was made and did not have the business revenue to cover the six-figure donation, Campaign Legal Center filed a complaint with the FEC in July 2018 alleging the company was used as a conduit to channel money derived from another source, in violation of the federal "straw donor" ban. Investigators tracked the money to the sale of Fruman's Miami condo to a Russian businessman.[52]

The dominance of super PAC spending exacerbates practically every ill of the US campaign finance system and its harm to governance. Candidates must raise even more money for their own campaign coffers to counter the influence of unlimited outside spending. For incumbents, this means even more time focused on fundraising instead of their official duties and dispensing more IOUs to special interest groups who pony up donations.

Some of the biggest super PACs are not "outside" spenders at all but tied to congressional leaders. The Senate Leadership Fund (Senate Republican leader), Senate Majority PAC (Senate Democratic leader), Congressional Leadership Fund (House GOP leaders), and House Majority Fund (House Democratic leader) were the top-spending super PACs in the 2018 and 2020 cycles, followed by other super PACs closely associated with candidates or party leaders.[53]

Super PACs have been joined by another and even less accountable mechanism for unlimited political money and one that promises anonymity to the donor. They are not-for-profit organizations that enjoy tax-exempt status under section 501(c) of the Internal Revenue Code; the subcategories are social welfare groups (c)(4), labor unions (c)(5), and business leagues (c)(6). Like super PACs, they can receive and spend unlimited contributions in elections and may not coordinate the spending with a political campaign. Unlike super PACs, donor disclosure is not required, provided that the 501(c) meets the "primary purpose" test. In practical terms, this means that if an organization spends slightly over half of its money on its primary purpose, then it can spend the remainder without limits and anonymously (and in the case of 501[c]4s with tax deductibility) on electioneering activities. The giant loophole means that vast sums can be transferred by the nonprofit to a super PAC to be used for negative attack ads without the public ever knowing the source of the money. Such organizations delivered over $660 million to super PACs in the 2020 cycle. Voila! Super PAC money becomes dark money.[54]

Numerous dummy 501(c)4s have been created for the purpose of allowing anonymized, huge-dollar contributions to flow into elective politics, proving that electioneers, big donors, and their lawyers are inventive and persistent in violating the spirit of campaign finance rules. Notable examples include the Democrats' Majority

Forward, Patriot Majority, Big Tent Project, and Duty & Honor; and the Republicans' One Nation, 45 Committee, and Crossroads GPS.

The Center for Responsive Politics notes that since 2010, "dark money" groups like 501(c)s and shell corporations that either don't disclose or obscure the source of contributions have spent over $1 billion to influence the outcome of federal elections.[55] They spent $350 million on political ads in the 2020 federal elections.[56] Senator Sheldon Whitehouse observed, "These entities have no purpose other than as a screening intermediary through which funds flow. . . . In go huge contributions from a donor, with instructions on how the money should be spent; out the money goes to electioneering groups that can spend it with no true record of where the money originated."[57]

In addition to ushering huge checks and undisclosed donations into partisan politics, the rise of independent expenditure will deepen other pathologies of US political culture, including weaker political parties, higher concentrations of negative partisanship, and pay to play in the nation's public affairs. In a report for the *Atlantic*, Jonathan Rauch found that both political parties are increasingly anxious about the trends involving independent expenditures. A party official told him, "We believe we are fighting for our lives in the current legal and judicial framework, and the super pacs and (c)(4)s really present a direct threat to the state parties' existence."[58]

Without viable, representative parties, the title fights in American politics will become rules-free and normless barroom brawls, yielding little more than disorder and unaccountability. As the hitmen of Politics Inc., outside spenders put their vast resources to work degrading national discourse. As already noted, super PAC-financed ads are typically far more noxious and far more negative than candidate- or party-sponsored appeals.

A growing but still modest percentage of the population takes part in financing runs for public office. In each federal election since 1990, when the Center for Responsive Politics started tracking political donations, no more than 1.5 percent of the population contributed more than $200 to a political campaign, party, or PAC. That is roughly the same number of Americans who play professional sports. Less than half of that number—a wafer-thin sliver of the electorate—contributed the maximum personal campaign donation allowed by the Federal Elections Commission ($2,800 as of 2019).[59] The top ten individual donors to super PACs accounted for 35.3 percent of their total outside spending of $1.06 billion during the 2016 congressional and presidential elections and 31.6 percent of the $2.111 billion spent in the 2020 elections.[60] A report by Issue One based on data supplied by the nonpartisan Center for Responsive Politics found that "the $3.4 billion contributed by the top 12 megadonors—six of whom generally supported Democrats and six of whom generally supported Republicans—amounts to 7.5% of the $45 billion that all federal candidates and political groups raised between January 2009 and December 2020."[61]

The 2020 election cycle produced a record-breaking upturn in small donations of $5 and $10 up to $200. Yet, the influential role of large special-interest contributors reinforces the public perception of a monied elite manipulating the levers of politics on the left and the right. Though presidents and congressional leaders come and go, George Soros and the Koch brothers have long been center ring influencing American politics, never having had to win an election or explain themselves to the nation. Eighty-seven percent of Americans believe that "campaign finance should be reformed so that a rich person does not have more influence than a person without money."[62] Despite the growth of internet fundraising based on small donations, nearly four out of five Americans think that government is "run by a few big interests looking out for themselves."[63] Such widespread cynicism is a recent phenomenon. "This question has been asked for decades in a national political science survey," says Trevor Potter, president of the Campaign Legal Center. "By comparison, in 1964, only 29 percent of us felt that way."[64]

Freedom of speech, especially political speech, is a sacred constitutional right that commands the highest level of legal protection. The Supreme Court's decisions in *Buckley v. Valeo*, *Citizens United v. FEC*, and *McCutcheon v. FEC* swung open the gate on unlimited and in some cases undisclosed political donations. The opinions are based on the highly controversial premise that money and speech are synonymous and that limiting the size of electioneering expenditures equates to an unconstitutional infringement on the right of free political speech. While Politics Inc. has pounced on the theory, clean government advocates are back on familiar ground—trying to eliminate from American politics big-dollar donations that confer outsized influence to big special interests.

The courts will face new cases testing the theory equating money and speech so long as the current system offends the public conscience. And legal challenges will also likely emanate from state-generated campaign finance reforms and novel controversies involving the use of technology in political advertising. In the 2019–2020 election cycle, spending on digital political ads broke the $1.5 billion barrier, five times the amount spent in 2016 federal elections and twice the amount spent in the 2017–2018 cycle.[65] The trend looks to accelerate, not only because the medium so efficiently connects with targeted audiences but also because online political appeals—unlike print and broadcast ads—are not required to disclose who sponsored and paid for them. Law and policy need to catch up.

The internet has proven a powerful engine for generating small-dollar contributions from a broad group of donors. That's good for democracy. Not so positive are the divisive appeals accompanying online fundraising campaigns. "Money bomb" events became an online sensation as a grassroots means of bringing small-dollar contributors into the system—looking to democratize campaign finance. The fundraisers are virtual events featuring collection goals within a set time period in association with some thematic historical event or occasion.[66] Like so many other aspects of the internet, the grass roots are shaded over and choked by the grass tops. Look for big operators in Politics Inc. to use internet money bomb campaigns tied to staged events on the House or Senate floor in what promises to be the ultimate abuse and the ultimate irony—turning the legislative process itself into another gimmicky fundraiser.

EARNING TRUST

As the policy, regulatory, and judicial communities confront the many issues at the intersection of money and politics, three paradoxes arising from court decisions must be resolved. One, if money and speech are equivalent, as the Supreme Court says in *Buckley v. Valeo*, how is it that using the megaphone of money to drown out other voices does not infringe on the right of others to speak and be heard?

Two, in striking down laws restricting politicians from self-funding their campaigns, the high court reasoned that a candidate cannot corrupt themselves by self-contributing, opining that spending one's own money would reduce reliance on outside contributions, lessening the risk of corruption from outside contributions.[67] How can super PACs not be corruptive when unlimited outside contributions can be made with the full knowledge and gratitude of the elected official benefited, even if the money is not spent in coordination with the campaign?

Three, the high court has recognized the government's prerogative to legislate against the "appearance of corruption" and to meet the "compelling government interest" of clean elections with narrowly tailored rules.[68] What could appear more corrupt than a fundraising-obsessed political system? What government interest could be more compelling than restoring the public's faith in the integrity of civic processes, channelling the focus of our elected officials on their appointed duties, and making elections more a battle of ideas instead of money?

Righting the role of money in politics is an age old challenge, but with new imperatives given the public's distrust in the political process weighing heavy on America's democracy. Needed most, of course, is the reversal of the court's decision in *Citizens United*, restoring the ability to enforce two main pillars of clean campaign finance: limits on the size of donations for electioneering purposes and bans on donations from organizations most likely to invite or appear to invite corruption. The Supreme Court is supreme but not impervious to logic and strong public demand to protect the fundamental integrity of our democracy. Without faith in the campaign finance system, there will be little faith in our system of politics and government and eventually in our nation.

In the meantime, five steps can start to right the role of money in politics and government:

1. **Upgrade and enforce rules barring the coordination of super PAC spending** with candidates and their campaign committees, as well as their other interactions and associations that foster the public perception of corruption.
2. **Separate government functions from political fundraising.** Utah bans campaign contributions to its governor, state legislators, and other officials while its state legislature is in session.[69] Alaska bars lobbyists from holding fundraising events for state lawmakers (except those from within the area the lawmaker represents).[70] Both reforms would meet fierce resistance in Washington but benefit the nation, and separating lobbying and the fundraising function

altogether would be better. Ending the practice of assigning fundraising dues to committee chairs could be accomplished by changes in congressional rules and practices without necessitating any change in law. An Issue One report said it best: "Those who are expected to handle the government's most important work should be selected primarily for their knowledge and skill, not their fundraising prowess. Doing otherwise further erodes the people's trust in government."[71]

3. **Clean up who can donate money to a political campaign.** Much good could be accomplished by restricting congressional campaign contributors to residents of the district or state and to PACs composed predominantly of individuals eligible to vote in the election they are seeking to influence. If wealthy individuals take advantage of the restriction by personally outspending their opponent, allow challengers to raise outside money up to the limit a candidate self-funds.

4. **Improve the transparency of donors seeking to influence elections.** Require disclosure of dollars donated to 501(c)s used for electioneering. Likewise, name the sponsors of paid online electioneering ads. Moreover, the FEC should promulgate a rule requiring that a copy of all fundraising appeals such as direct mail (snail and electronic) be posted on campaign websites for all voters to evaluate.

5. **Expand public financing options.** As a means of controlling campaign costs and avoiding the perpetual private fundraising for public office, fourteen states have instituted public financing of campaigns for state office—mostly in the form of spending limits in exchange for matching funds.[72] The city of Seattle has implemented a system providing publicly financed vouchers to citizens for each to allocate to the candidate of their choice.[73]

The idea of public finance was first proposed by Republican president Theodore Roosevelt in 1907. The 1974 Federal Election Campaign Act amendments put the idea into practice, establishing a public financing mechanism for primary and general presidential campaigns. They were used in every election until Barack Obama determined that raising unlimited money would give him an advantage in his 2008 race against John McCain. The mechanism has not been used since.[74] In 1978, nearly 25 percent of taxpayers checked off the voluntary three-dollar contribution to finance the Presidential Election Campaign Fund. Participation has been on the steady decline since. A scant 4 percent of filers did so in 2018.[75] States and cities will continue to be the incubators of the most creative and practical methods. Such systems could be configured in many different ways, but to achieve their objective must provide for voluntary adherence to spending limits, encourage small donations, reduce financial barriers to candidacy, and broaden public participation and trust in the integrity of campaigns and elections. What's abundantly clear is that the impetus for reform—the best ideas and the commitment to make them work—must come from a public demand, not be left to a conflicted Congress and a self-interested political duopoly.

Despite the parties' public posturing and rationalizations on how campaigns are financed, in the end both are interested in just one thing: whatever will most likely advantage their side. Absent tough, committed reform, each election will continue to set new fundraising and campaign spending records. The tone of campaigns and national political discourse will grow more strident. The additional time needed to fundraise will divert incumbents further from their official duties. More money will wash in from out of district; out of state; and, though illegal, probably from out of country, untethering elected officials from the people they are supposed to represent.

Political parties will grow weaker while independent operators pursuing narrow agendas will hijack the party brands, outmanning, outspending, and out-influencing organized political movements. The ugliness and high cost of running will repel our best from elective service. The public will grow more splintered and further alienated from the system.

Meanwhile Politics Inc. will keep laughing all the way to the bank, making efforts to heal America's political culture harder.

5

Running in Place (Structural Gear)

O, it is excellent to have a giant's strength, but it is tyrannous to use it like a giant.

—Shakespeare

Healing the country's deteriorating political culture will require more than correcting the nation's unseemly campaign finance practices on which Politics Inc. thrives. Reform must come to the structures and practices that the stale party duopoly has put in place to perpetuate its hold on power and prosecute its destructive rivalry across the continuum of representative government—running for office, electing our leaders, and making law. Modernizing the nation's democratic architecture by putting public interest ahead of party interest will not only make America's politics far better but our government and future as well.

In designing a radical new form of government, the country's founders were greatly influenced by the French philosopher Montesquieu, who in his 1748 treatise *Spirit of the Laws* set forth the doctrine of *trias politica* advocating the division of government into three branches.[1] In the American version of *trias politica*, the first and most important element is the "people's branch" of Congress by merit of its direct link to the governed—the heart and soul of representative democracy. Through regularly elected representatives, the will of the people and the individual states would be translated into the nation's laws and policies for the executive branch to administer and the judicial branch to interpret and adjudicate.

Among the seminal questions in framing the Constitution's first article, which established the Congress of the United States, was how best to provide for representation. After much wrangling and compromise, the framers opted for a bicameral legislative branch. Seats in the House of Representatives would be allocated to each state proportionally by its share of the nation's population. Representatives to fill them would be elected directly by the people. In the Senate, each state would be granted two senators so that large states could not run roughshod over the smaller ones.

When the gavel dropped calling the first Congress in March 1789 into session, the House had sixty-five seats apportioned among the thirteen states. As the nation's population grew and states were added to the union, the number of representatives also rose. Not until passage of the 1929 Permanent Apportionment Act was the current limit of a 435-member House of Representatives, to accompany each state's two senators, set by law.[2] Like previous apportionment laws, the 1929 act left responsibility for congressional boundary drawing to the individual states, providing little guidance on how the lines should be fixed.[3]

At that time, the US population stood at almost 122 million, and each member of Congress represented about 250,000 people. Today, in a country of 350 million people, the per district population exceeds 700,000 individuals. At the beginning of every decade, the federal government conducts a constitutionally mandated count that provides the basis for reapportioning the 435 congressional districts.[4] States whose share of the total population decreased from the previous census may lose a congressional district or two, which shift to states whose share has increased.

LINING OUT COMPETITION AND CENTRISM

The architects of American government did not supply detailed guidance on how congressional districts should be determined, but James Madison in *Federalist* 56 spoke to the matter broadly yet succinctly. "Divide the largest State into ten or twelve districts," wrote Madison, "and it will be found that there will be no peculiar local interests in either, which will not be within the knowledge of the representative of the district."[5] Nothing in Madison's words, the Constitution, or the *Federalist Papers* at large suggests that the framers meant, or even contemplated, the emergence of political parties that would game the system for partisan advantage or to secure the reelection of incumbent politicians. But in many cases today, that is precisely how districting works. The political party holding power in the state when the decennial census is taken plots congressional boundaries to maximize its political advantage until the next redistricting ten years hence—a procedure famously known as "gerrymandering" in honor of its founding practitioner.

Between representing Massachusetts in Congress and serving as James Madison's vice president, Elbridge Gerry won a long-sought term in 1810 as governor. There he became famous for tailoring Massachusetts district lines specifically to favor his Democratic-Republican Party over the rival Federalists. Among the artistically shaped creations he devised was a district resembling a tall, winged salamander, inspiring political cartoonists and pundits to create the clever tag.[6] Like most political mischief, the practice of gerrymandering has grown more sophisticated and insidious with time and know-how. Its prime objective, however, hasn't budged since Gerry took up his quill: to pack the state's congressional delegation with as many members of one's own political tribe as possible and to minimize the opposition.

Modern data analytics and software applications have brought digital precision to the process. The Brennan Center for Justice spells out some of the key objectives of modern gerrymandering, including "the fracturing of communities of interest, the protection of incumbents, the targeting of political foes, and/or the lack of competition in districts."[7] The tactics for achieving these and other machinations have labels as colorful as their aims. "Cracking" is weakening the opposing party or voting bloc by spreading their voters over multiple districts. "Packing" puts as many members of the opposing party into one district as possible to dilute their overall voting power. When doing so becomes race-based, the practice—banned by the Voting Rights Act—is called "bleaching."[8] "Hijacking" is the redrawing of two districts to force two incumbent members of the opposing party to face off, thereby eliminating one. "Kidnapping" creates a district that leaves the incumbent outside its boundaries, making their reelection more difficult.[9] Another districting abuse is what we might call "crowning": ensuring the safe reelection of incumbents, whether from the majority party drawing the lines or from the minority party in packed districts. Crowning plays a significant role in congressional gridlock and other political pathologies.

The contorted geometry required to perform all this magic is why many congressional and state legislative district maps look like deranged jigsaw puzzles. Gerrymandering combined with the money advantage enjoyed by officeholders largely explains why House incumbency remains in the ninetieth percentile election after election, despite a perpetually dismal congressional approval rating from a reform-hungry electorate.[10]

Cook Political Report's David Wasserman found that in the 2016 elections, only 40 of the 435 US House races were competitive, and just a handful could be classified as true toss-ups.[11] In 72 percent of the races, "the winner was effectively decided in the primary."[12] The 2018 and 2020 elections served up a larger number of toss-ups and competitive races, but incumbency still triumphed.[13] Even in a wild-card election like 2020, 380 out of 388 incumbents were rewarded with a new term.[14] In the lead-up to the 2018 contest, Lee Drutman of the New America Foundation advised that "only about one in 20 Americans lives in a place that appears likely to have a competitive House election."[15]

Incumbent members are winning not just with high frequency but by widening margins. The number of congressional elections won in a landslide (defined as a twenty-percentage-point victory or greater) rose steadily each cycle from 1992 to 2012. Over that period, Republican landslides jumped from 58 to 125; Democrats' blowouts kept pace, soaring from 65 to 117. Over the same period, the number of contested "swing districts" plunged from 103 to 35.[16] The *average* margin of victory in the Senate and House in the four federal elections between 2012 and 2018 was a stout twenty percentage points and thirty percentage points, respectively.[17]

In a nation that has long prized competition as the best way to drive improvement, the prevalence of uncompetitive congressional elections reveals troubling dynamics and systemic defects. Moreover, incumbent cakewalk victories promote the career-ification of congressional service, a trend borne out by data: the average years of service of the winners has been steadily rising.[18] Experience is a huge asset, no less in lawmaking than any other demanding enterprise; however, a professional class of politicians is removed from the founders' democratic ideal of the citizen-legislator. Meanwhile, the public's aversion to career politicians in Congress grows.

But an even greater menace of gerrymandering is its role in making Congress more extreme, more polarized, and less effective by driving out moderates. "Walled safely inside their gerrymandered districts," says Jonathan Rauch of the Brookings Institution, "incumbents are insulated from general-election challenges that might pull them toward the political center, but they are perpetually vulnerable to primary challenges from extremists who pull them toward the fringes."[19]

A study conducted at the University of Georgia found that in the 1950s, 80 percent of congressional Democrats and 47 percent of Republicans were moderates: in 2015, the respective figures had fallen to 14 percent and 4 percent.[20] By some calculations, only about twenty moderates remain in the House, evenly split between Republicans and Democrats. As centrists disappear, compromise declines. It's no coincidence that a strong majority of the relatively small Congressional Problem Solvers Caucus come from competitive districts.[21] Without compromise problems fester, leading to yet more partisan finger-pointing and polarizing rhetoric. The public channels the conflict, growing more divided and partisan itself. Within gerrymandered districts, the party activists push their primary election choices further to the extreme, helping to drive a negative feedback loop arranged, sponsored, and capitalized upon by Politics Inc.

Because the Republican Party currently controls the greater number of state legislatures, it benefits more from gerrymandering today than does the Democratic Party. That has not always been the case. As majorities shift, today's beneficiaries can be tomorrow's aggrieved. President Ronald Reagan called gerrymandering "a national scandal."[22] President Barack Obama described it as a practice that enables "politicians to pick their voters and not the other way around."[23] The public doesn't like it any better. Seventy-one percent of the respondents to a Harris poll said that "those who stand to benefit from redrawing congressional districts should not have a say in how they are redrawn."[24] The view was equally strong among Republicans, Democrats, and Independents, and among those describing themselves as conservative, moderate, and liberal.

Reformers have long hoped that the Supreme Court would step in to drive a stake through the heart of partisan districting. Those hopes were dashed in 2019. In a 5–4 decision, the high court declined to rule, declaring that "partisan gerrymandering claims present political questions beyond the reach of the federal courts. Federal judges have no license to reallocate political power between the two major political parties, with no plausible grant of authority in the Constitution, and no legal standards to limit and direct their decisions."[25] Thus, the practice remains intact. Empowered partisans soldier on. Millions of voters stuck in gerrymandered districts remain disenfranchised.

But the fault for gerrymandering sits with the state legislators and majority parties who make the districting decisions, not with judges. Federal law could be passed to curb the practice, but too many incumbents are products and beneficiaries of the status quo. Other than hearings in the mid-1990s and the following decade on race-based gerrymandering, Congress has shown little interest in reform.[26] Leaders at the state level, however, are stepping up. Larry Hogan, Maryland's GOP governor, and Roy Cooper, North Carolina's Democratic governor, lead two of the most gerrymandered states in the country, Maryland and North Carolina. In 2019, they penned a joint editorial calling for an end to the practice, adroitly summing up its damaging effects on those elected from gerrymandered districts: "They become less responsive to the full spectrum of needs in their district, and common ground and the common good take a back seat to a safe seat. It is just wrong."[27]

Governors around the country must follow their example and push for transferring districting power to independent commissions free of partisan bias. In such hands, the districting pen could be guided by public goods such as accommodating communities of interest, maintaining partisan balance, and creating sensible geographical and local jurisdictional boundaries. Citizen movements are cropping up in states across the nation to push referenda and ballot initiatives for districting reform—strongly opposed by elected officials and party machines in power who benefit from the status quo.

The stakes are enormous. The end of cracking, packing, hijacking, kidnapping, and crowning would mean stronger democracy and less division. It would temper extreme and inflammatory partisan rhetoric. Above all, public-interest districting would provide a desperately needed shot in the arm for the cross-aisle cooperation vital if Congress is to help move the country forward.

BATTLING FOR THE BALLOT

Democrat Joe Lieberman was elected by the people of Connecticut in 1988 to represent them in the US Senate, and in his 1994 reelection he enjoyed the largest margin of victory for a US senator in the state's history.[28] Lieberman chaired important Senate committees as a Democrat and earned a reputation as a serious and effective legislator. Nearing the end of his third six-year Senate term, he was tapped by Al Gore to be the vice presidential candidate on the party's unsuccessful 2000 ticket.[29] Vying for a fourth Senate term in 2006, Lieberman was upset in the party's primary by challenger Ned Lamont. The winning margin was 10,000, in an election in which only 283,000 of the state's 700,000 registered Democrats voted. The primary voters represented just one-seventh of the Constitution State's two million voters, a third of whom were neither Democrats nor Republicans.[30]

Nicknamed Cowboy Joe because of his candid but kindly style and boundless energy, Lieberman was convinced he enjoyed a far greater share of support among Democrats who vote in general elections. He knew that primary elections are notoriously low turnout and dominated by each party's extreme elements—a noisy but activist minority who have outsized say in the public's general ballot choices across the nation each election cycle. Further, he was certain he would receive significant backing from the state's independent voters and a creditable share of aisle-crossing Republicans. He determined to make an independent Senate run. Lieberman's instinct was correct: He went on to win the general election by ten percentage points over Lamont and forty points over the Republican nominee.[31]

If the parties had had their way, Lieberman never would have appeared on the general election ballot, and Connecticut voters would have been denied a demonstrably desirable choice. Had he run in any one of forty-four other states, the partisan desire to exclude him from the ballot would have been granted, because all but three US states have "sore loser" laws prohibiting a candidate defeated in a party primary from otherwise qualifying to be on November's general ballot.[32] Not long after Lieberman's victory, Connecticut's secretary of state, an elected Democrat eyeing a run for higher office, announced her intent to push the Connecticut state legislature to add a "sore loser" prohibition to the state constitution.[33]

To the party faithful, Lieberman was heretical for declaring, "I agree more often than not with Democrats on domestic policy. I agree more often than not with Republicans on foreign and defense policy."[34] No matter how much a balanced point of view might appeal to the general electorate, its impurity constitutes sacrilege for party firebrands, who prefer ideologues far more skilled at making partisan points than shaping policy. The duopoly prefers to maintain complete control over access to the general ballot. Had it succeeded in Connecticut, the nation would have suffered further loss in the ranks of a disappearing breed—independent-minded politicians willing to work across the aisle. Indeed, political scientists from the University of Wisconsin and Northwestern University found that the congressional candidates in states without "sore loser" laws are demonstrably less polarized than those with them, concluding that "by removing any subsequent reentry options for candidates [the latter states] place greater pressure on primary candidates to cater to the polarized preferences of the party bases."[35]

Sadly, Lieberman's example is an outlier. Mike Castle was a respected nine-term House member representative from Delaware, where he had been popular as governor. In 2010, he was defeated in the Republican primary for a special election called to fill the Senate seat vacated when Joe Biden became vice president under President Barack Obama in 2008.[36] Castle's opponent from the GOP's Tea Party wing, Christine O'Donnell, won the Republican nomination with a total of thirty thousand votes.[37] The primary voters accounted for about 16 percent of Delaware's registered Republicans and just 6.5 percent of the state's total electorate. Living in a "sore loser" state, Castle had no reasonable path to the general election ballot. After the primary, O'Donnell demonstrated serious shortcomings, including a faulty understanding of basic elements of the US Constitution and an admission that she had dabbled in witchcraft as a youth. She was defeated handily.

Sore loser law is just one of the many obstacles Politics Inc. has erected across the country to thwart competition. Others include onerous signature requirements, filing fees, deadlines, and support thresholds. States have not just the right but an obligation to ensure that campaigns and elections are orderly and that ballots present voters with choices they understand. The party system enables voters to at least have a notion of the candidates' philosophical bent, even if they may know little about the candidates themselves. But under the fig leaf of making ballots comprehensible, the parties have succeeded in making them uncompetitive and unfair.

Randy Barnett, director of Georgetown University's Center for the Constitution, observes that "just as poll taxes were set up to keep certain citizens from expressing their right to vote, current ballot-access laws are deliberately designed to provide a similar obstacle to those who might challenge the two prevailing parties."[38] Indeed, some states have never had an independent on a federal ballot for Congress.[39] The Coalition for Free and Open Elections found that the "requirements for a minor party candidate to get on the ballot increased tenfold from 1930 to 1980."[40]

For example, an independent or third-party candidate needs almost 180,000 valid signatures to get on the ballot in California, 69,500 in Maryland, and over 89,000 in North Carolina.[41] According to the coalition, it takes nearly seven hundred thousand petition signatures for an independent or minor party presidential candidate to get on the ballot in all fifty states—twenty-six times the number required by a major party presidential candidate.[42]

In 1992, Ross Perot was one of the few third-party candidates in the nation's history able to obtain enough signatures to get on the ballot for president in every state. *New York Times* editor and reporter Steven A. Holmes described the difficulty that such candidates encounter in running a "labyrinth of rules, regulations and procedures . . . mind-numbing in their complexity [and varying] widely from state to state. . . . Not only are the required numbers of signatures on petitions different in every state, but there are different rules regarding who can sign them, who can circulate the petitions and when and where the names can be collected."[43]

To get on Illinois's presidential ballot, for instance, a third-party candidate is required to present a petition signed by twenty-five thousand registered voters. Republican and Democratic candidates need only file a petition with at least three thousand signatures.[44] In 2006, the federal courts rebuked the state for imposing restrictive burdens on independent candidates trying to run for the state assembly. It pointed to provisions that "required nominating petitions to be filed 92 days before the March primary for that office, or 323 days before the November general election, required the obtaining of signatures from voters equaling 10% of the vote in the last general election (raised in 1979 from 5%), and disqualified anyone who signs such a petition for an independent candidate from voting in the primary."[45] Some states apparently don't even like the word "independent." In February 2019, the California

State Assembly approved legislation barring any political party from using the word "independent" in any form in its name.[46]

Diversity, choice, and competition are the magic behind America's economic success and social vibrancy. Diversity ensures choice. Choice promotes competition. Competition drives innovation and excellence. American consumers can choose from 2,500 different kinds of beer. Americans voters should have more choice at the ballot box than a pair of party primary survivors, most likely elected by a plurality of an unrepresentative sliver of the electorate. Choice is the very heart of democracy and the essence of the Helsinki Accords to which the United States is a party, binding signatories

> to respect the right of citizens to seek political or public office, individually or as representatives of political parties or organizations, without discrimination; respect the right of individuals and groups to establish, in full freedom, their own political parties or other political organizations and provide such political parties and organizations with the necessary legal guarantees to enable them to compete with each other on a basis of equal treatment before the law and by the authorities.[47]

In 2019, Pew Research found that at least seven states had recently rejected legislation to make it easier for third parties and independent candidates to get on the ballot, while several states were making it more difficult.[48] Of course, the decisions were made by state legislators composed exclusively of Republicans and Democrats. Sore loser laws need to go. Ballot access should be eased to give independent politicians and third parties a fairer shot. Given their druthers, McDonalds and Burger King would prefer not to compete with so many other national chains and local boutiques, but they are better for the competition, and the public is better served. Democrats and Republicans aren't forced to compete for one simple reason: They write the rules.

DEBATABLE DEBATES

Among the most anticipated rites of American political campaigns are debates, when the contenders square off face to face. Whether in presidential or congressional contests, debates offer the country a fleeting opportunity to take a candidate's measure in a relatively unscripted environment and to comparison shop. We get to see how would-be lawmakers and leaders think on their feet and interact under pressure. The exercise stands in stark contrast to the continuous blitz of press coverage and punditry and to the saturation bombing of the public by campaigns with scripted political ads and annoying robocalls.

At its best, official campaign debates are supposed to be a tool helping the voting public evaluate their choices. As they are, or more accurately as Politics Inc. has engineered them to be, debates serve the parties, candidates, and media far better than the voting public. Modern presidential debates are ninety minutes of cosmetic, sound-bite-centered, content-starved national embarrassment—the political version of the *Jerry Springer Show*—two or three times per election season. Surveys show that the public views them as one of the main ways of assessing and deciding between the candidates, but the percentage of voting-age Americans who watch televised debates has continued to plummet almost since their first appearance, as voters choose to forgo the constant interruptions, generalizations, exaggerations, and complaints about the moderator's fairness, political leanings, and officiating.[49]

Contrary to popular belief, campaign debates appeared fairly late in American politics. For much of the country's early history, personal electioneering was regarded as vulgar and inappropriate—beneath the dignity of the principal, whose conspicuous merit, not vain self-promotion should decide the election. Campaign-type activities were undertaken mainly by third parties, including surrogates, faction-friendly newspapers, and party organs. If candidates spoke up for themselves to tout their election-worthiness, they typically did so through anonymous or pseudonymous public letters. Personal efforts stayed behind the scenes.

As political parties matured, they became the hub of electioneering. Party-sponsored rallies designed to enthuse the faithful, recruit new supporters, and entertain the community were big events meant to help build momentum to carry their standard-bearer into office. Speakers sometimes stood on stumps to be readily seen and heard, thereby creating the stump speech.[50]

The first historically significant debate occurred in 1858 during Illinois's US Senate race between Abraham Lincoln and Stephen Douglas. Lincoln followed Douglas around the state, speaking on the major topics of the time—slavery and the politics of US territorial expansion—wherever Douglas had appeared. Some elites disparaged this unusual tactic as unseemly self-promotion. Eventually Lincoln and Douglas took the stage together in a series of seven three-hour debates. The proceedings featured an orderly process of speaking and rebutting, accompanied by heavy doses of sarcasm and personal invective.[51] Though Lincoln lost the Senate election, he defeated Douglas two years later in the 1860 presidential race—without further head-to-head debate.

Harold Stassen and Thomas Dewey were the first presidential candidates to tangle, engaging in a radio debate during the 1948 Republican primary. The next presidential debate—the first ever televised—took place in 1956 between two surrogates of the Republican Dwight Eisenhower and his opponent Adlai Stevenson. Maine's senior senator Margaret Chase Smith represented Eisenhower and former First Lady Eleanor Roosevelt stood in for Stevenson in a debate that aired on the infant TV show *Face the Nation* two days before the election.[52]

The match-up set the stage for Richard Nixon and John F. Kennedy, who in the next election took part in four televised debates simulcast by each of the nation's networks—ABC, CBS, and NBC. The debates are remembered for the contrast between the perspiring, ill-at-ease Nixon and the smooth, dashing young Kennedy. Presidential scholars wrangle over whether the imagery alone tipped the balance in the election. Not in dispute, however, is that they launched television as a dominant tool of mass communication and a major force in US elective politics. The medium revolutionized political news coverage and the art of politicking as TV became a high-powered channel for political advertising.[53]

The norm of presidential campaign debates was not yet established, however, in part because broadcasting them bumped up against the Fairness Doctrine—a federal rule requiring networks to provide equal time to all candidates for elected office. Congress temporarily waived the rule for Nixon and Kennedy so the two major party candidates could have the debate stage to themselves. But after 1976, special waivers would no longer be required. The Federal Communications Commission determined that the Fairness Doctrine did not apply to bona fide news events not sponsored by the networks.[54] The ruling permanently cleared the way for the two major party candidates to go head-to-head in nationally televised debates.

The League of Women Voters (LWV)—a nonprofit organization founded by leaders of the women's suffrage movement—volunteered to become the independent sponsor. It hosted the 1976 face-off between Republican president Gerald Ford and Democratic challenger Jimmy Carter and sponsored presidential debates in the following two elections. In 1980, the first debate was boycotted by President Carter because third-party candidate John Anderson was invited to take part along with Republican nominee Ronald Reagan. Carter participated in the second and final debate with Reagan when Anderson was excluded. Four years later, Reagan—now the incumbent—debated his opponent Walter Mondale twice under LWV auspices.[55]

That's when Politics Inc. stepped in. The two major party campaigns decided they, not LWV, should control the debate process. Operatives for Republican presidential candidate George H. W. Bush and his Democratic opponent Michael Dukakis met discreetly, some would say "secretly." They forged a memorandum of understanding structuring how the 1988 presidential debates would be run. The agreement included an approved list of panelists, the composition of the audience, and a prohibition on follow-up questions.[56]

The LWV swiftly resigned, calling the parties' maneuver a "fraud on the American voter" and declaring it had "no intention of becoming an accessory to the hoodwinking of the American public."[57] In response, the Republican and Democratic National Committees formed the Commission on Presidential Debates (CPD) to sponsor, organize, and conduct general election presidential and vice presidential debates.[58] Established as a nonprofit organization by the parties, the commission holds no legal duty to the public. In 1996, the CPD barred third-party candidate Ross Perot from joining Bill Clinton and Bob Dole in a televised debate, though 19 percent of the electorate supported Perot's bid for the presidency.

Under its rules today, a third-party candidate may take part in a presidential debate only if he or she possesses at least 15 percent of the electorate's support and a statistical chance of winning a majority of electoral votes. Presidential candidates Gary Johnson of the Libertarian Party and Jill Stein of the Green Party sued the commission, the Republican and Democratic Parties, and presidential candidates Barack Obama and Mitt Romney for barring them from taking part in the 2012 presidential debates. Their suit maintained that both appeared on a sufficient number of state ballots meeting the electoral vote test and that collusion between the CPD and the major parties to bar them violated antitrust law.[59] The suit failed.

Whatever its legal merits, their underlying complaint was right on. The debate system stinks. Campaign debates, whether for president or Congress, are the equivalent of an interview for the profoundly important job of deciding matters of law and policy that affect every American, shape global affairs, and even determine war or peace. A former chairman of the Republican National Committee called them "the super bowl" of presidential politics.[60]

Their seriousness and utility are dwindling partly because the parties and campaign chieftains have claimed for themselves the right to determine how, when, and on what issues candidates face off—a prerogative that should belong to the electorate. It should offend public sensibilities that the campaign gurus, party chieftains, and media moguls get to dictate how would-be public officials audition for their job. The formats typically mirror the worst characteristics of American politics. Big questions are given little time for reply and answered with platitudes, while the candidates routinely exceed their time, talk over one another, or both.

The tone of campaign debates—boorish and ad hominem—is echoed in the coarseness of the nation's political discourse, whether on the floor of Congress, on the political talk shows, in internet chat rooms, or increasingly in the nation's civic and social venues. The *Princeton Review* assessed the grade level of the language and the concepts discussed in key presidential debates. The study found that the Lincoln-Douglas debates were conducted at about the level of a high school senior. The Nixon-Kennedy debates registered at a tenth-grade level, and by 2000, "the two contenders were speaking like sixth graders."[61]

The media seem to find new and creative ways of ensuring debates emphasize the worst aspects of the nation's political culture, making them commercial, sensational, and not terribly informative—focused on who is winning the horse race rather than making the most horse sense. As Gary Johnson's pleading to the US courts noted, "Debate sites throughout the United States have become 'corporate carnivals' where sponsors provide their marketing and lobbying materials and products to journalists and politicians."[62]

During its coverage of a presidential debate, one major network put together focus groups and hooked up the participants to biometric monitors. Their breathing, heart rate, and other indicators controlled a rolling display that showed which words or phrases used by the candidates registered positively or negatively. The viewing audience watched the needles pulsing up and down as if on a hospital monitor while a political consultant interpreted the results.[63] Emphasis on sensation and emotion was alive and well, but substance and thoughtfulness had a less promising prognosis. And, of course, almost before the debate moderator falls silent, the network talking heads are telling the public who won and why. FOX reassures Republicans that their candidate triumphed. MSNBC and CNN explain to Democrats why theirs came out on top. Polling companies rush out surveys to announce who their sampling says ruled the night.

Even as Americans are turned off by the sideshow, the world watches and wonders how the US model is a worthy one. Following the execrable first presidential debate between Donald Trump and Joe Biden in September 2020, adversaries gloated while the rest of the world gasped. For the Chinese, it was an example of US hypocrisy regarding its values and a demonstration of the greater stability of one-party rule.[64] The Russian government highlighted the spectacle in public-information campaigns to disgrace democracy.[65] Foreign press accounts used such descriptions as ill tempered, incomprehensible, chaotic, childish, grueling, and low, likening it to a "car accident" and—most often—a "national embarrassment." The international reaction was summed up by US analysts with a single word description—"worry."[66]

Ironically, the CPD touts its international programming, providing "technical assistance to emerging democracies and others interested in establishing debate traditions in their countries."[67] It's hard to imagine young democracies and the worldwide audience tuning in to any of our national political debates and exclaiming, "Yes, that's the tradition we need!"

The public deserves far better means of assessing candidates' qualifications and head-to-head performance. American democracy needs fewer precanned speeches, partisan rallies, and contrived photo-ops and better ways to explore the quality and public-worthiness of office seekers—meaning not just their ability to campaign effectively and deliver a good sound bite or a staggering political uppercut but the talents and character to lead and govern well.

Reform begins with reassessing who controls debates. Why should Politics Inc. determine the parameters of debates? Its why US presidential debates are too few, too short, and uninformative. In congressional races, too, candidate debates are structured by agreements between the two campaigns, the parties, the sponsoring institution, and perhaps the media outlet(s) covering the event. Nowhere is the electorate truly represented.

While the duopoly stays focused on how to make debates work better for the candidates and parties, the call for reform is growing louder. In 2012, the Annenberg Public Policy Center's Working Group on Presidential Debate Reform released "Democratizing the Debates," which set forth three compelling objectives: expanding and enriching debate content, broadening the accessibility of the debates, and improving the transparency and accountability of the debate process.[68] Anyone who tuned in to the 2020 debates, whether in the primary or the general election, knows that these important goals remain aspirational.

Public interest coalitions and citizen groups are looking for and proposing ways to make the debates work better for the voters. The Open Debate Coalition is a diverse, nonpartisan coalition created to improve political debates by harnessing the internet to make them "more of the people."[69] It has helped arrange more participatory and informative debates for federal, state, and local elections, in which the public drives the questions. The organization's support from left to right demonstrates the broad hunger for change. In its words: "This is not a matter of right versus left, but new versus old. Participatory democracy is a driving principle of the open Internet.

The best ideas rise to the top, and the wisdom of crowds prevails. Moderators can choose from among the top questions proposed and voted on by the public—and have discretion to ask follow-up questions. Many formats can be experimented with, some typical and others so innovative they have yet to be conceived."[70] Though the programming and platforms inspired by the coalition do not yet rival the networks' scale and reach, they provide a model for reform.

In his book *By Popular Demand, Revitalizing Representative Democracy through Deliberative Election*, John Gastil suggests convening diverse citizen groups to consider and evaluate candidates and ballot initiatives; their perspectives, provided to the broader electorate, could supplement journalistic, party, and special interest voting guides and analyses.[71] Social media platforms such as Facebook and YouTube have sponsored electronic town halls that offer a more conversational and productive voter learning experience, enabling candidates to make points rather than score points in a televised blood match.

Imagine if presidential debates, by public demand and legal mandate, were made to be comprehensive, substantive, and dignified: perhaps seven two-hour debates, each focused on a specific policy area—national security, foreign policy, the economy, energy, the environment, and so on. Further, how much more informative could such debates be if they were moderated by a subject-matter expert with excellent journalistic skills (there are lots of them) rather than celebrity media personalities sometimes more eager to make an impression than to elicit one? Naturally, the campaigns and party establishments prefer limiting candidates' exposure to potential embarrassment. They do not benefit when the public sees candidates' knowledge gaps, difficulty thinking on their feet, and lack of composure—serious liabilities in elective office. The duopoly likes things just the way they are, no matter the cost to the country.

6

Suffering Suffrage (Structural Gear)

The will of the people shall be the basis of the authority of government.

—UN Declaration of Human Rights

On December 10, 1948, the world was still staggering from the horrors of a world war that had claimed the lives of eighty-five million human beings. From the ashes of unimaginable suffering rose the Universal Declaration of Human Rights, which enshrined the right of every person "to take part in the government of his country, directly or through freely chosen representatives," as a means of ensuring freedom, equality, and government licensed by the will of the governed.[1] "This will," declared Article 21 of the charter, "shall be expressed in periodic and genuine elections which shall be by universal and equal suffrage and shall be held by secret vote or by equivalent free voting procedures."[2] The concept of democracy as a basic human right was stated with more plainspoken wisdom almost a century earlier by Abraham Lincoln, who said, "No man is good enough to govern another man, *without that other's consent.*"[3]

Redistricting that serves the public interest, fair ballot access for legitimate political parties and independents, clean campaigns, and informative debates culminate in the act that makes a government "of, by, and for the people"—*voting. The vote* is what elevates democracy above every other form of government conceived by man. *The vote* ensures that government serves the governed, not the other way around. *The vote* gives each citizen a voice in the affairs that shape their lives and communities. *The vote* is what Americans started a revolution to achieve and have endured untold sacrifices to defend.

As the Constitutional Convention drew to a close in 1787, Benjamin Franklin was asked by a friend, "Well, Doctor, what have we got, a republic or a monarchy?" He replied, "A republic if you can keep it."[4] American generations since the nation's birth have sought to meet that challenge. Whether the present one will pass a vibrant, strong democracy on to the next generation will depend largely on how well it preserves the integrity of voting, measured by three fundamental criteria:

1. Is every eligible individual empowered to vote?
2. Is every vote counted accurately?
3. Does every vote count?

Anything less than a decisive yes to each menaces the national enterprise and ultimately our freedom. Getting to yes requires overcoming Politics Inc.

EMPOWERING THE VOTE

Condoleezza Rice, former US secretary of state and first female national security adviser, is a Black American. In the 1960s, she grew up in Birmingham, Alabama—a city that had earned the nickname Bombingham because of the violence and terror born of racist opposition to desegregation and voting rights.

On September 15, 1963, a bomb planted by the Ku Klux Klan detonated at the 16th Street Baptist Church, killing four little girls and injuring dozens of other parishioners. Among the children murdered that day was seven-year-old Denise McNair, a playmate of Condoleezza's. Rice's father, John—a minister and educator— had awarded Denise her kindergarten graduation certificate. Twelve years before the murders, he attempted to exercise his basic right to vote, hoping to add his voice to the call for positive change. When Rice tried to register to vote, a clerk pointed to a jar of jellybeans and asked him how many it contained. As he could not answer correctly, he was denied registration. Later, on the advice of a parishioner, he sought out an alternative registrar, a Republican in a state dominated by the Democratic and Dixiecrat Parties, who duly registered him.

The right to vote was one of many civil liberties that the South's Jim Crow laws were intended to obstruct. Named after a fictional character in a racially charged comedy act from the 1830s, "Jim Crow" sought to institutionalize racial discrimination at the state level and circumvent constitutional and federal civil rights protections. The tactics aimed at voting included restrictive poll taxes and literacy tests, all-White Democratic primaries, and assorted acts of violence and intimidation. In 1965, Congress moved to end these abuses with passage of the Voting Rights Act, proposed by Democratic president Lyndon Johnson and introduced in the Senate by Democrat Mike Mansfield and Republican leader Everett Dirksen.

Despite many years of fitful progress, voting rules have once again become a source of national conflict inflamed by partisan politics. Tensions over President Trump's bogus claims of a stolen 2020 presidential election boiled over into violence that resulted in an unprecedented second presidential impeachment. And today's voting controversies, however distinctive, have deep roots in Jim Crow, Tammany Hall corruption, and the 2000 presidential election.

Well after election day, the outcome in the 2000 presidential race between Democrat Al Gore and Republican George W. Bush remained in doubt. Disputes over Florida's vote count that would determine who won the state's twenty-five electoral votes and with them the presidency caused electoral chaos, lawsuits, countersuits, and delay in forming a new government. Ultimately, the Supreme Court was called on to sort out the catastrophe, stopping the recount and producing Bush's victory. The parties drew differing and ultimately contradictory conclusions from the debacle.

Although significant voter fraud was not proved in Florida's controversial election administration, public confidence in its integrity had been deeply shaken.[5] Perceiving a need, as well as political opportunity, Republicans pushed for clean election reforms, including measures toughening fraudulent voting tactics such as impersonation, double voting, mailing in someone else's ballot, mail-in ballot stealing, and noncitizen voting. The left perceived a need for greater voter participation, and believing it was robbed of the victory saw a new phalanx of election integrity measures as backdoor means of suppressing Democratic votes. Both sides viewed voting controversies through disparate historical lenses. Democrats recalled the long, shameful history of race-based voter suppression and Jim Crow; Republicans see them predominantly through the legacy of Tammany Hall and Lyndon Johnson.

Most of the big-city political bosses of the nineteenth and twentieth centuries were Democrats who ruled by corruption and maintained their fiefdoms by vote rigging. One of the most notorious was Tammany Hall in New York City, run by "Boss" Tweed. He used every scandalous tactic imaginable to steal elections, including voter intimidation, ballot stuffing, bribery, and premarking ballots issued to voters, with stunning success.[6] Tweed also managed to amass an impressive personal fortune through bribery. In his later years, Tweed was called to public account. At a hearing on his various vote-rigging tactics, he was asked whether a particular election in the city had been fixed. Tweed's reply was striking for its candor and criminality: "I don't think there was ever a fair or honest election in the City of New York."[7] The situation was little different in Cleveland, Chicago, Kansas City, Memphis, Boston, and elsewhere.[8]

Even after public backlash and legal reform greatly diminished the power of big-city machines, their legacy cast a long shadow on elective politics. Lyndon Johnson won an early election in Texas thanks to a box of votes that mysteriously materialized in a remote area. Each ballot bore a signature in the same handwriting.[9] Richard Nixon believed that illegal voting in Illinois and Texas swung the 1960 presidential election to Kennedy.[10] Though election law prosecutions took place in Cook County, Illinois, the offenses were not proved to be result altering.[11] But the controversy created enough smoke to suggest a fire to the losing side, and that fire continues to smolder. Some observers believed that Nixon's sense of being cheated inclined him to sanction illegal tactics such as the Watergate break-in as necessary to right a wrong.[12] His motivations cannot be known, but we can say with some confidence that partisan politics has a long, destructive, and still-thriving tradition of "doing unto the other what you believe was done unto you." The deep distrust between the two parties regarding election reform is based on the understandable suspicion that the other is interested in reform only to the extent it promotes their election prospects.

REGISTERING CONCERN

Distrust and partisan ambition hang over every debate on voting rules and procedures, including the first step in the balloting process: voter registration. Registering to vote, instituted in the nineteenth century, is designed to ensure that each voter is eligible to cast a ballot by meeting requirements on age, citizenship, and residence, and votes only once. The Voluntary Voting System Guidelines, produced by the federal, bipartisan Election Assistance Commission (EAC), formed in 2002, call on states to make the process as easy as possible so that registration is a reasonable safeguard, not an impediment to exercise the franchise.[13]

In 1993, Bill Clinton signed legislation, passed by Congress largely on party lines, that required states to enable individuals to register to vote when applying for a driver's license, on the premise that increased registration would boost voting.[14] Republicans opposed the practice on grounds related to election administration and integrity—but their real motivation was fear that the law would increase Democratic turnout. Nine years after the bill was enacted, a witness from the CATO Institute, a conservative Washington think tank, presented evidence to Congress that despite increasing voter registration rolls, the Motor Voter Act did not result in the hoped-for increase in voting. He further pointed out that rather than helping states maintain more accurate registration rolls—another advertised benefit—the law in fact made matters worse.[15] In any event, the EAC reported that, as of 2018, motor vehicle licensing agencies remained "the most common source" of voter registration applications.[16]

The battle lines continue to form as Democrats look to take the next step in motor voter: automatic registration of any citizen who applies for a driver's license. According to a leader of the movement, President Obama's former voter turnout director, "Many of those new voters would be young, poor or minorities—groups that tend to support Democratic candidates."[17] Seventeen states have implemented automatic voter registration on their own authority.

Proponents argue that the government should make registering to vote as easy as possible, and nothing is easier than automatic enrollment. Opponents argue that voting is a choice as well as a right, and registration should be no different. Further, they contend that the mandate will again worsen the quality of state voter rolls, noting the ability of noncitizens to obtain driver's licenses. Problems with misregistration encountered in California's and Illinois's automatic voter registration rollouts bolstered their case.[18] Moreover, since licensure and voter registration connect to internet-based databases, cybersecurity risks abound.

The public can expect little movement toward legitimate progress on this front so long as both parties evaluate voting reform by how it affects their party rather than how well it serves people's rights and the strength of American democracy. The same observation applies to challenges over procedures for how votes are cast.

Among the prominent post-2000 election reforms pushed mainly by Republican-controlled legislatures was tightening voter identification rules. When the Supreme Court issued its ruling in *Bush v. Gore*, only fifteen states required government-issued ID to vote. As of 2020, only fourteen states lacked such requirements, and of the states that do have it, most stipulate that the ID contain a photo.[19] From the Republicans' perspective, even if most known fraud cases would not have been prevented by the ID requirement, one can imagine schemes that have gone undiscovered or that might be possible without it. Moreover, matching a voter's confirmed identity against the registration rolls is a small inconvenience if it helps reassure the public our elections are clean.

Or does it? Many Democrats oppose such rules as voter suppression, citing the lack of evidence of widespread voter fraud. Known instances of fraud, they point out, are exaggerated, inconsequential, and typically turn out to be clerical errors.[20] The Brennan Center calculates that voter fraud occurs in a microscopic 0.0025 percent of votes cast.[21] The real problem, say Democrats, is the harm the unnecessary solution to the nonproblem has on legitimate voting. Photo ID requirements disproportionately affect the poor and minorities, who typically face greater obstacles to exercising their franchise, are less likely for economic reasons to possess a government-issued ID, and are more likely to vote Democratic.[22]

Furthermore, not all voter ID requirements are created equal. Some, such as Texas, appear designed to favor partisan interests: it defines acceptable government photo IDs to include concealed weapons permits but to exclude state-issued college or university IDs. By contrast, Virginia law now allows a broad range of IDs to prove identity, including private as well as public educational institutions, with a failsafe provision of a sworn voter affidavit if required. Thus, the key controversy is less about whether a state requires voter ID and more about the kind of proof required and whether the particular procedures discriminate against a specific subset of voters.

Data on the percentage of Americans who do not possess a government-issued photo ID are sketchy, but the Brennan Center estimates that 25 percent of Black Americans and perhaps up to 16 percent of Hispanics are without one, compared to 8 percent of Whites.[23] This means that photo ID requirements disproportionately harm a particular segment of society more likely to be without ID (the poor), adversely affecting racial and ethnic minorities, who comprise a lopsided share of people living in poverty.[24]

Voter fraud is not unknown in the United States. The conservative Washington-based think tank Heritage Foundation maintains a database including 1,296 "proven instances of voter fraud" since 1992, almost 90 percent of which resulted in criminal convictions.[25] Only one had the result—indirectly—of flipping an election. In 2019, a North Carolina campaign contractor was arrested for fraudulent vote casting, which resulted in overturning the Republican-won election and the election of a Democrat in the ensuing rerun.[26] A case prosecuted in the summer of 2020 resulted in the arrest and conviction of a former Democratic congressman; the charges included ballot stuffing during three separate primary elections (2014, 2015, and 2016) to help favored candidates.[27]

One would hope that the parties could agree, as do most Americans, that the law should ensure the fullest possible citizen participation in elections and the unquestioned integrity of the process. But one would be naïve. Republicans and Democrats seek their advantage and mold their purpose and message to their partisan ends, including rallying their voters with false claims of stolen elections and duplicity by the other side, degrading public trust in the system and in one another. Kim Wyman, the state of Washington's secretary of state, told the *Atlantic*, "I have met many Democrats that are convinced that Republicans are trying to keep their party from voting, and I've met many Republicans that are convinced that Democrats are cheating and it's really hard to convince either side otherwise."[28]

That might be because neither side wants to be convinced. Partisan identity is more important if the other side is wicked and out to get you. The parties like it that way. Facts and fairness are immaterial if fibs and fig leaves can be used to partisan advantage and a sense of victimization can be weaponized. Without evidence, Donald Trump repeatedly peddled the fiction that several million votes were cast illegally in 2016, costing him the "popular vote" in his match-up against Hillary Clinton.[29] After his 2020 defeat by Joe Biden, Trump's election fraud claims not only threw the nation into chaos but delayed the presidential transition and sharpened partisan distrust and animosity that will outlive him.

The scandalmongers were in full force, seeking donations to right the invented wrong, and 2020's legacy of distrust and hostility will surely persist as subsidiaries of Politics Inc. scent political and financial opportunity. Accusations of wrongdoing will stick among hardcore partisans even absent hard evidence. Legitimate concerns about the discriminatory potential of new election security and voter integrity rules will be dismissed by some Republicans as proof that Democrats intend to cheat.

Democratic appeals will press that photo ID laws and other forms of election integrity measures are aimed solely at suppressing minority voters. They won't acknowledge that voter fraud can't be waved away. Nor will they explain why Hawaii, run by a Democratic governor and legislature, and the most racially diverse state in the nation, saw fit to implement a photo ID law.[30] They won't mention that Georgia and Virginia offer free voter ID cards or that a commission chaired by former president Jimmy Carter, a Democrat, recommended creating a photo ID system.[31]

Democrats point out that Republicans use election law to lower the turnout of Americans unlikely to support them, but they too manage turnout to their advantage. A prime example is local elections that are "off-cycle," or held at different days and times than the federal election, as happens in forty-four states.[32] Eitan Hersh, an assistant professor of political science at Yale University, calls the US election calendar "an insane mess," and "Exhibit A is New Jersey. New Jersey holds federal elections with the rest of the country on the first Tuesday after the first Monday in November of even-numbered years. But elections for state office in New Jersey are held in November of odd-numbered years. School district elections are held on the third Tuesday in April or else in November. And fire district commissioner elections are held on the third Saturday in February."[33]

Voters prefer to have consolidated federal, state, and local elections. They can increase voter participation, including among minorities who face greater obstacles getting to the polls. Yet, Democrats vehemently oppose consolidation efforts. From the party's perspective, lowering turnout for local offices like school boards is just fine, because those who do turn out are more likely to be constituencies that favor Democrats.[34] In *Timing and Turnout: How Off-Cycle Elections Favor Organized Groups*, UC Berkeley professor Sarah Anzia examined 203 bills to consolidate elections introduced in state legislatures between 2001 and 2011—the lion's share sponsored by Republicans.[35] Examining 102 bills that included school board elections, Anzia found they were principally defeated by Democratic opposition.[36] Opposing parties included teacher unions, school board associations, and "interest groups that align with the Democratic Party."[37] Moreover, Democrats in the South preferred to spread out elections so that the region's penchant to vote Republican in the presidential race would not carry down ballot to other elective offices.[38]

No democracy can remain great without ensuring both the integrity of votes and maximum citizen participation. Finding the right balance begins with looking for it. Such a search isn't likely without both parties recognizing that both objectives are crucial and committing to see voting reforms through the lens of national interest rather than partisan advantage. Such leadership is more likely to come from governors than members of Congress, given states' responsibility for managing elections. A strong, bipartisan group of governors could establish a template for the nation that's based on three principles:

1. Minimal impediments to voting
2. Maximal opportunity to register and vote voluntarily
3. Reasonable safeguards against fraud and illegal voting in response to bona fide risks

COUNTING THE VOTE

Solving the tension between illegal voting and voter suppression is difficult enough before we layer on the mistrust created by the enormous complexity of the nation's state-run, multiform, and technology-reliant voting systems. A problem anywhere in the continuum is fodder for viral partisan suspicion. According to a February 2020 Gallup poll, nearly 60 percent of Americans say they lack confidence in the honesty of US elections.[39] Republicans are not the only distrustful voters. In 2016, while Donald Trump claimed illegal Clinton votes, a group of computer scientists and election lawyers purported to have discovered results-altering manipulations in Michigan, Wisconsin, and Pennsylvania. They unsuccessfully lobbied Hillary Clinton to initiate a court challenge to the election.[40]

Whether accusations are spurred by partisan sour grapes or legitimate irregularities, there is no denying the complexities of counting almost 160 million ballots in the nation's several thousand counties and well over two hundred thousand polling sites across fifty states that use many different methods of casting and tabulating votes, or that such disparity invites controversy. In a hyperpartisan environment, Politics Inc. will pounce on any glitch as foul play, no matter how innocent.

Partisan doubts about the outcome of the 2000, 2016, and 2020 presidential elections and the ensuing lawsuits and inquiries continue to hang heavily over our political culture. Many Democrats remain convinced a recount in Florida would have reversed Bush's 537-vote victory and that the 2016 Trump win was a fraud. Many Republicans came to believe that Trump was victimized in 2020 and that Biden's election was not legitimate.[41] Even greater challenges to the public's trust in our elections may be yet to come given the cybervulnerabilities of the nation's election system.

What neither party could ignore following the 2000 election was the inadequacy of election recording, tabulating, and reporting across the country. The Bush versus Gore debacle spawned bipartisan accord on preventing future chaos over hanging chads and uncertain election results. Congress passed the Help America Vote Act of 2002, offering funds to help states transition from antiquated paper ballots to more reliable electronic and internet-dependent vote casting and counting equipment. The Help America Vote Act also created the bipartisan Election Assistance Commission to help improve election administration and promote voter participation without impinging on the states' authority to manage elections. Among the EAC's primary duties was to set guidelines for certifying and decertifying voting equipment.

Expectations were high that the transition to digital voting and tabulating systems would be the end of human error and the potential for duplicity, which could restore public trust in the integrity of elections. Instead, new and more menacing threats emerged, created by digital error, domestic software hackers, and foreign cyberattackers, not to mention vulnerability to natural and manmade electrical disruptions.

In a 2010 report, the Brennan Center for Justice catalogued two hundred known cases of electronic voting system failure, including instances in which the equipment failed to accurately record, count, or tabulate votes.[42] Because of one technical glitch, tens of thousands of votes went uncounted during a 2004 election in Broward County, Florida. Foul play could wreak far more havoc. The multiple connection points in electronic voting systems offer many openings to cybervillains trying to attack. Appearing before an audience at MIT in autumn 2018, J. Alex Halderman, director of the University of Michigan's Center for Computer Security and Society, demonstrated the ease with which a knowledgeable hacker could use malicious software to alter election results.[43] A national election could be decided by digital mischief in a single county or even a precinct in a swing state, plunging the nation into political crisis.

For all its flaws, the traditional punch card voting system enabled observers from both parties to verify results and compliance with proper procedures at polling stations and counting areas. The transition to software-based and internet-dependent voting administration created an enormous vulnerability to disruption by foreign adversaries. As a result, election administrators and experts pushed for the adoption of standards requiring a "paper trail" for all voting machines. This is often accomplished by voting on computer-readable paper ballots, which are preserved, although some systems generate a paper copy of the machine entries for voters to verify and deposit in a sealed box for future potential audit. Today all but eight states require such a paper trail, and those that do not are being pushed to do so.[44] In addition, a number of states have begun requiring random auditing of machine totals to try to detect any machine malfunctions.

According to the Senate Intelligence Committee investigation on foreign interference in the 2016 election, Russian hackers had probed for weaknesses on the internet-connected voter registration systems in all fifty states.[45] The panel concluded that the hackers had an opportunity to "modify or destroy" data but held back.[46] The massive 2020 Solar Winds hack of US networks provided a taste of what's possible when malefactors decide to take the plunge. Foreign agents infiltrated digital systems serving the Department of Defense, the Department of Treasury, and the Department of Homeland Security, the agency responsible for cybersecuring national critical infrastructure.[47]

Cybersecurity expert Kim Zetter warns, "It's not too grand to say that if there's a failure in the ballot box, then democracy fails."[48] It matters little whether the failure is accidental or intentional, home based or foreign sourced, or even if it's perceived rather than real. Foreign powers know that actually manipulating votes isn't necessary to achieve their ends. Even the suggestion of foul play can help tip the nation into partisan-fueled disorder.

As ominous as were the events at the US Capitol on January 6, 2021, the turmoil surrounding the election could have been far worse had it not been for private intervention. An organization sponsored by Mark Zuckerberg and his wife, Priscilla Chang, gave $400 million to over 2,500 voting jurisdictions for staffing, training, and equipment to cope with early voting and the massive influx of mail-in ballots.[49] The funding, which matched sums appropriated by Congress, is credited with staving off greater controversy certain to have fed partisan paranoia and wider violence. In any case, 2020 opened a predictably nastier front in partisan hostilities. Allegations of stolen elections play big for Politics Inc., particularly when, as law professor Richard Hasen notes, "election law has become a political strategy."[50]

The parties remain united in at least one important aspect of election law: keeping it in the hands of partisan administrators. In forty-five states, the top election administration official, typically the secretary of state, is an elected Republican or Democrat.[51] Most discharge their duties honorably, but they quite naturally look to distinguish themselves with their party. The look doesn't inspire public confidence, particularly when secretaries of state, some eying higher office, engage in overtly partisan election activities. When Florida was embroiled in election controversy in 2000, its secretary of state also served as cochair of George W. Bush's Florida campaign.[52]

The National Association of Secretaries of State (NASS) strongly opposed the establishment of the Election Assistance Commission and worked to limit its authority to issuing only guidelines, not directives, on standards for federal election administration. NASS's opposition to the Department of Homeland Security's effort in 2017 to designate the election system as national critical infrastructure attracted greater scrutiny, given its public assurance several months before the 2016 national vote that "hacking of the election is highly improbable due to our unique, decentralized process."[53] Decentralization can have merit from a security perspective, but a hash of election systems with disparate reliability standards overseen by partisan officials does not, particularly when a single problem in a lone precinct of a single swing state can throw the entire nation into constitutional crisis.

Ensuring election integrity is far too important to American democracy to languish as another national imperative lost to partisan gridlock. Five fundamental reforms would go far toward restoring confidence in the electoral system and disarming divisions that the excesses of Politics Inc. could turn into national disaster:

1. Transitioning to nonpartisan, independent, and professionalized election administration chiefs, in accordance with the recommendations of the Carter-Baker Commission on Federal Election Reform[54]
2. Ensuring state compliance with national norms and performance-based standards of cybersecurity and best practice election administration procedures codeveloped by the EAC and the NASS and certified by the Department of Homeland Security and Congress
3. Providing oversight, monitoring, and quality assurance of election software algorithms and codes used by voting system equipment software providers
4. Instituting a multilayered system validating vote accuracy, including an auditable trail and use of artificial intelligence and mathematical models to identify anomalies and verify tally accuracy
5. Resourcing fully the upgrade of election systems and administration. The nation spends $700 billion a year on defending democracy from outside threats. We should be able to afford the necessary costs to provide for the integrity of its most essential practice.

VOTES THAT COUNT

A strong democracy not only welcomes every voter and properly counts every vote but also ensures that every vote counts. Politics Inc. has put in place rules making that impossible. Taxpayer-funded presidential and congressional primary elections are crucial in determining the choices the electorate have on General Election Day. Yet, under current law, more than thirty million Americans—those not registered as either Republican or Democrat and not living in one of the twenty-four states that have some form of open primary—are not permitted to participate in primary voting.[55]

Opponents of opening primary voting to nonparty members believe that doing so defeats the notion of "party" and enables gamesmanship such as partisans crossing over to vote for the weaker candidate. The country must decide which is fairer—limiting the ability to determine who will appear on the nation's presidential ballot to party members (who compose only 60 percent of the country's registered voters) or opening that right to all Americans. The public's preference is clear. Polls show that 70 percent of Americans cast their vote for the latter: allowing registered Independents to vote in the primary of their choice.[56]

Expanding the practice would encourage more federal office seekers to court a broader spectrum of voters, beyond the stouter partisans who exert outsized influence in primary elections. As it is, a small fraction of the electorate decides what choice voters have on General Election Day. In the 2018 midterm (nonpresidential election year) elections, just 20 percent of registered voters took part in the House primaries, a significant increase over the 2014 midterms, when only 14 percent showed up. The Senate primaries were little better: 22 percent and 16 percent participated in 2018 and 2014, respectively.[57] In 2008, a presidential election year, only 11 percent of Republicans and 19 percent of Democrats cast primary votes.[58] Though 2020 set records for voter participation, fewer than half of party registrants went to the primary polls.[59]

A common refrain in congressional circles is that no member wants to "get primaried"—meaning outflanked by a more extreme candidate who may be more attractive to the hardest core primary voters. The danger of being primaried remains especially acute in congressional districts gerrymandered for one-party dominance. In 2012, because some of his members feared it could subject them to a primary challenge from the right, Republican leader John Boehner was forced to pull a budget proposal he negotiated with the Democratic leadership to prevent some but not all tax hikes scheduled to go into effect automatically. Fellow Republican Mike Coffman admitted to the press, "There were members that are so gun shy about primaries that they weren't willing to take a risk" to support their own party leader in a major vote. The reason was that the substance of the vote could be misperceived, leaving a supporter vulnerable to attack.[60] An incumbent seeking reelection must take care not to arouse the ire of party activists by committing the sin of working with the other side or the ultimate heresy of agreed-to compromise. The fight against centrists is fully engaged within the party caucuses. Jim DeMint, a conservative firebrand and former Republican senator from South Carolina, established a super PAC to raise money for conservative challengers against Republican colleagues he deemed too soft. The fiery liberal representative Alexandria Ocasio-Cortez has done the same to dislodge centrist Democrats.[61]

So long as independents and centrists are marginalized by the primary system, moderate members of Congress will grow scarcer. As they disappear, and the parties migrate closer to their fringes, the choices presented by two parties for the general election will be less and less acceptable to the broader electorate, even in gerrymandered districts. These trends feed the growing cynicism infecting the nation's reasonable center. And it will be complemented by the public's increasing antipathy toward the most arcane, misunderstood, and maligned idiosyncrasy of the American political system—the Electoral College.

GRADUATING THE ELECTORAL COLLEGE

Established by Article II of the Constitution, the Electoral College is currently composed of 538 electors apportioned to the states.[62] Each state's number of electoral votes corresponds to its total number of congressional districts (435 in all) plus its two US senators (100 in all). Three additional electoral votes are apportioned to Washington, DC. A candidate who achieves a majority of the 538 total electoral votes—270—is elected president. If no candidate wins a majority, a "contingency vote" is triggered. The House of Representatives—with each state's congressional delegation allotted a single vote—votes for one of the top three candidates as determined by the Electoral College. The candidate with the most votes is elected.

Most Americans would be shocked to learn there is no constitutional right to vote for president or even for the electors. State law controls voting for president, or more precisely voting for the electors who vote for the party's candidate.[63] The Democratic and Republican Parties choose their slates of electors in each state. The winning candidate is assigned the electors from his or her party, who are expected (but not in all cases legally bound) to vote for their party's candidate if that candidate wins the state's popular vote.

The Electoral College casts its ballots in December, following the federal general elections, which are held on the first Tuesday after the first Monday in November. The early November date, established when the economy was mainly agricultural, set election day after the fall harvest but before harsh winter weather.[64] Tuesday was selected so that farmers, who usually devoted Sundays to church and Wednesdays to market day, could travel to distant polling places. The tradition has persisted even though weekend voting and longer poll hours would be more convenient for individuals who find it difficult to take time off work.

Since the nation's founding, only five presidents lost the popular vote but won the Electoral College, but two did so within the past three presidencies. George W. Bush had five hundred thousand fewer votes than Al Gore in 2000; Donald Trump had almost three million votes fewer than Hillary Clinton in 2016. The other three were John Quincy Adams (1824), Rutherford B. Hayes (1876), and Benjamin Harrison (1888). Many Americans do not understand the reason behind this seemingly undemocratic mechanism, and the perception of injustice contributes to public distrust in the political process.

The founders wrangled at length during the Constitutional Convention about how to choose the nation's chief magistrate. Proposals to make the selection by popular vote drew three main objections. First, delegates feared the highly populated states would have undue power over their smaller counterparts. The founders' vision was of a federal republic composed of equal, independent states—such imbalance would not suffice or garner the support necessary for ratification of the Constitution. The desire to balance state power explains why the union's least populous state (Wyoming, 578,000 people) and most populous (California, 39.6 million) send an equal number of senators to Washington. Second, the southern states feared the more populated northern states would dominate the executive, threatening their regional interests, including slavery. And third, some delegates believed that even under the framers' cramped definition of "voter," too many of them lacked the temperament and intellect to choose a national leader wisely. Delegate Elbridge Gerry of gerrymandering fame dismissed the idea as too democratic owing to "the ignorance of the people."[65] An alternative mechanism called for Congress to choose the president. This idea was shelved as too undemocratic and at odds with the doctrine of *trias politica*—separate branches of government that can check one another rather than be beholden to one another.

Eventually, a "Committee of Eleven on Postponed Matters" was appointed to develop a proposal acceptable to all.[66] The Electoral College was conceived as an independent body of wise people, selected by each state in a manner of its own choosing, to elect a chief executive. Tying the number of each state's electors to the size of its congressional delegation took advantage of the already-settled question on representational balance. Allowing each state to determine how it would select its electors satisfied the desire to maintain federalism. A mechanism was included—the "contingency vote" described above—that tossed the decision to the House of Representatives should no candidate receive a majority of Electoral College votes. The founders anticipated that use of the contingency mechanism would be a regular occurrence.

Convoluted? Yes. Controversial? From its origins. Bipartisan support for changing the system has waxed and waned over the past two and a half centuries. In 1969, legislation to shift to a direct popular vote was passed in the House but not taken up in the Senate, despite the urging of President Richard Nixon. Public opinion polls have consistently favored Electoral College reform for many decades. In *Why Do We Still Have the Electoral College?*, Alexander Keyssar ascribes the inability to change the Electoral College to the high procedural hurdles involved in amending the Constitution, reluctance by the states to give up constitutional power, regional jockeying, and, of course, partisan politics—as each party's support shifts depending on whether reform is seen as helping or hindering it.[67]

What stays constant is the harm done to the voters and the country, not so much by the Electoral College itself but by the way the states choose the electors. Millions of voters are marginalized every four years by "winner take all" laws in forty-eight states. (In Maine and Nebraska, the exceptions, two votes go to the winner of the statewide popular vote and one to the winner of each congressional district). Even if a presidential candidate wins a state's popular vote by just a single ballot, the state's entire allotment of electoral votes is credited to the victor. As a result, a highly Democratic state like California reliably gives all its electoral votes to the Democratic candidate (fifty-five in 2020), and a reliably Republican state like Texas unfailingly gives all its votes to the Republican candidate (thirty-four in 2020), no matter the popular vote margin of victory.[68]

In the 2012 presidential election, Republican Mitt Romney received 4.2 million votes (38.3 percent of the total votes cast) in California.[69] His opponent Barack Obama received 3.3 million votes (41 percent of the total votes cast) in Texas.[70] Four years later, over 4.4 million Californians voted for Republican Donald Trump, while Texans cast nearly 3.9 million votes for his opponent Hillary Clinton.[71] But all fifty-five of California's Electoral College votes were awarded to Obama and Clinton.[72] All of Texas's electoral votes went to Romney in 2012, and thirty-six of thirty-eight voted for Trump in 2016.[73]

In practical terms, winner-take-all electoral voting means that no Republican presidential nominee need step foot in California except to fundraise, and no Democratic nominee need campaign in Texas. This ability to ignore many states—including the nation's largest—diminishes the political influence of voters living in uncompetitive states, which is yet another disincentive to centrism and moderation. Were both parties' candidates to compete for votes in California and Texas, it would likely have a moderating effect on them. The system should encourage candidates for the land's highest office to compete for votes everywhere, not just in "swing states."

The simplest way to cure these serious deficiencies is to replace the winner-take-all system with a proportional one in which electoral votes would be awarded by each state in proportion to its popular vote. Such reform could be accomplished without the Herculean task of amending the Constitution, which requires either a constitutional convention (a method so far never used) or a two-thirds supermajority in the House and Senate and ratification by three-fourths (thirty-eight out of fifty) of the states. Congress could pass legislation requiring that electoral votes be prorated, or states could take the step independently or by compact. The prime caveat would be ensuring that apportionments are based on the state's total popular vote rather than by a "districting system" that allocates each electoral vote per congressional district and would further incentivize gerrymandering.

Though not generally considered as such, the sweepstakes approach is really an institutionalized form of ballot rigging and voter suppression. Despite its injurious defects, and no matter how well change would serve American democracy, the chances for Electoral College reform are vanishingly small. Neither party looks to forfeit electoral vote jackpots in the states they control. Both will fight any reform perceived as threatening their grip. Such fights include standing in the way of other key electoral reforms, such as fusion voting and ranked-choice voting, that would accomplish two important objectives: granting alternative parties a stronger voice and ensuring that US elections are decided by genuine majorities, not partisan pluralities.

Fusion voting, also called cross-nomination, cross-endorsement, and open-ballot voting, allows candidates to appear on a ballot as the nominee of more than one party. In the 1800s, many states allowed this practice, and New York, Connecticut, and six other states (plus California for presidential elections only) still do. It gives alternative parties and their followers a place in the process and encourages major candidates to address their priorities. Yet, to stifle the competition it would create, the duopoly has used its power to ban fusion voting from spreading beyond those few states where it has enjoyed a long tradition.[74]

Fusion voting enables voters to align with minority parties that best reflect their values and still vote for a candidate who has a chance of winning. It brings new voices to the political arena and offers people a political home that better suits them while encouraging candidates to appeal to a broad array of political movements rather than focus exclusively on their traditional bases. New parties can produce change. The Republican Party was founded in 1854 as a third party devoted to the issue of abolition, challenging the Whig and Democratic Parties, setting in motion reform resulting in the salvation of freedom and the Union.

Ranked-choice voting (RCV), also called instant run-off, alternative vote, and preferential voting, would likewise welcome more people and ideas into the system and ensure that victors represent a true consensus. In this method, voters rank each candidate on the ballot in the order they favor. When the first preferences are tallied, the winner is declared if a candidate wins a majority of the vote. Otherwise, the candidate receiving the fewest votes is eliminated, the second choice votes of those who voted for the eliminated candidate are reapportioned to the remaining competitors, and the vote retabulated. The process is repeated as necessary until a majority vote produces the winner.

RCV has key democracy-strengthening advantages. It ensures that all votes matter. A voter who prefers a minority party candidate can cast a vote to express that preference without wasting it if their second choice is needed to form a majority. It also eliminates the possibility, now common in the US system, that candidates can win with a plurality of the votes, carrying the day even though the majority of voters oppose them. In ranked voting, third parties aren't spoilers robbing votes from one of the two major party candidates. They're participants in the pursuit of consensus.

Numerous good government groups pushing for reform are ranked voting advocates. "We are really settling on ranked-choice voting as the most promising reform to democratize and depolarize our politics," says Larry Diamond, the former director of Stanford's Center on Democracy, Development, and the Rule of Law. "I think it's not only here to stay but that it's gaining support across the country."[75] Studies show that RCV both decreases the negativity in campaigns and increases voter satisfaction as candidates seek to appeal to a broader group of voters.[76] *New York Times* columnist

David Brooks observes, "Right now our politics is heading in a truly horrendous direction—with vicious, binary political divisions overlapping with and exacerbating historical racial divisions. If we're going to have just one structural reform to head off that nightmare, ranked-choice voting in multimember districts is the one to choose."[77]

The United States is the most innovative nation on earth. The time has come to apply our creative energies to modernize the electoral process on which ride the nation's aspirations for more effective political leadership, better government, and stronger democracy.

7

Laws and Sausages (Structural Gear)

Beware of my partisanship, my mistakes of fact and the distortion inevitably caused by my having seen only one corner of events.

—George Orwell

When political campaigns have run their course, the votes have been cast and counted, winners declared, and oaths of office sworn, a new Congress is born. The "people's branch" is where the electorate fulfills its right to participate in government through its freely chosen representatives. The founders designed the legislative branch to emulate the Constitutional Convention—citizen legislators contesting ideas in orderly, even if contentious, debate in search of consensus.

From the first Congress that met in New York City on March 4, 1789, to the present, every important matter of American life has come before it. The *Congressional Record*, a daily transcript of House and Senate proceedings, is a sort of national diary, chronicling the country's aspirations and controversies, great questions and debates, and its glories and failures. The gaveling in of a new Congress should be a time for renewed hope in our great constitutional purpose: "to form a more perfect Union, establish Justice, insure domestic Tranquility, provide for the common defence, promote the general Welfare, and secure the Blessings of Liberty to ourselves and our Posterity."[1] But Americans' sense of optimism is strained and exhausted. Ordained to be the grand staging ground for democratic governance, each Congress—convened for a two-year period—seems more carnival than caucus and more performance theater than policy shop. Its structures and practices, hijacked by Politics Inc., look to be better suited for campaigning than problem-solving.

Congress has never enjoyed heartfelt approval from a many-minded public. Griping about lawmakers and government is among Americans' most cherished traditions. But public antipathy for the legislative branch's poor performance goes far beyond reflexive disdain for its authority.[2] Political scientists find that, apart from the lead-up to the Civil War, Congress has never been more polarized and ineffectual.[3] Legislating may be like sausage making, but far worse is how they are not made. Something is fundamentally wrong when fifty-six members of Congress, frustrated by partisan gamesmanship and stalemate, are compelled to establish a "Problem Solvers Caucus."[4] A caucus of problem solvers is what the 535 voting members of the House and Senate are meant to be.

Acts of Congress cannot solve every national ill despite extravagant political rhetoric to the contrary. Many challenges are better tackled by the states and localities, the private sector, civil society, families, or individuals. The most difficult national problems require whole-of-society approaches. Finding the best solutions for securing the general welfare while protecting personal rights and liberties is an exacting test, challenged by diverse views on the proper role and core competencies of the central government. However, if the purpose of a full-time Congress, supported by over 12,500 staff members and $3 billion per year, is not to solve public problems, what exactly is it doing?[5]

To be sure, Congress was never a paradise of interparty harmony and productivity. Bitter partisan fights and political intrigues are as old as the oath of office and have even come to violence at times. In *The Field of Blood*, Yale historian Joanne Freeman chronicled eighty acts of physical violence in Congress in the three decades leading up to the Civil War.[6] Among the colorful instances is one that occurred on February 28, 1838, when congressman John Cilley of Maine was cut down by a bullet in a duel with his colleague William Graves of Kentucky over charges of bribery. The actions of Graves and his seconds in the duel, fellow members of Congress, drew a recommendation of censure, but the House declined to punish them.[7]

In 1856, proslavery representative Preston Brooks of South Carolina famously charged onto the Senate floor and clubbed abolitionist senator Charles Sumner of Massachusetts over the head with a steel-tipped cane. The vicious assault was triggered by Senator Sumner's denunciation of the possibility that Kansas might enter the union as a slave state, which he salted with harsh words on the Senate floor about congressman Andrew Butler, Brooks's fellow South Carolinian. Sumner had called Butler a "noise-some, squat, and nameless animal."[8] Two years later, thirty members of Congress were involved in a brawl on the House floor. Amid the melee, "Wisconsin Republicans John 'Bowie Knife' Potter and Cadwallader Washburn ripped the hairpiece from the head of William Barksdale, a Democrat from Mississippi."[9]

While Mitch McConnell and Nancy Pelosi might detest each other's politics, they have yet to charge across the Capitol with dueling pistols or canes, and, mercifully, unless it takes place in private corridors, wig snatching has remained out of bounds. Physical altercations aside, every Congress has known the ferocious collision of competing wills, ideas, and interests. Still, the institution generally found a way to perform its essential duties. Today, under the sway of Politics Inc., the national legislature is so broken that its ineffectiveness is weakening the three-legged stool of

American government, exciting fears it is wobbling to a tipping point. Broken as it is, Congress's core responsibilities, few of which it performs well, remain unchanged:

- Legislating annual federal spending limits and revenue levels (budget bills)
- Appropriating budgeted funds to the various federal departments and programs[10]
- Establishing federal laws, policies, and programs, including the reauthorization, reform, or elimination of federal agencies and initiatives approved by previous Congresses, typically passed with sunset provisions so they may be periodically reevaluated
- Providing "advice and consent"—constitutional language for the Senate's duty to approve or disapprove treaties and the president's nominations to fill high-level executive branch positions and federal judgeships
- Overseeing the conduct of the executive branch and ensuring the nation's laws are faithfully and effectively administered

For decades Congress could be generally relied on to pass a national budget, all thirteen of its spending bills, and a range of authorizations and reauthorizations. In the modern House and Senate, riven by partisan hostility, the only legislation the country can have confidence Congress will send to the president are huge catch-all spending bills and the annual National Defense Authorization Act. All else is a crapshoot.

The national budget process is a mess.[11] Determining how much taxpayer money to spend each year, on what, and how to raise the revenue is one of Congress's chief constitutional responsibilities and the cause of some of its harshest interparty fights, reflecting deep disagreement between liberals and conservatives on fiscal policy and the role of government. Instead of responsibly ironing out their differences, Congress has on occasion resorted to a kind of self-debasement unknown in other legislatures—shutting down the central government. Government closures damage the nation's economy, taking a bite out of GDP, and harm vital national programs and operations, including national security.

Between the mid-1970s (when new budgeting rules were adopted) and 1995, congressional failure to approve a federal budgeting measure resulted in the furlough of at least some federal employees only four times. The partial shutdowns lasted a total of seven days, costing the federal government about $215 million. Between 1995 and 2020, the shutdowns totaled eighty-three days at a cost of $75 billion. The House Government Affairs Committee studied the three government shutdowns between 2013 and 2019, including the thirty-five-day shutdown beginning in December 2018; it found that "rather than saving taxpayer money, shutdowns produce significant costs to the American taxpayer" as well as enormous loss of productivity.[12] The Government Accountability Office also found that closures cost the government more money than is saved by furloughing federal employees.[13]

The melodrama is fodder for press releases and partisan acrimony but at a steep price to the country. Spurred by deadlocked US budget negotiations in 2011,

Standard and Poor's downgraded the country's credit rating, stating, "The political brinksmanship of recent months highlights what we see as America's governance and policymaking becoming less stable, less effective, and less predictable than what we previously believed. The statutory debt ceiling and the threat of default have become political bargaining chips in the debate over fiscal policy."[14]

Budget debates have come to resemble a *Groundhog Day*–like recurrence of the same experience over and over again. Republicans denounce Democrats for fiscal irresponsibility, for ignoring the limitations and inefficiencies of government, and for promoting confiscatory tax rates. Democrats call Republicans heartless for blocking additional federal spending on social programs and higher taxes on the wealthy that could help pay for it. Both sides blamed Standard and Poor's for embarrassing them, as if government shutdown caused by partisan impasse is not embarrassment enough for the world's greatest democracy.[15] Meanwhile, the national debt-to-GDP ratio threatens to stall the economic activity responsible for generating tax dollars. Having for all practical purposes ditched the processes and disciplines imposed by the Congressional Budget and Impoundment Control Act established almost fifty years ago, the country chugs toward the looming fiscal cliff.[16]

Primarily because of partisan gridlock, two decades have passed since Congress took up and approved the full complement of required appropriations bills.[17] This failure has ushered in an era of massive spending measures, known as omnibus appropriations bills, cobbled together by party leaders and senior committee members. The bills are typically rushed to a vote without an opportunity for rank-and-file members to properly review the provisions and offer amendments. It's astonishing that members are able to lift these measures, much less read and evaluate their merits. Not infrequently members and staff are surprised to learn what was in them when reading newspaper accounts following their passage.

When omnibus bills prove too difficult to assemble, Congress relies on what it calls "continuing resolutions," which simply extend preexisting funding levels.[18] Often passed at the eleventh hour, they let Congress avoid hard decisions without defunding federal operations, but they afford no opportunity to adjust the national allocation of resources to meet evolving challenges. Used sparingly before the 1980s, they are now routine; Congress used the mechanism 117 times between 1997 and 2019, lasting from one day to an entire fiscal year.[19]

Other than the defense bill, formal program reauthorizations that update national policies have slowed to a trickle. Many departments, agencies, and programs have never been comprehensively modernized despite the social, economic, commercial, and technological changes that demand fresh approaches. As of 2021, the Federal Bureau of Investigation; the Drug Enforcement Administration; the Bureau of Alcohol, Tobacco, and Firearms; the State Department; the Federal Trade Commission; and the National Weather Service are all operating on expired authorizations. The Federal Elections Commission hasn't been reauthorized in forty years.[20] The Congressional Budget Office reported that in fiscal year 2020, Congress devoted nearly 20 percent of total federal discretionary spending (more than $332 billion) to funding

407 programs that lawmakers had not reauthorized.[21] By comparison, twenty-five years ago, funding of unauthorized programs totaled around $35 billion.[22]

DIVISION BY DESIGN

The breakdown in lawmaking is not caused by national challenges that have become more difficult or solutions that are beyond the reach of principled compromise. The impediments are structural and systemic, following a familiar recipe for institutional decline. It typically begins with a human element that replaces constructive norms and practices with new standards and customs, eventually spoiling the organization's culture and ability to function.

We have examined the factors that bring to Congress members beholden to extreme voter bases who devalue collaborative problem-solving. The ill effects on congressional norms, practices, and culture—even in members' physical interactions—are evident. An analysis of C-SPAN footage of the House of Representatives floor proceedings from 1997 to 2012 shows that members intermingled with their colleagues across the political aisle progressively less. The less they did, the more partisan the vote tallies.[23] A 2018 Michigan State University analysis of House and Senate bipartisanship found that cross-party sponsorship of legislation has steadily declined since 1973, regardless of whether Democrats or Republicans held the majority. Polarization, says Zach Neal, the study's author, has "hit the ceiling."[24]

Newly minted members are swiftly disillusioned as they are indoctrinated into the congressional ethos. Their certificates of election usher them into a culture fixated on incumbency, obsessed with financing and partisan gamesmanship. These days, the good of the country is usually perceived as the good of the party. Even the physical layout of Congress is designed to emphasize partisanship over teamwork. The parties operate in separate cloakrooms, caucuses, steering committees, conferences, and weekly lunches. In Congress's chambers and hearing rooms, Democrats sit on one side and Republicans on the other. Every trapping of the legislative body, including its rules and procedures, is used to foster apartness and prosecute interparty warfare. Social and professional customs that used to help bridge the partisan gap have fallen away.

Political scientists and scholars debate the origins of rabid partisanship and the decay of congressional capacity. Some point to Vietnam and the Watergate scandal, when distrust of Washington became the norm. Reagan-era messaging compounded the public suspicion of Washington that was seeded in the unrest of the Johnson and Nixon years and the failures of the Carter years, turning it into antipathy toward government itself—a theme still exploited by the extremes in both parties. The defeat of Robert Bork's nomination to the Supreme Court in 1987 sparked continuing partisan strife and political tit for tat over appointments to the High Court. Many ascribe today's hyperpartisanship to the Gingrich revolution in 1994, when Republicans took the House after six decades in the wilderness. The newly empowered majority eagerly sought to reverse the rapid growth of government and pursued vengeance for the humiliation of its former powerlessness. Compromise with the Democratic minority was considered sacrilege.

Polarization accelerated during the Obama administration, fed by the former senator's disdain for an inept Congress and by the sharp rhetoric of the Republican Party's emerging Tea Party wing. The parties themselves were splintering. The Freedom Caucus, waving the banner of Tea Party conservatism, considered Republican centrists as grave a threat to the country as Democrats—and they ran Republicans John Boehner and then Paul Ryan out of their speakerships. During Donald Trump's term, the Democratic version of the Tea Party emerged in a movement led by Bernie Sanders and Alexandria Ocasio-Cortez. Both party fringes gained traction in the backlash against a president from the other party. Amplified by mainstream and social media that monetize drama, the spin artists for both parties went to work rebranding the other side as the sum of its fringes. In the 2020 election, American politics became a caricature of right-wing fascists versus left-wing socialists, both sides calling the other traitors. Most Americans stood blinking in the rational center, wondering what had happened. Time will tell whether the extremes continue to define America's political landscape, driving the country closer to the abyss, or if we can regain a sense of national balance and move forward.

REGULAR DISORDER

Moving the country in the right direction will require that Congress revitalize lapsed traditions of interparty respect and orderly government procedures vital to the success of the American system. In the 1970s, an animated television series called *Schoolhouse Rock* used catchy children's tunes to teach children, including about how Congress works. "I'm Just a Bill" follows an anthropomorphic "Bill sitting here on Capitol Hill" as it goes from an idea to law. This clever lesson in applied civics is now a fairy tale. Bill was describing the process known as "regular order," now defunct. Model lawmaking was designed to follow seven sequential steps:

1. Public introduction of a legislative proposal
2. Referral to the committee of jurisdiction
3. Official public hearings on the proposal
4. Committee consideration of the measure and amendments to improve it offered by committee members
5. Committee vote approving the measure for referral to the House and Senate calendar for consideration
6. Floor debate and amendments by the full body
7. Upon the exhaustion of amendments, an up or down vote on final passage

The modern Congress has shelved regular order in favor of an ad hoc system administered by the majority's leadership. Major legislation is often written in relative secrecy by leadership staff and sprung on the full body without giving members sufficient time to assess its impact or amend it. Time and again the result is presented on the floor as a take-it-or-leave-it proposition. It is passed mainly along partisan lines, leaving the minority feeling cheated and alienated from the legislative process. The practice ensures the enactment of laws that have all manner of unintended consequences and tepid public support. Moreover, when the party in power changes, the new majority repays the favor with interest. The public is left trying to plan lives and businesses around laws that change every time majority shifts.

In their critical 2020 open letter warning that Congress is failing to fulfill its constitutional duties, a bipartisan group of retired US senators cited as one factor that "Senate committees have lost responsibility for writing legislation."[25] Representative Charlie Dent, a retired thirteen-year veteran of the House, echoed their sentiments: "I think it's fair to say the leadership exercises a lot more control on chairmen than they did in the bygone era," helping make congressional service miserable and unmeaningful for those aiming to do good things for the country.[26]

The fingerprints of Politics Inc. are all over the death of regular order and the procedures that have taken its place. In their book *It's Even Worse Than It Looks*, Thomas Mann and Norm Ornstein point out that many characteristics of the modern Congress resemble a parliamentary system (in which the members of the majority party operate in the legislature as an extension of the chief executive, and the opposition's task is to question and impede them) more than a coequal branch of government designed by the founders to perform a discrete set of functions.[27] The party leaders primarily see themselves as guardians of their respective parties' interests, not congressional prerogatives. For example, the so-called Hastert Rule, implemented by former Republican Speaker of the House Dennis Hastert, allowed bills to come to the floor only if the majority of his caucus supported the measure, without consideration for the will of the body at large.[28]

In the House of Representatives, the majority-controlled House Committee on Rules determines what bills come to the floor and under what rules of debate and procedure. Obedient to the partisan base, the leadership has increasingly resorted to what Congress calls "closed rules": no amendments may be offered to a measure when considered by the full House. The body is left to vote up or down on a bill crafted by the majority party and giving the other side little or no opportunity to address concerns with it.

The Senate employs its unique rules to accomplish the same end. The Senate has historically prided itself as being "the world's greatest deliberative body," one that allowed members unlimited debate and amendment in a spirit of collegiality. No longer. Party leaders increasingly rely on the uncollegial parliamentary maneuver called "filling up the tree," which blocks amendments from the opposition meant to hurt the reelection prospects of the majority and fend off any change to a bill that the party leadership favors as is.

The majority party's effort to exert total control leads to domination of the legislative process by relatively few senior members. Whichever their side of the aisle and whatever their particular ideological leanings, most senators would genuinely prefer to take part in the process. Marginalizing them is marginalizing the people who sent them there. The frustration this causes makes cooperation less likely and increases the institution's inertia. As a former senator explained to me, without the opportunity to help shape legislation, "there's nothing left but partisanship."

The relevance of rank-and-file members is further eroded by changes in how the appropriations process works. Gone are the days when all or most of the thirteen separate appropriations measures were passed in orderly fashion. Because the funds they allocated fell under preapproved budget spending caps, members were free to offer amendments directing federal funds to a designated purpose without concerns about budget busting. The process involved much bipartisan horse-trading.

Yes, appropriations earmarks could divert tax dollars to low-priority and often wasteful projects. The famous Alaskan "bridge to nowhere" came to symbolize congressional profligacy and prompted the 2011 rule change barring earmarks. But the practice had an unappreciated benefit: the opportunity to take part in a legislative process for the interests of a member's district or state got members in the habit of working together. Participation gave members a sense of ownership and an incentive to say yes when saying no because a bill isn't perfect is usually the politically safe option. If members could barter on the allocation of federal highway dollars, then perhaps they could come together on desperately needed legislation to modernize national infrastructure. As a veteran Senate leadership staffer told me, "Members have lost the muscle memory of amending legislation." "Us and them" has replaced "give and take" and built a road to nowhere.

GOING NUCLEAR

Some of the more destructive parliamentary maneuvers are prompted by persistent partisan obstruction to getting anything done at all. Under Senate rules, proceeding to business on the Senate floor requires either the membership's unanimous agreement to do so or, on the objection of a single senator, a majority vote in favor of proceeding to the business. The "motion to proceed," as it is officially called, is subject to debate; thus, a member can talk for as long as they wish to delay the matter, a maneuver called filibustering. The only way to end the debate is for at least sixteen senators to sign and file what is known as a cloture petition—bringing closure. A couple days after that petition is filed, the Senate votes on it: three-fifths of the Senate (sixty members) must agree to end the filibuster and get on with voting on the matter at hand.[29]

In November 2013, weary of Republican opposition to voting on President Obama's judicial nominees, Democratic majority leader Harry Reid employed what became known as "the nuclear option." Over Republican objections, he changed the Senate rules to require a simple majority to take up executive branch nominations, except for the Supreme Court. The change eliminated the ability for a single senator or small group of senators to talk a nomination to death or significantly delay its consideration. Republicans accused the Democrats of foul play. But of course, four years later, when Republicans took control of the Senate and Trump was president, the GOP used its majority to extend the nuclear option to nominations for the Supreme Court, providing a case study in tit for tat that keeps congressional norms and practices slipping further into the trenches.[30]

At present the nuclear option applies only to executive nominations. In the conduct of legislative business, a single senator can still object to consideration of a measure without having to identify themselves as the source of the hold. Filibusters, a tactic once used sparingly for the most controversial issues, have become standard partisan weaponry, sapping time and energy that Congress needs to perform its constitutional duties. The sclerosis partly explains why US policy can't keep up with national needs in a fast-changing world where speed and agility are necessary. A politician can win election by a bare plurality of the electorate but, once in office, be empowered to compel supermajority support for the Senate to do its work.

But tit once again proves as damaging as tat. Invocation of the "let's get on with it" cloture procedure to overcome the abuse of the filibuster has itself become an abuse. Wielding their prerogative to control the legislative schedule and agenda, Senate majority leaders, irrespective of party, often invoke cloture immediately after bringing a bill to the floor, thereby shutting down debate and curtailing amendments. Between 1917 and 1970, cloture was invoked a total of eight times. In the 116th Congress (2019–2020), the procedure was used no fewer than 270 times.[31] The procedure denies members their right to improve legislation every bit as effectively as it preempts obstructionists seeking to kill a measure by filibuster or poison pill amendment. Above all it spoils congressional culture by marginalizing the minority party, disenfranchising rank-and-file members on both sides of the aisle, and sharpening resentment and frustration.

In February 2020, a bipartisan group of seventy former senators signed an open letter denouncing congressional dysfunction. Its catalogue of mechanisms undermining the institution's work included abuse of the filibuster: "Rules allowing extended debate, a feature of the Senate that is essential to protecting the rights of minorities, have been abused. . . . It is now commonly said that it takes 60 votes to pass anything in the Senate. This is new and obstructionist. . . . Neither in committee nor on the floor do rank-and-file members have reasonable opportunities to advance their positions by voting on legislation."[32]

Floor votes are when many senators see one another and bond. Fewer votes mean fewer bonding opportunities and less collaboration. Congress is more than a legislative institution. The House and Senate are social organizations, no different than a school, workplace, or civic group. Election certificates do not alter human nature. People belonging to any organization in which they are ignored, disenfranchised, or bullied will disengage and lash out. When the power shifts from one party to the other, as it inevitably does, the abused become the abusers.

CONGRESSIONAL DISCOURTESY

The sense of cooperation and respect that once inspirited Congress has been replaced with cancerous distrust. Senate veterans wistfully recall past instances of comity and fairness. An example involved former senator Ted Stevens, a Republican who came to the Senate in 1968. As a junior senator, he believed he had an agreement with a powerful committee chairman to offer an amendment to a bill. By some turn of events, the vote on final passage commenced without Stevens getting his opportunity. Learning that the senator from Alaska felt slighted, majority leader Mike Mansfield, a Democrat from Montana, took the extraordinary step of stopping the roll call vote so his colleague from the other side of the aisle could offer his modification.[33]

It is nearly impossible to imagine such behavior in today's Congress, in part because members of the two parties now see themselves less as colleagues and more as adversaries. No longer do they have the time and opportunity to establish the professional and social relationships on which trust and cooperation rely. Before the 1990s, members of Congress typically lived in the Washington area while Congress was in session. Their families would come to know and socialize with one another, and members often commuted together to the Capitol. As congressional sessions lengthened and members began to fear accusations they had become creatures of Washington, they began traveling back to their home states and districts on Thursday night and returning on Monday, leaving little time for socializing.

In addition, many legislators point to C-SPAN's televising of House and Senate floor proceedings, which began in 1979, as dramatically changing congressional culture. Though the coverage was intended to enhance transparency and educate the public, veteran lawmakers say that it fueled partisan posturing and bogged down the legislative process. Congressional proceedings have turned into campaign theater. In this acrimonious daytime political drama, the parties conceive new ways to embarrass one another before the press and public. "The idea that Washington would work better if there were TV cameras monitoring every conversation gets it exactly wrong," says former Democratic Senate majority leader Tom Daschle in his book *City of Rivals*. "The lack of opportunities for honest dialogue and creative give-and-take lies at the root of today's dysfunction."[34] Chief Justice Louis Brandeis famously said that sunlight is the best disinfectant, but too much sun can blind and burn. One reason the Senate can regularly pass a well-considered annual defense authorization act is the fact that the Armed Services' markup proceedings are closed to the press and public due to the sensitive nature of the subject matter. Members may offer whatever amendments they deem appropriate, in a process refreshingly free of partisan gamesmanship. No one is posturing for an audience or interest.

When C-SPAN expanded its live television coverage to congressional committee hearing rooms, hyperpartisanship followed. Hearings vital for fact-finding were overwhelmed by partisan theatrics. Committee oversight gives way to partisan grandstanding. In many high-profile hearings, one must listen hard for a question in a speech aimed at scoring points rather than eliciting answers. In overseeing the executive branch, members all too often focus more on their party interests than their institutional duties—one side doing its best to tear down the administration of a president of the opposing party, the other side engaging in whatever contortions are necessary to defend it.

Politics works by creating contrasts. Governance works by constructing consensus. Unsurprisingly, under the bright lights of television and the sway of Politics Inc., the politics of contrast have gained the upper hand. Television cameras are in the House and Senate chambers to stay, but the culture must change to provide transparency and accountability without pandering and partisanship.

DEATH BY COMMITTEE

Congressional committees are an indispensable tool for analyzing issues and testing ideas among members responsible for developing an issue area expertise. They are platforms conferring a measure of influence and authority to their members. Seeking to get involved in the action, members clamor for seats on major standing committees and opportunities to gain a chairman's gavel. As a result, plum committees have grown too big and unwieldy and subcommittees too many in number.

John Hamre, president and CEO of the Center for Strategic and International Studies, believes that the bloat, along with changes in seniority rules, has played a role in diminishing the power of chairmen and the effectiveness of standing committees—for many years the repository of congressional expertise and influence. In a memo to his board of trustees made available to me, Hamre said, "The Senate Armed Services Committee now has 27 members [currently 26], over a quarter of the Senate. The House Armed Services Committee now numbers 61. And members of the Senate and the House now routinely serve on many more committees and subcommittees, diminishing their time and focus."[35]

Congressional oversight is an essential component of the constitutional system of checks and balances, but inefficient oversight is as harmful as too little oversight. Administration officials spend so much time and resources responding to Congress that their ability to manage their agency—and the agency's performance—suffers. The Department of Homeland Security, for example, reports to more than *ninety-three* congressional committees and subcommittees, not to mention several dozen congressionally sponsored commissions and task forces with overlapping jurisdiction.[36] The Heritage Foundation's Riley Walters observed, "Excessive oversight only hinders DHS's [Department of Homeland Security's] abilities, but meaningful reform would allow DHS officials the freedom of making our daily lives more secure. And it would allow members of Congress to stop fighting useless turf wars."[37] Years ago congressional icon Morris Udall quipped from his chair at a House Interior Committee hearing, "Everything that can be said has been said, but not everyone has said it."[38] Anyone who has viewed a congressional hearing knows exactly what he meant.

A witness told the 9/11 Commission that the multiplicity of reporting lines for the Department of Homeland Security to the Hill served as "perhaps the single largest obstacle impeding the department's successful development."[39] The commission offered its recommendation: "Through not more than one authorizing committee and one appropriating subcommittee in each house, Congress should be able to ask the secretary of homeland security whether he or she has the resources to provide reasonable security against major terrorist acts within the United States and to hold the secretary accountable for the department's performance."[40]

The committee structure itself is dangerously outdated. While modern challenges demand comprehensive, multidisciplinary approaches, congressional committee structure remains largely unchanged, stovepiped by function. No committees are designed to comprehensively tackle multidimensional national problems. Cyber-security, energy security, environmental protection, homeland security, economic development, and other key issues cut across the jurisdictions of numerous committees that need to be more effectively synchronized. Because bills in the Senate are referred to a single committee for consideration, other committees with relevant expertise typically weigh in once a matter has reached the Senate calendar or is called up for floor action when time is short and business is rushed. Committee chairmen don't typically hold regular meetings to learn from one another and bridge gaps. This lack of coordination extends beyond committees. No formal mechanisms exist to promote serious agenda setting and planning involving the two parties' leaders, much less involving congressional leaders and the president of the United States. Collaboration is almost exclusively ad hoc, relying on personal relationships.

UNCHECKS AND IMBALANCES

The partisan games and archaic structures impeding Congress from performing its constitutional role pose a long-term problem for American democracy. In their open letter, the seventy former senators raised alarms about Congress's remarkable concession of authority to the executive branch, including "the power to regulate international trade, the power to authorize the use of military force in foreign conflicts and, when the president declares national emergencies, the power of the purse. In addition, the partisan gridlock that is all too routine in recent decades has led the executive branch to effectively 'legislate' on its own terms through executive order and administrative regulation."[41]

The exercise of greater presidential powers to fill the void left by Congress becomes a point of partisan conflict and resentment. The 2001 and 2002 authorizations for the use of military force against Al Qaeda and Iraq have been distorted beyond recognition by presidents of both parties for almost twenty years, yet Congress can't reassert its constitutional authority in spite of broad agreement that both authorizations need to be replaced. Republicans called Obama's use of executive orders dictatorial. Democrats repeated the charge against Trump. Though executive orders have come to play a growing role in national policy because of congressional incapacity and lack of bipartisan teamwork, Congress doesn't see itself as the source of the problem.

Government by executive order is arbitrary and fleeting in its effects. When control of the White House shifts, so do the previous incumbent's executive orders, destroying any semblance of continuity in pursuing strategic objectives. Congress's failure to set a credible policy confronting climate change prompted President Obama to resort to executive order to make good on a campaign promise. He put in place extensive rules to curtail the use of coal and cut power plant emissions.[42] Upon election, Donald Trump promptly moved to rescind the orders. Joe Biden acted quickly to put them back in place. The same pattern holds in assorted other policy areas. Had Congress taken up the issues to work out mutually acceptable plans, more durable policies would be in effect, and those affected could plan and move on.

Congress, of course, has a responsibility to oversee the executive branch's vast rule-making authority. Oversight was once the domain of experienced committee chairs and ranking minority members who knew the agencies, government programs, and issues under their jurisdiction better than many of the officials appointed to manage them. Fellow members trusted their expertise. Today, House committee chairmen are chosen for their fundraising prowess and instead of vigorously exercising the lost art of oversight, members mainly employ executive action as ammunition for criticism and politicking. Safeguarding their domain while monetizing it leaves chairmen insufficient time and energy to perform effective oversight so essential for ensuring government accountability.

Moreover, many chairmen are term limited and take their experience with them when the gavel goes to the next in line. The staff they depend on for expertise pass through the revolving door on their way to better-paying jobs in the private sector. The brain drain requires legislators to rely even more heavily on the expertise of the executive branch itself and on lobbyists.

DOWN HILL

A deficient Congress translates into not only poor governance but also defective government. A Government Accountability Office study on duplication in the federal government outlined a vast web of redundancy and inefficiency, including eighty-two federal programs to improve teacher quality, eighty to improve services for those who need transportation, and fifty-six focused on financial literacy. "Reducing or eliminating duplication, overlap, or fragmentation," the agency pointed out, "could potentially save billions of tax dollars annually and help agencies provide more efficient and effective services."[43] The mishmash of arbitrary policies and poor oversight of executive action together have enabled the buildup of rules sapping the nation's economic strength. A comprehensive 1999 study by the Organisation for Economic Co-operation and Development found that "the complexity of the national regulatory system, the interplay of federal, state and local regulatory activities, and the fact that certain areas of the economy remain heavily regulated present both domestic and foreign firms with formidable challenges regarding regulatory coherence, cost of regulatory compliance, and transparency."[44] These are serious shortcomings from either party's perspective. A Congress dutifully performing its Article One responsibilities would not be making things worse.

For the three-legged stool of American democracy to work the way it was intended, political culture must break from the practices cultivated by Politics Inc. The people's branch must be reformed to serve the public interest, not the duopoly; to focus on governing, not campaigning; and to protect its integrity as a coequal branch of government. Pundits and political scientists argue that Congress should look more like America, usually referring to race, creed, color, income bracket, and background, but the same holds for expertise and political views. Forty percent of Congress are lawyers; less than 0.0004 percent of Americans practice law. Forty percent of American voters are political Independents; only 0.0037 percent of Congress can say the same. The party duopoly ensures that Congress and state legislatures are run almost exclusively by Republicans and Democrats who are organized, led, and conditioned to fight each other.[45]

Issue One associate former representative Frank LoBiondo says, "Today a vocal and obstinate minority within both parties has hijacked good legislation in pursuit of no legislation." His colleague representative Lynn Jenkins laments that some members of Congress "just oppose the other side for no other reason than they don't like the other side."[46] Upon his departure from the Senate, Jeff Flake observed that the "tribal nature of politics" leaves "no room for compromise or doubt."[47] The instinct to fight is why almost every issue that must be addressed gets reframed and run aground by debate easier to politicize and fight over. Immigration policy and border protection is converted into a fight between racism and violent crime. Fiscal responsibility becomes a referendum on compassion versus greed. Environmental protection is made into war over prosperity versus sustainability.

"If I have learned anything from my time in Congress," said former congressman Will Hurd, "it is that the only way we are going to solve the big problems our country faces is by working together."[48] Many members of Congress past and present share his conviction. Increasing numbers of them are calling for reform of Congress' rules, procedures, and culture. In 2019, the House of Representatives established a Select Committee on the Modernization of Congress composed of an equal number of Democrats and Republicans. The panel issued ninety-seven recommendations, revealing bipartisan hunger to make Congress more effective.[49] The suggestions heavily emphasized training and programming to upgrade member and staff expertise, not just in law and government but disciplines necessary to understand issues. While the 116th Congress contained 192 lawyers, members with other skill sets, such as economics, science, and technology, were in short supply.[50] "The best defense against partisanship," wrote American essayist Roger Angell, "is expertise."[51] The Select Committee offered other defenses, including joint planning and activities to break down partisan barriers; it also called for technological innovations to improve the quality of hearings and promote fact-based legislation as well as an internal commitment to "reclaim Article One responsibilities." Harnessing big data analytics and artificial intelligence can inform better policy and eliminate some of the conjecture that contributes to policy disputes and partisan divide. A blue-ribbon group of former members of Congress empaneled by the Bipartisan Policy Center— a Washington think tank—urged a return to regular order so that elected members of Congress could do what their voters sent them to do.[52] No new laws or constitutional amendments are required to make these reforms, only the willingness of people's representatives is required to make it so.

UPGRADING DEMOCRACY'S SOFTWARE

Long needed modernization of Congress' structures and practices begins with adopting a new operating system built around greater jointness and interoperability much as we expect from the country's military services. In a great democracy, it must not be too much for the country to expect that the parties' congressional leadership gather at the beginning of each session to publicly lay out a comprehensive joint agenda and principles to guide their collaborations. The country would benefit immeasurably if instead of conducting political combat via press releases and social media posts, policy makers instituted mechanisms to enhance cooperation such as regularly scheduled coordination sessions: interparty, intercommittee, intercameral, and interbranch. These should include formal and regular meetings between the bipartisan congressional leadership and the president of the United States. Separation of powers and parties must not mean estrangement when national interest is at stake. National and state leadership, too, should strengthen the intergovernmental partnership required to meet critical needs. The COVID-19 pandemic proved the importance of better intergovernmental collaboration between levels of government to tackle shared threats and achieve common public interest objectives.

Bringing the congressional committee system into the twenty-first century and building greater institutional accountability would significantly improve congressional culture and national problem-solving. Cross-jurisdictional committees should be organized to address multifaceted challenges holistically rather than in silos—something the best organizations in academia and business recognized long ago.

Congress needs one-stop shopping for members, the press, and the public who seek to know what agencies and programs are due for reauthorization, reform, or elimination, and to chart legislative progress in fulfilling these duties. Every bill Congress passes should contain a well-defined set of objectives, clear benchmarks, and criteria enabling better evaluation of federal laws and programs under Congress's purview. Bringing greater discipline to congressional procedures can boost the institution's functionality and begin to restore the political system's capacity for progress.

Above all, the quality of Congress depends on the quality of its human capital. Acting with simple decency—respecting one another and listening to one another—does not require that leaders yield their conviction. But it will make all the difference in determining whether the grand principles we share endure or fall victim to our relatively petty squabbles and temporary passions. Upon his retirement from Congress, representative Sam Johnson decried the status quo: "What I will miss least is the current polarization and common refusal to listen to or respect others' ideas."[53] These tired conditions have taken a stranglehold on the legislative branch and "we the people" it is constituted to serve, a grip tightened by the handiwork of Politics Inc.'s codependent—the mercenary media.

8

Mercenary Media (Media Gear)

A cynical, mercenary, demagogic press will produce in time a people as base as itself.

—Joseph Pulitzer

The US Constitution expressly references but one industry—the press. Extolling the importance of a vigorous free press, Thomas Jefferson declared, "No experiment can be more interesting than that we are now trying, & which we trust will end in establishing the fact that man may be governed by reason and truth. Our first object should therefore be to leave open to him all the avenues to truth. The most effectual hitherto found is the freedom of the press. It is therefore the first shut up by those who fear the investigation of their actions."[1]

The proponents of free expression understood that democratic government, even if equipped with internal checks and balances, would not safeguard the governed from abuse of power. Representative democracy would require an external check that only a free and independent press could provide. Jefferson and Madison knew that maintaining open avenues of truth would be exploited by scoundrels and demagogues trafficking distortion and deceit. Nevertheless, they placed their faith in the wisdom of free people to distinguish between reason and folly. In a measure of courage that should inspire officeholders today, young America's political leadership sanctioned press freedom because it was good for democracy, despite that its power would be used as a check upon themselves.

In 2017, the *Washington Post*, one of the country's largest and most influential newspapers, announced it was adopting the motto "Democracy Dies in Darkness." Detractors perceived pretension. Others saw a thinly veiled broadside at President Trump for calling the press an "enemy of the people" and habitually dismissing unfavorable coverage as "fake news."[2] In fact, the paper was moving to incorporate the dictum in its masthead well before Trump became president. It was drawn from a decades-old court decision issued by federal judge Damon Keith, the grandson of slaves, requiring the government to obtain a judicial warrant to conduct a wiretap.[3] His words—"Democracy dies in the dark"—spoke to the fragility of democracy and that the fate of freedom rested on responsible overwatch of government. Equally true, however, is that democracy can perish in broad daylight when irresponsible press become party to the abuse of the public trust it is obliged to expose.

Most Americans have come to believe that the press no longer serve the public interest, any more than the politicians they cover, and that "journalists and reporters are purposely trying to mislead people by saying things they know are false or gross exaggerations."[4] When first measured in 1972, Gallup polling found that about seven in ten Americans trusted the mass media to report the news "fully, accurately, and fairly." By 2020, only four of ten felt the same.[5] Other polls show almost three-quarters believe news outlets are politically biased.[6]

Many members of the press don't disagree with the poor appraisal of its performance. "As politicians have become more polarized," says journalist and author Amanda Ripley, "we have increasingly allowed ourselves to be used by demagogues on both sides of the aisle, amplifying their insults instead of exposing their motivations. Again and again, we have escalated the conflict and snuffed the complexity out of the conversation."[7]

In some ways, American mainstream media and other elements of the industry are back to the future, imitating their eighteenth- and nineteenth-century forebears before press independence, fairness, and objectivity were recognized as important ethical standards for the profession. In the early days of the Republic, broadside newspapers, handbills, and pamphlets were the cable TV and political pulpits of their time, operating as mouthpieces for their affiliated political team, purveying their propaganda, and savaging their opponents. In the nation's infancy, John Fenno's *Gazette of the United States* plied the Federalist platform, and Philip Freneau's *National Gazette* spun for the anti-Federalist camp. A surplus of small and medium-sized newspapers served readers with similar ideological slant. Like many digital platforms today, broadsheets delivered a mix of reportage, politicking, and entertainment, often with lively invective.

Over the following decades, the newspaper industry paced the nation's growth. The written word was the primary means of mass communication, and political advocacy was expected in news and public affairs coverage. By the late 1800s, fierce competition for print circulation ushered in the era of "yellow journalism," titillating the public with sensationalism, scandalmongering, and incendiary editorial. The circulation-seeking melodrama inflamed public passions and prejudices; by some estimates it even goaded the United States into war with Spain in 1898. But public weariness with the excesses of a manipulative and irresponsible press converged with a professional reform movement, and in the early 1900s, a code of ethics for the news business emphasizing truthfulness and responsibility began to take shape.[8]

Soon the advent of commercial radio and network television revolutionized mass communication, posing new and complex public interest challenges. Foremost was providing for the responsible use of limited, publicly owned airwaves. To meet the challenge, in 1934, Congress created the Federal Communications Commission (FCC) to license and regulate broadcasters to ensure they operated in the "public interest, convenience, and necessity."[9] The mandate resulted in rules requiring that licensees devoting airtime to endorse a candidate for elective office provide qualified opponents with access to "equal time"—a major regulatory foray into public and political communications.[10] The move set the stage for implementation in 1949 of the "fairness doctrine," obliging broadcasters to present issues of community importance in a fair and balanced manner.[11]

Following World War II, network television became king of American mass communication. By 1980, 90 percent of the population was tuning in to primetime programming sponsored by one of the three major national networks: ABC, CBS, and NBC.[12] The country's news, public affairs, and information ecosystem was rounded out by magazines, city and community newspapers, and network radio and TV affiliates offering local news and public affairs programming. Legal scuffles over press rights were accompanied by growing public expectations of greater press responsibility, giving rise to a professional code of ethics obliging journalists to adhere to truth, accuracy, and balance in reportage and to the separation of news and opinion.[13]

But public perceptions of political bias and other flawed practices by the media persisted. Liberals came to see conflict of interest in the ownership of mass communication companies by wealthy, conservative businessmen dependent on corporations for advertising revenue. Conservatives were convinced that newsrooms and broadcast studios teemed with left-leaning journalists skewing reportage to fit political agendas hostile to the free enterprise system and traditional American values. These contradictory but not mutually exclusive perceptions budged little over time.

Technology, however, took a leap, upending mass communication as a business and as a cultural force. Cable television, satellite TV and radio, and the internet emerged in succession offering a multitude of channels and a diverse mix of news and public affairs programming—and creating increasingly fierce media competition for audience. No longer did broadcast television and radio dominate mass communication. Determining in 1987 that the conditions warranting the fairness doctrine no longer existed, the FCC withdrew the rule. By 2017, fifty national free-to-air national networks and over 1,700 commercial television stations operated in the United States, more than double the number in 2000.[14]

Year over year, internet access and online sources of information have multiplied, providing users with an inconceivably diverse selection of content. Not only could anyone with a device and an internet connection receive masses of information on demand, but they could also produce and disseminate it. The freedom to speak and publish was being enabled beyond anything the founders could have imagined.

Consumers have come to enjoy a profusion of sports, movies, and entertainment programming and multiple modes and channels to access it. The glut of news and public affairs choices, however, has not benefited national political culture or the economics of the news business quite so generously. Stiff competition for audience and revenue has generated forces deeply impairing the quality and character of journalism and the performance of its duties in democracy. In fairness, "media" is an exceedingly broad term encompassing a wide spectrum of channels, outlets, and practitioners, including many outstanding broadcast and print journalists. It is hard to point to a golden age of the news business that did not exhibit many of the shortcomings now in evidence. The difference is their scale and intensity today, and the accelerating trends worsening them.

Key elements of the media—particularly cable news—have gained outsized influence on American culture and politics, obscuring the wealth of truly great journalism produced every day. They have become codependent bedfellows with Politics Inc., all too often utilizing and amplifying its tactics and degrading the practice of professional journalism by

- Sensationalizing content and exploiting human emotions to attract attention and audience
- Blurring the line between fact and falsehood and between news and commentary
- Emphasizing opinion and advocacy over objectivity
- Exercising haste over responsibility
- Catering to and reinforcing partisan bias to win market share and brand loyalty
- Driving social and political division to feed on the proceeds

The tragic story of Seth Rich is a case study in the corrosive implications of journalism that has lost its way in the era of manic competition and hyperpartisanship. Rich, a twenty-seven-year-old DNC staffer, was murdered outside his Washington, DC, home in June 2016. Online propagandists and conspiracy theorists quickly picked up on the story, concocting a connection between the murder and the Wikileaks release of the hacked DNC emails that had made such a splash earlier in the campaign to the embarrassment of Hillary Clinton and other top Democrats. Simply imagining that the young man was murdered by Democratic operatives in a revenge plot and posting the erroneous conjecture online conspiracists brought the falsehood to life. Fox News picked up the internet speculation and gave it credence by reporting the "story." The Trump campaign picked up on the fake news and amplified it further. From there the myth went viral. The media kept the tale going because political figures were talking about it. Political operatives echoed it because it was in the press. The public was engrossed by the dramatic nature of the story helping it spread across the internet.

All in all, Politics Inc. had a field day. The news business had an emotionally arresting story that could titillate viewers and increase ratings. A political campaign had a manufactured scandal that could be used against the opposition. Interparty distrust was nicely fueled. One party despised the other even more for being party to a sordid "scandal," and the other reciprocated for its opposition being party to a vile sham. The damage to Seth Rich's reputation and the further pain inflicted on his family and friends mattered not at all. And it did not concern Politics Inc. that American culture had been further degraded and the parties further divided by the debacle. In November 2020, Fox News settled the civil defamation suit filed by Seth Rich's family.[15]

Left unaddressed were the dynamics behind such miscarriages and the troubling direction of so much news coverage and journalism—beginning with how the industry even defines news. In its purest form, news is the factual verification that something happened or is true. The mainstay of journalism was finding and reporting facts, even if much else is needed for those facts to make sense. "There can be no higher law in journalism," said Walter Lippman, "than to tell the truth and shame the devil."[16]

Today, in the tsunami of public communications in abbreviated news cycles, the fact that something outrageous or spectacular was said, posted, or tweeted, no matter how untruthful or irrelevant, qualifies as news. Such a standard gives misinformation, disinformation, and propaganda currency and power. Lies used to be called out. Now they are repeated. And when responsible journalism leavens the story with the fuller context, it hardly matters since the "media" are distrusted. What remains are untruths for partisans to exploit and the question: How did we get here?

EARS, EYEBALLS, AND CLICKS

Respected journalist and longtime host of *PBS NewsHour* Jim Lehrer listed among his professional rules "I am not in the entertainment business."[17] For many media outlets, including their news and public affairs function, however, that has become precisely their business. In the mad scramble to win ears, eyeballs, and clicks from stiffening competition, entertaining the audience with emotional, conflict-heavy sensation is the winning formula.

Little is better at attracting and holding the attention of audiences than the ability to stir emotions, especially by use of plotlines full of tension involving villains, victims, and heroes—the time-honored basis of good storytelling. Partisan politics, with its loyal team-like following, penchant for conflict, and emotional appeal, is ripe for exploitation, and it's unending. Stories covering the partisan firefight of the day churn constantly. How coincidental that the most earth-shaking political developments seem to break daily between commercials or at the top of the hour of the dominant cable news and public affairs programs, announced by startling gongs and alarming red screens as the host stares gravely into the camera. Politics Inc. is happy to oblige, given the many benefits it receives from the continuous coverage of its dramas.

Print media are not exempt from the tactics used by the cable giants and their online doppelgangers. Often readers find themselves drawn to a frothy headline only to find it misrepresents the facts in the story.[18] Given that nearly half of Americans read only headlines, how these practices help people truly comprehend the significant events affecting their lives is harder and harder to see.

Press irresponsibility is not new, nor are the difficulties it presents for democracy. Seventy-five years ago, the Commission on Freedom of the Press (known as the Hutchins Commission) was empaneled to better define and evaluate the press's role in strengthening the foundations of freedom and democracy. Its final report highlighted the dangers when the press emphasize "the exceptional rather than the representative, the sensational rather than the significant."[19] The charges and their dangers still apply, doubly so today in a far more competitive landscape, where the temptations are greater for an industry facing extreme financial challenges in a culture with disappearing limits on what public communicators will do to stand out in an exceptionally crowded and noisy electronic public square.

PITCHING THE NICHE

Regardless of how content is packaged or its medium, Americans are drawn to outlets that present news and information that reinforce their worldview and preconceptions. Writing for *Slate* in 2008, social commentator Bill Bishop observed, "It's not what people say that matters in today's politics. It's what people *hear*. Voters go out of their way *not* to hear what upsets their existing beliefs."[20] Bishop found that a shrinking number of Republicans listened to the State of the Union addresses during Bill Clinton's years in office, while Democrats began to tune out during the George W. Bush years.

Media is an industry, and like any other its businesses seek their niche and to curry a loyal customer base. All too many, imitating partisan politicians at a townhall in a gerrymandered district, know what their audience wants to hear, and they deliver the goods—bias-confirming information and commentary. In this way, broadcasters have become narrowcasters with an ideological brand. Significantly, the niche audience creates a well-profiled market segment for advertisers. The yellow journalism that plagued the early twentieth century has been replaced in the opening decades of the twenty-first century by *orange journalism* and *green journalism*—the colored reportage and public affairs coverage generated when mixing sensational yellow with Republican red by some highly influential outlets and with Democratic blue by others.

Viewer data substantiate what most people already know—Republicans tend to tune in to FOX, One America News, Newsmax, and their pick of favorite conservative radio jocks and websites, while Democrats patronize CNN and MSNBC, along with left-leaning radio and digital sources. Analyzing the "stark difference in the partisan composition of the Fox News Channel, CNN and MSNBC audiences," Pew Research found that "each cable network's audience profile differs from the partisan balance of the public at large by approximately the same amount."[21]

Presidential debate coverage offers an excellent case in point. Comparative analyses of how FOX, CNN, and MSNBC cover the debates show the differing tone and emphasis among the networks aligned with the political leanings of their target audience. In a study of how the three networks apportioned airtime and emphasis in their coverage of the 2016 debate between Donald Trump and Hillary Clinton, journalist Andrew McGill boiled it down: "Fox News largely showed Trump triumphant, while MSNBC savored Clinton's quips. Sometimes they agreed. . . . But so far, the recaps mostly split along three lines: 'Trump good,' 'Clinton smart,' and 'Everyone is interrupting.'"[22] In the macro sense, the predictably different tone of coverage and analysis created a kind of balance—useful perhaps, provided viewers could watch several networks simultaneously. Instead, partisan-minded Americans tuned in to their favored network. When the sparring was over, they tucked themselves comfortably into bed, having been generally reassured that their side prevailed.

As Americans sort themselves into their ideological clans and information ecosystems, shared understanding becomes more elusive. Media choices heavily influence how we see the world around us. Senior media writer Tom Jones of the Poynter Institute for Media Studies advised, "Watch CNN and see a very different country than the one you will see on Fox News. In fact, the network you turn to might say a lot about how you see the country. Or go to their websites."[23] Jones did that on a random evening in 2020 during social protest and racial unrest following the killing of George Floyd. CNN's headlines were "Massive protests in US largely peaceful now (though it warned of possible problems later in the night); Thousands march in protest in Floyd's hometown of Houston; Reverend: They turned holy ground into literal battle ground." Running simultaneously on the Fox News website: "Police may bust high-ranking Antifa members soon, amid concerns over riots hitting suburbia; Kellyanne Conway on 'outrage' over Trump's St. John's trip: 'Anarchists won't dissuade us'; Fleischer on Trump activating military: Governors are 'fools' not to call National Guard, 'do your job.'" Monitoring the two network broadcasts that evening, Jones noted, "While CNN's primetime hosts such as Don Lemon and Chris Cuomo and their guests criticize President Donald Trump, Fox News hosts such as Sean Hannity and Laura Ingraham and their guests vigorously defend him."

A smaller but oft-repeated vignette speaks volumes about the subtle and not-so-subtle nuances that make a big difference in the public's perception of politics and government. Following Election Day in 2016, the customary drumbeat of announcements began on cabinet appointments. Both cable networks were streaming news on the nominations to Trump's economic team. The FOX ticker proclaimed something to the effect of "Trump taps corporate titans for cabinet." CNN's scrolling banner announced something along the lines of "Trump appoints millionaires to economic team." The headlines covered the exact same story. Both were factually correct but intended to make very different impressions. The subtext of the FOX banner was: Rejoice! Experienced corporate leaders bring heavyweight business skills to government. CNN's was: Beware! Trump straps country with corrupt, wealthy corporatists.

Rabid FOX watchers likely nodded approvingly while CNN devotees shook their heads in disgust. Meanwhile the divide widened a little more. The loaded discrepancy repeats itself continuously across the politicized media landscape.

JOURNATORIALISM

The competitive imperative to connect ideologically and emotionally with a niche audience is why fact-based reporting, necessary for keeping the public properly informed, has been overwhelmed by opinion journalism offered by the cable giants and their like on talk radio, online, and in print. Analyzing the content of the three big cable news networks, Pew found that over half of Fox News programming was devoted to opinion, CNN 46 percent, and MSNBC 85 percent.[24] News, analysis, and opinion are so blended in cable TV news programming that telling them apart has become almost impossible. The emphasis on opinion performs double service. As an audience getter, opinion beats facts in dramatizing and sensationalizing storylines and keeping viewers emotionally aroused. Moreover, in a bottom-line industry, creating and airing opinion is much cheaper and quicker than finding facts and can be streamed continuously, filling monetizable airtime. Hard luck for the public, since political journatorialism comes at the expense of programming on economic, social, commercial, and technological matters of much greater relevance to most Americans' daily lives. In any event, facts themselves are less important in the era of hyperpartisanship. Their persuasive effect is lost on made-up minds often more interested in seeking the comforts of affirmation than the challenges presented by facts, truth, and rounded perspective. Goodbye, Chet Huntley, David Brinkley, and Walter Cronkite. Hello, Sean Hannity, Lou Dobbs, and Rachel Maddow.

SPEEDY, SHALLOW, AND SLOPPY

In the digital era, the stiff competition for audience and strong public demand for continuous content sharply magnifies performative pressure on the media. The compromises required to cope with it are destroying the professional norms vital for the press to fulfill their public interest responsibilities. News cycles have been reduced to mere minutes. Getting information out fast trumps getting it out right and risk losing out to speedier competitors.

Being pushed out urgently gives every morsel of news and information an artificial aura of importance. Worse, speed promotes sloppy reporting and oversimplification and further encourages commentary above reportage. In a Brookings Institution essay, veteran *Washington Post* reporter Robert Kaiser observed, "We seem to have adapted to the demise of the old expectations about accuracy, fairness, and reporting without much of a fight. . . . News as we know it is at risk."[25] Some in journalism seeking to keep up with speedy news cycles and demand for content have lowered their standards from two-source verification to a single source, diminishing accuracy and reliability. Most editors, journalists, and media executives polled in 1999 agreed not only that the "distinction between reporting and commentary has seriously eroded" but that "news reports are increasingly full of errors" and "sloppy reporting."[26] The industry's performance has only declined since the poll, as the competition for attention on social media has intensified.

Tweeting by journalists, like tweeting by politicians, seems like an ironic contradiction and ominous development, favoring impulsiveness over thoughtfulness and completeness befitting their respective roles. But they cater to an impatient and time-constrained public who want the bottom lines in simple sound bites and easily grasped memes. Those who fail to deliver content within the transient news cycle adapted to the immediacy required by social media risk being unheard.

The premium on speed and brevity means that both the producers and consumers of news and public affairs programming have less time to discern fact from viewpoint and truth from falsehood. Complex issues are presented to the public in simplistic extremes and false binary choices, bypassing important nuance, much like the duopoly does itself. "Obamacare" is good or bad. Trade is economic poison or antidote. Federal regulations are the tools of public benefit or the costly weapons of a nanny state. The fact is the Affordable Care Act has produced benefits and drawbacks. Certain aspects of trade policy promote our economy while other sectors suffer. Some government programs and regulations provide enormous social benefit; others are horribly wasteful and outdated. These are important nuances and distinctions meant for serious policy debate and responsible governance that the political industry, including many in the popular press, are loath to make. Rather than covering the meat and context of the issues, an inordinate amount of time and resources are devoted to covering the ad hominem political attacks and countercharges associated with the controversy. The public never quite gets its arms around the substance behind it.

In what has been called "the Super Bowl of American politics" during the presidential election every four years, we learn far more about the candidate's campaign and rhetorical skills than their ability to govern, lead, and unify while making tough, practical choices. The press predominantly interests itself in drawing a few major policy differences to create a contrast so it can turn its focus on the day-to-day horse race of fundraising and poll numbers, campaign stumbles and internal intrigues, character flaws, what the two sides are saying about each other, and hopefully a good scandal.[27] Thomas Patterson, the Bradlee Professor of Government and the Press at Harvard's Kennedy School of Government, calls the rise of horse-race journalism the "quiet revolution" in press coverage of political campaigns in which the "plot-like nature of the competitive game" has become the center of attention. In studying the focus on what he calls "game schema" versus policy and leadership qualifications, he found stark trends. In a sampling of press accounts covering the 1960 presidential election, 45 percent of the stories centered on campaign strategy and competitive dynamics. The percentage of such stories doubled by the 1992 contest. Conversely, stories centered on "policy schema" plummeted to 10 percent in 1992 from 50 percent in 1960.[28] Like opinion journalism, horse-race coverage is cheaper and easier and needs just enough substance to create distinctions to frame the fight. Covering the tactics of the brawl dominates from there.

BEDFELLOWS

The relationship between politics and media is an endlessly fascinating one—seemingly adversarial but fundamentally synergistic, incestuous, and financially codependent. They share an enormous financial stake in maintaining and exploiting partisan combat—the nastier the better. For the duopoly, the tension creates larger campaign contributions to finance political combat. For the media, covering partisan warfare produces higher ratings and revenue. Both exploit the same tactics to garner attention and resources: sensation, hyperbole, and half-truth.

The ideology-based market segmentation offered by the media is gangbusters for Politics Inc. A study by Emory University political scientists Alan Abramowitz and Steven Webster substantiates that "Democrats and Republicans have never been as divided as they are today."[29] According to a 2016 study cited in *Journalist's Resource*, the increase in media partisanship within the past few years has played a significant role.[30] Among the reasons why is the neat partisan segmentation of the audience. Partisan messaging echoed by media outlets entrenches views, making for more loyal disciples and enabling parties to target and fire up their base more efficiently. For the media, campaign and issue advocacy ads are goldmines, making up a significant portion of the revenue for the biggest and most influential networks and programs.

TheStreet's Chris Nolter says, "During times of peak demand, stations can sell political ads for 40 to 50 times more than the rates for the run of the mill car ad, making political spots disproportionately valuable." Moody's analyst Carl Salas told him, "It has become increasingly important because, for one, political advertising is now over 10% or 12% of average revenue and it's growing fast."[31] Each national election cycle sets new records in spending on political advertising. New highs were hit in 2020 as the presidential candidates spent over $2.5 billion to run over five million ads over the election year, over twice the amount spent in 2016. The total cost of the 2020 election reached $15 billion, compared to $7 billion in 2016, $6.5 billion in 2012, and $4.5 billion in 2008. As discussed in chapter 4, the money spigot to pay for political ads was opened to full blast by the Supreme Court's *Citizens United* decision. CBS president and CEO Les Moonves candidly observed, "Super PACs may be bad for America, but they're very good for CBS."[32]

Cable TV and Donald Trump were very good for one another. Nothing aided Donald Trump's prospects as a presidential candidate more than CNN—the network he pointed to as the fountainhead of fake news—and MSNBC's *Morning Joe*. The excessive coverage and free airtime candidate Trump received compared to his competitors in 2016 presidential TV catapulted his campaign.[33] The attention came not because he had better vision and ideas, demonstrated greater command of the issues than his competitors, or showed finer leadership skills. The mic and camera were his because he was famous, brash, controversial, and attention-getting. He was the star of a running political reality show, and cable news cashed in on the sweeps. Some people binged in delighted agreement; others were transfixed by the spectacle. Even if horrified and disapproving, they kept watching, which is what the networks care about most. Candidate Trump artfully used the unprecedented platform to help him trounce his party competition and win the general election.

Conversely, no one did more for the ratings and earnings of the top cable network and the MSNBC shows than Donald Trump. As *Forbes* trumpeted, "Donald Trump was not the only winner of this year's election. The three major cable news networks earned record profits and attracted record audiences, as millions of Americans tuned in to watch the dramatic showdown between Trump and Hillary Clinton."[34] In the process, he helped save CNN financially—a spectacular irony considering President Trump's oft-repeated charge of news fakery.[35] Having earned money helping to build him up, CNN and MSNBC cashed in on the sideshow they helped create and in programming to bring him down, as if either was the press's job. By spring 2021, after Trump left office, Fox News, CNN, and MSNBC all booked loss of viewership from the fourth quarter of the previous year. The lesson is clear. Big political drama equals big viewership and the revenue it produces. When you want more of something, says classic economic theory, financially incentivize it.[36] Bad news indeed for the country's political culture.

Before turning on him, Joe Scarborough openly provided Donald Trump with political and campaign advice while covering politics on his MSNBC show. Understanding the value of the precious airtime and positive coverage, Trump went so far as to publicly express appreciation to Scarborough and his cohost for being "supporters."[37] A *Washington Post* media critic called the setup a "cozy social club."[38]

The club is a well-populated one. The pattern of incestuous relationship between press and pol is a well-practiced but still troubling element of political culture that must be reexamined. Many prominent on-air figures in news and public affairs programming first had long careers in partisan politics, and others moved in the reverse direction. *Time* magazine's Washington Bureau chief left to become Vice President Joe Biden's director of communications and then President Obama's press secretary. Matt Gertz of *Media Matters* chronicled how the Trump administration hired "over a dozen current and former Fox News reporters and contributors to serve in both high-level cabinet and deputy chief of staff posts, as ambassadors, and in communications roles at federal agencies."[39] Roger Ailes was a longtime political operative before becoming chairman and CEO of Fox News and Fox Television Group. After stepping down from that influential post, he returned to partisan political consultancy.

A newer and more corrosive element is the dual-hatting of partisans and journalists in the form of so-called news contributors seen nightly on cable public affairs programming. The nomenclature is itself deceiving since most in this rapidly proliferating species of commentator don't contribute to the news with objective facts and information. Mostly they provide partisan perspectives, views, and opinions: journatorialism. Many "news contributors" populating the airwaves operate political and campaign consultancies, hold partisan positions, or otherwise play a role in the partisan ecosystem.

Longtime Democratic strategist Donna Brazile chaired the Democratic National Committee and managed high-profile political campaigns before becoming a CNN commentator. As part of its campaign coverage of the 2016 presidential election, the network sponsored a "townhall" debate among the contenders for the Democratic nomination. Found in the Wikileaks dump of campaign emails in 2016 was clear evidence that Brazile had shared with Hillary Clinton's campaign questions that would be asked of the candidates. Though terminated by CNN for the infraction, Brazile later signed a lucrative contract with Fox News as a "news contributor."[40] The well-beaten path between elective politics and the networks marks waning reverence for the critical but distinct and incompatible roles played by these institutions in our system.

Even when they appear to be at odds, the media and Politics Inc. seem to benefit one another at the public's expense. A 2010 study by the Shorenstein Center on the Press, Politics and Public Policy at Harvard's Kennedy School charted the dramatic increase in negative advertising between 1970 and 2008, finding it largely due to media's increasing coverage of such ads. The overwhelming majority of Americans who saw the ads did so not when they aired but during news coverage of them, which provided the "free" messaging campaigns covet. Political scientist John Geer observes, "The core idea is that the news media now cover negative ads so extensively that they have given candidates extra incentive to produce and air them. Candidates want to get their message out."[41] And the media want to get out theirs. The arithmetic ensures that political campaigns and the media benefit from the cycle of negativity. The loser in the deal is the electorate and American political culture worn down by negativity.

Politicians and the media also mutually benefit from using one another as foils. Blaming journalists for policy trip-ups or failure is a time-honored political tactic. Once the fault is affixed, the press is turned into another demon from which the party and the country, synonymous in today's partisan mindset, must be saved.[42] The more partisan media outlets become, the easier to make charges of bias stick. Media critic and CNN host Brian Stelter quoted a top Obama White House staffer's comments regarding Fox News: "We're going to treat them the way we would treat an opponent. . . . We don't need to pretend that this is the way that legitimate news organizations behave."[43]

As a candidate, Obama called out FOX for its bias as a mouthpiece for hateful opponents.[44] Democrats cheered his straight talk. Donald Trump called the press "truly an enemy of the people" and revoked White House press privileges for reporters he found offensive.[45] He criticized CNN and the other elements of the press for exhibiting Trump Derangement Syndrome, decrying their overwhelming "anger and hatred."[46] To the delight of his supporters, Trump's repeated verbal assaults on the press burnished his chops as a bare-knuckled outsider who wouldn't be bullied by the deep state's friends in the media. To be sure, when journalists perform by scolding or provoking instead of questioning officialdom, they make themselves part of the story inviting the criticism they receive. Unfortunately, the incentives today are in the wrong direction. Young media professionals know that the path to big professional success and high dollars is making it to television. Exceptionally fair and balanced reporting is not necessarily the fastest route to the studio and celebrity.

Politics Inc. and its press element share another trait: their exploitation of public cynicism and negativity. "The mainstream press highlights what's wrong with politics without also telling us what's right," says Thomas Patterson of the Shorenstein Center. "It's a version of politics that rewards a particular brand of politics. When everything and everybody is portrayed as deeply flawed, there's no sense making distinctions on that score, which works to the advantage of those who are more deeply flawed. Civility and sound proposals are no longer the stuff of headlines, which instead give voice to those who are skilled in the art of destruction."[47]

The climate this creates is another factor helping drive many good people from elective service, and it greatly discourages those who would serve admirably from even considering the prospect. And it discourages the public. David Broder, the longtime political reporter, noted that "cynicism is epidemic right now. It saps people's confidence in politics and public officials, and it erodes both the standing and standards of journalism. If the assumption is that nothing is on the level, nothing is what it seems, then citizenship becomes a game for fools, and there is no point in trying to stay informed."[48]

Villainization and the politics of animus and blame is a dangerous game not just for our civic health but quite literally for both sides of the public podium, in the political pulpit and at the press standup. Harassment, violence, and threats of violence against politicians and public servants are on the rise.[49] Trump's antipress applause lines ginned up supporters to the point that reporters covering his rallies were verbally and physically threatened. Reporters without Borders, an international nongovernmental organization established to defend freedom of information and protect journalists, documented nearly seventy attacks on the press during the nationwide protests following the killing of George Floyd by Minneapolis police in the spring of 2020. Members of the press were "shot by rubber bullets and pepper balls, exposed to tear gas and pepper spray, beaten, threatened and intimidated and had their news vehicles vandalized, simply for doing their jobs."[50] In Florida, reporters were hounded by protesters for covering the protests rather than participating in them.

PRESSING ON DEMOCRACY

Technological, commercial, and demographic trends are further complicating the ability of the press to fulfill its traditional role in democracy. The internet and social media enable politicians to message the public directly, bypassing journalistic filters and disciplines, among the reasons it is easier now for elected officials to thumb their nose at the press. That's because they can without paying a penalty. A top network journalist observed to me, "There was a time when politicians didn't pop off because they would be fact-checked. Now they are repeated. Any criticism falls flat on the ears of the public that no longer trust the press." And the criticism matters far less when politicians can message their base directly, cheaply, and immediately at will.

Younger generations prefer to obtain their news and information online and through social media that satisfy their desire for speed, brevity, and entertainment. Each of these market forces is hollowing out journalism on the community level. Local newspapers that have played such a significant role in community cohesion and public involvement are in trouble, shuttering across the country, their revenue model disrupted by online access to content and information. The circulation of surviving community papers continues to plummet. Newsrooms are shrinking, cutting staffs by almost half between 2008 and 2017, and local TV focuses more and more on sports, weather, and traffic.[51] "News deserts" are created by the disappearance of local press.[52] With it go important training grounds where professional journalists formerly learned their tradecraft and paid their dues before progressing to bigger outlets.

The loss of the community press matches declines in civic engagement, including fewer people running for public office and taking part in community civic and service organizations, and it further loosens the bonds of participatory democracy.[53] There is evidence that municipal administration deteriorates when locally focused watchdog journalism disappears, adding to public disaffection with government. Not the least of the damage from the loss of local journalism is the shifting public focus from state and local affairs to more polarized national news and coverage of partisan politics.

The competitive forces eroding journalistic discipline and professionalism and undermining community press are not a problem for the media alone. They are an American problem and a disaster for democracy. The experiment in representative government is built on a foundation of sacred trusts and responsibilities apportioned among the governed, the governors, and the government. Instrumental to this triad is a free and independent press entrusted to properly inform the governed so they can choose wisely, to inform and oversee the governors to ensure they serve faithfully, and to watchdog the government so it performs well.

Americans wonder how the press can fulfill these duties when it is so weakened by distrust and compromised by its financial dependence on sensationalism, partisanship, and social division.[54] Truth can't travel the avenues of public discourse when it is sideswiped by falsehood that the press seems more effective at amplifying than correcting. Media outlets can't be effective watchdogs when they choose to play lap dog to one political party and attack dog to its opponent. The public can hardly expect a more honorable political culture when it's shaped by media whose bankroll swells in proportion to domestic political tensions, partisan rivalry, crisis, and fear.

How is democracy served by news outlets that are party organs rather than public servants? Walter Lippman noted, "The news is the chief source of opinion by which government now proceeds. . . . In so far as those who purvey the news make of their own beliefs a higher law than truth, they are attacking the foundations of our constitutional system."[55]

A term used frequently to define good journalism is "balance." The FCC withdrew the fairness doctrine on the premise that the numerous channels of information and public affairs programming technology has produced created an overall balance in the content and viewpoints available to the public. "Balance" has become an imprecise and misleading word to encompass impartiality, fairness, and fullness in storytelling, which is not the same as balance. None of these attributes are achieved because slanted stories dished by the two dominant cable networks, one leaning Democratic and the other Republican, cancel each other out. Opposing half-truths do not combine to make whole truth. Nor is balance achieved by wrapping a few facts in opinion and calling it news when strictly separating the two and clearly labeling them is the chief obligation. Good reporting isn't truly measured in balance, anyway. There are full facts and whole truth, not balanced facts and balanced truth. Accuracy is simply about getting the story straight and right, not equally weighted to the satisfaction of all stakeholders.

The adversaries of freedom understand the important role the press plays in American democracy and culture and the gaping vulnerability created by the decline in its professionalism and trust. Garrett Graff, author of "A Guide to Russia's High Tech Tool Box for Subverting US Democracy," points out that the goal of Russia's extensive disinformation campaign against the United States "is not necessarily to convince people that the Russian view of the world is the right one or that their interpretation of events is better, but rather to destroy and undermine confidence in the Western media."[56] We are succeeding at doing that ourselves.

In 1947, the Hutchins Commission called for professional journalism to reform.[57] The panel of experts had been organized by *Time* magazine's founder and publisher, Henry Luce. Seeing the existential threat posed by fascism in World War II, he saw an urgent necessity to better define and evaluate the press's role in strengthening the foundations of freedom and democracy. Operating independently under the auspices of the University of Chicago, the national commission was asked "to study the role of the agencies of mass communication in the education of the people in public affairs." The time had come, it concluded, for the press to embrace a renewed responsibility to public interest grounded in a "scrupulous . . . regard for the wholeness of its truth and fairness of its presentation."[58]

The time has come again. Freedom is under threat in a geopolitical environment far more complex than when Luce's commission made its report. The nation's need for a free and responsible press accountable to the public interest is greater than ever. The media's job number one must be restoring its credibility and reestablishing public trust lest democracy die not in darkness but in the light of day.

CORRECTING THE RECORD

French philosopher Albert Camus had it right: "A free press can of course be good or bad, but, most certainly, without freedom, it will never be anything but bad."[59] Restoring the bonds of trust between the public and professional journalism is not a job for government that could only do damage by infringing on press freedoms it is sworn to protect.

The press's ability to restrain governmental abuse begins with restraining its own, matching press liberty with press responsibility. It begins with modernizing and reemphasizing professional principles, norms, and standards of conduct for journalists and press organizations, perhaps even with the help of a new Hutchins Commission. The emphasis should be placed on keeping faith with the worthy objective it set seven decades ago: "the information provided must be provided in such a form, and with so scrupulous a regard for the wholeness of the truth and the fairness of its presentation, that the American people may make for themselves, by the exercise of reason and of conscience, the fundamental decisions necessary to the direction of their government and of their lives."[60]

The panel observed prophetically, "We cannot assume that the mere increase in quantity and variety of mass communication will increase mutual understanding. It may give wider currency to reports which intensify prejudice and hatred. Nevertheless, the new instruments exist and will be used in any case. The cure for distorted information would seem to be more information not less."[61]

Right on! And not just more information but better information from sources that can be trusted because of the conduit's adherence to unimpeachable norms and standards—most of which are enshrined now in the Society of Professional Journalists' code of ethics. The country needs a nonprofit accrediting body through which affiliated professional journalists, press organizations, and media enterprises are credentialed after demonstrating their commitment and adherence to best practices. Among the priorities should be presentation that complies with Jim Lehrer's top rules of journalism: "Carefully separate opinion and analysis from straight news stories, and clearly label everything."[62] Such a body, composed of respected journalists, prominent subject-matter experts, and public representatives, should also

- Set accreditation standards and provide a seal of affiliation and good standing
- Establish a mechanism to identify and publicize serious and serial breaches
- Provide standards-based training and curricula for practitioners and news organizations—including how to report on disinformation, a skill in which only 15 percent of journalists have been trained[63]
- Establish awards and means of recognizing journalists and news organizations that meet the highest industry standards
- Rank journals and journalists according to their adherence to the highest standards of conduct and performance

Such an effort must be complemented by fact-checking services that expand their focus to include the professional media, not just campaigns and other sources propagating false information. A broader and better array of web-based tools are needed to identify and publicize media performance, including outlets trafficking in hoaxes and fake news. Journalists play an important role in grading the homework of public officials and public affairs. It's time to better grade the grader and watch the watcher to elevate good journalism and call out the bad.

Private foundations can play a role in providing viable alternatives to corporate-owned news and public affairs programming. ProPublica is a privately led and funded nonprofit enterprise devoted to investigative journalism, filling an important niche. The public also needs more daily resources. Schools and religious and civic institutions can be instrumental in training people to be better consumers of information and to track the provenance of the content we consume.

None of these measures should or would stop individuals, groups, or organizations from publishing, posting, and publicizing what they please. Those that show to be a public-serving professional news organization, however, should have the opportunity to be credentialed by a private, independent, and trusted body as committing to and adhering to the industry's code of ethics and professional standards. Corporations can play an influential role by placing advertising with responsible media who are properly credentialed.

Access to information about the entities that provide the news and content we receive serves the underlying premise of the First Amendment—the public's right to know. Enormous challenges lie ahead in decommissioning the media in the gearworks of Politics Inc. The scope and success of the mission will be heavily influenced by the X factor influencing so many aspects of modern society—the power of technology.

9

High Tech and Low Down (Technology Gear)

The human spirit must prevail over technology.

—Albert Einstein

The saga of human social evolution is largely written in the chapters of technological change. From stone tools to artificial neural networks, invention has continuously shaped and reshaped the patterns and structures of culture and life. The benefits of transformational change are typically accompanied by new challenges and unwelcome consequences. Harnessing technology to maximize social good is difficult enough. The complementary challenge, and, in some cases, the more urgent necessity, is to avert the use of powerful high-tech tools to inflict harm. Such a challenge has materialized at the intersection of digital age wizardry and liberal democracy.

In the pantheon of invention, modern information and communications technologies (ICT) are the crown jewels.[1] Internet-connected personal computers and mobile devices have transformed how people learn, work, and interact. Wireless and satellite networks enable us to stay connected on the go. Fifth-generation broadband networks compose an electronic central nervous system, bringing to life smart cities, machine learning, and an emerging Internet of Things. Digital superconnection creates the big data from which computer science and analytics extract insights and solutions benefiting practically every area of human interest.

At its inception, hopes soared that the internet's powers could be harnessed to strengthen democracy and governance. An open and accessible digital commons could bring more vibrant and participatory democracy and give voice to silenced communities. Ready access to Web-based content would lead to a better-informed electorate and spawn new ideas and approaches to old public problems.

E-government would provide easier and more satisfying citizen access and engagement with officialdom. On the policy front, data science could yield evidence-based insight and answers, helping sort poor proposals from good ones, perhaps wringing out a measure of the speculation that feeds partisan politics. Greater connectedness would enable the disparate segments of society and professional disciplines to collaborate on solving big national challenges.

Hopes run high that these aspirations can be fully attained, but they are accompanied by fear and concern over how to manage technology's unintended consequences and vulnerabilities. As anticipated, the internet has toppled long-standing barriers, broadening the boulevards of public discourse; but it has eliminated important guardrails and opened wide new lanes for misinformation and disinformation. Even as insights produced by big data analytics inform public policy and governance, they also reveal better ways to manipulate public opinion. E-government is bringing new efficiencies to public administration but creating new risks from cybersecurity threats including in the software-dependent, internet-based systems used increasingly to conduct US elections. As political campaigns and public discourse move online, they are becoming more uncivil and divisive.

The high technology that should be bringing society closer together is being exploited by Politics Inc. and foreign adversaries to drive us apart, helping twist the country's pluralism into factionalism. The question of how the internet and modern technology can strengthen democracy has been eclipsed by concerns that democracy can even survive it.

If the health of democracy were measured in the volume of political communication, thanks to ICT we would be doing marvelously. In a 2009 TED Talk, New York University professor Clay Shirky noted, "The internet is the first medium in history that has native support for groups and conversation at the same time. Whereas the phone gave us the one-to-one pattern, and television, radio, magazines, books, gave us the one-to-many pattern, the internet gives us the many-to-many pattern."[2]

In the early 1960s, an aide to President John Kennedy exuberated, "We don't need the press anymore. We've got TV."[3] Not exactly. TV, like radio, was a one-to-many capability benefiting politicians. But neither government nor politicians controlled the media; the television broadcast networks did. Speech coverage was hosted by professional journalists who helped interpret and fill out the bigger picture for the viewing public. The internet eliminated the need for such traditional media intermediaries, replacing them with open platforms. Barriers to producing and exchanging high volumes of information at scale evaporated, ushering in the Web-enabled many-to-many form of communication. News and information could be accessed quickly and easily on an array of devices and from a universe of sources, bona fide and bogus, and directly from sources.

Little could Kennedy's staff imagine a future president communicating at will, anytime, anywhere, filter-free from a self-governed platform. Nor could even the most imaginative futurist predict that as of 2021, ICT would be producing 2.5 quintillion bytes of data every twenty-four hours (accelerating algorithmically). Each day, six billion texts are sent. Each minute, more than 525,000 photos are shared over Snapchat, 4.1 million YouTube videos are viewed, and 450,000 tweets are launched.[4] Astoundingly, by 2021, 90 percent of the world's data had been generated in the previous two years! Engaging with our devices for hours a day, Americans are swamped by a mounting volume of messaging—including political content in pop-up ads, social media posts, tweets, texts, and news—all competing for attention.

The volume of digital communication is impressive. But some of the kinds and quality of information enabled by ICT today are not so wowing. Misinformation, hoaxes, conspiracy theories, rumor, and propaganda flow in torrents across the internet's filter-free avenues and byways. The public finds it increasingly difficult to cut through the noise to determine what is true and significant.

Garnering attention in the teeming online information ecosystem begets the worst in Politics Inc. Sensationalism is rewarded and amplified. The brevity and speed demanded by the streaming culture empower misinformation and oversimplification. Thoughtful debate is stampeded by propagandists disinterested in whether audiences receive what radio legend Paul Harvey called "the rest of the story."

Philosopher and communications theorist Marshall McLuhan theorized that "the medium is the message," meaning that the channels transmitting information themselves shape how people think and interact, influencing society more profoundly than the message itself.[5] McLuhan would likely point to Twitter as a prime example. The impetuous and emotive communication it fosters, especially political sniper fire, contains a message all its own about society in the digital era influencing the way we think, act, and engage.

In early American politics, the proverbial tree stump or wood-planked political platform was used for addressing fellow citizens on the issues of the day. That medium created distinct patterns of political speech and engagement. Civic interactions were personal and social. While often spirited and contentious, the dialogue was participatory and democratic, infusing a sense of community.

Newspapers and journals in this period, of course, delivered public information less intimately and interactively. Over time, the city paper became an ever more important community resource and reference point, providing a kind of civic glue. The maturation of broadcasting sharply increased passivity, but the three big TV networks supplied a dominant, common frame of reference for Americans.

Today's channels of communication draw from all three traditions but with seismic differences. We no longer have a social center. The community's glue has weakened, and our frames of reference grow more splintered by the day. We spread out and team up in cyberspace in an endless electronic forest of stumps abuzz with a greater abundance of talkers than listeners, where truths and falsehoods are less distinguishable, and it's harder to tell who and what is authentic. No one really has the floor. So, to command attention in the electronic commons, partisans shout. Rather than rationalizing, they emote. Without shared facts and frames of reference, the roar from the information superhighway makes it harder to listen, understand, and find consensus.

Society is confronted with three fundamental choices at the junction of modern technology and self-government:

- Will the message in today's powerful digital media be about greater inclusion and transparency that strengthens the political process or the empowerment of Politics Inc. and forms of communication that misinform and splinter the country?
- Will data analytics aid the political system to serve the public with practical solutions, or will it advance the art and science of manipulation to foster an even more destructive brand of politics?
- Will we better protect cyber systems used to conduct public communications, government, and the electoral process from fraud and manipulation, or will we allow their exploitation to subvert public trust?

The underlying existential riddle is whether technology will be harnessed to promote democracy or undermine it.

MICROTARGETING AND COMPUTERIZED PANDERING

Few topics excite hotter debate than the proper limits on how one's personal digital information may be used. The proliferation of Web-connected devices—phones, tablets, and laptops—and the staggering amount of time most people are connected to communication networks generate enormous intelligence about each of us. Americans' personal electronic data, anonymized or not, are continuously collected and processed to learn how we live and think; where we go in both the virtual and physical domains; the language we use; our connections and patterns of behavior; and what we do, buy, and value. The granularity is astonishing, as are the enormous sums involved and at stake. The intelligence helps marketers target pitches and time them to maximize their effectiveness.[6]

The same kind of algorithms that can tell product marketers about an individual in microscopic detail tell Politics Inc. whom to target with political messaging and how. The practice that in 2002 political strategist Alexander Gage labeled "microtargeting" empowers the election industry to identify and effectively influence potential donors, supporters, and voters—even pinpointing swing neighborhoods and households that can shift the vote in critical election battleground states and congressional districts.[7] More broadly, as Kathryn Montgomery and Jeff Chester at the Center for Digital Democracy note, "The same commercial digital media and marketing ecosystem that has dramatically altered how corporations engage with consumers is now transforming the ways in which campaigns engage with citizens."[8]

Cambridge Analytica became infamous for its endeavors to manipulate election outcomes including the UK's anti-EU Brexit vote and the 2016 US presidential race. The company boasted having four to five thousand data points harvested from social media and other sources on 230 million American adults to frame and target persuasive communications to influence election outcomes.[9] The information helped them classify individuals and shape communications according to personality traits—levels of openness, conscientiousness, extroversion, agreeableness, and neuroticism.[10] Cambridge's methods were drawn from the techniques used by its parent company, SCL Group, in defense intelligence and counterterrorism.

The 2016 presidential campaign was rife with "suspicious advertisers" sponsoring nearly five million political ads on social media and targeting voters in key swing states. Of the 228 groups that bought ads on Facebook examined by researchers, one in six was connected with the Internet Research Agency and Cambridge Analytica.[11]

The methods that pull microtargeting together are technically complex but follow a logical sequence:

- The commercial world *tracks* your spending habits, online activity, and other discoverable personal information.
- Data analytics *cracks* you by coding your activities into a psychographic profile.
- Social media *packs* you into an algorithm-based demographic for microtargeting.
- Politics Inc., like other marketers, *feeds back* messages tailored according to the information you, in many cases, unwittingly provide.

Political microtargeters are enabled by the same intelligence gathering tools marketers use to track their virtual and physical meanderings, activities, and interactions. Data analytics turn the information into actionable insight. Proponents of such digital age marketing research on voters argue that when political parties and candidates better understand the public and its preferences, democracy is strengthened. That is nonsense when the knowledge is exploited to pit groups against one another for partisan gain, to pander just right, or to suppress the opposition by alienating them from the political process. Even people not terribly offended that their data are used to target them for sales pitches oppose the practice for political purposes. In a survey conducted by the University of Pennsylvania's Annenberg School of Communication, 86 percent of the respondents said they do not want political advertising tailored to their interests.[12] Moreover, "sixty-four percent said their support for a candidate would decrease if they found out a candidate was microtargeting them differently than their neighbor. The study also found that 20% more respondents reacted more strongly to political targeting than they did to being targeted as a consumer."[13] Perhaps that is because most Americans understand that political appeals shaped by intelligence on what you want to hear versus what you need to hear lead to stronger partisans rather than better-informed citizens, and to craftier politics but poorer democracy.

Despite public misgivings about the practice, microtargeting has been a feature of political campaigns since the late 1990s, taking on a prominent role beginning in the 2012 presidential contest between Barack Obama and Mitt Romney.[14] Zac Moffatt, the Romney campaign's digital director, told the *New York Times*, "Two people in the same house could get different messages. Not only will the message change, the type of content will change."[15] That year produced the launch of Google Political Toolkit and Google AdWords. The services enabled campaigns to target YouTube videos and other campaign appeals to reach the demographically desired audience.[16] Facebook does something similar, not by allowing marketers to use personally identifiable information but by allowing marketers to target groups by demographic preferences.[17] Political strategy companies including Democratic DSPolitical and Republican CampaignGrid have become eager buyers, purchasing massive amounts of the personal data to inform computer-based campaign analytics.[18] The insights that result are why, as a CNN feature story on microtargeting declared, "campaigns know you better than you know yourself."[19]

Barack Obama's 2012 presidential campaign set a new standard of sophistication in political microtargeting. The campaign formed a highly advanced analytics cell composed of "behavioral scientists, data technologists, and mathematicians."[20] The team pored over the personal data of key demographic groups. By examining the segment's online activity and details, like what charities they support or magazines they receive, the team generated insight and intelligence to shape customized appeals.

The campaign found that winning the support of women between the ages of forty and forty-nine was essential for winning the election. Analytics found that among the most popular celebrities with this slice of the population was *Sex in the City* star Sarah Jessica Parker. Obama campaign staff recruited the celebrity to host an event in New York City. Fundraising appeals touting the event were sent to individuals fitting the profile. The letter helped leverage donations by offering an opportunity for big donors and a few lucky selectees to attend the star-studded affair.[21] Psychographic profiling helped the campaign boost fundraising and influence influencers, persuade persuadables, and spur supportive voters to the polls. The performance set a new norm for big-time political campaign operations.

Are the tactics smart? Yes. Are they effective? Demonstrably so. Is everyone doing it? They soon will be. The question is whether thoughtful, substance-based politics is served by campaign practices combining the habit tracking, online profiling, and customer segmenting techniques of direct marketing firms with the superficiality of the computer dating industry.

Providing a glimpse of what's coming, data analytics are helping to identify not only whom to target but precisely what to tell them, turbocharging the age-old political practice of pandering. *Wired*, a publication that follows the cultural effects of emerging technologies, observed, "It's no secret that politicians pander. They cling to trite concepts and overused buzzwords because they've got polls, focus groups, and an ever-growing deluge of data from social media sites telling them that those terms are the ones we want to hear."[22]

Artificial intelligence can test exactly which terms those might be.[23] Software-defined political appeals drew significantly higher approval from listeners in focus group tests than nonprocessed messaging. While the code was developed by a college professor to study political communications, the implications for Politics Inc.

is clear—computer-aided pandering and software-enhanced mudslinging.[24] One wonders how the public opinion poll on microtargeting would have registered if respondents had been informed that technology not only can tell electioneers what topics strike home for each individual but also is on the cusp of telling them precisely what to say. Something is deeply ironic and troubling when computers can advise political communicators what words will elicit their desired response and can teach them how to sound more sincere.

Chuck Todd, the moderator of *Meet the Press*, and his fellow NBC journalist Carrie Dann maintain that microtargeting has played a major role in widening the partisan divide.[25] They observe that before the era of computerized campaign analytics, the key to victory was winning over a larger share of the political center than one's opponent. No longer. Microtargeting makes mobilizing the base the favored strategy. Todd and Dann note lawmakers have "concluded (with ample electoral evidence) that they don't need centrist or swing voters to win." That's also why "the halls of Congress [are] populated by lawmakers who feel beholden not to all of their constituents, but only to their supporters."[26]

The same big data analytics and artificial intelligence used to shape and microtarget political communications can be employed in helping the parties macrotarget communities, for the purpose of ensuring that their supporters and opponents are favorably arrayed on the electoral map. Computer algorithms can spit out congressional maps drawn more precisely to maximize the majority party's advantage at the voting booth.

The staggering amount of time Americans spend online gives data collectors and analysts near continuous opportunity to extract intelligence on our individual patterns and profile, and for content creators to access us. Quartz Media reported that by 2015, Americans were spending an average of eight hours per day consuming media.[27] The San Diego Supercomputer Center (SDSC) at the University of California, San Diego, estimated that "the sum of media asked for and delivered to consumers on mobile devices and to their homes (also in 2015) would take more than 15 hours a day to see or hear."[28] The demand is more than matched by the massive and constantly expanding supply of digital data. The SDSC noted that with the greater number of media streams into the home, our multitasking will increase: "And as we increase our level of multi-tasking, we have to expect that total hours will grow even as the total number of physical hours a viewer can consume media will remain roughly constant. Moreover, this increasing level of multi-tasking is creating competition between media streams to be the dominant stream at any one time."[29]

Breaking through the competitive noise in the digital space best suits and strongly reinforces the negative qualities of partisan political messaging, and this appears primed to get far worse as the fight for attention intensifies. More extreme rhetoric and uglier politics are coming, courtesy of the "five Ps" of political communications: messaging that is provocative, pithy, pleasing, patronizing, and propulsive. The implications are not encouraging.

Provocative

Communicators must lean ever harder on arousing powerful emotions to grab and hold public attention. The professionals of Politics Inc. are not the only purveyors of online shock and awe. They are competing with freelancers who traffic in extreme messaging with a political dimension. In cyberspace, radical views are aired and amplified far more than is possible in the physical domain. The publicity enables extremists to find one another, organize, and exert undue influence making outliers seem mainstream. The imprinting made from the noisy political poles is why in the eyes of their opposition Democrats are socialists and Republicans are fascists—big news to the core of both parties.

The sensational aspect of politically charged myths gives them a leg up on the internet over plain fact. The fallacy spread online that COVID-19 was a deep state political trick resonated with a segment of the population who ignored public health protocols and spread the disease at a high cost to human life. The fantasy that the 2020 election was rigged incited extremists to threaten election officials who did their job and certified a true outcome. A Georgia elections official who worked for a Republican secretary of state pleaded for the disinformation over rigged voting to stop, predicting, "Someone is going to get killed. And it's not right."[30] He was right. People died during the mob's 2021 assault on the Capitol. Of course, extraordinary online attention to the excesses of hyperpartisans, political extremists, and myth peddlers warrants coverage by the mainstream media, multiplying their influence. So long as sensation sells with cashable clicks, sensation will be for sale, with politics center stage.

Pithy

The online scrolling culture places a premium on delivering short, hard-hitting messages; those who don't deliver risk being bypassed. Genuine debate is supplanted by electronic bumper sticker slogans, ad hominem tweets, disappearing Snapchat images, nine-second sound bites, and other forms of communication that can fit into fleeting digital windows.[31] The deceptive generalizations cannot possibly do justice to today's complex issues. It is why the other side of the story so often goes dismissed or untold, and facts get short shrift. At a time when public policy challenges would be better managed through deeper dialogue and mutual understanding, political discourse looks to grow ever shorter, shallower, and shriller.

Pleasing

Above all, if content is to be consumed, it must be entertaining. Vincent Harris, a top Republican operative with deep expertise in how politicians can most effectively harness the internet and social networks, asserts that politicians must figure out how to get noticed in a "24-second news cycle." To do this, says Harris, a politician must be entertaining, unique, and visual. "Entertainment" is a catch-all for material that shocks the senses or otherwise creates a stir by being exceptionally novel, extreme, combative, humorous, degrading, or humiliating. As Harris points out, "Buzz online equals money online. Money online equals money off-line. Money off-line equals GOTV [get out the vote], which equals votes. This is a very close-knit, tied-together thing."[32] Helping to create the buzz is digital political ad spending, which jumped from $22 million in 2008 to over $1.5 billion in 2020.[33]

Patronizing

Human nature attracts us to content that affirms our views and biases. We avoid messages that don't reinforce them or that challenge the rectitude of our civic associations and political team. Messages that pander to these instincts, quite often by lampooning, delegitimizing, or savaging the other team, are likelier to gain notice.

Propulsive

Hitting the mark on the foregoing qualities ups the chances that a message can go viral, creating economies of scale by propagating cost-free across the Net. The temptations to exploit half-truth or exaggeration to make it happen are great and growing. An MIT study found that "falsehoods are 70% more likely to be retweeted on Twitter than the truth, and reach their first 1,500 people six times faster."[34]

A sixth "P"—*profitable*—ensures that both Politics Inc. and the sites that host the ads will continue these practices. This is not to say that electioneers corner the market on 5P political messaging. The internet's openness and lack of accountability invite superspreaders of misinformation and partisan animus for fun and profit. People tend to speak disrespectfully, unfairly, and crudely on social media and in chat rooms, often anonymously or pseudonymously, in a way they never would face-to-face.[35] Psychologists have labeled this phenomenon the "online disinhibition effect, in which factors like anonymity, invisibility, a lack of authority and not communicating in real time strip away the mores society spent millennia building. And it's seeping from our smartphones into every aspect of our lives."[36] The more the country's politics play out in the virtual domain rather than eye to eye, the likelier political trolling and its consequences will worsen.

SOCIAL MEDIA AND THE ECHO CHAMBER

The millennial generation surpassed the baby boom generation in 2019 to become the largest generational grouping, nearly seventy-five million people strong. They have come of age using digital communication devices nearly as a fifth limb, following generation X, who engineered them. Eighty-six percent of millennials use social media, and just a few percentage points lower have Facebook accounts.[37] Three-quarters of them get their news online and through social media, compared to 62 percent of the population at large who do.[38]

Like its analogue in the arachnid world, the Web not only meshes and connects but can also trap. Individuals tend to stick to their digital comfort zone, seeking information that aligns with their personal views, and they tend to socialize on Facebook, Snapchat, and Instagram with those who see the world as they do.[39] As people huddle in cloistered communities of the likeminded, where their biases tend to harden, contrarian opinion gets short shrift.

In their book *Connected*, Nicholas Christakis and James Fowler explore how social media facilitates this tendency called "homophily."[40] Their studies demonstrate that "social media networks concretize what is seen in offline social networks, as well— birds of a feather flock together." While more recent studies question the power of the echo chamber, Christakis and Fowler and others have found "this segregation often leads to users seeking out and consuming news aligned with individual and group views cementing them unchallenged."[41]

One might think that homophily notwithstanding, the broad spectrum of infor- mation on the internet exposes people to a diversity of opinion. But even when that's so, psychologists and social scientists nevertheless find "that when confronted with diverse information choices, people rarely act like rational, civic-minded automatons. Instead, we are roiled by preconceptions and biases, and we usually do what feels easiest—we gorge on information that confirms our ideas, and we shun what does not."[42] People cling to their beliefs, and there are plenty of places in social networks and on the internet to find comforting and entertaining content that confirms them. Whether they are true or not is another matter. A BuzzFeed analysis of Facebook's leading political pages found that "three big right-wing Facebook pages published false or misleading information 38% of the time during the period analyzed, and three large left-wing pages did so in nearly 20% of posts."[43]

BOTS AND PHANTOMS

Internet bots (also known as Web robots or bots) are specialized software that can perform many legitimate high-speed functions online, such as crawling the internet to mark data for searches. Political influencers use them far less innocently—by deploying them to manufacture phony online poll results, creating bogus online accounts and messaging, and impersonating live humans tweeting to create false impressions of support or opposition to a person or ideas. Alessandro Bessi and Emilio Ferrara of the University of Southern California's Information Sciences Institute found that bots deployed to either support one candidate or smear another were adroit at creating phony tweets "pointing to Web sites with fake news."[44] The practice dates to the 2010 midterm elections and was used extensively in the 2016 presidential election. Studying Twitter data for a preelection period covering all three debates, the team discovered nearly half a million bots responsible for nearly four million of the twenty million tweets they studied.[45] That's massive fraud by anyone's calculus, and it's unsettling to know that a popular tweet on US policy or politics was manufactured by software, not a human being, or that a viral meme or hashtag has been popularized by digital phantoms. Consistent with Bessi and Ferrara's findings, *The Atlantic* reported that "more than a third of pro-Trump tweets and nearly a fifth of pro-Clinton tweets between the first and second debates came from automated accounts, which produced more than 1 million tweets in total."[46] According to *Bloomberg*, electronic forensics found that nearly half of Trump's Twitter followers were electronic phantoms created by bots.[47]

In April 2017, the former FBI agent Clint Watts described for the Senate Intelligence Committee how Russia used bots "to spread false news using accounts that seem to be Midwestern swing-voter Republicans." The purpose, of course, was to influence real Midwestern swing-voter Republicans.[48] Reuters reported that Russian operatives made about eighty thousand Facebook posts over the two years prior to the 2016 US election and that these posts were seen by roughly 126 million Americans.[49] Foreign interference in elections is an old story, but it used to be expensive and risky. More alarming than the Russians pulling it off was the ease with which they did so.

The use of fakery to exploit social media for political purposes doesn't necessarily demand technical know-how, however. Money and old-school methodology can serve the purpose almost as well. In 2018, an investigative news team successfully bought ads on Facebook on behalf of all one hundred US senators.[50] Trustworthy content and bona fide public opinion are vital to the proper functioning of representative democracy. Whether by using high tech means or the low side, the misrepresentation of identities and phony messaging to manipulate public opinion is an assault on the integrity of our public debates and democratic processes.

DIGITAL DIRTY TRICKS

Brooks Jackson, director of FactCheck.org—a nonpartisan organization that monitors and reports on the truthfulness of political discussion—observed that the internet has taken "the old-fashioned slanderous whispering campaign to a completely new level." The dirty tricks that have always been part of politics have been made "more dangerous and more insidious."[51] On the internet, unlike in human networks, rumor, innuendo, and deceptive messages aren't whispered. Online they are able to barge into our chat rooms, news feeds, and social media. Once posted, whether the messaging is video, audio, or text, they assume a kind of digital immortality, persisting long after facts and fairness have been dismissed. The exploitation of these qualities is why, says Joan Donovan, research director of Harvard's Shorenstein Center on Media, Politics and Public Policy Center, argues that online platforms are geared toward "controlling minds, not expanding them."

Digital audio, images, and video are highly vulnerable to electronic manipulation, using widely available tools. The appearance of practically anything someone says, does, or intends can be electronically doctored to create a manufactured impression.

In some cases, the alteration is meant to be humorous or satirical, a legitimate and sometimes entertaining form of political commentary. But with increasing frequency the purpose of doctored material is to deceive. The high quality of digital fakery can make it nearly indistinguishable from the real thing, enhancing its credibility, transmissibility, and deceptive power.

Three signature characteristics of the internet make it highly vulnerable to exploitation and an exceptionally effective medium for digitally empowered fabulists, mudslingers, and fraudsters. One is the inherent openness and accessibility of online platforms, and their weakness in screening fabrication. Two is the internet's high speed and reach, giving bogus content exceptional velocity and reach. By the time information can be fact checked, it may have already gone viral and lodged in the public consciousness before the truth can come out. Three, once in the digital commons, the material abides in electronic immortality. Bringing it altogether, social media platforms offer broad boulevards and targetable side streets through which misleading material can find its pre-packaged, well-profiled audiences in a nearly norm-free environment.

Jonathan Taplin, author of *Move Fast and Break Things: How Google, Facebook and Amazon Cornered Culture and Undermined Democracy*, warns, "Social media will continue to enable new and more-sophisticated forms of propaganda and disinformation. Artificial intelligence will enable deep fake videos that the average citizen will be taken in by. Facebook, YouTube and Twitter will continue to enable this content in their unending chase for revenue. Politicians will make noises about regulation, but since these platforms will become their primary source of advertising and publicity, they will never commit to the elimination of Safe Harbor and other rules that protect the social networks."[52]

Whether viewing them online or on television, the public is accustomed to campaign commercials that use video and audio manipulations to play on emotions and prejudices. Compared to what's possible now, the hoary practice of altering light, pixilation, and speed of motion to make an opponent look sinister or deranged while bathing the favored candidate in a halo of goodness and charm seems quaint. The deep bag of high-tech online tricks runs the gamut from artifice, using snowflake fakes, deep fakes, and spamming, to criminality in hacking, spoofing, and jamming networks, tactics pioneered by computer hackers, adopted by online grifters, and exploited by the warriors of Politics Inc.

The powers of manipulation aren't wielded only by organized political groups. Because almost anyone with technical savvy can slime at scale, and monetize the clicks they induce, the volume of digital illusion indistinguishable from reality will likely soar. Shams like the picture of Democratic presidential nominee Barack Obama swearing his oath as a US senator on the Quran and a phony 2008 photo of Republican vice presidential nominee Sarah Palin brandishing a rifle while wearing a US flag can be pulled off with greater ease and frequency. Satire and snow jobs will be indiscernible.[53]

YouTube will draw eyeballs and ad revenue from even more realistic-looking and -sounding fabrications, like the video of a top Hillary Clinton adviser doctored to look like he was cursing and uttering a slur, or of Nancy Pelosi altered to appear that she was intoxicated and rambling.[54] Laws will be broken with greater skill, like the Wikileaks attack on the DNC database and release of email or the hacking of George W. Bush's campaign website on the eve of the 2000 presidential election that inserted a link to the Gore for President website.[55]

False tweeting will become commonplace, like a post that made for Facebook chatter purported to be minority leader Chuck Schumer criticizing President Trump for imposing an air travel ban from China as part of the coronavirus containment policy. The lack of evidence from his account that such a tweet existed fed a conspiracy theory—also proven false—that he deleted it.[56]

"Many people believe that they can spot false news and propaganda," says the Shorenstein Center's Donovan, "but the reality is that it is much more difficult because the very design of social media and the incentives to plant misinformation are weighted in favor of the disinformers. In an environment when novel claims travel far and fast the truth is at a disadvantage."[57]

The ability to deceive is so refined, and the level of public skepticism so high, that no one really knows what data, images, or utterances are authentic. The prevalence of bogus content, say public opinion polls, leaves people confused about basic facts.[58] The ease of creating the appearance of scandal can't help but blind the public to legitimate cases of misconduct. Scoundrels and criminals will be able to easily sow doubt in practically any form of evidence by credibly claiming partisan fakery.

Elected representatives admit a growing reluctance to publicly interact with constituents, fearing their words or image will be manipulated or that something someone might say or do in their presence could create a digital meme. Once captured by cell phone video, the imagery can be digitally altered or enhanced by software to create the desired effect. Launched wildly into the electronic commons, the meme may race across the internet, finding its way into the fast lanes of social media. With a big enough splash, the content will be picked up by the mainstream media, reaching new audiences and levels of believability. Eventually it may appear in the opposition's political ad in the next campaign. However far it goes, the imagery is preserved in the world's digital archives in perpetuity. With all that to worry about, as one US senator put it, "you stick to safe bromides." The combination of a public unable to trust facts and elected officials hesitant to authentically engage constituents is a crippling development.

For better or worse, digital technology will continue to figure prominently in every aspect of the democratic process, including how the electorate learns and interacts, how ideas are socialized and debated, and how campaigns and elections are run. Politics is moving online in a big way that many older statesmen and pols can barely comprehend much less keep step with.

Adversaries understand the internet's central role in America's social, economic, and political life—making it the juiciest of targets. It is an open utility, expensive to defend, cheap to attack, easily accessed remotely and anonymously, and can be attacked with deniability often without risk. US national security doctrine classifies cyberspace as the fifth domain of warfare (joining land, sea, air, and space).[59] For now, the prime objective for hybrid warriors is not to destroy the internet and our communication networks but to weaponize them against assets of far greater strategic value to democracy—truth, trust, social order, national unity, faith in one another, and public confidence in the integrity of our institutions. Amid the COVID-19 pandemic, China was using fake accounts on social media to sow panic while expanding operations to the use of mobile phone text messaging in the United States to spread propaganda and disinformation.[60] Ironically, the ploy followed Beijing's reliable playbook of copying intellectual property developed by the United States, in this case by Politics Inc., against the United States.

The weaponization of freedom to destroy freedom is truly the pacing threat of our times. Ensuring that neither the schemes of foreign adversaries nor the extremes of Politics Inc. use technology to succeed should be a national priority. Meeting the challenge requires a whole-of-society campaign centered on a modern national security triad: improving the security of our cybersystems, ensuring the authenticity of online content, and giving greater power to accurate information over deception. In this campaign, technology must be used to defend freedom and democracy against the exploitation of technology to undermine it.

ORGANIZING AND EDUCATING

Step one is organizing and educating ourselves for this mission. The country needs political leadership that better understands advanced technology. While serving as staff director of the US Senate Commerce Committee, I took interest in thumbing through congressional records of old House and Senate proceedings, hoping to learn what issues occupied the early Congresses. What matters confronted the Commerce Committee, and how they were dealt with, was of particular interest. Among the first proceedings was a debate in the early 1800s over the allocation of federal money for lighthouses used to safely guide ships. Coincidentally, that week the Commerce Committee was debating aviation legislation, including allocation of air traffic control facilities to safely guide traffic in America's skies. Other than the more elegant prose employed by legislators of old, the nature of the two debates was strikingly similar. It was an aha! moment. Human nature and the fundaments of representative democracy don't really change; just the technology changes.

What is certain is that nineteenth-century elected leaders knew far more about lighthouses than their counterparts today know about complex twenty-first-century information and communications technology and things such as how algorithms move search results and bots perform online trickery. Despite technology's outsized influence over almost every aspect of American life, the skill set of most representatives and staff isn't in tech. It's hard to get the right answers when you don't even know what questions to ask. Making the knowledge gap worse, twenty-five years ago, Congress shuttered the Office of Technology Assessment (OTA), created in the early 1970s to inform representatives and senators on science and technology issues. OTA's implementing law stated, "As technology continues to change and expand rapidly . . . it is necessary for the Congress to equip itself with effective means for securing competent, unbiased information concerning the physical, biological, economic, social, and political effects of such applications."[61] The need has never been greater.

A revived OTA should be commissioned to significantly upgrade the legislative branch's tech literacy. Such savvy must be a core competency of political leaders and government officials. Because private-sector-led technological change is accelerating at warp speed, a new OTA must be empowered to regularly rotate in private-sector technologists to keep the enterprise current. It must be a dynamic agency of experts vigorously protected from careerist inertia.

The country can no longer afford for cybersecurity to be a sideline for dozens of congressional committees. It must be an urgent priority for the legislative branch, working in sync with the executive branch and the private sector as if the future of the country and democracy depends on it. Because it does. That's the only way to produce the kind of layered cybersecurity recommended by the bipartisan Cyberspace Solarium Commission in 2020.[62] The centerpiece of national initiative should be a modern and ongoing public-private-sector Manhattan project to continuously develop and deploy steps-ahead cyber protections.

The same committed public-private collaboration and expertise that brought information and communications technologies to market must be channeled to develop better capabilities to protect and police them. Better bots can be developed to detect and neutralize their deceptive cousins. Just as artificial intelligence creates deep fakes, it can be engineered and deployed to ferret them out. In 2015, the Defense Advanced Research Projects Agency, an arm of the US Department of Defense, initiated the Media Forensic program to improve the detection of telltale anomalies in digital content. In a similar vein of fighting tech with tech, advanced mathematics, data science, and artificial intelligence must be harnessed to help courts detect political gerrymandering and help draw congressional boundaries that serve the public interest. These and similar efforts should compose a comprehensive research, development, and deployment program for solutions to digital challenges that cut to the heart of America's democracy and political process.

Employing technology to defeat the abuse of technology must work in combination with policies and mechanisms for cleaning up how our ITC systems deliver content, beginning with the sanitizing powers of transparency. Search engines like Google use proprietary algorithms that largely determine what Americans see on their Web pages and information searches. Social media titans the likes of Facebook, YouTube, Snapchat, and Twitter, and all purveyors of online ads, are revenue-maximizing businesses that similarly hold their systems close to their vest. Notes historian Yuval Noah Harrari, "People have come to entrust Google's search algorithm with one of the most important tasks of all: finding relevant and trustworthy information. As we rely more on Google for answers, our ability to locate information independently diminishes. Already today, 'truth' is defined by the top results of a Google search."[63] The public has a need and right to know how online content is curated and distributed, including the principles, values, and factors that determine content feeds and the trade-offs involved as well as how personal information is used to shape content and target advertising. The algorithms involved should be explained and made available for public inspection by experts who can publicly report their evaluations without violating intellectual property rights.

The public's right to know extends to the provenance and sponsorship of paid political ads. Whether solicited or not, any electioneering advertisement that transits the information highway and speeds into your electronic driveway should be required to ring the bell and announce who paid for the visit before barging into your life. Inexplicably, the FEC rule requiring political ads to disclose their sponsor is not enforced when it comes to online ads. It should be.

Of course, inspection and knowledge of algorithms doesn't mitigate their shortcomings. Knowing who funded a dishonest message doesn't make misinformation right or a lie true. Sunlight must be complemented by stronger norms and effective oversight. Setting norms and principles underlying how information flows and promoting accuracy and truth in political content are not powers to be entrusted to government. For a freedom-loving people, government censorship is a cure worse than the disease. The duty falls to "we the people," whose interests are at stake. Norm setting and oversight should be the province of a private, not-for-profit board of trustees. Composed of multidisciplinarian experts, such a panel should be commissioned to set and certify compliance with public interest norms, best practices, and codes of conduct in how online platforms flow information. The social media platforms have a hash of policies, standards, and procedures when it comes to political advertising, microtargeting, and deceptive content and hate speech. By setting best practices and reporting regularly to the public, such a panel would put strong pressure on internet platforms, their customers, and users to comply with best practices and keep the public informed. This is where two other elements of reform come into play—market pressure and competition.

Nothing will bring about reform faster than institutional and citizen activism—democracy's most motivational force. Bowing to public demand, Google, Facebook, Twitter, and others have devoted significant financial and technical resources to develop and deploy better tools for labeling and weeding out deceptive content, and it's having an effect. A study coauthored by an MIT researcher found a 75 percent reduction in the sharing of fake news stories on Facebook after the company rolled out a new system designed to intercept such articles.[64] Companies and nonprofit organizations sent a $56 billion message to Facebook and its subsidiary Instagram when advertisers, exercising their freedom of speech as part of the #StopHate4Profit campaign, dropped ads because of the platform's role in facilitating hateful speech.[65] The exercise of freedom of speech to improve speech and protect democracy—that is a beautiful thing.

Stopping fakery, misinformation, disinformation, and hate speech before it enters the country's electronic bloodstream is, of course, a key objective worthy of our strongest efforts, but prevention has its limits. Layered security is the only truly effective safeguard. One of the most essential layers of defense is at the user level through personal awareness and empowerment. Whether by norm or statute, the public must be armed with stronger rights and tools. A start is granting individuals a clearer say in whether and how their data can be sold and used, including for the development and targeting of political ads. And internet users need readier access to more truly independent and trusted fact-checking and crowdsourced verification services to validate the online information they receive. Authentication should be as easy and automatic for internet users as spell check or the scroll bar, so information can be validated in real time before, not after, a user pushes "send," launching digital deception further into the cybersphere for multiplication.

Such capabilities will foster the ultimate defense—responsible human judgment. A national public information and education campaign is needed to bolster public awareness of the dangers of misinformation and disinformation, how to identify it, the tools available to help stop and report it, and the personal responsibilities of online citizenship. The mantra "Pause before you post" should become as engrained in the public consciousness as "Give a hoot, don't pollute." It may sound corny, but it makes a difference.

Clear norms backed by energetic oversight and personal empowerment policies and tools will create the strong leverage necessary to improve internet platforms and their practices. But, importantly, it will stimulate competition that can bust the monopolistic business model of corralling people onto "free" services, collecting and monetizing the personal data they generate by using the platform, and maximizing revenue by feeding back tailored advertising. Competition must be matched by choice, including the ability for the public to select from a broader menu of pre-loaded search engine options.

The information superhighway is an apt metaphor for the internet. Like highways, if it is to remain a safe, open, helpful, and efficient public utility, the internet needs sensible rules of the road, lanes, guardrails, and the cooperation and good judgment of responsible users. Reckless use by irresponsible operators or sabotage by adversaries endangers us all. What will make matters worse is the emergence of two segregated internets, one for Republicans and another for Democrats, with rigid ideology and confirmation bias built in—the stuff that despots and demagogues dream of.

Securing and cleaning up US cyberspace and harnessing technology to protect and strengthen democracy has implications far beyond American shores. Two clashing visions of the global future are emerging with technology at the core. In the autocratic model proffered by China, cybersystems are a weapon for distributing state propaganda, surveilling its citizens, and enforcing government will by monitoring and scoring good and bad political behavior. In the Western, liberty-based model, ICT is a tool to empower citizens, including the ability to surveil the state, critique it, and exercise economic, political, and expressive freedom. Soon every country's character will be known by the kind of internet and digital communications it operates, whether they serve freedom or autocracy.

The stark differences in these two visions make plain the need for ensuring that the US internet culture reflects our democratic ideals. Keeping Google (which owns YouTube) and Facebook (which owns WhatsApp and Instagram) and other US-based social media and search engine companies sizeable and strong is important if the Western model is to compete on a global scale with its state-supported Chinese and Russian counterparts. With that in mind, cleaning up these companies is preferable to breaking them up. But they cannot and should not stay large, strong, and financially viable if they contribute to the undermining of America's ideals. Values and principles are all that can ensure the human spirit prevails over technology. Seeing that they do is a job for democracies and their people.

10

We the Problem (Cultural Gear)

It is in the voting booth not the presidential desk that the buck finally stops.

—Arthur Schlesinger

The checks and balances built into American government go beyond *trias politica* and the free press. The ultimate check, of course, is the power of the vote. But the vote itself is a check on us. Representative democracy, as distinct from pure democracy where the population rules directly by plebiscite, was specifically designed to curb the power of "we the people." James Madison spoke to this point in Federalist Paper No. 10. The delegation of government to elected representatives, he said, would

> refine and enlarge the public views, by passing them through the medium of a chosen body of citizens, whose wisdom may best discern the true interest of their country, and whose patriotism and love of justice will be least likely to sacrifice it to temporary or partial considerations. Under such a regulation, it may well happen that the public voice pronounced by the representatives of the people, will be more consonant to the public good than if pronounced by the people themselves, convened for the purpose.[1]

The expectation was that our elected leaders would keep an eye on the broader interest and the longer haul. That works fine—provided, of course, that the public chooses to elevate those who are "consonant to the public good." If that's not predominantly the case, then we know where the fault lies. "In democracy," observed eighteenth-century French philosopher Joseph de Maistre, "the people get the leaders they deserve."[2]

If lawmakers and leaders are shortsighted, parochial, hyperpartisan, and uncompromising, we need to see these qualities in ourselves. If the nation is divided, that is because we allow ourselves to be divided. If democratic institutions are failing the country, then the voters and nonvoters responsible for electing our leadership bear the blame. We the people are a cog in the machinery degrading American democracy.

INSTANT GRATIFICATION NOW!

The public appetite for instant satisfaction in the "delivery economy" extends to political expectations.[3] We dismiss those who do not offer easy answers and quick fixes—even though patient, longer-term approaches may provide the only solutions. If tough medicine is required, we blame the doctor. The confluence of popular desire for instant gratification and politicians' impetus for self-preservation exposes the soft underbelly of democracy. Politicians who do not pander to our temporary and partial considerations either cannot get elected or do not survive in office. Most of our elected officials surely empathize with the admission of an EU politician who lamented, "We all know what to do, we just don't know how to get reelected after we've done it."[4]

It is hardly surprising that candor is disappearing from the public dais. Sam Greene of King's College observed, "Many voters have stopped seeing government as a tool for the production of the common good, and have instead turned to politicians (and others) who at least make them feel good. Thus, the news we consume has become as much about emotion and identity as about facts. That's where the vulnerability comes in, and its roots are in our politics—not in the internet."[5]

Politics Inc. is happy to oblige the feel-good support the public demands. It's why convincing the country that long-term threats are real—much less that they require action—is so difficult. Dismissing COVID-19 as a hoax was a pleasing alternative to accepting its harsh reality. Plenty of overopinionated but underinformed influencers were happy to reinforce the myth with deadly results—because it's what their audience wanted to hear. The same brand of denialism hampers efforts to deal with climate change, massive debt, and the internal threats to democracy. In an *American Scholar* essay, Paul Roberts, author of *The Impulse Society: America in the Age of Instant Gratification*, wrote, "Under the escalating drive for quick, efficient 'returns,' our whole socioeconomic system is adopting an almost childlike impulsiveness, wholly obsessed with short-term gain and narrow self-interest and increasingly oblivious to long-term consequences."[6]

Business leaders are preoccupied by the next quarterly earnings report. Journalists fixate on the transient news cycle. Politicians look no further than the coming election. "Short-termism is basically political expediency," says Eric Cantor, former majority leader of the House of Representatives. "It is not being willing to go home to constituents and explain to them the reason you need to affect a change—to essentially reduce the fear of that change so that it is less than the fear of the status quo."[7] Impulsiveness translates into the nation's public life and an inability to factor in the important question, And then what? Some Democrats' calls to defund police sounded immediately gratifying without any consideration of the dire consequences to public safety the day after. Most Republicans were pleased to toss aside the Affordable Care Act without any attempt to decide what would come next. The wars in Iraq and Afghanistan and military action in Libya were undertaken without due consideration and planning of what would follow.

NATIONAL ATTENTION DEFICIT

While reinforcing the cult of instant gratification, today's hyperconnectivity to digital technology and scrolling obsession have fostered a national attention deficit that makes it harder to engage the public on complex issues that require time and thought to understand. Weaned on the internet, screen-struck millennials have earned the nickname the "impatient generation," habituated to instant everything. For generation Z (individuals born between 1997 and the early 2010s), coming of age right behind them, mobile devices are nothing less than a personal appendage. Generation A coming next is referred to as the "glass generation" for the devices that will dominate their forms of communication, entertainment, and activities. On average, students spend six minutes on homework before diverting their attention to social media or texting with friends.[8] According to a 2012 study by Common Sense Media, "More than 70 percent of elementary, middle and high school teachers say media use has hurt students' attention spans, while more than 40 percent believe it has interfered with students' critical thinking and their ability to engage with subject matter."[9]

If a message is to pierce the veil of public distraction, it must be quick and attention-grabbing, euphemisms for incomplete and sensational. Points must be made within the stingy character limits of a tweet or the fleeting seconds of a sound bite, and with scroll-stopping novelty. The constraints favor opinion and stream of consciousness over reason and the time-consuming task of mustering facts, whether for a politician being interviewed, a journalist on a TV segment, or a Facebooker surfing the news of the day. Little wonder politicians and political marketers deal in buzz words and depend on emotional appeals to connect with us rather than risk not connecting at all, and why issues are presented and debated in tightly packaged but misleading absolutes.

If members of Congress do not take time to read and fully understand the legislation they must vote on, it is not solely because they are preoccupied with politicking and fundraising. They are bombarded with issues relentlessly. The press, public, and special interests demand a continuous flow of opinion on every event and issue. Constantly under the public spotlight, they are expected to be knowledgeable and have a position on all matters in the moment, leaving them little time to learn, think, or do.

Once the mainstream press wrings issues and stories of their drama, they race to the next crisis. Amid the mad shuffle of issues, rare is the politician who can admit being insufficiently informed to justify a position. Such candor would come at enormous risk. Time constraints put a premium on keeping it simple and defaulting to reliable messaging—if the other party is for it, you are against it. Moreover, conceding an unfixed position is politically dangerous, providing ammunition for political attack as being a waffler or out of touch—among other trusty election-time potshots.

The pressures to write script for continuous political theater and to satisfy the press and public's hunger for content has made Washington a communications war zone. The proliferation of internet news services and social media channels has widened the front. Winning the daily communications fight takes precedence over all other activities. Press releases, tweets, and posts gush from Capitol Hill, consuming more time and energy than negotiating sessions. Congressional press secretaries—at least 550, with their deputies easily doubling the count—vastly outnumber the bona fide staff experts in any policy field. This game is why Washington churns out more sound bites and quotes than good ideas and answers. Leaders must have the capacity to multitask and are obliged to share points of view on public matters, but having to channel so much of their energies into communications whack-a-mole and respond to demands for commentary on the crisis of the day is destructive.

FEARING FEAR ITSELF

The false alarms Washington warned of in his farewell address find fertile soil in modern America. In *The Culture of Fear*, Barry Glassner chronicles the prominent role of fear in selling anything and everything—goods, services, news stories, and entertainment—noting, "The short answer to why Americans harbor so many misbegotten fears is that immense power and money await those who tap into our moral insecurities and supply us with symbolic substitutes."[10] Campaigns and politics emulate the same pattern. Richard Nixon declared, "People react to fear, not love. They don't teach that in Sunday school, but it's true."[11]

To be sure, not all fear is paranoia. We live in intensely anxiety-filled times. Economic and cultural change happens at breakneck velocity. Many American baby boomers recall a life far more stable than it is today. People were more rooted in their communities, jobs, and patterns of life. Employment was durable, worker benefits were defined, and for many, life had a reassuring level of predictability. Globalization and technology now threaten their livelihoods and ways of life. People worry their jobs will be taken by robots, immigrants, or offshore labor; their money by the government, hackers, or financial crises; their culture by newcomers; their lives by terrorists or gun-wielding psychopaths; and their identities by cybersneaks.

As uncertainty and apprehension grow about the effects of change, people retreat into their tribes and villages for comfort and a sense of belonging. We quit seeing ourselves as part of something much larger because we no longer recognize it or understand how we fit in. Above all, we look for someone above us to blame. Uncertainty begets anger at leadership and political and economic elites perceived as causing or contributing to the threats bearing down on us. Toxic anxiety explains the rise of antiestablishment populism not just in the United States but in Europe and elsewhere.

The parties play on the passions and sense of victimhood that permeates society, offering alternative theories of who to blame. The Republican Party places responsibility at the doorstep of government that it views as far too liberal, involved in our lives, and in thrall to a power-grabbing bureaucratic elite. The Democratic Party blames government that it views as far too passive, indifferent, and in the pocket of a corporate and financial elite. For all their differences, Bernie Sanders and Donald Trump both talked about the country's institutions having been "rigged" against the little guy. The dueling narratives of who is doing the rigging keep us in fear and fighting over politics often out of touch with or irrelevant to the forces more immediately shaping the economy and culture, our community, and the quality of our lives.

CYNICAL CYNICS

Fear breeds distrust and vice versa. Public trust in government has been measured since 1958 by the American National Election Studies survey. In 2021, only 24 percent of Americans said they could trust the government in Washington to do what is right "just about always" (2 percent) or "most of the time" (22 percent)—up seven percentage points from the results in 2019, the lowest ever recorded and a fraction of the population who felt that way fifty years ago.[12] Distrust of those in power arises from unfulfilled political promises and the accumulating sense of vulnerability to the effects of globalization and modernization. The cynicism feeds populism and vice versa, creating a powerful feedback loop. Distrust is not just a response to institutional breakdown but a cause, driving too many good people out of elective and public service. Absent trust, forging grand solutions to big problems is not doable. The chain reaction, however, is unavoidable. Failure breeds greater cynicism begetting more malfunction.

Negativity has become hardwired into culture and is socially en vogue. Distrust of anything mainstream has gone mainstream, and it's infectious. The alienation is reinforced at every turn. Political commentary online is mostly negative. Party rhetoric is based on sowing distrust of the other side's motives, and it dominates the color of journalism, the entertainment media, and popular culture. "Politicians fib to get elected; they pander to particular constituencies; they leave principle at the door in favor of convenience in order to maintain power and position," says Ben Shapiro of the *Daily Wire*, but "if you watch *House of Cards*, you're likely to believe that top-level politicians off each other on a regular basis—and you might be more willing to believe conspiracy theories about the murder of former Democratic National Committee staffer Seth Rich. If you've seen *The Manchurian Candidate*, you're more likely to believe that either former President Obama or President Trump is one."[13]

Cynicism fires moral outrage that justifies stepping over norms of fairness, civility, and democratic order—even to justify political violence like the intermittent clashes between Trump and Biden supporters in 2020. Members of Congress attempting to hold a townhall with constituents find them invaded by cranks who show up to disrupt the proceedings. Counterculture movements divine the right to disrupt House and Senate hearings in self-absorbed bouts of cheap and wholly unproductive attention-getting. Trump supporters whipped into a frenzy at a South Florida airport in 2020 chanted "Fire Fauci! Fire Fauci!"—for the sin of being a competent expert on public health and voice of reason.[14] Like a cancer, cynicism about public servants has spread to our attitude toward one another, and even to human nature itself.[15] Perhaps worst of all, the mindset is taking root in youths.[16] "There is nothing quite so tragic as a young cynic," wrote Maya Angelou, "because it means the person has gone from knowing nothing to believing nothing."[17]

CONSPIRACY

Epidemic cynicism has conditioned the public to spy conspiracies, cabals, and cover-ups around every corner. Conspiracy mongers thrive in the presence of uncertainty, fear, and distrust. The crisis in confidence is why so many people believe nothing they hear, and yet, paradoxically, so many Americans are willing to believe almost anything. One reason why conspiracy laden fake news is so powerful is that people enjoy it and want to believe it. Nearly one-third of the country believes that the 9/11 attacks were staged by the US government. An even higher percentage are convinced climate change is a put-up job. Over one in four are certain that transnational elites are plotting to take control of the world.

Social scientists say that the attraction to conspiracy theories is a response to the public's sense of alienation, stress, vulnerability, and loss of control in modern society. The desire to supply the theories is rooted in money. Clever entrepreneurs have found a way to cash in on conspiracy, selling it like crack cocaine, helping addicts escape reality and poisoning the public mind. QAnon of Pizzagate fame sells the idea that Donald Trump is leading the fight against "deep state" collaborators—elites including the likes of Hollywood billionaires, Hillary Clinton, and Pope Francis II—who are running the world "while engaging in pedophilia, human trafficking and the harvesting of a supposedly life-extending chemical from the blood of abused children."[18] The movement began in the remote backwaters of the internet and spread on social media, while also creating a marketing sensation that hawks T-shirts, hats, and merchandise. Alex Jones, host of the radio show *Infowars*, has accumulated an estimated $10 million of personal net worth entertaining the audience with a stream of whoppers, including that the US government staged the Orlando Pulse nightclub shooting; Barack Obama is the global head of Al Qaeda; Antonin Scalia was murdered; the FBI was behind the Boston bombing; and the US government is using juice boxes to "make children gay."[19] A QAnon adherent was elected to Congress in 2020. Truth is often prosaic, presenting too many tones of gray to arouse passions. Absurdity is regularly accepted by a public conditioned to distrust. A 2020 poll by Chapman University in Orange, California, asked respondents what conspiracy theories they believe to be true. They decided to test public response to a made-up incident the social scientists called the "North Dakota crash." When asked if they agreed with the statement "The government is concealing what they know about the North Dakota Crash," one-third of the respondents said yes.[20]

LET YOU ENTERTAIN ME

Among the allures of conspiracy theory is its ability to meet a deeply ingrained need in American culture to be entertained. The public mania for constant entertainment has made us a nation of screen watchers and voyeurs in an endless sea of apps and content. Almost every aspect of life has been gamified to amuse us with fantasy and alternative reality.

Polls show that many Americans receive their news about politics and government from entertainment media—not from *Meet the Press* and *Face the Nation* but from news parodies and political satires on Comedy Central.[21] Political humorists and satirists play a fun and important role in culture and politics. The emergence of entertainment media as a key source of news and information for the electorate, however, is not simply a magnifying glass aimed at trivialized national political culture; it is a contributor.[22]

The public's appetite for entertainment has given rise to a national obsession with celebrity. Fame and infamy have become indistinguishable and equally monetizable. Many great professional baseball players are interesting, well-spoken, and knowledgeable experts who played by the rules. The country did not bat an eye when, to provide color commentary for its broadcast of the World Series, Fox tapped two former players, one who had been banned from baseball for a year for illegal steroid use, the other for life for gambling on games he participated in. Seemingly what matters most in popular culture is name identification, no matter how it is achieved. Celebrity arises from notice. Notice arises from being controversial, by saying and doing the extraordinary and outrageous, regardless of whether it is meritorious or notorious. This dynamic in part explains how a reality TV star who mocked the disabled and war heroes, bragged about not paying taxes, and demonstrated few of the traits associated with good leadership defined over two centuries by the US military became president and commander in chief.

We want to watch celebrity journalists who make themselves part of the story, contrary to all standards of professional journalistic conduct. We want celebrity influencers to follow and "like," whether they know what they're talking about or not. When all the world's a stage and image is everything, appearance has come to count more than reality, words are more powerful than deeds, fame is more valued than experience and expertise, and endorsing virtue suffices for practicing it.

APATHETIC AT A PRICE

For many years, political scientists have studied the reasons behind the United States' increasingly anemic voter turnout without coming to much consensus. Those deciding not to vote often cite a belief that their vote doesn't matter, the system is too corrupt, or there's no point because the political elite don't care about the average voter; an aversion to casting an uninformed vote; or dislike of the candidates.[23] Beyond such attitudes, voting experts point to legal and administrative impediments such as the requirement to register (a step unique to the United States) and to present ID to cast a ballot, along with practical factors such as difficulty getting time off work to get to the polls.

On average, 60 percent of eligible voters take part in presidential elections and 40 percent in midterm congressional balloting, placing the United States a pathetic thirty-first among thirty-five democracies in voter participation.[24] Over sixty million age-eligible Americans typically do not bother registering to vote. The 2020 presidential elections bucked the downward trend, recording the highest voter turnout in 120 years. Almost 160 million people—over 66 percent of eligible voters—cast ballots. Casting doubt on the hope of a trend is the highly unusual confluence of circumstances involved—a particularly polarizing incumbent, a major global public crisis thrusting government center stage in people's lives, severe social and racial strife on a scale not seen in half a century, and an energetic get out the vote campaign. The public viewed it as an election that truly mattered. It's a free country so each US citizen is at liberty to exercise their franchise or not, but, hopefully, keeping in mind the decades-old observation of magazine editor George Jean Nathan, "Bad officials are elected by good citizens who do not vote."[25]

Only a small sliver of the population are political activists. Most people are busy making a living, raising families, contributing to society in myriad ways, and trying to live by the rules rather than make them. But the ability to do those things well is shaped by policy and politics. When the sensible center checks out, politics is dominated by the more extreme elements in society, amplifying the influence from the polar regions of the national political spectrum. If national political discourse is shrill and extreme, then the buck stops in the distracted and apathetic middle more than the noisy margins.

The fact is that politicians cater to those who vote and take part in the democratic process and marginalize those who do not. Voting data show that between 1990 and 2010, nearly 84 percent of Americans over the age of seventy were regular voters. The percentage drops with each decade to the point that only 16 percent of those aged twenty to twenty-nine bother to cast ballots.[26] One need not be a supersleuth to explain why Congress maintains a well-funded phalanx of retiree support programs authorized by the Older Americans Act of 1965 and why Social Security and Medicare benefits are assured no matter how imbalanced the system's finances or the burden it places on younger generations. It's pretty simple: older Americans vote; younger people do not.

"If people don't participate," asked a 2018 *PBS NewsHour* segment on political apathy, "at what point does a democracy cease to be democratic?"[27] Participation means more than just voting. It encompasses adopting the habits of good citizenship. Fewer citizens are willing to run for public office at the federal, state, and local levels, and the patterns and quality of citizen participation in civic organizations have changed. In his book *Bowling Alone*, Robert Putnam spotlighted the role that "mediating institutions" play in our sense of community. They are defined as "those institutions standing between the individual in his private life and the large institutions of public life."[28] Putnam postulated that declining membership in such organizations, caused by preoccupation with television and the internet, has depleted the social capital vital to a healthy democracy. Evidence suggests the story may be more nuanced. Unlike television, the internet readily connects people to social engagements and participatory activities. Still, in a world in which we increasingly engage one another through our devices, the quality of engagement is different. Human interaction is richer and more intimate face-to-face than pixel to pixel. Perhaps that will change as technology bridges the experiential gap between virtual and nonvirtual interaction. As it is, the digital life mediated online is encouraging a corrosive voyeurism.

As addressed in the previous chapter, social echo chambers reinforce the personal biases and groupthink that fuel real-world civic division. The echoes are decidedly uglier in cyberspace than in the flesh-and-blood domain. The anonymity, pseudonymity, and distance provided by the internet make it easier for people to conspicuously judge, criticize, dismiss, bully, and insult those with whom they disagree, creating a coarseness in social dialogue that finds its way into our political culture. It's more acceptable to call one another and even entire groups of fellow Americans things like traitors, irredeemables, deplorables, fascists, racists, and communists in a tweet or post than eye to eye. When members of society engage in such exchanges in the digital common, politicians find it much easier to do so at the speech podium and in their ads. Trolling alone and its contribution to digitally enhanced hatred and disrespect are bigger factors in eroding the nation's social capital and in curdling disagreement into discord than how we might bowl alone.

The future of freedom and democracy remains, as always, in the hands of youth. Millennials are at an experiential disadvantage. Older Americans, I believe, vote not just because they have more time on their hands but, more importantly, because they have more experience under their belt. The baby boom generation has a stronger recollection of the Cold War, the threat of nuclear annihilation, and the grim alternatives to the democratic form of government. As this historical perspective fades, so does the value of democracy in the eyes of those who have enjoyed its benefits to the point of taking them for granted.

As the baby boom generation ages out, younger generations are likelier to grow up in a family where voting is not so much the norm. The hopeful news is that young people are intensely altruistic and care deeply about their fellow human beings. Curtis Gans, director of the Committee for the Study of the American Electorate, points out that younger generations' aversion to politics is driven by "disgust and discouragement and frustration, but not apathy."[29] If young people do not see politics as an agent for change or entering elected service as the best way to improve lives, fair enough. But we delude ourselves if we believe that politics is irrelevant to improving lives or destroying them. "War," said French statesman Georges Clemenceau, "is too important to leave to the generals." For the same reasons, politics is too important to leave to the politicians.

Americans have more information at their fingertips than ever, but we seem more ill-informed and confused. The country's student body is woefully ignorant about basic US history and civics. In a survey of youth from working-class families, Kei Kawashima-Ginsberg of Tufts University found that one in five didn't believe they knew enough to vote.[30] That is a problem for the nation at large, not just youth. "It is testimony to the failure of the country's education system," says Jonathan Cole in the *Atlantic*, "that a high percentage of the voting-age population is simply ignorant of basic facts—knowledge that is necessary to act reasonably and rationally in the political process."[31] The American Council of Trustees and Alumni found that only 20 percent of college seniors at fifty-five highly ranked colleges and universities would have received better than a D grade on testing based on "standard high-school-civics curricula."[32] Only one in two adults can name the three branches of government.[33] While three-quarters of us can name each of the Three Stooges, less than 40 percent can name a single Supreme Court justice.[34]

An American public high school student drops out every eight seconds. The deficit is not just in knowledge of civics but in understanding history, economics, and other disciplines necessary to make well-informed self-governance work. The implications go from the concerning to the frightening. Only 15 percent of US eighth graders are proficient in history.[35] A Woodrow Wilson National Fellowship Foundation survey found only 36 percent of Americans could pass a test drawn from questions that appear on the US citizenship test.[36] More frightening is a survey that found only 63 percent of Americans polled knew that six million Jews were murdered during the Holocaust under Nazi fascism; and ignorant or indifferent that a hundred million people were murdered by communist regimes, one in three millennials views communism favorably.[37] While the American system has placed more democratic responsibility in the hands of voters, such as through primary voting and referendums, it is not properly preparing the public to fulfill them responsibly. "The only sure bulwark of continuing liberty," observed Teddy Roosevelt, "is a government strong enough to protect the interests of the people, and a people strong enough and well enough informed to maintain its sovereign control over its government."[38]

Americans choose to refrain from civic participation and literacy because of a view that political culture is tainted and illegitimate. Greater consideration must be given to the inverse. Political culture has soured and lost its legitimacy because of the lack of participation and civic literacy.

TEAM RIVALRY

What Americans indulge in ardently and often with an unquenchable passion is devotion to our teams—athletic, organizational, occupational, and religious. Common is the rabid sports fan. Rare is one whose bias doesn't create illusions of unfair officials and rigged contests, as they pillory the other side for offenses they overlook when committed by their own. Many Democrats were convinced that the 2016 election was stolen. Many Republicans were convinced the 2020 election was stolen. We wuz robbed! The nation has come to treat its politics and party preferences the same way as its athletic teams, without an iota of objectivity and where "just win, baby" is all that matters. Like love of our teams, party affiliation is often a family tradition, a function of where we live and who we associate with, and a part of personal identity defended and protected, sometimes beyond reason or self-interest. In the effort to distinguish ourselves from rivals, differences are exaggerated and sometimes manufactured.

Though the partisan faithful would be loath to admit it, their respective parties' centrists have a great deal in common. Both sides generally agree that private-sector-led growth is the most desirable and sustainable, though they may differ on how best to stimulate it. They concur on the need for sensible tax and regulatory policy to foster economic growth and fill the national treasury. They are in accord on the importance of a strong national defense as a guarantor of peace and security, and that strong US leadership in the world serves US interests and betters the world. Among the nation's centrist majority, the policy debate in these areas generally focuses far more on tactics and degrees than overall objectives. Veteran journalist Tom Jacobs observed, "Many studies suggest we routinely overestimate just how different our positions are from those of our opponents. Bad, oversimplified journalism, along with the tendency of many high-profile political candidates to take extreme positions, has obscured the fact that many of our differences are, in fact, bridgeable."[39]

Even in presidential elections, the difference on the wedge issue of tax policy is not nearly as large as the political combatants would have us believe. During the 2008 and 2012 presidential elections, the debate often boiled down to disagreement over a top tax rate of 35 percent versus 39.6 percent. Meanwhile, Obama, Romney, Clinton, and Trump all expressed some level of support or sympathy for lowering business tax rates to improve US global economic competitiveness. The difference between Trump's and Clinton's tax plans with respect to the nation's top earning tax bracket was 6 percent (though Clinton's plan included a 4 percent surcharge on earnings above $5 million per year). The differences between their plans for the lowest-earning tax bracket were also not as vast as their rhetoric would make it seem. Trump recommended lowering the tax by three percentage points to 12 percent, while Clinton left it at 15 percent but proposed several new child and caregiver tax credits.[40]

Many of the largest political action committees give money to candidates on both sides of the aisle. The narrowing of the policy lanes is among the reasons that political campaigns have become nastier and more ad hominem. Differences must be magnified and where necessary manufactured to create political edge, to fan partisan passion that can be translated into money and votes. The focal points of divergence today are mainly social issues and identity politics that run high on emotion capitalized on by Politics Inc.

The team mentality informs our social interactions. When people flock with the like-minded, they are less likely to engage authentically with people outside their milieu, reinforcing groupthink. University of Notre Dame professor James S. O'Rourke IV mused about democracy in the digital age:

> Jesuits have long cautioned "No man can understand his own argument until he has visited the position of a man who disagrees." Such visits are increasingly rare. The long-predicted "filter bubble" effect is increasingly visible. People will simply not seek out, read or take time to understand positions they do not understand or do not agree with. A sizeable majority now live with a thin collection of facts, distorted information and an insufficient cognitive base from which to make a thoughtful decision. Accurate information is no longer driving out false ideas, propaganda, innuendo or deceit.[41]

THE MIRROR

In democracy, politics and government take on the character of the people, or at least the character of those who vote and take part in the political process. The crisis of trust in government is really a crisis of trust in ourselves and one another. Politics is a national mirror, and the reflection will not change until we do. We must become better consumers of information; fairer-minded evaluators of others' ideas; and more open to understanding the hopes, dreams, fears, and frustrations of others. Above all, we must understand more clearly that democracy works better as a verb than a noun. It is not something we get. It is something we do and earn by the habits of good citizenship.

Maybe if we quit treating politicians and government like cash registers, they will quit doing the same to us. Maybe if we stop treating elected officials like piñatas and punching bags, they will stop doing the same to one another. And maybe if families, schools, and civic organizations do a better job of teaching history, economics, civics, and government, the democracy will be more participatory and the electorate will make better-informed choices.

"The preservation of liberty," said John Adams, "depends upon the intellectual and moral character of the people. As long as Knowledge and Virtue are diffused generally among the body of a nation, it is impossible they should be enslaved."[42] The public is the great army of democracy. Building a culture that promotes a well-informed and participatory electorate and the habits of good citizenship will translate into a more united country, more functional politics, and better governance.

Once again, states, nongovernmental organizations, and academic institutions are leading the way. Florida, Illinois, and Massachusetts are making strong moves to institute civics education into middle and high school. The sunshine state's program focuses on four main pillars: "the origins and purposes of law and governments; citizens' rights and responsibilities, the political process, and the organization and function of government. Starting it early in middle school."[43] Dozens of bills to enact similar programs are pending in state legislatures looking to bring a renaissance to civics education.[44] Coalitions like CivXNow with the help of nongovernmental organizations like ICivics are developing model curricula, teacher training material, and programs that help students not only learn about democracy but practice it in their schools. It's hard to conceive of an initiative more instrumental to the salvation of American democracy than a well-resourced, whole-of-society campaign to raise levels of civic literacy and of the skills vital to functional self-government. Hand in hand with greatly improved civic literacy must be a renaissance in national and community service to strengthen Americans' connection to civic responsibility.

More and more educational institutions at all levels are finding value in school-sponsored community service ("community service activities that are non-curriculum-based and are recognized by and/or arranged through the school") and service learning curricula ("curriculum-based community service that integrates classroom instruction with community service activities").[45]

The report of the National Commission on Military, National, and Public Service, issued March 2020, stated that performing a term of service, either in civilian or military capacity, will "strengthen the civic fabric of the Nation"—something profoundly needed when the nation seems to be straining at its seams.[46] The commission's recommendations centered on the broad adoption of initiatives to facilitate civic education, service learning, and national service opportunities. The objective, in the commission's words, would be to create "a robust culture of service characterized by an expectation that all Americans participate in service of some kind, at some point in their lifetime so that no one is surprised by the questions 'How have you served?' or 'How will you serve?'"[47] Our leaders can do their part by adopting the commission's thoughtful proposals.

The norm of national service sought by the commission would bring greater civic cohesiveness, foster a stronger sense of shared stakes, and enkindle mutual respect that will go a long way toward restoring virtues vital to a healthy democracy. Whether it is sponsored by government, civil society, or public-private partnerships, the country would benefit tremendously by establishing a corps of national service recruiters who can engage with youth in every community, educating them on ways to serve the nation that marry their interests with public needs and ample service opportunities.

Service and education are at the core of strengthening the long-term prospects of self-governance. A culture of service reinforces the individual bonds to the community, and education prepares each person both to fulfill the obligations of citizenship. The American education reformer Horace Mann observed in 1848, "It may be an easy thing to make a Republic; but it is a very laborious thing to make Republicans; and woe to the republic that rests upon no better foundations than ignorance, selfishness, and passion."[48] If the people provide a stronger foundation for politics and government, then our politics and government will more clearly exhibit the best in democracy.

11

The Casualty of Virtues

The Soul or Spirit of Democracy, is virtue. No state can long preserve its Liberty where Virtue is not supremely honored.

—Samuel Adams

The severe damage to the nation caused by Politics Inc. is deepening from the accumulating effects of nonstop and dirty political campaigns abetted by a broken campaign finance system, and the self-serving structures it has put in place. Intensified by mercenary media, the darker consequences of modern technology, and cultural accelerants, the danger is becoming existential. The pillars of functional representative government—teamwork, compromise, and consensus—are strained to the breaking point. But these effects are the consequence of still deeper dynamics imperiling American democracy: the obliteration of core virtues and ethics unspecified in the Constitution but that permeate its every syllable. Without them, democracy can't work. If the American experiment is to have a tombstone, "a casualty of lost virtue" would be the epitaph and the gearworks of Politics Inc. its cause.

CASUALTY OF TRUTH AND FACTS

Inspired by the fact-resistant character of American politics, in 2016 the nearly 140-year-old *Oxford English Dictionary* formally added to the language the term "post-truth": "relating to or denoting circumstances in which objective facts are less influential in shaping public opinion than appeals to emotion and personal belief."[1] Those who rely on simple facts and whole truths to persuade hardly have a chance against the methods of Politics Inc.

Rumors, half-truths, and outright whoppers have always played a role in elective politics and civic affairs and had an edge on truth. "Falsehood flies," said Jonathan Swift, "and the truth comes limping after it; so that when Men come to be undeceiv'd, it is too late; the Jest is over, and the Tale has had its Effect."[2] The speed and interconnectedness of modern communication technology give balderdash unprecedented power. And in the social media domain, says the senior technology reporter for *Guardian US*, "the truth of a piece of content is less important than whether it is shared, liked, and monetized."[3]

Most Americans, continuously bombarded by hyperbole, spin, and "alternative facts," hardly know who or what to believe anymore. So, they don't. Conversely, too many political party loyalists believe almost any half-truth or falsehood dished by their team. In a survey taken before the 2016 presidential election, 81 percent of respondents said that partisans differed not only about policies but also about "basic facts."[4]

The heated debate over highly complex and nuanced immigration policy offers a classic case study in real-world implications of post-truth politics. Republican talking points came to assure the party faithful that illegal immigration posed a grave threat to US national security and prosperity and that Democrats are to blame. Democratic politicians convince their followers that illegal crossings were of little consequence to public safety or the economy and that Republicans simply fabricate the problem to be cruel.[5]

Republican audiences might be surprised to learn that between 2007 and 2020, net illegal immigration decreased.[6] The Government Accountability Office and even the Trump administration's State Department reported that no credible evidence showed that terrorists were using the southern border to enter the country.[7] In most cases, undocumented workers fill jobs shunned by US citizens. And overall, legal immigration has been a boon to the national economy.[8]

Democrats ignore the public safety disaster on our porous southern border, where between 1998 and 2017 over 7,200 people died attempting to cross illegally.[9] Not included in the statistic are the untold numbers who perished en route from Central America. "Along the way," says Amnesty International, "many of these men, women and children suffer assaults, robbery and abduction by criminal gangs." Mexico's human rights commission estimates that twenty thousand migrants a year are kidnapped and held for ransom as they transit.[10] And, in some cases, children are used as pawns, forced to accompany unrelated adults across the border to help them avoid lengthy detention or deportation if apprehended. Though undocumented workers often fill jobs shunned by US citizens, illegal immigration depresses wages in some industries and regions, hurting the most vulnerable US citizens. Even though 50 percent of undocumented workers pay federal, state, and local taxes, many do not, straining state and municipal services and budgets.[11] And, lack of proof that terrorists are exploiting the southern border doesn't mean it can't happen.

Large swaths of border wall along the US-Mexico border were erected during the administrations of Bill Clinton and Barack Obama. Republican icon Ronald Reagan opposed border fences altogether, advising, "Rather than talking about putting up a fence why don't we work out some recognition of our mutual problems?"[12]

More people were deported during Obama's first term than in Trump's four years, though the Trump administration made more border apprehensions than his predecessor over the same period. Ironically, the indication given by both parties that post-Trump border policies would be liberalized resulted in a rush of migrants to the southern border creating a crisis in 2021. Most Americans would prefer a rational national debate about immigration, informed by a common set of acknowledged facts. Honest discussion would more likely result in policy that aligns with the country's interest in upholding rule of law and with its character favoring fairness, compassion, and attaining sustainable solutions to include helping improve the quality of life in troubled countries to our south. For the political industry, however, campaigning on problems is preferable to solving them.

Politifact, a Pulitzer Prize–winning fact-checking service, fact-checked Donald Trump and Hillary Clinton 509 times by Election Day in 2016. Of Trump's 313 statements fact-checked, approximately 84 percent qualified as either "half true, mostly false, false, and 'pants on fire,'" while Clinton's 196 statements fact-checked registered 49 percent.[13] Both sides were much more concerned about the other team's falsehoods than their own, demonstrating the "whatever it takes to win" ethos of today's manic partisanship. Postelection events showed that post-truth was around to stay. The newly elected Congress and president immediately locked in battle over whether the Trump campaign colluded with Russia's interference in the election. To Republicans, the accusations were just lies. To Democrats, only lies kept the full truth from being revealed. And Donald Trump would go on to spend the remainder of his presidency setting records for falsehoods.

In 2018, the *New York Times* asked readers to submit examples of misleading political content they experienced online via social media accounts, apps, and emails. The newspaper received four thousand examples.[14] The fabricators ran a wide gamut: official campaign and political advocacy organizations, plausible-sounding but fictitious groups, and lone wolves wielding digital megaphones. Each election, the fact-checkers must keep a feverish pace. Americans are rightfully outraged at foreign manipulation campaigns and the use of disinformation to advance its objectives. Puzzling is why the country would be less offended and roused to action when similar tactics are employed by domestic political parties to advance theirs. In the national scrum of alternative facts, fake news, and post-truth politics, the ominous warning issued by civil rights leader and former US ambassador to the United Nations Andrew Young remains largely unheeded: "There can be no democracy without truth."[15]

THE CASUALTY OF TRUST

Post-truth leads to a phenomenon that merits its own spot in the dictionary—post-trust. Distrust is America's political pandemic, propagated by Politics Inc.'s core business strategy to sow cynicism about the country's civic institutions and leader-ship, our national political processes, and one another.

In the *Federalist Papers*, John Jay expressed the danger clearly: "Distrust natu-rally creates distrust, and by nothing is good-will and kind conduct more speedily changed."[16] Democratic governance is about collaborative problem-solving depen-dent on the establishment and maintenance of trust.[17] Every fact-free political attack impugning the opposition's motives, ethics, and competence, or the integrity of its constituencies, weakens the parties' confidence in one another, widens national division, and thwarts consensus-building. Former senators and representatives point to the growing penchant for questioning each other's motives as the pathology in congressional culture most responsible for gridlock. Almost no one is spared charges of malintent—election opponents, the press, subject-matter experts, businesspeople, labor unions, foreigners—so long as they hold a differing point of view.

The climate change debate offers a case in point. In 2018, thirteen US govern-ment agencies issued a major report affirming the long-standing consensus in the scientific community that human-caused climate change threatens our national security and prosperity. Rather than address the substance of the report, Republican skeptics attacked the scientists' motives. "The report is nothing more than a rehash of age-old 10- to 20-year assumptions made by scientists that get paid to further the politics of global warming," former Speaker of the House Tom Delay told CNN. "The reality is that a lot of these scientists are driven by the money that they receive," warned former Republican senator and two-time presidential candidate Rick Santo-rum. "And, of course," said Santorum, "they don't receive money from corporations and Exxon and the like."[18] Clearly, expert scientists are worse than wrong: they are corrupt, greedy, and can't be trusted!

The Green New Deal sponsored by several dozen Democrats called for a national transition from fossil fuels to an all-renewable energy mix within ten years. Upon its release, experts including renewable energy supporters like Ernie Moniz, secretary of energy in the Obama administration, observed that the timeline was technically and practically impossible. Others noted that the measure ignored alternative carbon control measures that could help solve the problem and aid the transition to clean energy.[19] Fair-minded economists pointed out that the resolution was a statement of goals, and without a specific set of implementing policies, no one could accurately calculate the measure's probable cost, much less assess its efficacy. Nevertheless, to some of its supporters, questioning the measure was an act of villainy. In an edito-rial welcoming a campaign fight over the Green New Deal, former Clinton and Obama administration official John Podesta and climate activist Varshini Prakash argued that the Republican Party's approach to the climate crisis was "further lining the pockets of oil and gas executives."[20] In other words, dissenters are worse than mistaken: they are corrupt, greedy, and can't be trusted!

The rampant impugning of motives offers vanishing hope we'll ever agree on sensible climate change policy. As the parties drift further toward their ideologi-cal extremes, distrust becomes more entrenched, and we're stuck in an unyielding dispute between protectors of the unsustainable status quo and proponents of the unrealistic. Both sides are content with trading accusations rather than exchanging ideas that could make a difference. That same playbook is employed across public policy. "Before impugning an opponent's motives, even when they legitimately may be impugned," counseled educator and philosopher Sidney Hook, "answer his arguments."[21] Politics Inc.'s counsel is attack, attack, attack.

Amid the cross-party attacks over who is in whose pocket, the American mainstream loses more trust in both sides. The public understands the damage inflicted by the contagion of cynicism, telling pollsters that lack of trust inhibits the country's ability to solve problems and that they hunger for bipartisan cooperation and confidence in the nation's institutions.[22]

THE CASUALTY OF BALANCE

The revolutionaries who gathered in Philadelphia to shape a new nation took counsel from ancient thinkers such as Aristotle, who espoused the virtue of the "golden mean" that has proved its worth in human affairs down through the ages. The framers knew that successful self-government would hinge on the maintenance of essential balances. Governmental powers had to be carefully distributed among separate branches to check abuse of authority. The purview and powers of the federal government needed to be squared with those of state and local administration. Nationhood required harmonizing the influence of big states with the interests of small ones. Majority rule needed to be balanced with minority rights, and public prerogatives reconciled with personal rights and responsibilities.

While democracy at its best synthesizes and balances interests, in search of principled compromise satisfactory to the strongest possible majority. Hyperpartisanship, conversely, rends and devotes itself to winner-take-all competition. Its practitioners in Politics Inc. have thrown democracy off kilter allowing bare pluralities to rule and sweepstakes processes to persist. Fringe-driven primary elections sacrifice representation that reflects the general electorate's attitudes and views. Skewed congressional redistricting sends to Congress a surplus of ideologically rigid representatives who see bipartisan cooperation as betrayal likely to cost them their seat. Electoral College apportionment skews the weight of each vote.

The sweepstakes approach bleeds over to newly elected administrations and congressional majorities, who presume that victory excuses them from bipartisan collaboration. Julia Azari, a political scientist who has carefully studied presidential communications, traced the notion of a postelection presidential "mandate" to Andrew Jackson but credited Nixon and Carter with explicitly claiming one—a practice that "became especially pronounced" in the administrations of George W. Bush and Barack Obama, who "frequently used mandate rhetoric to respond to critics." She argued that it reflects a kind of "defensive posture, born of polarization and shaky trust in institutions."[23]

Their vote margins, however, don't really suggest mandate. Richard Nixon won the presidency in 1968 by a plurality of the popular vote (43 percent) followed by a 60 percent tally in his 1972 victory. Jimmy Carter won 50 percent of the vote in his lone triumph in 1976. In his two presidential wins in the 1990s, Bill Clinton won 43 percent and 49 percent of the vote, respectively; George W. Bush won his by 48 percent and 50.7 percent. Barack Obama carried his elections with 53 percent and 51 percent of the vote, Donald Trump with 46 percent, and Joe Biden with just over 51 percent.

During the 2016 presidential election, Donald Trump divined a "mandate" from his supporters to be disruptive and inflammatory during the campaign and carried the approach into office. Yet, in claiming grand presidential and congressional mandates, the parties alternately yank at the reins of government so that it careens left then right and back again, dismissing the balance and consensus necessary to keep the country steadily moving forward.

As more ideological members of Congress and an increasingly partisan electorate abjure compromise and consensus, power flows from the incapacitated "people's branch" to the executive and judicial branches, upsetting the equilibrium of the US tripartite system. President Obama and President Trump each resorted to highly controversial executive orders to implement significant policy changes meant to be under congressional purview; in his first two weeks in office, President Biden signed twenty-eight executive orders, the most since FDR in 1933. Government by executive order sharpens the resentment of the out party, sets policy that can be easily overturned by subsequent executive orders, and heightens partisan tensions. As noted in chapter 7, a bipartisan group of seventy former US senators decried this pattern and blamed their own institution: "The Senate's abdication of its legislative and oversight responsibilities erodes the checks and balances of the separate powers that are designed to protect the liberties on which our democracy depends."[24]

Power in American politics is no longer centered in the moderate middle but has split in two, one piece within each party and moving toward the extremes. Every shift toward its fringe by one party seems to excite an opposite shift by the other party in response. As the center is hollowed out, there is no longer any place to meet and address national problems. Michael Porter of Harvard Business School addressed the practical effects: "Effective solutions are almost never purely 'right' or purely 'left.' For example, the question is not 'big government' or 'small government,' but how to strike the right balance across the various roles that government must play. Similarly, the issue is not 'regulation' or 'no regulation,' but how to craft regulations that deliver the desired social or economic benefits."[25]

Republican rhetoric often plays to the party base by expressing contempt for government, while Democratic themes often impress the base by demonizing business. The reality that good government and private-sector-led economic growth are codependent elements of national success is rarely acknowledged in the parties' rhetoric,[26] though heretical but important moments of political candor do occur. A decade before he ran for president, Paul Tsongas, a Massachusetts Democrat, spoke up to his party, saying, "You can't have employment and despise employers."[27] Al From, founder of the Democratic Leadership Council and top adviser to Bill Clinton, recalls Tsongas's lament: "The problem with the Democratic Party is that we spend so much time worrying about passing out the golden eggs that we forget to worry about the health of the goose."[28] The honesty earned Tsongas the antipathy of some Democratic stalwarts and likely cost him a place on his party's presidential ticket.

Tsongas's colleague Bob Michel served as the Republic leader in the House of Representatives from 1981 to 1995. In a speech titled "Change, Politics, and the Future: A Challenge to Republicans," delivered at a Forum called "Congress of Tomorrow," Michel argued, "We Republicans have to rid ourselves of the clichés and platitudes of yesteryear and realize that most Americans don't believe government is the enemy—most Americans believe bad government is the enemy. Our job is to make limited Government work for the betterment of our communities all across America. That should be our battle-cry."[29]

Through it all, both parties deceive the country and their constituencies with promises based on the asymmetry of something for nothing. At their extreme, Democratic appeals are rooted in the dogma that more government is the answer to most every need, minimizing the rights of taxpayers and employers and discounting the need for robust private initiative to fund the treasury and safeguard general welfare. At their margins, Republican appeals ply the misleading proposition that human needs can be met by market function and private initiative alone, minimizing the rights of employees and the needs of the disadvantaged, and underestimating the importance of general welfare to a strong private sector and individual initiative.

Fundamental imbalances in the nation's political culture contribute to corrosive national disparities in the federal budget, income and resources, the burdens of military service, the mix of public entitlements versus personal responsibilities, and in the widening gap between the nation's aspirations and the capacities of a system at risk.

THE CASUALTY OF INCLUSION

Government "of the people, by the people, and for the people" is none of those things unless it is inclusive and participatory. Almost forty years ago, Congress established the National Endowment for Democracy (NED) to help fledgling democracies establish strong democratic institutions and political processes. NED programs emphasize inclusion and citizen participation as pillars of strong democratic society. Their lack is as damaging to the United States as to the young democracies it mentors. Yet, many aspects of the US political process remain unrepresentative and exclusive.

A prime example is the role played by money in campaigning for public office and for attracting the attention of office seekers and incumbents.[30] As noted in chapter 4, while the number of small political donors is on the rise, large donations from the small fraction of Americans who make them account for a large portion of the total spending. At the same time, the number of self-funded candidates has grown, and their attractiveness to party leaders elbows out less moneyed potential candidates.

Among the reasons Americans give for not voting, cited in chapter 10, is not liking either candidate. And one reason voters regularly dislike their options is that, by rule, millions have no say in what the choice will be. Democratic and Republican primary elections and caucuses decide the options for the entire electorate. Those contests might be more representative if every American voter was a registered Democrat or Republican, but not when more voters are registered as Independents than affiliate with either of the two major parties.[31] Twenty-six states bar nonparty members from voting in the primary, leaving nearly twenty-two million independent voters without a say in who will top the federal election ballots.[32] Moreover, most party registrants— particularly moderate members—don't take part in primary elections. Pew Research Center found that in the first dozen presidential primary elections in 2016, "only 17 percent of eligible voters participated in Republican primaries, and only 12 percent in Democratic primaries."[33] The 2020 primaries, with pandemic-driven mail-in voting and a highly charged election, saw a modest and anomalous uptick. Still, a relatively small sliver of the American populace decides the binary choice presented to the rest of the country.

THE CASUALTY OF SUBSTANCE

The world has never been more complex, nor has navigating the difficult public policy and governance terrain to cope with its complexities. Yet, national political discourse is dominated by simplistic eight-second sound bites and 280-character tweets, crowding out thoughtful debate. Studies of social media show a deepening focus by the political culture on the "personalities and personal traits of politicians" rather than their policies and ability to lead.[34]

Brian Ott, chair of communications studies at Texas Tech University, observes, "Twitter infects public discourse like a social cancer. It destroys dialog and delibera-tion, fosters farce and fanaticism, and contributes to callousness and contempt."[35] Twitter "demands simplicity . . . promotes impulsivity . . . [and] fosters incivility," and social media puts a premium on speed to capture fleeting public attention spans and encourages shock to make messages stand out in the torrents of internet commentary.[36] The electronic commons are a riot of monologue, propaganda, ad hominem diatribes, and dumbed-down rhetoric.

Instant communications in the digital era emphasize appearance over substance. Politicians are under 24/7 scrutiny, and demands from the public and press for immediate comment drive reflexive, superficial rhetoric. Hyperexposure leads them to overemphasize image management and the theater of politics rather than the hard work of good governance. Politicians rely on base-pleasing bromides and generalities for fear anything they say will be recorded, distorted, and go viral.

Political reporting in general is captivated by horse-race journalism, covered like ESPN sports. Team versus team. Who's winning and who's losing and why? Play-by-play. Real-time scoring and analysis. Reports are so busy dissecting the game that the country has lost sight of the purpose of the sport. The performative nature of politics has overtaken core legislative functions in a parliament of pundits and pod-casters, sound bites and bumper stickers. Meanwhile, analysis of the bills passed by the 115th Congress (2017–2019) found that about 30 percent were ceremonial—"renam[ing] post offices, courthouses, and the like."[37]

Perhaps nothing better illustrates the lack of substance in the nation's political life than presidential campaign debates. Intended as an exercise in voter education, they have become an unedifying exchange of slogans and insults—the political imitation of a Ultimate Fighting Championship weigh-in. Their vapidness plumbed new depths during the 2016 Republican primary debate, which at one point devolved into a schoolyard dispute over the size of candidates' body parts.

The 2019 Democratic primary debates weren't much better. A reporter called them a "silly microcosm of absurdity."[38] Asked whether they were worth the effort they require, one operative for a leading Democratic candidate replied, "Absolutely not. It's so much on the performance art of this, and we've lost the substantive debates we should have."[39] Another aide found a little personal utility in the debates, noting, "I mean, it's fun to hang out and drink with friends in a city that's not D.C. Sucks otherwise on all levels."[40] Modern debates hit their nadir in the first televised debate of the 2020 general election. Ninety minutes of national embarrassment featured Trump repeatedly interrupting his opponent, cutting off the moderator, and being in turn called a "clown" and told to "shut up."

Candidates and their debate teams rehearse one-liners, hoping to create a juicy sound bite or viral hashtag. Meanwhile, their campaigns busy themselves with other high-tech-enabled assaults on substance including use of data analytics to determine what segments of the electorate want to hear. The Madison Avenue approach carries over from campaigning to governance in the use of colorful packaging and good marketing to obscure questionable aspects of legislation. Congress passed legislation titled the Affordable Care Act, which has raised insurance premiums by as much as 30 percent.[41] Substance was in short supply when, in 2016, Republicans, after using Obamacare as a punching bag for six years, captured both houses of Congress and the presidency but had produced nothing substantive to replace it. As of 2019, thirty million Americans were still without health insurance.[42]

Veterans of Capitol Hill will tell you that ideas are not so much good or bad as they are either Republican or Democrat. Merit is evaluated by which party is advantaged. The ethos is illustrated by a telling exchange I had early in my tenure at the Senate Committee on Commerce, Science, and Transportation. The Senate was taking up a transportation bill referred by the committee for action. During the floor proceedings, one of the committee's Republican staff approached me, upset about an amendment offered by a Democrat. He asked for direction on how to block it. I asked him for a description of the proposal and whether it had merit. He explained the content and conceded it was a good idea. When I noted that perhaps that meant we should recommend the amendment's adoption to the Republican chairman of the committee, the staffer was dumbfounded. "But it's a Democratic amendment," he pleaded. Small anecdote. Big problem.

THE CASUALTY OF CIVILITY AND RESPECT

Unanimity has always been hard to achieve in our raucous politics, but there is near universal agreement that civility is near extinction in our political discourse, and norms of dignity and respect in the democratic process are vanishing.

Washington was shocked when a member of Congress shouted "you lie" at President Obama during a State of the Union address in 2009 and when a senator called another a liar on the Senate floor.[43] Today, lapses in civility like these have lost their ability to surprise us, much less shock.

In the era of full-time, negative campaigning, opponents are not just misguided or wrong: they are morally flawed and unpatriotic. In the words of candidates, the 2016 presidential campaign was a battle between "losers" and "deplorables." Not since President Eisenhower called the US Communist Party treasonous has a sitting president used the word to describe an American political party or an elected official.[44] The accusation is now employed regularly by both sides. In an article for *Reason* magazine entitled "In Today's America, Everybody Who Disagrees with You Is a Traitor," J. D. Tuccille wrote,

> Throwing the word "treason" around, unmoored from its actual meaning, is a weapon for delegitimizing political opposition and dissent. . . . Except in those rare circumstances when the charge is accurate, tagging your enemies as traitors lazily bypasses debating their ideas and actions and goes straight for accusations of betraying the nation on behalf of its enemies to such a heinous degree that it warrants punishment with a bullet or a noose.[45]

Rather than touting their own qualifications, vision, and policy agenda, most candidates rely on attack ads and direct mail appeals for money and support focused on the evils of their opponent. The practice pits segments of society against one another and turns honest disagreement into such hostility that one in four partisans attests to harboring "hatred" for members of the other party.[46]

For many decades, Congress conducted business part time but intensively and in person. Though debates could be heated, members tried to maintain a level of decorum and civility. Republican icon Barry Goldwater called it disagreeing without being disagreeable.[47] Today the legislative branch is a full-time, high-intensity, low-productivity operation. Members monitor floor proceedings and committee hearings on television. More and more they communicate with constituents and colleagues digitally and through staff surrogates. The world may operate increasingly in the virtual domain, but human understanding and political compromise—the soul of democratic governance—remains an eye-to-eye enterprise that is fast disappearing.

Congressional observers point to the loss of weekend socializing beginning in the mid-1990s, when Washington legislators began traveling home every weekend. Today, many members don't know one another. Even colleagues who have served in the body over many years may have never met. Yet, representatives and senators attest to how important personal relationships are to building consensus and trust. Missouri Democrat Emanuel Cleaver II shared, "Republicans sit on one side of the floor, we sit on one. The only time I see a Republican is when I come up here (to the Capitol) to vote. Or go to a committee hearing. That's probably the biggest reason things have turned nasty. All of the incivility, all of the difficulty working together."[48]

Former members note that in earlier times, members of differing parties got to know one another best during votes and when working together on legislation. Beginning in the mid-1990s, bipartisan legislation grew rarer as arcane parliamentary maneuvers by party leaders to limit amendments and incumbents' exposure to politically dangerous votes diminished opportunities to build constructive relationships.

Other norms supporting a collegial and constructive political environment are disappearing as well and unlikely to be restored even in the long term. Despite the prohibition on electioneering in government workspace, Donald Trump used the White House for partisan rallies.[49] Conversely, the Republican National Convention was used as a platform to announce official national policy.[50] In a breach of good manners and interparty respect, many Democrats boycotted Trump's inauguration in 2016. Trump returned the favor by refusing to take part in Biden's ceremony. This ungracious act occurred after his false, norm-busting, self-declaration of victory.

For decades following World War II, an unwritten rule constrained political opponents from criticizing a president of the United States on travel abroad. On the other hand, presidents refrained from talking partisan politics in foreign capitals. The concept was expressed in 1947 by Republican senator Arthur Vandenberg, chairman of the Senate Foreign Relations Committee, who argued that partisan politics must stop "at the water's edge" lest it show division to foreign powers.[51]

Once taboo, salvos now fire across seas. Nearing the end of his first term while preparing for the 2012 challenge from Mitt Romney, Obama was asked to respond to criticisms he received from a Romney adviser in a German newspaper. The president demurred, saying, "I think traditionally the notion has been that America's political differences end at the water's edge."[52] But while at an economic summit in the Philippines in 2015 and again later while traveling in Africa, President Obama shot back at his critics seeking the GOP nomination to succeed him for their poor policy ideas.[53] That same year while in the United Kingdom, New Jersey governor Chris Christie criticized Obama's skills as a negotiator.[54]

In December 2019, Democrats held presidential impeachment hearings while Donald Trump was traveling in Europe. Trump vehemently protested the breach. Yet, six months earlier, during a news conference with the prime minister of Japan in Tokyo, Trump echoed an insult hurled by North Korea's dictator questioning

Joe Biden's intelligence. For good measure, Trump lashed out at Republican Robert Mueller, who had headed the Justice Department's Russia investigation, and at
"the angry Democrats" who sought his impeachment. The stunned prime minister
looked on quietly while the president of the United States aired America's dirty
laundry on the world stage.[55]

Republicans and Democrats each have core convictions that stir passion and activism. That is the American way. Pro-life Republicans argue passionately that laws
should be changed to prevent the loss of life from abortion. Pro-choice Democrats
passionately counter that the question of abortion is a protected personal matter that
the state has no right to interfere with. Pro–gun control Democrats are adamant
that laws should be changed to restrict gun ownership to prevent the loss of life
from gun violence. Republicans counter that the right to bear arms is constitutionally protected. These are issues of perpetual disagreement between the parties. What
both sides did agree to, however, are the House of Representatives' rules intended to
maintain the dignity and decorum of the House chamber by prohibiting the use of
cell phones on the House floor. In early 2016, Democrats staged a sit-in in the well
of the House following the mass shooting at an Orlando bar that killed forty-nine
people and wounded fifty-three others, refusing to budge until Speaker Paul Ryan
allowed a vote on gun legislation.[56]

The protesters used cell phones to take pictures and stream the event live. Andrew
McGill of the *Atlantic* reported that Representative John Lewis sent an email blast
calling for public support. The mail linked to a petition sponsored by the Democratic Congressional Campaign Committee (DCCC), "featuring a rather unflattering photo of Ryan."[57] The front page of the DCCC's website is cluttered with
"donate" tabs and displays a running total of donations. Republicans decried the
maneuver as a publicity stunt. *The Hill* reported that during the sit-in, the DCCC
sent at least six fundraising emails with a goal of attracting six thousand donations,
one signed by then minority leader Nancy Pelosi taking Republicans to task for not
lifting a finger on gun violence and telling prospective donors, "I need your help to
defeat them once and for all."[58]

None of this is to suggest that preventing gun violence isn't a worthy cause. The
protesters knew they were not going to succeed, but it made for high drama. One
can imagine pro-life Republicans will conduct a sit-in issuing tweets from the House
floor that link to the National Republican Campaign Committee and its donation tabs. Many issues are "sit-in-worthy" for both sides of the aisle. But using the
House floor as a prop deepens divisions between the parties and further damages the
chances for action that can make a difference to the country.

One of the most damaging effects of the incivility gripping American political
culture is the disappearance of respect and a willingness to listen. Partisans talk at
and over one another instead of to one another. The great American artist Norman
Rockwell's famous 1943 painting *Freedom of Speech* portrays a humble citizen rising,
hat in hand, to express himself before a town meeting of fellow citizens courteously
listening. The twenty-first-century version could accurately depict members of a

mob shouting one another down. In 1978, Jesse Jackson was invited to speak at a Republican National Committee conference, where he was received respectfully and enthusiastically.[59] Such a thing happening today in either camp seems unimaginable.

Democrat Lee Hamilton, a leading member of Congress for thirty-five years, stated both the distressing trends and the high stakes involved: "Walking into a room or chamber where the differences are sharply drawn and finding a way to bring people together is political skill of the highest order. And it's pretty much impossible to exercise without civility."[60]

THE CASUALTY OF DUTY

The American system of government is built on a framework of distinct roles and responsibilities requiring focused devotion to duty.

Preoccupation with filling campaign coffers to get reelected steals enormous time and energy from performing core official functions such as studying issues, understanding legislation, and collaborating with colleagues to solve problems. It is why, in the words of Nancy Pelosi, Congress must "pass legislation before you can know what's in it."

While Pelosi's words may not have been intended exactly as they sounded, they contained an irrefutable truth. Most members do not read and comprehend the bills and amendments they vote on. In many instances, they simply can't. No one could. The Affordable Care Act, containing highly complex policy provisions that affect every American and over 17 percent of the country's $21 trillion economy, covered 906 pages.[61] The National Defense Authorization Act typically covers over one thousand pages. Mega-spending bills can be even longer.

Although responsible for overseeing government and assuring that the executive branch is doing its job, a polarized Congress is no longer capable of fulfilling its own basic duties. Its preoccupation with partisan wrangling is why the budget and appropriations process is a mess, why many government agencies and programs built for another era persist, why many high-level government posts and judgeships go vacant, and why its capacity for effective oversight of government has weakened. These and other examples of the legislative branch's failure to fulfill its constitutional responsibilities largely explain why the executive and judicial branches exceed theirs, creating partisan fights over "imperial" presidents and "activist" judges.

Attention to duty is an essential element of good leadership. One of the most important tasks of a dutiful political leader is to define what they want to do, why, and how. Throughout much of the twentieth century, presidents would send to Congress draft bills necessary to implement their priorities. The practice shows seriousness of purpose, and the specificity enables lawmakers, the press, and the public to properly assess the merits of proposed policy. John F. Kennedy didn't just say he wanted new statutory civil rights protections for minorities; he sent Congress draft legislation to implement what eventually became the Civil Rights Act of 1964. Lyndon Johnson sent specific legislative proposals to Congress to implement his Great Society policies. Nixon, Ford, and Carter did the same with their priorities. One of Ronald Reagan's first actions after taking the oath of office was sending to Congress his pro-federalism proposals, providing block grants to the states so they could implement various community improvement functions that the federal government had assumed, and he provided the same level of specificity with other policy priorities. Likewise, when George H. W. Bush sought to comprehensively strengthen the Clean Air Act, tackling acid rain and poor urban air quality—one of his biggest legislative achievements—he presented Congress with a draft bill to implement every aspect of his plan, as he did other major proposals.

The practice of presidents sending Congress detailed proposals in legislative form (other than spelling out the specifics of federal spending and revenue in legally required budget submissions) tapered off beginning with Bill Clinton. Among Clinton's major policy priorities upon taking office in January 1993 was universal health care insurance coverage. He put First Lady Hillary Clinton in charge of a task force to develop a comprehensive plan. After months of intensive discussions with stakeholders, the task force produced a thousand-page package of detailed proposals. The plan ran into immediate opposition and eventually died without ever coming to a House or Senate vote.

A former Clinton aide says that the smackdown discouraged the administration from submitting fine-grained legislative proposals to Congress that could be picked apart over details and used as partisan fodder. From that point on, Clinton was inclined to articulate the objectives of legislation while leaving Congress to figure out and fight over the specifics. Except in rare cases, subsequent administrations have followed the practice. The political reasons for doing so remain strong. Vagueness provides a measure of deniability and deprives Congress, the press, and the public of specific ammunition to attack the shortcomings inevitably part of any significant change in public policy. Abandoned, however, is an important duty of leadership, dealing a serious blow to the proper function of democracy.

The casualty of duty has infected the fourth estate, as described in chapter 8. Broadcast journalism was once the province of devoted, lifelong professional newspeople. The industry endeavored to keep separate news and commentary and to inform the public objectively. Accuracy was a professional obligation, and the dividing line between partisan politics and professional journalism was respected if not always maintained. Today, televised news and current events coverage teems with on-air talent whose roots are in elective politics rather than professional journalism.

During the 2020 COVID-19 crisis, a nationwide audience watched Chris Cuomo, host of CNN's *Cuomo Prime Time*, yuk it up during an interview with his brother, Andrew Cuomo, the sitting governor of New York, and again several months later in a follow-up interview as conditions worsened. What would Walter Cronkite have thought about an award-winning journalist heaping praise on a relative for his performance as New York's chief executive then ignore allegations that the governor had covered up the number of pandemic-related nursing home deaths?[62] For that matter, what would Cronkite, "the most trusted man in America," think about how propaganda, infotainment, and news "analysis" crowd out authentic journalism that is supposed to objectively tell the story?

The decline of virtues critical to democracy and Politics Inc.'s false binary choices and tired patterns are crippling the country's ability to sustain its security, prosperity, and global influence in the years ahead. In particular, five imperatives for positioning America to thrive in the twenty-first century are drifting further out of reach: syncing the public and private sector to achieve national objectives, harnessing the nation's diversity to excel in every area of national endeavor, building on common cause and mutual interest to unify the country, striking and maintaining essential balances to strengthen American democracy, and elevating national strategy over tactical politics.

Syncing the Public and Private Sector

Republican rhetoric vilifying government and Democratic rhetoric demonizing business have generated dangerous antipathies in a country that needs both government and business at their best. Many of the projects and innovations fueling US prosperity, job creation, and global competitiveness in the twentieth century were the product of public-private-sector teamwork. Without it, we wouldn't have been able to build a national electric grid, telephone network, and the interstate highway system. The federal government was at the forefront in developing digital computers, satellite communications, weather forecasting, and the global positioning system. Many of the vaccines in use today were developed with federal support.

Through it all, America's private sector has served as the engine of US prosperity. The nongovernment sector is the enabler of the American dream, helping democratize the opportunity for each of us to make our own contribution. The strength and stability of America's private sector are what enable the country to weather poor governance and misguided political administrations.

The Democratic extremes must recognize that government isn't all-knowing and all-capable. When Republicans are hard on government, they have lots of reasons to be. Its inefficiencies are disrespectful to taxpayers and the public. Its excesses impinge on freedom and harm the economy, costing jobs, damaging dreams, and reducing the public wherewithal to do good. Its failures weaken the nation.

Studies produced by the Government Accountability Office on debilitating redundancies in the federal government's structure and the inefficiency of its service, and by the Organisation for Economic Cooperation and Development, on the numbing complexity and excessive burdens of the US regulatory system (Organisation for Economic Co-operation and Development), tell only part of the story. Since at least the mid-1990s, the US government has been on the decline in all but one category of the World Bank's Worldwide Governance Indicators, including accountability, regulation quality, rule of law, and control of corruption.[63]

The Republican extremes must recognize that markets are not omnipotent. Market failure produces adverse social, economic, environmental, and political consequences that hurt business as much as society at large. Business and industry that are too dominant in public affairs can create distortions as damaging as those caused by an overzealous government that exceeds its core competencies. Business and financial scandals inspired by greed have from time to time dragged the nation to the precipice.

Imagine the good made possible by atypical behavior—Democrats tougher on bureaucracy and Republicans harder on corporatocracy.[64] We must have our policy debates and disputes, but a political culture that creates antipathies rather than partnerships and clings to doctrinaire modalities rather than synthesizing all elements of national power to meet strategic objectives is guaranteed to fail.

Harnessing the Nation's Diversity

Diversity is among America's greatest assets and defining characteristics. Legal scholars Amy Chua and Jed Rubenfeld note, "In the United States, you can be Irish American, Syria American, or Japanese American, and be intensely patriotic at the same time. We take this for granted but consider how strange it would be to call someone 'Irish French' or 'Japanese Chinese.'"[65]

Innovation experts find that diversity fosters dynamism and creativity, yielding better ideas and solutions than homogeneity and groupthink. Mankind needs all the creativity it can muster given the challenges ahead. That will take harnessing our differences and diversity rather than exploiting them for partisan advantage. Senator John McCain observed,

> What makes America exceptional among the countries of the world is that we are bound together as citizens not by blood or class, not by sect or ethnicity, but by a set of enduring, universal, and equal rights that are the foundation of our constitution, our laws, our citizenry, and our identity. When anyone, not least a member of Congress, launches specious and degrading attacks against fellow Americans on the basis of nothing more than fear of who they are and ignorance of what they stand for, it defames the spirit of our nation, and we all grow poorer because of it.[66]

The country grows poorer still as Politics Inc. promotes adversaries over alliances and exploits social fission rather than harnessing the fusion necessary to succeed. National unity doesn't mean uniformity. The national melting pot must merge our interests in freedom and justice and foster mutual respect and affections, not erase the distinct identities and subcultures that enrich us.

Building on Common Cause and Mutual Interest

Partisan politics casts too many of the country's policy disputes as zero-sum propositions yielding a winner and a loser, when in many cases common cause and mutual interest are well aligned. Capital and labor need one another to thrive. Both do better when they work together fairly and efficiently to grow the economy. Commerce and conservation need one another. Poverty is a poor environmental steward, and sustainability in our natural systems provides the reliable supply chain of resources necessary to support human systems and industrial productivity for the long haul. A strong economy and strong social safety net are interdependent.

Efforts by Republicans to promote investment, productivity, and economic growth should not be dismissed as an assault on the poor, despite the political advantages gained by such charges. Job creation is the country's most powerful anti-poverty program. Conversely, an economy in which the upper crust enjoys advantages that add to its wealth without commensurate gains in the middle class does not serve the general welfare and will result in a more fractious and unstable society whose deterioration even gated communities can't ignore. So when Democrats spotlight skewed economic gains and the struggles of segments of society burdened with uncertainty and being left behind, the complaint is not necessarily an attack on the economic system than a challenge of how we can make it work better and more sustainably.

Striking and Maintaining Essential Balances

Exercising democracy is about striking proper balances, making equitable accommodations, and engaging in give-and-take. Majority rule must be balanced against minority rights and public interest against private prerogatives. Freedom has to be complemented by self-restraint and liberty by responsibility. The executive, legislative, and judicial powers must be commensurate and authorities properly allocated among federal, state, and local governments. The efficiencies of centralization must be measured against the benefits of devolution. The interests of capital and labor, producers and consumers, taxpayers and beneficiaries must be responsibly and justly reconciled.

The main tensions in the US political system arise from partisans who too frequently view the national purposes set forth in the Constitution's preamble as an à la carte menu. Generally speaking, Republicans tend to emphasize national defense and domestic tranquility, while Democrats emphasize justice and general welfare. In fact, the constitutional objective of "forming a more perfect Union, establishing Justice, ensuring domestic Tranquility, providing for the common defense, promoting the general Welfare, and securing the Blessings of Liberty to ourselves and our Posterity" is not a list of options for partisans to pick over and choose. It is a recipe of coequal and interbraided national ingredients for success.

Studies show that conservatives and liberals differ in their personality types and even brain function. They emphasize different values. Conservatives focus on personal responsibility and public order, liberals on public compassion and personal freedom. Each of these goods is important to the nation—something perhaps inherently understood by the four in ten Americans who prefer divided government to bring the parties and their respective priorities into balance since they will not balance themselves.[67] Nineteenth-century philosopher and political economist John Stuart Mill observed that "a party of order or stability, and a party of progress or reform, are both necessary elements of a healthy state of political life."[68]

Elevating National Strategy over Tactical Politics

China and its authoritarian brethren contend their model has more to offer than democracies, including the ability to set strategy, implement policy, and sustain focus on achieving national objectives. The point should not be dismissed because of its source. Henry Adams, one of America's most accomplished and respected historians, compared the American president to a commander of a ship at sea who must have "a helm to grasp, a course to steer, a port to seek."[69] The US ship of state cannot fix on a worthy port and a general course to get there when the parties take turns yanking the helm back and forth and the country finds itself careening, not moving forward. The political system must find the ability to forge common objectives and set national strategy we can stick with, even while we tussle over the details and tactics. Doing so will require the parties to retire their practiced contrarianism and find satisfaction not only in achieving strong policy consensus but in sustaining it. This will be easier to do if the country can lift its focus from the tactical politics of the day to the horizon and apply itself to the comprehensive national strategies necessary to navigate the challenges ahead.

Sam Rayburn, longtime Speaker of the House, remarked, "Any jackass can kick a barn down. But it takes a good carpenter to build one."[70] The political system needs more bipartisan carpenters who have the discipline and focus to devise practical, long-term solutions that meet national needs rather than rash expedients that serve shortsighted political agendas.

Rebuilding the country's fidelity to its democratic ideals and reviving the virtues necessary to put them into practice is the starting block for American evolution.

12

The American Evolution

E pluribus unum.

Upon declaring independence in 1776, the Continental Congress delegated Benjamin Franklin, Thomas Jefferson, and John Adams to design a great seal that would symbolize the new country. The team's effort ran aground. Follow-on committees were established to carry the work forward. They, too, fell short. Eventually, the best elements and ideas drawn from the collective efforts were successfully combined. Established in 1782, the Great Seal of the United States stands as a global emblem of liberty, bearing the Latin inscription "*E pluribus unum*"—out of many, one. These three simple words manifest the power and promise of democracy.

Faith that *unum* could be forged from *plures* was rooted in the conviction that individual differences, no matter how formidable, pale in comparison to the universal human passion for freedom and self-determination. Constituting a nation based on this conviction and supplanting the divine right of kings with the radical concept of divinely endowed human rights were risky propositions for the founders. But it was a project they embraced even at the menace of their lives and fortunes. The true miracle of Philadelphia is that they translated the dream into a living charter inspired by ideals much greater and better than their times and prejudices.

The Constitution has thrived for nearly two and a half centuries not because the framers were unimpeachable but because the principles they enshrined in it are—powerful enough to command changes in the charter itself. The framers recognized that perfecting the union and securing the blessings of liberty would be a continuous work in progress. And since 1791, the charter has been altered twenty-seven times.

From the moment Washington raised his right hand to swear the oath of office and the first Congress was gaveled into session, the American idea has endured monumental trials and challenges. To come was a civil war, two world wars, the Great Depression, the ongoing struggle for equally shared civil rights, the Cold War, severe economic crises, social upheavals, and intermittent political strife—still, the lamp of liberty stayed lit, guiding the nation forward.

Despite our mistakes and shortcomings, the United States has earned admiration and gratitude around the globe. America has demonstrated the power of free people, free institutions, and free enterprise and stood as a bulwark against the evils of stolen, concentrated political power. Along the way, we built the largest economy ever known, nearly one-third larger than any other. Largely following the US model of economic freedom, one billion people have been lifted out of extreme poverty over the past twenty-five years. Through it all, the country has endured and thrived not primarily by virtue of its wealth and military might but because of the legitimacy of its ideals—the same reason people from every continent still aspire to call America home.

As mightily as previous generations have been tested in keeping the American idea alive, the most difficult challenges lay ahead. New threats are emerging and old ones reasserting themselves. Autocracy is again on the rise worldwide, seeking to replace democracy as the template for governance, claiming to offer the world a better future based on old and discredited concepts of state control. Advanced technology is arming authoritarians with new and powerful tools to propagandize, surveil, and control their populations as well as threaten others. The sharp rise expected in global population, potentially doubling in the next fifty years, will intensify already severe challenges—among them providing energy, food, and water security; defeating extreme poverty and violent extremism; and protecting global health. Solving them will set the foundation for keeping the peace, fostering human development, and sustaining freedom in the twenty-first century. In a world of high-velocity change and rapidly scalable threats, stability has never been so fragile nor instability so treacherous.

More than ever, the world needs an America at its absolute best—but the country seems intent on presenting its worst. Indicators are blinking red across the US economic, social, and political domains. Line charts on the growth of national debt and deficits, health care costs, income inequality, and the costs of modernizing the nation's crumbling infrastructure continue to climb. The country has flatlined on improving student performance in the skills of the future, reforming an anticompetitive tax and regulatory system, bolstering middle-class income, and helping pull families and communities out of generational poverty.

On the social front, the percentage of people who trust civic institutions, believe in one another, and are optimistic about the future continues to slide. Race relations have not been so poor in half a century. As explored in preceding chapters, political culture is being degraded by steep rises in the length, cost, and negativity of campaigns. Matching them is the steady increase of one-party votes, budget impasses, unauthorized spending, congressional gridlock, interparty animus, and demand for a third party. Plummeting slopes depict the continuing decline in the favorability of the Republican and Democratic Parties; centrists in Congress; bipartisanship; and public trust in the nation's leaders, government, and political process. The electorate wonders where the return on investment is from a colossal government and substantial tax burden. Year after year, the country fails to perceive any semblance of bipartisan priority setting or comprehensive joint strategies to tackle big, obvious problems. The combination of unmet challenges and ugly politics largely accounts for what is the most troubling metric of all—distrust in the nation's institutions and gathering indifference toward democracy itself.

After every national election, analysts, political scientists, and historians scrutinize the campaign strategies and seek lessons from the results about the electorate's mood and attitudes. The political message may not be the outcome of any election—as Marshall McLuhan wrote of the media, the process is the message: its cost, negativity, divisiveness, and lack of substance.

Major national campaigns typically ring with calls for "revolution" and the choruses of "time for a change." Talk of revolution certainly has dramatic and even demagogic appeal. Revolution sponsored by one extreme of the American political spectrum or the other, however, won't make the country a better place. Revolving takes us back to where we have already been, to recommit old mistakes and relearn old lessons. "Change" is a lousy, near meaningless term. The country needs evolution, not revolution, and less campaign rhetoric about change and more focus on improvement.

As Justice Sandra Day O'Connor advised, we need to use "what is right with America to remedy what is wrong with it."[1] The nature of the problem today makes that difficult. What's wrong with America, Politics Inc. and its gearworks, is undermining what's right with America: the virtues Washington described as the "necessary spring of popular government" and the values that Martin Luther King believed could be found in the "great wells of democracy which were dug deep by the founding fathers in the formulation of the Constitution and the Declaration of Independence."

If Politics Inc. won't accommodate reform to save democracy, then it's time to reform Politics Inc. and its machinery. Without restoring the system's virtues, values, and functionality, we can't expect to add to the number of good people in elective politics and public service and to make it worthy of those already laboring within it. We will be unable to rise above partisan combat to craft the strategies, make the decisions, and maintain the momentum necessary to meet the enormous challenges ahead. Systemic reform is the foundation on which all other national improvement rests and the key to realizing our aspirations for a better future.

THE CAMPAIGN

The mission to dismantle the machinery responsible for driving national division, public dysfunction, and the decay of our democracy evokes the experience of Jack

Port and June 6, 1944. Once again, the eyes of the world are turning to the United States at a time of peril, this time one of our own making but having everything to do with preparing ourselves for greater trials to come. The internal divisions the nation nurses and the deep political dysfunctions it tolerates, but particularly the essential virtues we abandon, pose a clearer and more present danger to the country than any external threat. How the United States responds to these forces will greatly determine its fate and the future of democracy. Victory will require a smart and committed campaign plan looking to the future but guided by the past.

Astride the entrance to the National Archives in Washington, DC, stand two ten-foot limestone statues. On the right is the statue *Future*, featuring a young woman "gazing in contemplation of things to come . . . hold[ing] an open book symbolizing what has yet to be written." On the base is written "WHAT IS PAST IS PROLOGUE" from Shakespeare's *The Tempest*. To the left is the statue *Past*, symbolized by "an old man gazing down the corridors of time . . . hold[ing] a closed book representing history." Its base is inscribed "STUDY THE PAST," drawn from the Confucian wisdom of looking to the past to understand the future.[2]

Historians study ancient civilizations looking for lessons that might instruct America on how to remain a strong and consequential nation. The search for insight, however, need not be restricted to ancient history. America's own history offers instructive prologue for a strategic campaign plan centered on the "four Cs" of political reform: competition, collaboration, content, and citizenship.

Harnessing Stronger, Better, Cleaner Competition to Break the Party Duopoly and Better Serve the Country

In the late nineteenth and early twentieth centuries, the nation was dogged by business trusts exploiting concentrated market power to crowd out competition for self-benefit at public expense. Monied interests fought hard to maintain their undue privilege. Yet, with public interest clearly at stake, Congress found its way to pass a series of landmark measures to foster healthy market competition. Bipartisan majorities approved the Sherman Antitrust Act, outlawing monopolies, the Clayton Antitrust Act prohibited anticompetitive mergers, and the Federal Trade Commission Act instituted authorities to investigate and prevent "anti-competitive activities and unfair or deceptive acts or practices affecting commerce."[3]

Just as stifled economic competition sustained corrupt business trusts, so restraint of political competition has perpetuated an unhealthy party duopoly. The time has come to apply the principle of competition that stimulated US economic prosperity to the nation's political culture so that it can better serve the public interest:

- Make legislative races more competitive by putting the pen for drawing congressional boundaries in the hands of independent bodies responsible for applying public interest criteria to the maps.

- Open primary elections in every state so Independents can take part in deciding what candidates appear on the general election ballot.
- Foster ballot access for third parties and Independents.
- Adopt fusion voting and ranked choice voting.
- Replace winner-take-all electoral vote apportionment with a prorated system.
- Keep testing the Citizens United decision until the courts outlaw the ability of Super PACs and other organizations to receive and spend unlimited and undisclosed contributions from corporations, unions, and individuals to influence elections.
- Strengthen and enforce court-sanctioned rules and standards to rid the public perception that Super PAC spending is coordinated with candidates or their campaigns.
- Require congressional campaigns to raise the bulk of their contributions from their home districts (House) and states (Senate).
- Require candidates to publicly post their fundraising (physical and electronic) mailings and their fundraising event schedules.
- Establish public campaign financing alternatives that provide for voluntary adherence to spending limits, encourage small donations, reduce barriers to candidacy, and broaden citizen participation and trust in campaigns and elections.

Strengthening Collaboration, Cohesion, and Mission Focus

Until the mid-1980s, the military services (then composed of the Air Force, Army, Coast Guard, Marine Corps, and Navy) operated in autonomous and often competitive stovepipes. Interservice rivalry and uncoordinated operations impaired mission success and endangered national security. In 1986, against the Department of Defense's rigid opposition, Congress overwhelmingly approved the Goldwater-Nichols Department of Defense Reorganization Act.[4] The law overhauled the defense establishment to improve the interoperability and unity of effort among the services to facilitate mission success. The time has arrived to flip the script and bring greater jointness and focus on mission into our civilian and political services:

- Establish strategic planning and coordination bodies and mechanisms between the Republican and Democratic congressional leadership; House and Senate leaders; Congress and the administration; and among federal, state, and local elected leaders.
- Streamline congressional committees and establish inter-committee task forces purposed to address complex problems comprehensively rather than through disciplinary and jurisdictional stovepipes.
- Return to congressional "regular order" of processing legislation.
- Formalize advanced training and continuing education for elected officials in mission-critical subject matter.

- Require Congress to regularly report to the public on the status of legislation to update departments, agencies, programs, and policies with expired or expiring authorizations.
- Ban congressional campaign fundraisers and electioneering activities while Congress is in session.
- Protect the public from congressional dereliction of duty by eliminating government shutdown and brinkmanship, including through two-year budgeting and automatic continuing resolution funding.
- Eliminate the ability of a solitary member to anonymously hold up the Senate from proceeding to consider bills and nominations.

Improving the Content Informing the Nation's Politics and Public Debate

Nothing is more instrumental to social stability and to personal and public health than a reliable, safe, and healthy food supply. From its inception in the early twentieth century, the Food and Drug Administration took incremental action to compel ingredient and nutrition labeling. As the public call for transparency intensified, so did Food and Drug Administration efforts to provide better consumer information. Food and beverage companies responded to the pressure by providing more information and offering healthier options. In 1990, Congress passed the Nutrition Labeling and Education Act to require informative nutrition labeling. There is clear public demand for accurate public affairs news and information and a more trustworthy information supply chain and for making truth, facts, and agendas more transparent to the electorate. Just as the public has a right to know the provenance and content of what the food industry offers to put into our bodies, people need and deserve to know more about what the political and information industries offer to put into our minds.

- Label media content as news, opinion, or hybrid journalism.
- Establish a civil society sponsored service to badge news services that profess and practice adherence to professional journalism ethics and standards.
- Clearly identify the sponsor of all political ads and electioneering communications.
- Promote public access to and use of trusted third-party verification services that spotlight and label fake news, disinformation, and hoaxes, including in news feeds and electioneering content.
- Develop and deploy technology to identify doctored video and audio, and weed out bots impersonating human beings sharing news and political commentary.
- Employ bipartisan or nonpartisan citizen commissions to set the number, format, and topics to be covered in candidate debates for public office.

Promoting Good Citizenship, Civics Literacy, and Public Service

The need for a well-educated public properly prepared to assume its obligations in democracy was well established from the nation's infancy. Over time, compulsory elementary and some level of secondary education became a legal requirement in every state. Personal empowerment is provided by a strong education, a connection reinforced within families, communities, the workplace, and civic and religious institutions. It's time to embrace the reality that civics literacy and a strong sense of citizenship, like proficiency in the three Rs and basic arts and sciences, is vital to an individual's preparation for the responsibilities of self-government and to national success. Democracy thrives when the public possesses a strong understanding of its principles and values, and knowledge of the country's civic institutions and processes. A prerequisite going hand in hand with civic literacy toward a stronger union and better future was expressed with perfect clarity by the National Commission on Military, National, and Public Service: to establish a "robust culture of service characterized by an expectation that all Americans participate in service of some kind, at some point in their lifetime."[5] Doing so will strengthen the bonds of citizenship and sharpen our sense of common purpose and shared fate core to the country's general welfare and, ultimately, to the maintenance of our personal freedoms.

- Implement a comprehensive national campaign to improve civics education through rigorous elementary, secondary, and university requirements and standards; curriculum; and accessible public information programming.
- Enact the recommendations of the National Commission on Military, National, and Public Service published on March 25, 2020, centered on programming increased civic education and service learning as well as expansion of programs under AmeriCorps.[6]
- Establish a US Civil Service Academy modeled after the US military academies, and modernize public sector human capital management and professional development.

EVOLUTION

The major reform movements from the twentieth-century described above is prologue to the fight for political modernization today. Each sought fundamental change at odds with entrenched powers and patterns. In all four cases, the country was able to rise above partisanship and the resistance of narrow interests to serve the public good, fulfilling the whole hope of democracy in the capacity for peaceful, positive evolution.

Fundamental reform, however, is impossible without a committed people's movement to advance it. On this point, US history provides another model. A resolute civil rights movement energized by righteous and ultimately irresistible principles produced the reforms instituted by the major civil rights acts and measures of the 1960s. When the nation's integrity hung in the balance, constitutional values and national character overcame an intractable status quo.

Then as now, the movement demanded that the nation look not only to its laws but also to its conscience. Political reform requires kindred national introspection and boldness. Fundamentally, clean politics and good government are civil rights. Securing them requires evolutionary thinking and public demand to overcome ignorant and deeply rooted political prejudices and injustice.

Successful movements possess common characteristics that set them in motion and see them through. "Ships" are needed to overcome "isms." The first is courageous *leadership* at both ends of Pennsylvania Avenue and from our governors, mayors, and tribal leaders; the private sector; and civil society. Nothing about modernizing the US political system will be easy given the scope of change required and the obstinate resistance that will require courageous, visionary leaders across the country to overcome.

Success in restoring the health and vibrancy of American democracy has little chance without resuscitating respect for *citizenship* in which the enjoyment of personal liberties is matched by common reverence for community responsibilities. The Constitution begins with the word "we" not "they," "them," or "others." In his first message to Congress, Lincoln said of the struggle for union, "This is essentially a people's contest . . . it is a struggle for maintaining in the world, that form and substance of government, whose leading object is, to elevate the condition of men—to lift artificial weights from all shoulders—to clear the paths of laudable pursuit for all—to afford all, an unfettered start, and a fair chance, in the race of life."[7] His words state the struggle before us. It, too, is a people's contest. Without good, participatory citizenship, the quality of our politics and the public institutions of, by, and for we the people will further decline. And until every American sees that the fate of our individual freedoms and pursuit of happiness is vested in the strength of our teamwork and unity, we risk all.

Hopes for the integrity of politics, competency of government, and future of the American experiment require superb *partnership*. Many of the essential reforms must be implemented by government at all levels. Each requires the active participation of the country's nongovernment and civic institutions. Particularly when the country is in peril, jurisdictional turf and bureaucratic stovepipes must give way to common purpose. Partisans have a political right to fight for their views but a patriotic duty to measure reform not by how it helps one party over the other but by its fairness and effectiveness at promoting stronger democracy. "Where the integrity and honor of the nation is involved," said House Republican leader Joe Martin to FDR following the attack on Pearl Harbor, "there is only one party."[8]

Democracy typically works slowly. Public opinion takes time to gain momentum. Though gradually, energy builds—and when the need is undeniable, reform becomes irresistible. The conviction that Washington is broken has never been stronger. Four of five voters polled in 2018 favored bipartisan political reform (85 percent of Democrats, 81 percent of Independents, and 78 percent of Republicans).[9] Calls for reform are gaining steam from the growing number of former members of Congress and senior officials who perceive a nation jeopardized by a political system that no longer serves the country or the cause of democracy as it should. We owe it to those who submit themselves to elective service to make the system worthy of their sacrifices. And success will attract many more of our best citizens to service.

OPPORTUNITY IN CRISIS

The accumulation of unsolved national problems is evidence enough of the need, but the degraded character of the political process and the normalization of partisan animosity bleeding into hatred have created an urgency for action. Immediately following a crisis is often the choicest time for national reset and reform. The years after World War II saw a battery of legislation setting the nation's course with clear and convincing strategic vision. The Employment Act of 1947 established the aims of national economic policy to maximize employment, productivity, and purchasing power, setting the stage for the prosperity to follow. The National Security Act of 1947 transformed the nation's military and intelligence establishment, laying the groundwork to win the Cold War. Racial integration of the military that same year helped lay the foundation for broader civil rights measures to come.

The nation must seize the opportunity to pivot from the internal strife and the death and devastation of the COVID-19 pandemic to find its better self. Glimpsing how quickly circumstances can turn against us should inspire the energy and will to mend political and social divisions, reverse the political culture's dysfunction, and reinvigorate democratic processes to make us stronger and more resilient. The hope of success rests in the fact that despite the ugliness of today's politics, Americans still have far more commonalities than differences—most importantly, shared principles. But even amid deep division over social and cultural issues and what seems like an unbridgeable red and blue American political map, less actually separates the two major parties than at any time in our history. After the rhetoric is peeled away and policy differences are boiled down to their essentials, they can most often be measured in degrees rather than compass points. The real question is where we are going not as parties but as a nation. Two other "ships" will be necessary to carry us forward: *bipartisanship* and *kinship*.

Reform will likely not yield a new major party to save the day anytime soon. Fostering greater choice and competition, however, will take bipartisan commitment to break the grip of Politics Inc. and make the parties more responsive to public interest and national need. Undoing its structures that empower the political fringes should make democracy more representative and restore a rational center in Congress. Reform will make the role of money in politics less dominant and corrosive. Campaigns will be cleaner. The good achieved by responsible media and advanced technology will prevail over their darker sides. A more engaged and better-informed citizenry will serve as the foundation for sustaining and accelerating progress. Overall, an improved political culture will restore American kinship and foster the human capital and sound democratic processes needed to meet challenges now and in the future.

RESTORING TRUST

If reform accomplishes but one thing, it must be to restore trust and reverse the sense of alienation permeating the country. By far the most dangerous deficit plaguing America is the accelerating shortfall in public confidence in our institutions, leaders, and public processes. Without restoring trust, very little good is possible.

A curious and unique feature of American politics is that often a president's most celebrated accomplishments are those not entirely consistent with their party's philosophical bent or priorities. To give just a few examples, only Lyndon Johnson, a southern Democrat, could have led passage of the major civil rights laws of the 1960s, and only Nixon, the staunch anticommunist, could have opened the door to US-China relations in the 1970s. In the following decade, only Ronald Reagan, the hawk, could have accomplished arms control with the Soviets. George H. W. Bush, a pro-business Republican, led a major strengthening of the Clean Air Act in the late 1980s, and his successor, Democrat Bill Clinton, produced welfare reform. The X factor in each case was trust. Leaders used their influence and authority to bring their respective party along in a project it was disinclined to embrace. Concern that the initiative might be damaging was assuaged by the political stripes of the leader taking up the charge. History suggests that it will take a Republican to marshal the nation to address climate change and a Democrat to overhaul America's global economic competitiveness. Imagine the possibilities if the political system cultivated the bipartisan trust necessary for each side to overcome party biases to do what must be done for the good of the country other than in the most extraordinary circumstances.

SUNRISE OR SUNSET

During the precarious months in 1787 as the delegates to the Constitutional Convention toiled over their difficult and uncertain task, George Washington presided over the assembly from a mahogany chair still on display at Independence National Historical Park in Philadelphia. The chair's backing is inlaid with a shining half sun perched on a horizon.[10] For Benjamin Franklin, completion of the charter answered a question that had nagged him throughout the proceedings. "I have often looked at that behind the president without being able to tell whether it was rising or setting," said Franklin. "But now I . . . know that it is a rising . . . sun."[11]

The same question, whether it will be national dawn or dusk, tries and tests every American generation in its own way. Then, the trial was establishing democracy. The test now is keeping it. Can the United States ensure that democracy survives the internet age? Even more, can we seize the opportunity to make it an epoch of unrivaled human advancement? If the answer is to be yes and the country is to pass the gift of freedom to the next generation stronger and better than we received it, political reform is the only path.

America's global standing and influence for the remainder of this century will be shaped by the decisions we make today. Ours is more than a struggle for the country's own liberty, prosperity, and security. A US exit from global leadership would be a tragedy for civilization and for the cause of human rights and freedom. The country must get out ahead of change in a fast-evolving world—making our politics more responsive and dutiful and our government more agile, strategic, and decisive. Otherwise, we cannot possibly hope to meet the gathering challenges ahead.

The difficulty of the task cannot be overestimated, but it can be overcome by marshalling the country's signature courage and passion, inspired by a sober understanding of the stakes—all that is to be gained if we get it right and all that will be lost if we do not. As formidable as the mission might be, we have every cause to embark on it with a sense of optimism. History shows that nothing is beyond the country's grasp when the stakes are clear and the nation's resolve is firm.

President Eisenhower liked to echo the admonition "America is great because it is good; if America ever ceases to be good, America will cease to be great."[12] For this reason, the path of reform must be lit by a reaffirmation of basic virtues that ennoble and sustain democracy, particularly decency and respect, the absence of which John Adams predicted would be the undoing of popular government.[13]

When listening to the partisan acrimony dominating the discourse in congressional chambers, on the political talk shows, and in the nation's chatrooms, it's hard not to think about how the bitterness and disrespect that characterizes our public discourse falls on the ears of young service members standing dangerous posts abroad. They know, as we know, that overcoming the enormous challenges we face requires national unity and sense of purpose, not wild partisan warfare. Reform should be inspired by them, by those who saved democracy and should never have to hate leaving the country the way it is, and by our children.

America is a work in progress and always will be. On the obverse side of the Great Seal of the United States is an unfinished pyramid. It signifies strength and duration but also more work to be done. The arc of history bends toward goodness and justice, provided we keep at what Lincoln referred to as the unfinished work of freedom such "that government of the people, by the people, for the people shall not perish from the earth." Above the pyramid is an eye, symbolizing Providence watching over humanity and the American cause. Below the pyramid is written "*novus ordo seclorum*," meaning "a new order for the ages."

The responsibility of carrying on our unfinished work will soon pass to a new generation. Fulfilling the mission will require them to be the next Greatest Generation and imposes on all Americans a duty to help prepare the way. Guided by a clear understanding of the past, a true respect for freedom and democracy, and a well-informed vision for the future, the new order can be renewed for the ages to come. The cause is just. The time is now.

E pluribus unum.

Notes

CHAPTER 1

1. Noemie Bisserbe, "'I Didn't Want Any Medals': Last D-Day Veterans Make Poignant Return to Normandy," *Wall Street Journal,* June 5, 2019, https://www.wsj.com/articles/d-day -veterans-and-world-leaders-converge-in-normandy-11559727001.

2. Kim Parker, Rich Morin, and Juliana Menasce Horowitz, "Looking to the Future Public Sees an America in Decline on Many Fronts," Pew Research Center, March 21, 2019, https:// www.pewsocialtrends.org/2019/03/21/worries-priorities-and-potential-problem-solvers/.

3. Lee Rainie, "Trust, Facts, Democracy," Pew Research Center, December 18, 2018, https://www.pewresearch.org/internet/2018/12/18/trust-facts-democracy/.

4. "Public Trust in Government: 1958–2019," Pew Research Center, April 11, 2019, https://www.pewresearch.org/politics/2019/04/11/public-trust-in-government-1958-2019/.

5. Lydia Saad, "Trump and Clinton Finish with Historically Poor Images," Gallup, November 8, 2016, https://news.gallup.com/poll/197231/trump-clinton-finish-historically -poor-images.aspx.

6. Ron Fournier, "The Worst of All Worlds," *Atlantic,* March 16, 2016, https://www.the atlantic.com/politics/archive/2016/03/clinton-vs-trump-the-worst-of-all-worlds/474024/.

7. Marian Currinder, Michael Beckel, Amisa Ratliff, and Sydney Richards (contributor), "Why We Left Congress, How the Legislative Branch Is Broken and What We Can Do about It," R Street / Issue One, accessed January 25, 2021, https://www.issueone.org/wp-content/ uploads/2018/12/Why-We-Left-Congress-Report.pdf.

8. Julie Steenhuysen, "Fauci Says U.S. Political Divisions Contributed to 500,000 Dead from COVID-19," Reuters, February 22, 2021, https://www.reuters.com/article/us-health-co ronavirus-fauci-idUSKBN2AM2O9.

9. "States of Play: Battleground & National Likely Voter Surveys on the Conventions & Protests," Change Research, September 9, 2020, https://changeresearch.com/post/states -of-play-battleground-wave-13/. *Note:* Please see the internal link entitled "Battleground Toplines" for the mentally fit/unfit polling data: https://changeresearch.com/wp-content/up

loads/2020/09/CNBC-CR_Battleground_Toplines_Wave-13_Sept-4-6-Wave-13_-9_4-9_6
.pdf.

10. Michael Balsamo, "Disputing Trump, Barr Says No Widespread Election Fraud," Associated Press, December 1, 2020, https://apnews.com/article/barr-no-widespread-election -fraud-b1f1488796c9a98c4b1a9061a6c7f49d.

11. Humeyra Pamuk and Arshad Mohammed, "NATO Secretary-General Calls for U.S. Election Outcome to Be Respected," Reuters, last modified January 6, 2021, https:// www.reuters.com/article/us-usa-election-nato/nato-secretary-general-calls-for-u-s-election -outcome-to-be-respected-idUSKBN29B2SU.

12. Steven Erlanger, "Trump-Biden Debate Prompts Shock, Despair and, in China, Glee," *New York Times*, September 30, 2020, https://www.nytimes.com/2020/09/30/world/europe/ trump-biden-debate-global-reaction.html?auth=login-google.

13. "The Budget and Economic Outlook: 2020 to 2030—Table 1-2: CBO's Baseline Projections of Federal Debt," Congressional Budget Office, January 2020, https://www.cbo .gov/publication/56073. *Note:* The estimated federal debt (subject to limit) is $36.231 trillion.

14. "As Debt Rises, Interest Costs Could Top $1 Trillion," Committee for a Responsible Federal Budget, February 13, 2019, https://www.crfb.org/blogs/debt-rises-interest-costs-could -top-1-trillion.

15. For eighth grade math and reading results, see "The Nation's Report Card," National Assessment of Educational Progress, 2019, https://www.nationsreportcard.gov/mathematics/ supportive_files/2019_infographic.pdf; for science results (fifteen-year-olds), see Programme for International Student Assessment, OECD, 2018, https://www.oecd.org/pisa/publications/ pisa-2018-results.htm.

16. "Transcript: Arne Duncan on 'Face the Nation,'" *Face the Nation*, August 5, 2018, https://www.cbsnews.com/news/transcript-arne-duncan-on-face-the-nation-august-5-2018/.

17. "The Growing Threat of Cyberattacks," The Heritage Foundation, accessed September 1, 2020, https://www.heritage.org/cybersecurity/heritage-explains/the-growing-threat -cyberattacks.

18. Angus King and Mike Gallagher, *United States of America, Cyberspace Solarium Commission*, U.S. Cyberspace Solarium Commission, CSC Final Report, 15, Washington, DC, March 2020, https://www.solarium.gov/home.

19. Lizzie Dearden, "Climate Change Is Destabilising the World and Becoming 'Threat to National Security,' US Security Chiefs Warn," Partnership for a Secure America, October 22, 2015, https://psaonline.org/climate-change-destabilising-world-becoming-threat-national -security-us-security-chiefs-warn/.

20. Samuel Issacharoff, "Democracy's Deficits," *The University of Chicago Law Review*, https://lawreview.uchicago.edu/sites/lawreview.uchicago.edu/files/09%20Issacharoff_SYMP_ Online.pdf, 485.

21. Michael J. Abramowitz, "Democracy in Crisis," Freedom House, accessed January 27, 2021, https://freedomhouse.org/report/freedom-world/2018/democracy-crisis.

22. "The Stories behind the Data 2018," Bill and Melinda Gates Foundation, accessed January 24, 2021, https://www.gatesfoundation.org/goalkeepers/report/2018-report/.

23. Nicholas Norbrook and Patrick Smith, "President Paul Kagame: 'Africa Has Been Struggling to Follow the West, and Now That System Is Crumbling,'" The Africa Report, July 9, 2019, https://www.theafricareport.com/15102/president-paul-kagame-africa-has-been -struggling-to-follow-the-west-and-now-that-system-is-crumbling/.

24. Sarah Repucci, "Freedom in the World 2020: A Leaderless Struggle for Democracy," Freedom House, accessed January 25, 2021, https://freedomhouse.org/sites/default/files/2020-02/FIW_2020_REPORT_BOOKLET_Final.pdf

25. Andrew Weisburd, Clint Watts, and Jim Berger, "Trolling for Trump: How Russia Is Trying to Destroy Our Democracy," War on the Rocks, November 6, 2016, https://waronthe rocks.com/2016/11/trolling-for-trump-how-russia-is-trying-to-destroy-our-democracy/.

26. Weisburd, Watts, and Berger, "Trolling for Trump."

27. Garrett M. Graff, "A Guide to Russia's High Tech Tool Box for Subverting US Democracy," *Wired*, August 13, 2017, https://www.wired.com/story/a-guide-to-russias-high-tech-tool-box-for-subverting-us-democracy/.

28. Christina Nemr and William Gangware, "Weapons of Mass Distraction: Foreign State-Sponsored Disinformation in the Digital Age," Park Advisors, March 2019, https://www.state.gov/wp-content/uploads/2019/05/Weapons-of-Mass-Distraction-Foreign-State-Sponsored-Disinformation-in-the-Digital-Age.pdf, 2.

29. George Washington, *Washington's Farewell Address to the People of the United States* (Washington, DC: U.S. Government Printing Office, 2000), https://www.govinfo.gov/content/pkg/GPO-CDOC-106sdoc21/pdf/GPO-CDOC-106sdoc21.pdf. *Note:* Per govinfo.gov, "George Washington's 'Farewell Address' is dated September 19, 1796, and was printed as a Senate Document in the 2nd session of the 106th Congress."

30. Washington, *Washington's Farewell Address*.

31. Washington, *Washington's Farewell Address*.

32. "Bono Turns Up the Volume for Social Enterprise," *Guardian*, November 14, 2012, https://www.theguardian.com/social-enterprise-network/2012/nov/14/social-enterpise-bono-georgetown.

33. Walt Kelly, "We Have Met the Enemy and He Is Us," Pogo, April 22, 1971, https://library.osu.edu/site/40stories/2020/01/05/we-have-met-the-enemy/.

34. Samuel Adams to Benjamin Kent, July 27, 1776, in *Collection: Samuel Adams Papers, Letter to Benjamin Kent*, Manuscripts and Archives Division, The New York Public Library, New York Public Library Digital Collections, https://digitalcollections.nypl.org/items/9076fc10-1a17-0134-93e7-00505686a51c#/?uuid=90896b10-1a17-0134-f5a6-00505686a51c.

35. D-day statement to soldiers, sailors, and airmen of the Allied Expeditionary Force, 6/44, Collection DDE-EPRE: Eisenhower, Dwight D: Papers, Pre-Presidential, 1916–1952; Dwight D. Eisenhower Library; National Archives and Records Administration.

36. Stephen E. Ambrose, *Citizen Soldiers: The US Army from the Normandy Beaches to the Bulge to the Surrender of Germany* (New York: Simon & Schuster, 1997), 473. See also: *Stephen E. Ambrose Legacy Society* (New Orleans: The National WWII Museum), accessed February 9, 2021, https://impact.nationalww2museum.org/wp-content/uploads/sites/72/2020/11/Stephen-E.-Ambrose-Legacy-Society-Brochure.pdf), 2.

37. "Third Inaugural Address of Franklin D. Roosevelt," The Avalon Project at Yale Law School, January 20, 1941, https://avalon.law.yale.edu/20th_century/froos3.asp.

CHAPTER 2

1. National Historical Publications and Records Commission, Founders Online, *From John Adams to Jonathan Jackson, 2 October 1780* (Washington, DC), accessed March 29, 2021,

https://founders.archives.gov/documents/Adams/06-10-02-0113. Original source: Gregg L. Lint and Richard Alan Ryerson, eds., *The Adams Papers, Papers of John Adams*, Vol. 10, *July 1780–December 1780* (Cambridge, MA: Harvard University Press, 1996), 192–93.

2. George Washington, *Washington's Farewell Address to the People of the United States* (Hartford, CT: Hudson and Goodwin, 1813), accessed September 25, 2017, Yale Law School, Lillian Goldman Law Library, The Avalon Project, http://avalon.law.yale.edu/18th_century/washing.asp.

3. "A Bad System Will Beat a Good Person Every Time," The W. Edwards Deming Institute, February 26, 2015, https://deming.org/a-bad-system-will-beat-a-good-person-every -time/. See also: Cecelia S. Kilian, *The World of W. Edwards Deming* (Knoxville, TN: SPC, 1992), 264, https://archive.org/details/worldofwedwardsd00demi/page/264/mode/2up?view=theater &q=bad+system.

4. U.S. Congress, Senate, *Party Division*, accessed August 7, 2021, https://www.cop.senate .gov/pagelayout/history/one_item_and_teasers/partydiv.htm.]

5. U.S. Congress, Senate, *Senators Representing Third or Minor Parties*, accessed February 6, 2021, https://www.cop.senate.gov/senators/SenatorsRepresentingThirdorMinorParties .htm; U.S. Congress, House of Representatives, *Party Divisions of the House of Representatives, 1789 to Present*, accessed February 6, 2021, https://history.house.gov/Institution/Party -Divisions/Party-Divisions/.

6. "Governors' Party Affiliation, 1900–2019," National Governors Association, revised December 14, 2018, Governors Affiliations 1900-2013, https://www.nga.org/wp-content/ uploads/2019/03/Governors-Affiliations-1900–2019.pdf. "State Partisan Composition," National Conference of State Legislatures, accessed February 6, 2021, https://www.ncsl.org/ research/about-state-legislatures/partisan-composition.aspx.

7. "Trends in Party Identification, 1939–2014," Pew Research Center, April 7, 2015, https://www.pewresearch.org/politics/interactives/party-id-trend/; Stephen Mihm, "The Easiest Political Force to Ignore Is Only Getting Bigger," *Bloomberg*, January 31, 2021, Political Polarization and Independent Voters in the U.S. - Bloomberg, https://www.bloombergquint .com/gadfly/political-polarization-and-independent-voters-in-the-u-s.

8. "Party Affiliation," Gallup, accessed February 5, 2021, Party Affiliation | Gallup Historical Trends, https://news.gallup.com/poll/15370/party-affiliation.aspx. *Note:* Data points from polling conducted January 4–15, 2021.

9. Lydia Saad, "Perceived Need for Third Major Party Remains High in U.S.," Gallup, September 27, 2017, https://news.gallup.com/poll/219953/perceived-need-third-major-party-remains-high.aspx.

10. Katherine M. Gehl and Michael E. Porter, *Why Competition in the Politics Industry Is Failing America: A Strategy for Reinvigorating Our Democracy* (Cambridge, MA: Harvard Business School, 2017), https://gehlporter.com/wp-content/uploads/2018/11/why-competition-in-the-politics-industry-is-failing-america.pdf, 1-2.

11. Gehl and Porter, *Why Competition in the Politics Industry Is Failing America*, 21.

12. Katherine M. Gehl and Michael E. Porter, *Why Competition in the Politics Industry Is Failing America: A Strategy for Reinvigorating Our Democracy* (Cambridge, MA: Harvard Business School, 2017).

13. "The Economist/YouGov Poll November 8-10, 2020 - 1500 U.S. Registered Voters," YouGov, accessed August 8, 2021, https://docs.cdn.yougov.com/q2rwpojo39/econTopline. pdf, 7.

14. Dwight D. Eisenhower, "Farewell Radio and Television Address to the American People—January 17, 1961," The American Presidency Project (UC Santa Barbara), https://www.presidency.ucsb.edu/documents/farewell-radio-and-television-address-the-american-people.

15. Gehl and Porter, *Why Competition in the Politics Industry Is Failing America*; John Raidt, *Whither America? A Strategy for Repairing America's Political Culture* (Washington, DC: Atlantic Council, November 2017), Whither_America_1115_web.pdf (atlanticcouncil.org).

16. "Party Committee Fundraising, 2019–2020," Ballotpedia, accessed December 28, 2020, https://ballotpedia.org/Party_committee_fundraising,_2019-2020.

17. *The Price of Power: A Deep-Dive Analysis into How Political Parties Squeeze Influential Lawmakers to Boost Campaign Coffers* (Washington, DC: Issue One, 2017), https://www.issueone.org/wp-content/uploads/2017/05/price-of-power-final.pdf. See also: "It's Time to Imagine a New Path Forward," Issue One, accessed February 22, 2021, https://www.issueone.org/imagine-a-new-path-forward/.

18. Marian Currinder, Michael Beckel, and Amisa Ratliff, Issue One, accessed August 9, 2021, https://www.issueone.org/wp-content/uploads/2018/12/Why-We-Left-Congress-Report.pdf, 10.

19. Daniel Hensel, "Reps. Massie and Kaptur Join the Rebellion," Issue One, May 26, 2016, https://www.issueone.org/reps-thomas-massie-and-marcy-kaptur-join-the-rebellion/. See also: Deirdre Shesgreen and Christopher Schnaars, "Lawmakers' Dues to Party: 'Extortion' or Team Effort?" *USA Today*, updated May 26, 2016, https://www.usatoday.com/story/news/politics/2016/05/25/lawmaker-dues-party-extortion-team-effort/84819738/.

20. Casey Burgat, "Problems with the 'Committee Tax' in Congress," The Brookings Institution, July 21, 2017, https://www.brookings.edu/blog/fixgov/2017/07/21/problems-with-the-committee-tax-in-congress/.

21. *The Price of Power*, 13.

22. Richard Harwood, "The Alienated American Voter: Are the News Media to Blame?" The Brookings Institution, September 1, 1996, https://www.brookings.edu/articles/the-alienated-american-voter-are-the-news-media-to-blame/.

23. Adam Sheingate, "The Political Consultant Racket," *New York Times*, December 30, 2015, https://www.nytimes.com/2015/12/30/opinion/campaign-stops/the-political-consultant-racket.html.

24. Shane Goldmacher, "Trump Lost the 2020 Election. He Has Raised $207.5 Million Since," *New York Times*, updated January 31, 2021, https://www.nytimes.com/2020/12/03/us/politics/trump-campaign-money.html.

25. Michael S. Rosenwald, "The NRA Once Believed in Gun Control and Had a Leader Who Pushed for It," *Washington Post*, February 22, 2018.

26. "National Rifle Association - Outside Spending," OpenSecrets.org, accessed August 10, 2021, https://www.opensecrets.org/orgs/national-rifle-assn/summary?id=d000000082.

27. Eileen A. J. Connelly, "NRA gives chief Wayne LaPierre 57% pay raise amid calls to step down," *New York Post*, November 16, 2019, https://nypost.com/2019/11/16/nra-gives-chief-wayne-lapierre-57-pay-raise-amid-calls-to-step-down/.

28. Christopher Moraff, "A Quick Timeline of the NRA's Descent into Madness," Phillymag.com, December 18, 2012, https://www.phillymag.com/news/2012/12/18/nra-timeline-gun-lobby/; see also: Peter Wallsten and Tom Hamburger, "Cautionary Tale for Obama: NRA's High Caliber Lobbying Bags Big Legislative Wins in States over Past Two Decades," *Washington Post*, January 16, 2013, https://www.washingtonpost.com/politics/cautionary-tale-for-obama-nras-high-caliber-lobbying-bags-big-legislative-wins-in-the-states

-over-past-two-decades/2013/01/16/410e2c5c-5f08-11e2-b05a-605528f6b712_story.html; Mike Weisser, "The NRA Wins Again on Armor-Piercing Bullets, but Common Sense Was Already Lost," *Huffington Post*, May 11, 2015, https://www.huffpost.com/entry/the-nra-wins -again_b_6846314.

29. Heidi Przybyla, "How the NRA Undercut the Last Big Gun Reform Effort," NBC News, updated March 1, 2018, https://www.nbcnews.com/politics/congress/ how-nra-undercut-last-big-gun-reform-effort-n852176.

30. Lydia Saad, "Americans Widely Support Tighter Regulations on Gun Sales," Gallup, October 17, 2017, https://news.gallup.com/poll/220637/americans-widely-support-tighter-regulations-gun-sales.aspx.

31. Erik Larson, "Private Planes for Family: NRA Spending That Drew Scrutiny," *Bloomberg Quint*, updated August 7, 2020, NRA's Long List of Financial Misdeeds as Claimed in N.Y. Lawsuit, https://www.bloombergquint.com/onweb/nra-s-long-list-of-financial-misdeeds -as-claimed-in-n-y-lawsuit. See also: Daniel Nass, "An Illustrated Guide to the NRA's Lavish Spending and Cozy Deals," The Trace, May 31, 2019, https://www.thetrace.org/2019/05/ nra-ackerman-lapierre-financial-misconduct-guide/.

32. Avik Roy, "How the AARP Made $2.8 Billion by Supporting Obamacare's Cuts to Medicare," Forbes, September 22, 2012, https://www.forbes.com/sites/theapothecary/ 2012/09/22/the-aarps-2-8-billion-reasons-for-supporting-obamacares-cuts-to-medicare/ ?sh=41202e8b5935.

33. Gerard Gianoli, "AARP's Interests Diverge from Its Members'," *Wall Street Journal*, August 29, 2019, https://www.wsj.com/articles/aarps-interests-diverge-from-its-members -11567120882.

34. "Can You Trust the A.A.R.P.?" *New York Times*, May 20, 1996, https://www.nytimes .com/1996/05/20/opinion/can-you-trust-the-aarp.html.

35. Patricia Barnes, "Once Again, Is AARP Advocating for Older Americans or for Itself?" *Forbes*, June 23, 2019, https://www.forbes.com/sites/patriciagbarnes/2019/06/23/ once-again-is-aarp-advocating-for-older-americans-or-for-itself/?sh=455b87f95795.

36. Louis DeNicola and Andrew Lisa, "Watch Out for These Scams Targeting Seniors," MSN.com, November 6, 2020, https://www.msn.com/en-us/money/personalfinance/watch -out-for-these-scams-targeting-seniors/ss-BB1aCi3l. See also: Russel Hanson, "AARP: Money First, Seniors Second," American Thinker, June 18, 2011, https://www.americanthinker.com/ articles/2011/06/aarp_money_first_seniors_second.html.

37. Kenneth P. Vogel, "The Rise of 'Scam PACs': Conservatives Sound Alarms about Self-Dealing Fundraisers," *Politico*, January 26, 2015, https://www.politico.com/story/2015/01/ super-pac-scams-114581.

38. "The Lincoln Project, Outside Spending Summary 2020," OpenSecrets.org / Center for Responsive Politics, accessed February 4, 2021, https://www.opensecrets.org/outsidespending/ detail.php?cmte=The+Lincoln+Project&cycle=2020; see also: Federal Election Commission, FEC Form 3X, Report of Receipts and Expenditures, FILING FEC-1498014 (Washington, DC, 2021), FEC Disclosure Form 3X for The Lincoln Project, https://docquery.fec.gov/ cgi-bin/forms/C00725820/1498014/.

39. Tamara Lytle, "Fraudsters Use Political Action Committees to Rip Off Older Americans," AARP, December 11, 2019, Fake PACs Cheat Campaign Donations from Older Americans, https://www.aarp.org/money/scams-fraud/info-2019/scam-pacs.html.

40. Sarah Kleiner, "'Scam PAC' Treasurer Sentenced to Federal Prison," The Center for Public Integrity, February 21, 2020, https://publicintegrity.org/politics/scam-pac

-scott-mackenzie-court-justice-prison/. See also: Megan Janetsky, "Scam PACs Line Pockets by Misleading Donors," OpenSecrets.org / Center for Responsible Politics, April 26, 2018, https://www.opensecrets.org/news/2018/04/scam-pacs-misleading-donors/.

41. Kleiner, "'Scam PAC' Treasurer Sentenced to Federal Prison."

42. Jennifer Bell, "About," *Drowning in Junk Mail* (blog), accessed February 3, 2021, https://drowninginmail.wordpress.com/tag/culturejamming/.

43. Bell, "About."

44. Thomas B. Edsall, "Democracy, Disrupted," *New York Times*, March 2, 2017, https://www.nytimes.com/2017/03/02/opinion/how-the-internet-threatens-democracy.html.

45. Samuel Issacharoff, *Outsourcing Politics: The Hostile Takeovers of Our Hollowed Out Political Parties* (New York: New York University School of Law, 2016), 2, https://www.ifs.org/wp-content/uploads/2017/01/Issacharoff-2016-Hostile-Takeover-Of-Political-Parties.pdf.

46. "The Waning Influence of American Political Parties," The Conversation US, March 31, 2016, https://theconversation.com/the-waning-influence-of-american-political-parties-56875.

47. Federal Election Commission, Democracy PAC, FEC Form 3X, Report of Receipts and Disbursements, Filing FEC-1494657 (Washington, DC, 2021), https://docquery.fec.gov/cgi-bin/forms/C00693382/1494657/.

48. Thomas B. Edsall, "What Motivates Voters More Than Loyalty? Loathing," *New York Times*, March 1, 2018, https://www.nytimes.com/2018/03/01/opinion/negative-partisanship -democrats-republicans.html.

49. National Archives, National Historical Publications and Records Commission, Founders Online, *John Adams to Thomas Boylston Adams, 2 September 1789* (Washington, DC), accessed March 29, 2021, https://founders.archives.gov/documents/Adams/04-08-02-0218. Original source: C. James Taylor, Margaret A. Hogan, Jessie May Rodrique, Gregg L. Lint, Hobson Woodward, and Mary T. Claffey, eds., *The Adams Papers, Adams Family Correspondence*, Vol. 8, *March 1787–December 1789* (Cambridge, MA: Harvard University Press, 2007), 407.

50. Edsall, "What Motivates Voters More Than Loyalty? Loathing." See also: Alexis Blue, "Political Scientist Describes the Rise of Negative Partisanship and How It Drives Voters," PHYS.org, October 22, 2020, https://phys.org/news/2020-10-political-scientist-negative -partisanship-voters.html; "Feelings about Partisans and the Parties," Pew Research Center, June 22, 2016, 1, https://www.pewresearch.org/politics/2016/06/22/1-feelings-about -partisans-and-the-parties/.

51. Richard Reeves, *Profile in Power* (New York: Simon & Schuster, 1993), 510.

52. E. E. Schattschneider, *Party Government* (New York: Farrar and Rinehart, 1942).

53. Sam Anderson, "The Media's Guide to Suppressing Voters - Here are five ways the media hurts third-party campaigns," Medium, July 28, 2020, https://medium.com/overt-politics/blame-the-media-for-americas-two-party-system-eb891d2d167a.

CHAPTER 3

1. Uri Friedman, "American Elections: How Long Is Too Long?" *Atlantic*, October 5, 2016, https://www.theatlantic.com/international/archive/2016/10/us-election-longest-world/501680/.

2. Dylan Grosz, "As Length of Presidential Campaigns Increases, 2020 Might Follow Suit," *Stanford Daily*, January 22, 2019, https://www.stanforddaily.com/2019/01/22/as-length

-of-presidential-campaigns-increases-2020-might-follow-suit/; Alex Seitz-Wald and National Journal, "Why the Presidential Race Starts Earlier Every Cycle," *Atlantic*, March 4, 2014, https://www.theatlantic.com/politics/archive/2014/03/why-the-presidential-race-starts-earlier -every-cycle/359535/?single_page=true.

3. Chester J. Pach Jr., "Dwight D. Eisenhower: Campaigns and Elections," UVA Miller Center, accessed February 5, 2021, https://millercenter.org/president/eisenhower/campaigns -and-elections.

4. The Upshot, "How Presidential Campaigns Became Two-Year Marathons," *New York Times*, April 17, 2015, https://www.nytimes.com/2015/04/17/upshot/how-presidential -campaigns-became-two-year-marathons.html.

5. Emma Roller, "Why This Election Feels Never-Ending," *New York Times*, September 6, 2016, https://www.nytimes.com/2016/09/06/opinion/campaign-stops/yes-it-does-feel-like -this-election-is-never-ending.html.

6. The Upshot, "How Presidential Campaigns."

7. Scott Piroth, "Selecting Presidential Nominees: The Evolution of the Current System and Prospect for Reform," *Social Education* 64, no. 5 (September 2000): 278, https://www .uvm.edu/~dguber/POLS125/articles/piroth.htm.

8. Elaine Kamarck, "The Urgent Need for Peer Review in the Presidential Nominating Process," The Brookings Institute, October 29, 2019, https://www.brookings.edu/policy2020/ bigideas/the-urgent-need-for-peer-review-in-the-presidential-nominating-process/.

9. Larry J. Sabato, "How the Campaign Season Got So Long," *Wall Street Journal*, October 11, 2011, https://www.wsj.com/articles/SB10001424052970203476804576615300476081190.

10. Sabato, "How the Campaign Season Got So Long."

11. "Partisans Agree: Presidential Election Will Be Exhausting," Pew Research Center, July 5, 2012, https://www.pewresearch.org/politics/2012/07/05/partisans-agree-presidential- election-will-be-exhausting/; Randolph T. Stevenson and Lynn Vavreck, "Does Campaign Length Matter? Testing for Cross-National Effects," *British Journal of Political Science* 30, no. 2 (2000): 217–35, https://econpapers.repec.org/article/cupbjposi/v_3a30_3ay_3a2000_3ai _3a02_3ap_3a217-235_5f00.htm.

12. Stephen M. Walt, "How Our Election Cycle Screws Up Our Foreign Policy," Foreign Policy, March 22, 2012, https://foreignpolicy.com/2012/03/22/how-our-election-cycle-screws -up-our-foreign-policy/.

13. Maksymilian Czuperski, John Herbst, Eliot Higgins, Frederic Hof, and Ben Nimmo, "Distract, Deceive, Destroy: Putin at War in Syria," Atlantic Council, April 2016, https:// publications.atlanticcouncil.org/distract-deceive-destroy/assets/download/ddd-report.pdf.

14. Rebecca Shabad, "Clinton Slams Four-Year Campaign Cycles," *The Hill*, December 3, 2013, https://thehill.com/blogs/ballot-box/presidential-races/191927-4-year-campaign-cycles -big-mistake-pres-clinton-says.

15. James Harvey Robinson, *The Human Comedy* (New York: Harper & Brothers, 1937).

16. Mark Leibovich, "'I'm the Last Thing Standing between You and the Apocalypse,'" *New York Times*, October 11, 2016, https://www.nytimes.com/2016/10/16/magazine/hillary -clinton-campaign-final-weeks.html.

17. Leslie Gornstein, "What Is Socialism? And What Do Socialists Really Want in 2020?," *CBSN Originals*, September 23, 2020, https://www.cbsnews.com/news/what-is-socialism/.

18. Martin Haselmayer, "Negative Campaigning and Its Consequences: A Review and a Look Ahead," *French Politics* 17 (2019): 355–72, https://link.springer.com/article/10.1057/ s41253-019-00084-8.

19. Jennifer D. Greer, "Evaluating the Credibility of Online Information: A Test of Source Advertising Influence," *Mass Communication and Society* 6, no. 1 (2003): 11–28, https://doi .org/10.1207/S15327825MCS0601_3.

20. Donald Green, "Do Negative Political Ads Work?," *Scientific American Mind*, September 1, 2013, https://www.scientificamerican.com/article/do-negative-political-ads-work/.

21. Denise-Marie Ordway and John Wihbey, "Negative Political Ads and Their Effect on Voters: Updated Collection of Research," *Journalist's Resource*, September 25, 2016, https:// journalistsresource.org/studies/politics/ads-public-opinion/negative-political-ads-effects -voters-research-roundup/.

22. John A. Henderson and Alexander Theodoridis, "Seeing Spots: An Experimental Examination of Voter Appetite for Partisan and Negative Campaign Ads," SSRN, July 14, 2015, SSRN-id2629915.

23. Frank Rich, "Nuke 'Em," *New York Magazine*, June 15, 2012, https://nymag.com/ news/frank-rich/negative-campaigning-2012-6/.

24. Jesse Byrnes, "Colin Powell to 2016 Candidates: 'Stop with the Nastiness,'" *The Hill*, March 7, 2016, https://thehill.com/blogs/blog-briefing-room/news/ 272042-colin-powell-to-2016-candidates-stop-with-the-nastiness.

25. Kyle Mattes and David P. Redlawsk, *The Positive Case for Negative Campaigning* (Chicago: University of Chicago Press, 2015); Denise-Marie Ordway and John Wihbey, "Negative Political Ads and Their Effect on Voters: Updated Collection of Research," *Journalist's Resource*, September 25, 2016, https://journalistsresource.org/studies/politics/ads -public-opinion/negative-political-ads-effects-voters-research-roundup/.

26. Mattes and Redlawsk, *The Positive Case for Negative Campaigning*; "2016 Election Study Published," Wesleyan Media Project, March 6, 2017, https://mediaproject.wesleyan .edu/2016-election-study-published/.

27. Erika Franklin Fowler, Michael Franz, and Travis N. Ridout, "The Big Lessons of Political Advertising in 2018," *The Conversation*, December 3, 2018, https://theconversation .com/the-big-lessons-of-political-advertising-in-2018-107673.

28. "Record Shattering 2020 Ad Volumes," Wesleyan Media Project, October 21, 2020, https://mediaproject.wesleyan.edu/releases-102120/.

29. Mattes and Redlawsk, *The Positive Case for Negative Campaigning*.

30. Seth McLaughlin, "Volume of Negative Political Ads Increased in 2018, Study Finds," *Washington Times*, October 30, 2018, https://www.washingtontimes.com/news/2018/oct/30/ volume-of-negative-political-ads-increased-in-2018/.

31. Erika Franklin Fowler and Travis N. Ridout, "Political Advertising in 2014: The Year of the Outside Group," *The Forum* 12, no. 4 (2014): 663–84, https://www.degruyter.com/ document/doi/10.1515/for-2014-5030/html; McLaughlin, "Volume of Negative Political Ads"; Karl Evers-Hillstrom, "Outside Spending in 2020 Election Surpasses $1 Billion, on Track to Break Records," Open Secrets, September 23, 2020, https://www.opensecrets.org/ news/2020/09/outside-spending-2020-on-track-to-break-record/.

32. Alan Abramowitz and Steven Webster, "'Negative Partisanship' Explains Everything," *Politico*, September/October 2017, https://www.politico.com/magazine/story/2017/09/05/ negative-partisanship-explains-everything-215534.

33. Harry Zahn, "Why 'Negative Partisanship' Is Flipping Politics on Its Head," *PBS NewsHour*, December 23, 2016, https://www.pbs.org/newshour/politics/negative-partisanship -flipping-politics-head.

34. Shanto Iyengar and Masha Krupenkin, "The Strengthening of Partisan Affect," *Advances in Political Psychology* 39, no. 1 (February 13, 2018): 201–18, https://doi.org/10.1111/pops.12487.

35. Nathaniel Rakich and Ryan Best, "There Wasn't *That* Much Split-Ticket Voting in 2020," FiveThirtyEight, December 2, 2020, https://fivethirtyeight.com/features/there-wasnt-that-much-split-ticket-voting-in-2020/.

36. Michael Lewis, "Has Anyone Seen the President?," *Bloomberg Opinion*, February 9, 2018, https://www.bloomberg.com/opinion/articles/2018-02-09/has-anyone-seen-the-president.

37. Doug Criss, "This Is the 30-Year-Old Willie Horton Ad Everybody Is Talking about Today," CNN, November 1, 2018, https://www.cnn.com/2018/11/01/politics/willie-horton-ad-1988-explainer-trnd/index.html.

38. Robert Mann, "How the 'Daisy' Ad Changed Everything about Political Advertising," *Smithsonian*, April 13, 2016, https://www.smithsonianmag.com/history/how-daisy-ad-changed-everything-about-political-advertising-180958741/.

39. Erika Fowler, "2012 Election Crushes Records for Campaign Advertising," Knight Foundation, February 14, 2013, https://knightfoundation.org/articles/2012-election-crushes-records-campaign-advertising/.

40. Lee Drutman, "How Hatred Came to Dominate American Politics," FiveThirtyEight, October 5, 2020, https://fivethirtyeight.com/features/how-hatred-negative-partisanship-came-to-dominate-american-politics/.

41. Matthew Finders, "Gotcha! Coronavirus, Crises and the Politics of Blame Games," *Political Insight* 11, no. 2 (May 27, 2020): 22–25, https://journals.sagepub.com/doi/full/10.1177/2041905820933371; Matthew Finders, "Democracy and the Politics of Coronavirus: Trust, Blame and Understanding," *Parliamentary Affairs*, June 23, 2020, https://doi.org/10.1093/pa/gsaa013.

42. Richard Harwood, "The Alienated American Voter: Are the News Media to Blame?," Brookings, September 1, 1996, https://www.brookings.edu/articles/the-alienated-american-voter-are-the-news-media-to-blame/.

43. Alex Isenstadt, "GOP Memo Urges anti-China Assault over Coronavirus," *Politico*, April 24, 2020, https://www.politico.com/news/2020/04/24/gop-memo-anti-china-coronavirus-207244.

44. "Trump Says Coronavirus Worse 'Attack' Than Pearl Harbor," *BBC News*, May 7, 2020, https://www.bbc.com/news/world-us-canada-52568405.

45. Jonathan Martin and Maggie Haberman, "A Key G.O.P. Strategy: Blame China. But Trump Goes Off Message," *New York Times*, October 6, 2020, https://www.nytimes.com/2020/04/18/us/politics/trump-china-virus.html.

46. Martin and Haberman, "A Key G.O.P. Strategy."

47. Kenneth P. Doyle, "Democratic Ad Surge Targets GOP Senators' Virus Response (1)," *Bloomberg Government*, August 18, 2020, https://about.bgov.com/news/democrats-target-gop-senators-virus-response-in-august-ad-surge/.

48. Janet Hook, "Campaigns Accentuate the Negative," *Los Angeles Times*, October 17, 2004, https://www.latimes.com/archives/la-xpm-2004-oct-17-na-attack17-story.html.

49. Lee Drutman, "This Voting Reform Solves 2 of America's Biggest Political Problems," *Vox*, July 26, 2017, https://www.vox.com/the-big-idea/2017/4/26/15425492/proportional-voting-polarization-urban-rural-third-parties.

50. Drutman, "How Hatred Came to Dominate American Politics."

51. Drutman, "How Hatred Came to Dominate American Politics."

52. Levi Boxwell, Matthew Gentzkow, and Jesse Shapiro, "Cross-Country Trends in Affective Polarization," Stanford University, June 2020, https://web.stanford.edu/~gentzkow/research/cross-polar.pdf.

53. "Political Polarization in the American Public," Pew Research Center, June 12, 2014, https://www.pewresearch.org/politics/2014/06/12/political-polarization-in-the-american-public/.

54. "How Partisans View Each Other," Pew Research Center, October 10, 2019, https://www.pewresearch.org/politics/2019/10/10/how-partisans-view-each-other/.

55. Edsall, "What Motivates Voters."

56. Edsall, "What Motivates Voters."

57. Lachlan Markay and Adam Rawnsley, "A Vile Website Doxxing Trump's Enemies Has Caught the Eye of the FBI," *Daily Beast*, December 11, 2020, https://www.thedailybeast.com/a-vile-website-doxxing-trumps-enemies-has-caught-the-eye-of-the-fbi.

58. Courtney Subramanian and Jordan Culver, "Donald Trump Sidesteps Call to Condemn White Supremacists—and the Proud Boys Were 'Extremely Excited' about It," *USA Today*, September 29, 2020, https://www.usatoday.com/story/news/politics/elections/2020/09/29/trump-debate-white-supremacists-stand-back-stand-by/3583339001/.

59. "George Floyd Protests: 'Boogaloo' Member Held in Precinct Attack," *BBC News*, October 24, 2020, https://www.bbc.com/news/world-us-canada-54670557.

60. Ann Banks, "Dirty Tricks, South Carolina and John McCain," *The Nation*, January 14, 2008, https://www.thenation.com/article/archive/dirty-tricks-south-carolina-and-john-mccain/.

61. "AAPOR Statements on 'Push' Polls," American Association for Public Opinion Research, accessed May 16, 2021, https://www.aapor.org/Education-Resources/Resources/AAPOR-Statements-on-Push-Polls.aspx.

62. Larry J. Sabato, "When Push Comes to Poll," *Washington Monthly* 28, no. 6 (June 1996): 26–31, https://www.uvm.edu/~dguber/POLS234/articles/sabato.htm; Evan Gerstmann and Matthew J. Streb, "Putting an End to Push Polling: Why It Should Be Banned and Why the First Amendment Lets Congress Ban It," *Election Law Journal* 3, no. 1 (2004), https://pdfs.semanticscholar.org/58e0/28ac58bc6a3ab1bd015bcc64bae6c9ea52a0.pdf.

63. Lauren Feeney, "Patterns of Ad Deception," Moyers & Company, May 11, 2012, https://billmoyers.com/content/patterns-of-ad-deception/.

64. Feeney, "Patterns of Ad Deception."

65. Elaine Kamarck, "A Short History of Campaign Dirty Tricks before Twitter and Facebook," Brookings, July 11, 2019, https://www.brookings.edu/blog/fixgov/2019/07/11/a-short-history-of-campaign-dirty-tricks-before-twitter-and-facebook/.

66. Alan I. Abramowitz and Steven Webster, "The Only Thing We Have to Fear Is the Other Party," Sabato's Crystal Ball, University of Virginia Center for Politics, June 4, 2015, https://centerforpolitics.org/crystalball/articles/the-only-thing-we-have-to-fear-is-the-other-party/.

67. Drew Desilver, "Near-Record Number of House Members Not Seeking Re-Election in 2018," Pew Research Center, April 11, 2018, https://www.pewresearch.org/fact-tank/2018/04/11/near-record-number-of-house-members-not-seeking-re-election-in-2018/.

68. David Freedlander, "An Unsettling New Theory: There Is No Swing Voter," *Politico*, February 6, 2020, https://www.politico.com/news/magazine/2020/02/06/rachel-bitecofer-profile-election-forecasting-new-theory-108944.

69. Kathleen Hall Jamieson, "PDF12: FlackChecking Political Sleaze," Personal Democracy Forum, YouTube video, 12:38, June 13, 2012, https://www.youtube.com/watch?v=zRqf9rAuvEM&feature=emb_title.

70. Jamieson, "PDF12: FlackChecking Political Sleaze."

71. Matthew Crain and Anthony Nadler, "Political Manipulation and Internet Advertising Infrastructure," *Journal of Information Policy* 9 (2019): 370–410, https://doi.org/10.5325/jinfopoli.9.2019.0370.

72. Fred Bergen, "West Virginia Push Poll Law," Insight Association, July 21, 2015, https://www.insightsassociation.org/legal-article/west-virginia-push-poll-law.

CHAPTER 4

1. U.S. Congress, Senate, Committee on Government Affairs, *Investigation of Illegal or Improper Activities in Connection with 1996 Federal Election Campaigns, Final Report*, 105th Cong., 2nd sess., 1998, S. Rep. 105-167, Vol. 1, 43, https://www.congress.gov/105/crpt/srpt167/CRPT-105srpt167-pt1.pdf.

2. U.S. Congress, Senate, Committee on Government Affairs, *Investigation of Illegal or Improper Activities in Connection with 1996 Federal Election Campaigns, Final Report*, 105th Cong., 2nd sess., 1998, S. Rep. 105-167, Vol. 1, 970, https://www.congress.gov/105/crpt/srpt167/CRPT-105srpt167-pt1.pdf.

3. U.S. Congress, Senate, Committee on Government Affairs, *Investigation of Illegal or Improper Activities in Connection with 1996 Federal Election Campaigns, Final Report*, 105th Cong., 2nd sess., 1998, S. Rep. 105-167, Vol. 2, 2914, https://www.congress.gov/105/crpt/srpt167/CRPT-105srpt167-pt2.pdf.

4. U.S. Congress, Senate, Committee on Government Affairs, *Investigation of Illegal or Improper Activities in Connection with 1996 Federal Election Campaigns, Final Report*, 105th Cong., 2nd sess., 1998, S. Rep. 105-167, Vol. 2, 2929, https://www.congress.gov/105/crpt/srpt167/CRPT-105srpt167-pt2.pdf.

5. "Integrity of the Institutions," Center for Security Policy, March 20, 1997, https://centerforsecuritypolicy.org/integrity-of-the-institutions-2/.

6. U.S. Congress, Senate, Committee on Government Affairs, *Investigation of Illegal or Improper Activities in Connection with 1996 Federal Election Campaigns, Final Report*, 105th Cong., 2nd sess., 1998, S. Rep. 105-167, Vol. 2, 2915, https://www.congress.gov/105/crpt/srpt167/CRPT-105srpt167-pt2.pdf.

7. *An Act to Regulate and Improve the Civil Service of the United States, U.S. Statutes at Large*, Vol. 22, 47th Cong., 2nd sess., Chap. 27 (1883): 403–7, https://www.loc.gov/law/help/statutes-at-large/47th-congress/session-2/c47s2ch27.pdf. See also: "Pendleton Act 1883," www.ourdocuments.gov, accessed May 17, 2021, https://www.ourdocuments.gov/doc.php?flash=false&doc=48.

8. "Federal Election Commission Annual Report 1980," Federal Exchange Commission (Commission's Office of Publications, 1981), 16, https://www.fec.gov/resources/cms-content/documents/ar80.pdf.

9. "Total Cost of Election (1998–2020)," OpenSecrets, Center for Responsive Politics, 2020, https://www.opensecrets.org/elections-overview/cost-of-election?cycle=2020&display=T&infl=Y.

10. "Total Cost of Election (1998–2020)," OpenSecrets, Center for Responsive Politics.

11. "Consumer Price Index (CPI) of All Urban Consumers in the United States from 1992 to 2020," Statista, January 2021, https://www.statista.com/statistics/190974/unadjusted-consumer-price-index-of-all-urban-consumers-in-the-us-since-1992/.

12. "Total Cost of Election (1998–2020)," OpenSecrets, Center for Responsive Politics.

13. John Oliver, "Congressional Fundraising," *Last Week Tonight*, April 3, 2016, YouTube video, 21:24, https://youtu.be/Ylomy1Aw9Hk.

14. Oliver, "Congressional Fundraising."

15. Trevor Potter, "A Republic—If You Can Keep It!: An Agenda for Our Democracy," speech presented at the Chautauqua Institution, Chautauqua, New York, July 4, 2016, https://campaignlegal.org/sites/default/files/Chautauqua percent202016 percent20Final.pdf.

16. Deirdre Shesgreen and Christopher Schnaars, "Lawmakers' Dues to Party: 'Extortion' or Team Effort?," *USA Today*, May 26, 2016, https://kaptur.house.gov/media-center/in-the-news/lawmakers-dues-party-extortion-or-team-effort.

17. William Gray, "Millions of Viewers Watch Issue One Explain the Price That Comes with Power in Washington," Issue One, May 31, 2017, https://www.issueone.org/millions-viewers-watch-issue-one-explain-price-comes-power-washington/.

18. Peter Schweizer, *Extortion: How Politicians Extract Your Money, Buy Votes, and Line Their Own Pockets* (Boston: Mariner Books, 2014).

19. Kate Ackley, "House Committee Leadership Is Becoming a Game of Musical Chairs," Roll Call, March 13, 2018, https://www.rollcall.com/2018/03/13/house-committee-leadership-is-becoming-a-game-of-musical-chairs/.

20. Andrea Seabrook and Alex Blumberg, "Take the Money and Run for Office," *Planet Money NPR*, March 30, 2012, http://www.npr.org/sections/money/2012/03/26/149390968/take-the-money-and-run-for-office.

21. Michael Beckel, "Behind the Price of Power: Q&A with former Rep. Jim Jones (D-OK)," Issue One, August 17, 2017, https://www.issueone.org/behind-price-power-qa-former-rep-jim-jones-d-ok/.

22. Michael J. Barber, Sharece Thrower, and Brandice Canes-Wrone, "For Congressional Donors, Politicians' Policy Preferences Are More Important Than Their Party," LSE US Centre, December 2, 2016, https://blogs.lse.ac.uk/usappblog/2016/12/02/for-congressional-donors-politicians-policy-preferences-are-more-important-than-their-party/.

23. Mitt Romney, "Massachusetts Senatorial Campaign Speech," C-SPAN, October 14, 1994, https://www.c-span.org/video/?60872-1/massachusetts-senatorial-campaign-speech.

24. "List of U.S. Congress Incumbents Who Did Not Run for Re-Election in 2020," Ballotpedia, accessed February 12, 2021, https://ballotpedia.org/List_of_U.S._Congress_incumbents_who_did_not_run_for_re-election_in_2020.

25. Norah O'Donnell, "Are Members of Congress Becoming Telemarketers?," CBSNews.com, April 24, 2016, https://www.cbsnews.com/news/60-minutes-are-members-of-congress-becoming-telemarketers/.

26. Steve Israel, "Confessions of a Congressman," *New York Times*, January 8, 2016, https://www.nytimes.com/2016/01/09/opinion/steve-israel-confessions-of-a-congressman.html.

27. Kate Ackley, "House Committee Leadership Is Becoming a Game of Musical Chairs," Roll Call, March 13, 2018, https://www.rollcall.com/2018/03/13/house-committee-leadership-is-becoming-a-game-of-musical-chairs/.

28. "Election Results, 2020: Incumbent Win Rates by State," Ballotpedia, updated February 11, 2021, https://ballotpedia.org/Election_results,_2020:_Incumbent_win_rates_by_state; "Reelection Rates Over the Years," OpenSecrets, Center for Responsive Politics, accessed February 12, 2021, https://www.opensecrets.org/elections-overview/reelection-rates.

29. Ryan Grim and Sabrina Siddiqui, "Call Time for Congress Shows How Fundraising Dominates Bleak Work Life," *Huffington Post*, December 6, 2017, https://www.huffpost.com/entry/call-time-congressional-fundraising_n_2427291.

30. Baxter Holmes, "Election 2020: How Sports Owners Hide Political Donations from Players and Fans," ESPN, October 29, 2020, https://www.espn.com/nba/story/_/id/30210730/election-2020-how-sports-owners-hide-political-donations-players-fans.

31. Jonathan Van Fleet, "Lawrence Lessig Compares the Number of Fundraisers between Presidents Reagan and Obama," Politifact, January 20, 2015, https://www.politifact.com/fact-checks/2015/jan/20/lawrence-lessig/lawrence-lessig-compares-number-fundraisers-betwee/.

32. Van Fleet, "Lawrence Lessig Compares."

33. "Donald Trump: Presidential Visits by State: Fundraisers—Detailed Schedule of Fundraisers," FactSquared, Inc., Factbase, accessed April 4, 2021, https://factba.se/topic/calendar-map#state-fundraiser.

34. Robert Pear, "In House, Many Spoke with One Voice: Lobbyists," *New York Times*, November 14, 2009, https://www.nytimes.com/2009/11/15/us/politics/15health.html.

35. Joshua L. Kalla and David E. Broockman, "Campaign Contributions Facilitate Access to Congressional Officials: A Randomized Field Experiment," *American Journal of Political Science* 60, no. 3 (2015): 454, https://onlinelibrary.wiley.com/doi/full/10.1111/ajps.12180.

36. Ira Glass, Alex Blumberg, Andrea Seabrook, and Ben Calhoun, "This American Life: 461: Take the Money and Run for Office," *Public Radio International*, transcript, March 30, 2012, https://www.thisamericanlife.org/461/transcript.

37. John W. Schoen, "Incumbents in Congress Are Hard to Beat—And a Lot of It Has to Do with Money," CNBC, April 26, 2018, https://www.cnbc.com/2018/04/26/here-is-why-incumbents-in-congress-are-hard-to-beat.html.

38. "In-District vs. Out-of-District," OpenSecrets, Center for Responsive Politics, accessed February 12, 2021, https://www.opensecrets.org/elections-overview/in-district-vs-out-of-district?cycle=2018&display=M.

39. "In-District vs. Out-of-District," OpenSecrets.org; see also: "Rep. Paul Ryan—Wisconsin District 01," OpenSecrets.org, Center for Responsive Politics, accessed February 12, 2021, https://www.opensecrets.org/members-of-congress/paul-ryan/contributors?cid=N00004357&cycle=CAREER.

40. "Report: 77% of Money in Senate Races Comes from Out-of-State," United States Public Interest Research Group, October 24, 2016, https://uspirg.org/news/usp/report-77-money-senate-races-comes-out-state; Lucia Geng, "From South Carolina to Maine, Out-of-State Donors Give Big in Senate Races," OpenSecrets.org, Center for Responsive Politics, October 22, 2020, https://www.opensecrets.org/news/2020/10/senate-races-outstate-donors.

41. "Buckly v. Valeo," Oyez, accessed February 12, 2021, https://www.oyez.org/cases/1975/75-436.

42. Stephanie Condon, "Why Is Congress a Millionaires Club?" CBS News, March 27, 2012, http://www.cbsnews.com/news/why-is-congress-a-millionaires-club/.

43. Soo Rin Kim, "The Price of Winning Just Got Higher, Especially in the Senate," OpenSecrets, Center for Responsive Politics, November 9, 2016, https://www.opensecrets.org/news/2016/11/the-price-of-winning-just-got-higher-especially-in-the-senate/.

44. Fredreka Schouten, "Trump Effect? Candidates Plow Record Amounts of Their Own Money into Congressional Bids," CNN.com, November 5, 2018, https://www.cnn.com/2018/11/05/politics/self-funding-candidates-record-midterms/index.html; "Top Self-Funding Candidates, 2017–2018," OpenSecrets.com, Center for Responsive

Politics, accessed January 31, 2021, https://www.opensecrets.org/elections-overview/top-self
-funders?cycle=2018.

45. "Top Self-Funding Candidates," OpenSecrets.org, Center for Responsive Politics.

46. Eliza Newlin Carney, "Senate Democrats Criticize Super PACS," Roll Call, February 1, 2012, http://www.rollcall.com/news/senate_democrats_criticize_super_pacs-212043-1.html
?pos=hbtxt.

47. Alina Selyukh, "McCain Predicts 'Huge' U.S. Campaign Finance Scandals," Reuters, March 27, 2012, https://www.reuters.com/article/us-usa-campaign-money/mccain-predicts
-huge-u-s-campaign-finance-scandals-idUSBRE82Q13P20120327; Jonathan Weisman, "Independent Senate Run in Maine Puts Parties in a Pinch," *New York Times*, May 6, 2012, https://www.nytimes.com/2012/05/07/us/politics/senate-control-could-hinge-on-angus-king
-of-maine.html.

48. Carney, "Senate Democrats Criticize Super PACS."

49. "Super PACs," OpenSecrets, Center for Responsive Politics, January 25, 2021, https://
www.opensecrets.org/political-action-committees-pacs/super-pacs/2020.

50. Ilya Marritz, "How Parnas and Fruman's Dodgy Donation Was Uncovered by Two People Using Google Translate," ProRepublica, February 5, 2020, https://www.propublica
.org/article/trump-inc-2020-how-parnas-and-frumans-dodgy-donation-was-uncovered-by
-two-people-using-google-translate.

51. Marritz, "How Parnas and Fruman's Dodgy Donation."

52. Brendan Fischer, "How Citizens United Led Directly to Trump's Impeachment," *Slate*, January 21, 2020, https://slate.com/news-and-politics/2020/01/citizens-united-john-roberts
-trump-impeachment.html.

53. Glass, Blumberg, Seabrook, and Calhoun, "Take the Money and Run for Office."

54. "Dark Money Basics," OpenSecrets, Center for Responsive Politics, accessed February 12, 2021, https://www.opensecrets.org/dark-money/basics.

55. "Dark Money Basics," OpenSecrets, Center for Responsive Politics.

56. Anna Massoglia, "'Dark Money' Groups Pouring Millions into 2020 Political Ads with Even Less Disclosure," OpenSecrets, Center for Responsive Politics, News & Analysis, September 11, 2020, https://www.opensecrets.org/news/2020/09/dark-money-pouring-920/.

57. Holmes, "Election 2020: How Sports Owners Hide Political Donations."

58. Jonathan Rauch, "How American Politics Went Insane," *Atlantic*, July/August 2016, https://www.theatlantic.com/magazine/archive/2016/07/how-american-politics-went-insane
/485570/.

59. "Donor Demographics," OpenSecrets.org, accessed January 30, 2021, https://www
.opensecrets.org/elections-overview/donor-demographics?cycle=2020&display=G.

60. "Who Are the Biggest Organization Donors? (see: Top Individual Contributors to Super PACs, 2019–2020)," Center for Responsive Politics, accessed January 30, 2021, https://
www.opensecrets.org/elections-overview/biggest-donors?cycle=2020&view=sp.

61. Michael Beckel, "Outsized Influence," Issue One, accessed May 17, 2021, https://www
.issueone.org/wp-content/uploads/2021/04/Issue-One-Outsized-Influence-Report-final.pdf.

62. Potter, "A Republic—If You Can Keep It!"

63. "Trust in Government: 1958–2015," in *Beyond Distrust: How Americans View Their Government*, ed. Pew Research Center, November 23, 2015, 2, https://www.pewresearch.org/
politics/2015/11/23/1-trust-in-government-1958-2015/.

64. Potter, "A Republic—If You Can Keep It!"; Molly Ball, "Obama Is Spending an Unprecedented Amount of Time Fundraising: Scandal?," *Atlantic*, June 14,

2012, https://www.theatlantic.com/politics/archive/2012/06/obama-is-spending-an-unprecedented-amount-of-time-fundraising-scandal/258526/; Lee Ann Potter, "A Republic—If You Can Keep It!," Library of Congress, September 8, 2016, https://blogs.loc.gov/teachers/2016/09/a-republic-if-you-can-keep-it/.

65. Howard Homonoff, "2020 Political Ad Spending Exploded: Did It Work?," *Forbes*, December 8, 2020, https://www.forbes.com/sites/howardhomonoff/2020/12/08/2020-political-ad-spending-exploded-did-it-work/?sh=286a1d043ce0.

66. Andrew Kreighbaum, "Bombs Away!," *Texas Tribune*, May 13, 2010, https://www.texastribune.org/2010/05/03/money-bombs-a-new-political-organizing-tool/.

67. "Buckly v. Valeo," *Oyez*.

68. "Williams-Yulee v. Florida Bar," Legal Information Institute, accessed February 12, 2021, https://www.law.cornell.edu/supremecourt/text/13-1499.

69. Dennis Romboy, "Utah House Votes to Ban A.G., Other State Offices from Fundraising during Legislative Session," DeseretNews, February 22, 2018, https://www.deseret.com/2018/2/22/20640484/utah-house-votes-to-ban-a-g-other-state-offices-from-fundraising-during-legislative-session.

70. Nathaniel Herz, "As Clock Ticked toward Session, Alaska Lawmakers Turned to Lobbyists for Cash," *Anchorage Daily News*, December 2, 2017, https://www.adn.com/politics/2017/01/21/as-clock-ticked-toward-session-alaska-lawmakers-turned-to-lobbyists-for-cash/.

71. *The Price of Power: A Deep-Dive Analysis into How Political Parties Squeeze Influential Lawmakers to Boost Campaign Coffers* (Washington, DC: Issue One, 2017), 19, https://www.issueone.org/wp-content/uploads/2017/05/price-of-power-final.pdf.

72. "Public Financing of Campaigns: Overview," National Conference of State Legislators, February 8, 2019, https://www.ncsl.org/research/elections-and-campaigns/public-financing-of-campaigns-overview.aspx.

73. Sarah Kliff, "Seattle's Radical Plan to Fight Big Money in Politics," *Vox*, November 5, 2018, https://www.vox.com/2018/11/5/17058970/seattle-democracy-vouchers.

74. "History of Campaign Finance Regulation," Ballotpedia, accessed February 12, 2021, https://ballotpedia.org/History_of_campaign_finance_regulation.

75. Aravind Boddupalli and Erin Huffer, "Rethinking the Presidential Election Campaign Fund," Tax Policy Center, July 25, 2019, https://www.taxpolicycenter.org/taxvox/rethinking-presidential-election-campaign-fund.

CHAPTER 5

1. "Separation of Powers—An Overview," National Conference of State Legislatures, May 1, 2019, https://www.ncsl.org/research/about-state-legislatures/separation-of-powers-an-overview.aspx.

2. "Reapportionment Act of 1929," PL 71-73, June 18, 1929, 46 *U.S. Statutes at Large*, 21–27.

3. The Public Law 17-13, the Reapportionment Act of 1929, permitted states to have an "at-large" district encompassing the full state, which a handful of states did until the early 1960s.

4. The District of Columbia and five US territories (American Samoa, Guam, Northern Mariana Islands, Puerto Rico, and US Virgin Islands) each elect a representative to Congress

who may vote in committees and on procedural matters but not on legislative matters taken up on the House floor.

5. James Madison, "Federalist No. 56: The Same Subject: The Total Number of the House of Representatives," New York Packet, February 19, 1788, http://avalon.law.yale.edu/18th_century/fed56.asp.

6. Erick Trickey, "Where Did the Term 'Gerrymander' Come From?," *Smithsonian*, July 20, 2017, https://www.smithsonianmag.com/history/where-did-term-gerrymander-come -180964118/.

7. Laura Royden and Michael Li, *Extreme Maps* (New York: Brennan Center for Justice, 2017), https://www.brennancenter.org/sites/default/files/publications/Extreme%20Maps%20 5.16.pdf.

8. Olga Pierce, Jeff Larson, and Lois Beckett, "Redistricting, a Devil's Dictionary," ProPublica, November 2, 2011, https://www.propublica.org/article/redistricting-a-devils -dictionary.

9. Pierce, Larson, and Beckett, "Redistricting, a Devil's Dictionary."

10. Megan Brenan, "Congress' Approval Drops to 18%, Trump's Steady at 41%," Gallup, July 30, 2020, https://news.gallup.com/poll/316448/congress-approval-drops -trump-steady.aspx?utm_source=alert&utm_medium=email&utm_content=morelink&utm _campaign=syndication; "Reelection Rate Over the Years," OpenSecrets.org, accessed February 19, 2021, https://www.opensecrets.org/elections-overview/reelection-rates.

11. "2016 House Race Ratings," *The Cook Political Report*, November 7, 2016, https:// cookpolitical.com/ratings/house-race-ratings/139361.

12. "2016 House Race Ratings," *The Cook Political Report*.

13. "2018 House Race Ratings," *The Cook Political Report*, November 5, 2018, https:// cookpolitical.com/ratings/house-race-ratings/187562; "2020 House Race Ratings," *The Cook Political Report*, November 2, 2020, https://cookpolitical.com/ratings/house-race-ratings.

14. Nathaniel Rakich, "Ed Markey Won, but It's Still Been a Rough Year for Incumbents," FiveThirtyEight, September 2, 2020, https://fivethirtyeight.com/features/ed-markey-won-but-its-still-been-a-rough-year-for-incumbents/.

15. Lee Drutman, "This Voting Reform Solves 2 of America's Biggest Political Problems," *Vox*, July 26, 2017, https://www.vox.com/the-big-idea/2017/4/26/15425492/proportional -voting-polarization-urban-rural-third-parties.

16. Nate Silver, "As Swing Districts Dwindle, Can a Divided House Stand?," *New York Times*, December 12, 2012, https://fivethirtyeight.blogs.nytimes.com/2012/12/27/as-swing -districts-dwindle-can-a-divided-house-stand?mtrref=undefined&gwh=E47478DC3EFE8FC F17E8E1B9113D809C&gwt=pay&assetType=PAYWALL.

17. "Margin of Victory Analysis for the 2018 Congressional Elections," Ballotpedia, accessed February 19, 2021, https://ballotpedia.org/Margin_of_victory_analysis_for_the _2018_congressional_elections.

18. "Congressional Careers: Service Tenure and Patterns of Member Service, 1789–2021," Congressional Research Service, January 5, 2021, https://www.everycrsreport.com/reports/ R41545.html#_Toc533777305.

19. Jonathan Rauch, "How American Politics Went Insane," *Atlantic*, July 2016, https://www .theatlantic.com/magazine/archive/2016/07/how-american-politics-went-insane/485570/.

20. Keith Poole, "The Decline and Rise of Polarization in Congress during the Twentieth Century," San Diego, University of California, January 1, 2008, https://www.researchgate .net/publication/253147367_The_Decline_and_Rise_of_Party_Polarization_in_Congress _During_the_Twentieth_Century.

21. "Featured Members," Problem Solvers Caucus, February 19, 2021, https://problem solverscaucus-gottheimer.house.gov/members.

22. Ronald Reagan, "Remarks at the Republican Governors Club Annual Dinner," October 15, 1987, http://www.presidency.ucsb.edu/ws/?pid=33559.

23. Christopher Ingraham, "This Is Actually What America Would Look Like without Gerrymandering," *Washington Post*, January 13, 2016, https://www.washingtonpost.com/news/wonk/wp/2016/01/13/this-is-actually-what-america-would-look-like-without-gerrymandering/?utm_term=.7bc2508160b5.

24. Harris Poll, "Americans Across Party Lines Oppose Common Gerrymandering Practices," November 7, 2013, https://theharrispoll.com/new-york-n-y-november-7-2013-ask-a-person-on-the-street-what-they-think-of-congress-and-you-likely-know-what-sort-of-response-youll-get-the-harris-poll-did-and-the-response-was-more-.

25. *Rucho v. Common Cause*, 588 U.S. 30 (2019).

26. Voting rights: Hearings before the Subcommittee on Civil and Constitutional Rights of the Committee on the Judiciary, 103rd Cong., 1st and 2nd sess. (1993 and 1994); U.S. Congress, Senate, Committee on the Judiciary, Understanding the Benefits and Costs of Section 5 Pre-Clearance, Hearing Before the Committee on the Judiciary, 109th Cong., 2nd sess., 2006, S. HRG. 109–545, Serial No. J–109–76, https://www.govinfo.gov/content/pkg/CHRG-109shrg29625/pdf/CHRG-109shrg29625.pdf.; U.S. Congress, House of Representatives, Committee on the Judiciary, Voting Rights Act: The Judicial Evolution of the Retrogression Standard, Hearing Before the Subcommittee on the Constitution, 109th Cong., 1st sess., 2005, Serial No. 109–74, 33, https://www.govinfo.gov/content/pkg/CHRG-109hhrg24504/pdf/CHRG-109hhrg24504.pdf.

27. Roy Cooper and Larry Hogan, "Take It from Us Governors: Politicians Shouldn't Draw Electoral Maps," *Washington Post*, March 24, 2019, https://www.washingtonpost.com/opinions/take-it-from-us-politicians-cant-be-trusted-to-draw-electoral-maps/2019/03/24/afd587b0-4cce-11e9-9663-00ac73f49662_story.html.

28. Nick Ravo, "The 1988 Elections: Connecticut; Lieberman Upsets Weicker in Close Race; Margin of Victory Spurs Recount," *New York Times*, November 9, 1988, https://www.nytimes.com/1988/11/09/nyregion/1988-elections-connecticut-lieberman-upsets-weicker-close-race-margin-victory.html.

29. Katherine Q. Seelye, "The 2000 Campaign: The Vice President; Lieberman Will Run with Gore; First Jew on a Major U.S. Ticket," *New York Times*, August 8, 2008, https://www.nytimes.com/2000/08/08/us/2000-campaign-vice-president-lieberman-will-run-with-gore-first-jew-major-us.html.

30. Associated Press, "Lieberman Concedes; Lamont Wins Primary," NBC News, August 7, 2006, https://www.nbcnews.com/id/wbna14228351.

31. Frank James, "Sen. Joe Lieberman Leaves Divided Legacy," NPR, January 19, 2011, https://www.npr.org/sections/itsallpolitics/2011/01/21/133056239/joe-lieberman-its-time-to-turn-page.

32. "Sore Loser Laws in the 50 States," Ballotpedia, accessed February 21, 2021, https://ballotpedia.org/Sore_loser_laws_in_the_50_states.

33. "Let Losers Try to Win," *Hartford Courant*, August 20, 2006, https://www.courant.com/news/connecticut/hc-xpm-2006-08-20-0608200102-story.html.

34. Chris McGreal, "Why Joe Lieberman Is Holding Barack Obama to Ransom over Healthcare," *Guardian*, December 16, 2009, https://www.theguardian.com/world/2009/dec/16/joe-lieberman-barack-obama-us-healthcare.

35. Barry C. Burden, Bradley Jones, and Michael S. Kang, "Sore Loser Laws and Congressional Polarization," *Legislative Studies Quarterly* 39 (2014): 302, https://ssrn.com/abstract =2354168.

36. Ron Elving, "Castle's Loss Is Victory for Partisanship," NPR, September 15, 2010, https://www.npr.org/sections/itsallpolitics/2010/09/15/129877484/castle.

37. Elving, "Castle's Loss Is Victory for Partisanship."

38. Randy E. Barnett and Lawrence Lessig, "The Real Reason You Can't Vote for an Independent Candidate," *Time*, August 3, 2016, https://time.com/4436805/lawrence -lessig-randy-barnett/.

39. Richard Winger, "Only Three States Have Never Had a Party on the Ballot without 'Independent' or 'Independence' in Party Name," Ballot Access News, July 6, 2019, https:// ballot-access.org/2019/07/06/only-three-states-have-never-had-a-party-on-the-ballot-without -independent-or-independence-in-party-name/.

40. "Coalition for Free and Open Elections," Coalition for Free and Open Elections, accessed February 20, 2021, http://www.cofoe.org/.

41. "Do We Really Have Free Elections?" Coalition for Free and Open Elections, accessed April 4, 2021, http://www.cofoe.org/.

42. "Coalition for Free and Open Elections," Coalition for Free and Open Elections.

43. Steven A. Holmes, "The 1992 Campaign: Third-Party Candidate; Perot Encounters Maze of Ballot Rules," *New York Times*, May 14, 1992, https://www.nytimes.com/1992/05/14/ us/the-1992-campaign-third-party-candidate-perot-encounters-maze-of-ballot-rules.html.

44. "Ballot Access for Presidential Candidates," Ballotpedia, accessed February 20, 2021, https://ballotpedia.org/Ballot_access_for_presidential_candidates.

45. "Lee v. Keith," Find Law, Thomson Reuters, accessed May 12, 2021, https://caselaw .findlaw.com/us-7th-circuit/1273720.html; U.S. Library of Congress, Congressional Research Service, Substitution of Nominees on the Ballot for Congressional Office, "Sore Loser" Laws, and Other "Ballot Access" Issues, RL33678 (Washington, DC, 2006), 13, accessed May 10, 2021, https://www.everycrsreport.com/files/20060929_RL33678_4525f99c7469b517512bb a909127a678cb44a8eb.pdf.

46. CA, S. 696, Sess. (2019–2020), https://legiscan.com/CA/text/SB696/2019; the stated purpose of the prohibition is to avoid "voter confusion"; Section 1. (a) (1) "When a qualified political party's name includes the phrase 'no party preference' or 'decline to state' or the word 'independent' it inherently misleads voters and creates voter confusion for voters who wish to not register with any political party and stay independent of political parties."

47. Office of the Spokesman, "Annex 3: Agreement on Elections" to *The Dayton Peace Agreement*, opened for signature on December 1, 1995: 7.5–7.6.

48. Marsha Mercer, "Progress Stalls for Minor Parties to Get on State Ballots," Pew Research, July 1, 2019, https://www.pewtrusts.org/en/research-and-analysis/blogs/ stateline/2019/07/01/progress-stalls-for-minor-parties-to-get-on-state-ballots.

49. Joe Holz, Heather Akin, and Kathleen Hall Jamieson, "Presidential Debates: What's Behind the Numbers?," Annenberg Public Policy Center, September 2016, https://cdn .annenbergpublicpolicycenter.org/wp-content/uploads/Presidential_Debates_white_paper _Sept2016.pdf.

50. "The Origins of Modern Campaigning: 1860–1932," Roosevelt House, Hunter College, accessed February 20, 2021, http://www.roosevelthouse.hunter.cuny.edu/seehowthey ran/portfolios/origins-of-modern-campaigning/.

51. Fergus M. Bordewich, "How Lincoln Bested Douglas in Their Famous Debates," *Smithsonian*, September 2008, https://www.smithsonianmag.com/history/how-lincoln-bested -douglas-in-their-famous-debates-7558180/.

52. "The First Televised Presidential Debate," United States Senate, November 4, 1956, https://www.senate.gov/artandhistory/history/minute/The_First_Televised_Presidential_ Debate.htm#:~:text=The%20typical%20answer%20to%20that,not%20appear%20in%20 the%20debate.

53. Bill Newcott, "Behind the Scenes of the First Televised Presidential Debates 60 Years Ago," *National Geographic*, September 25, 2020, https://www.nationalgeographic.com/ history/article/behind-scenes-first-televised-presidential-debates-nixon-jfk-1960.

54. "Fairness Doctrine," Reagan Library, January 6, 2021, https://www.reaganlibrary.gov/ archives/topic-guide/fairness-doctrine.

55. "The League of Women Voters and Candidate Debates: A Changing Relationship," League of Women Voters, accessed February 20, 2021, https://www.lwv.org/league-women -voters-and-candidate-debates-changing-relationship.

56. Michael Oreskes, "Dukakis and Bush Agree on the Rules for Debates on TV," *New York Times*, September 15, 1988, https://www.nytimes.com/1988/09/15/us/dukakis-and-bush -agree-on-the-rules-for-debates-on-tv.html.

57. "The League of Women Voters and Candidate Debates," League of Women Voters.

58. "The Commission on Presidential Debates: An Overview," Commission on Presiden- tial Debates, accessed February 20, 2021, https://www.debates.org/about-cpd/overview/.

59. Brian Doherty, "The Commission on Presidential Debate's 15 Percent Polling Crite- rion Must Go, Argues Lawsuit from Gary Johnson," *Reason* (blog), April 21, 2017, http:// reason.com/blog/2017/04/21/the-commission-on-presidential-debates-1.

60. Doherty, "The Commission on Presidential Debate's 15 Percent Polling Criterion Must Go."

61. Timothy Egan, "The Dumbed Down Democracy," *New York Times*, August 26, 2016, https://www.nytimes.com/2016/08/26/opinion/the-dumbed-down-democracy.html.

62. *Gary E. Johnson v. Commission on Presidential Debates*, No. 16-7107, U.S. Court of Appeals, 2017.

63. Mark Schreiner, "USF Researchers Use Biometric Sensors to Measure the Emotional Response to a Presidential Debate," WUSF Public Media, March 4, 2020, https://wusfnews .wusf.usf.edu/university-beat/2020-03-04/usf-researchers-use-biometric-sensors-to-measure -the-emotional-response-to-a-presidential-debate.

64. Chris Buckley, "For China's Leaders, U.S. Election Scandals Make the Case for One- Party Rule," *New York Times*, October 11, 2016, https://www.nytimes.com/2016/10/12/ world/asia/us-presidential-election-china.html?mcubz=1&_r=0.

65. Sarah Rainsford, "US Election 2016: Why Russia Is Celebrating Trump Win," BBC News, November 9, 2016, http://www.bbc.com/news/election-us-2016-37928171.

66. Jamey Keaten and Rod McGuirk, "World Reacts with Surprise, Worry to 1st Biden- Trump Debate," Associated Press, September 30, 2020, https://apnews.com/article/election -2020-joe-biden-virus-outbreak-donald-trump-japanese-yen-68ee6e1d6d3ae065afb37968fc a52f6b.

67. "Our Mission," Commission on Presidential Debates, accessed February 22, 2021, https://www.debates.org/about-cpd/.

68. Annenberg Working Group on Presidential Campaign Debate Reform, "Democratizing the Debates," Annenberg Public Policy Center, 2015, http://cdn.annenbergpublicpolicy center.org/wp-content/uploads/Democratizing-The-Debates.pdf.

69. "Coalition Statement," Open Debate Coalition, accessed February 22, 2021, http:// opendebatecoalition.com/coalition-statement.

70. "Coalition Statement," Open Debate Coalition.

71. John Gastil, *By Popular Demand: Revitalizing Representative Democracy through Deliberative Elections* (Berkeley: University of California Press, 2000).

CHAPTER 6

1. "The Universal Declaration of Human Rights," Universal Declaration of Human Rights, United Nations, accessed February 15, 2021, Universal Declaration of Human Rights | United Nations. See Article 21.1.

2. "The Universal Declaration of Human Rights," Universal Declaration of Human Rights.

3. Roy P. Basler, ed., *The Collected Works of Abraham Lincoln*, Vol. 2, 247–83 (Speech at Peoria, October 16, 1854) (New Brunswick, NJ: Rutgers University Press, 1953). See also: "Speech at Peoria, October 16, 1854," Abraham Lincoln.org, accessed February 21, 2021, http://abrahamlincoln.org/abraham-lincoln-freedom/speech-peoria-october-16-1854/.

4. Richard R. Beeman, "Perspectives on the Constitution: A Republic, If You Can Keep It," National Constitution Center, accessed August 6, 2021, https://constitution center.org/learn/educational-resources/historical-documents/perspectives-on-the-constitution -a-republic-if-you-can-keep-it.

5. James W. Ceaser and Andrew E. Busch, *The Perfect Tie: The True Story of the 2000 Presidential Election* (Lanham, MD: Rowman & Littlefield, 2001), 2–3, 180.

6. John Fund, "From the Magazine 'How to Steal an Election,'" *City Journal*, Autumn 2004, How to Steal an Election | Election Fraud is Expanding | Voting SSystem, https:// www.city-journal.org/html/how-steal-election-12824.html. See also: Kenneth Ackerman, *Boss Tweed: The Rise and Fall of the Corrupt Pol Who Conceived the Soul of Modern New York* (New York: Carroll and Graf, 2005).

7. Fund, "From the Magazine 'How to Steal an Election.'"

8. Ralph G. Martin, *The Bosses: The Flamboyant Story of America's Political Bosses, from Tammany to Today* (New York: Putnam, 1964); Alfred Steinberg, *The Bosses* (New York: Macmillan, 1972).

9. Irwin Unger and Debi Unger, *LBJ: A Life* (New York: Wiley, 1999), 139.

10. Stephen E. Ambrose, *Nixon, The Education of a Politician* (New York: Simon & Schuster, 1987), 606–7. See also: Edmund F. Kallina, "Was the 1960 Presidential Election Stolen? The Case of Illinois," *Presidential Studies Quarterly* 15, no. 1 (1985): 113–18, http://www.jstor.org/stable/27550168; Scott Bomboy, "The Drama behind President Kennedy's 1960 Election Win," *Constitution Daily*, National Constitution Center, November 7, 2017, https://constitutioncenter.org/amp/blog/the-drama-behind-president-kennedys-1960-election-win; Josh Zeitz, "Worried about a Rigged Election? Here's One Way to Handle It," *Politico*, October 27, 2016, https://www.politico.com/magazine/story/2016/10/donald-trump-2016-rigged-nixon-kennedy-1960-214395/.

11. David Greenberg, "Voter Fraud Is Nothing New: The 1960 Election of JFK," Helleniscope, November 5, 2020, https://www.helleniscope.com/2020/11/05/voter-fraud-is-nothing-new-the-1960-election-of-jfk/.

12. David Greenberg, *Nixon's Shadow* (New York: W. W. Norton, 2003), 189. See also: Greenberg, "Voter Fraud Is Nothing New."

13. U.S. Election Assistance Commission, *Election Official and Voter Toolkit*, Toolkit Resource, https://www.eac.gov/election-officials/election-official-voter-toolkit; "Voluntary Voting System Guidelines," U.S. Election Assistance Commission, accessed August 6, 2021, https://www.eac.gov/voting-equipment/voluntary-voting-system-guidelines. U.S. Library of Congress, Congressional Research Service, *Voluntary Voting System Guidelines* (VVSG): An Overview, by Karen L. Shanton, IN11592 Version 3 (updated February 11, 2021), https://crsreports.congress.gov/product/pdf/IN/IN11592. "Turbovote: We Help You Vote, No Matter What," accessed February 16, 2021, https://turbovote.org/.

14. *An Act to Establish National Voter Registration Procedures for Federal Elections, and for Other Purposes*, Public Law 103-31, *U.S. Statutes at Large* 107 (1993): 77–89.

15. John Samples, "On the Motor Voter Act and Voter Fraud," CATO Institute, March 14, 2001, https://www.cato.org/testimony/motor-voter-act-voter-fraud.

16. U.S. Election Assistance Commission, *Election Administration and Voting Survey, 2018 Comprehensive Report, A Report to the 116th Congress*, Silver Spring, Maryland, 2019, 18, accessed February 16, 2021, https://www.eac.gov/sites/default/files/eac_assets/1/6/2018_EAVS_Report.pdf.

17. Michael D. Shear, "Democratic Group Called iVote Pushes Automatic Voter Registration," *New York Times*, November 9, 2015, https://www.nytimes.com/2015/11/10/us/politics/democratic-group-called-ivote-pushes-automatic-voter-registration.html.

18. Matt Vasilogambros, "Glitches in California Embolden Automatic Voter Registration Foes," The Pew Charitable Trusts, Stateline, October 17, 2019, https://www.pewtrusts.org/en/research-and-analysis/blogs/stateline/2019/10/17/glitches-in-california-embolden-automatic-voter-registration-foes. See also: Shelby Fleig, "Concerns Mount over Implementation of Illinois' Historic Automatic Voter Registration Law," Social Justice News Nexus, December 14, 2017, https://sjnnchicago.medill.northwestern.edu/blog/2017/12/14/concerns-mount-implementation-illinois-historic-automatic-voter-registration-law/; Dan Petrella, "Illinois Election Officials Reveal More Issues with Automatic Voter Registration—This Time with Information from 16-Year-Olds Being Forwarded," Chicagotribune.com, January 30, 2020, https://www.chicagotribune.com/politics/ct-illinois-automatic-voter-registration-16-year-olds-20200130-wqooin23vff23cqrldgp2rrcbe-story.html.

19. "Voter Identification Requirements | Voter ID Laws," National Conference of State Legislatures, August 25, 2020, https://www.ncsl.org/research/elections-and-campaigns/voter-id.aspx#Two.

20. Justin Levitt, *The Truth about Voter Fraud*, Brennan Center for Justice at New York University School of Law, 2007, SSRN-id1647224.pdf, https://www.brennancenter.org/our-work/research-reports/truth-about-voter-fraud, 7.

21. *Debunking the Voter Fraud Myth* (New York: Brennan Center for Justice at NYU School of Law, undated), 1, https://www.brennancenter.org/sites/default/files/analysis/Briefing_Memo_Debunking_Voter_Fraud_Myth.pdf.

22. Zoltan L. Hajnal, Nazita Lajevardi, and Lindsay Nielson, "Do Voter Identification Laws Suppress Minority Voting? Yes. We Did the Research," *Washington Post*, February 15, 2017, https://www.washingtonpost.com/news/monkey-cage/wp/2017/02/15/do-voter-identification-laws-suppress-minority-voting-yes-we-did-the-research/.

23. *Citizens without Proof: A Survey of Americans' Possession of Documentary Proof of Citizenship and Photo Identification* (New York: Brennan Center for Justice at NYU School of Law, November 2006), 3, https://www.brennancenter.org/sites/default/files/legacy/d/download_file_39242.pdf; Emily Larsen, "Fact Check: Do Millions of Americans Not Have Government Photo ID?" Checkyourfact, December 2, 2018, https://checkyourfact.com/2018/12/02/fact-check-millions-government-photo-id/. See also: Denise-Marie Ordway, "New Insights on US Voters Who Don't Have Photo ID," *Journalist's Resource*, Harvard's Kennedy School Shorenstein Center on Media, Politics and Public Policy, August 16, 2018, https://journalistsresource.org/politics-and-government/voter-photo-id-law-research/.

24. Benjamin Highton, "Voter Identification Laws and Turnout in the United States," *Annual Review of Political Science* 20 (January 25, 2017): 149–67, 160.

25. "About the Election Fraud Database," The Heritage Foundation, accessed May 11, 2021, https://www.heritage.org/article/about-the-election-fraud-database.

26. Alan Blinder, "North Carolina Operative Indicted in Connection with Election Fraud," *New York Times*, February 27, 2019, https://www.nytimes.com/2019/02/27/us/mcrae-dowless-indicted.html.

27. "U.S. Attorney William M. McSwain Announces Election Fraud Charges Against Former U.S. Congressman and Philadelphia Political Operative," United States Department of Justice, United States Attorney's Office, Eastern District of Pennsylvania, July 23, 2020, https://www.justice.gov/usao-edpa/pr/us-attorney-william-m-mcswain-announces-election-fraud-charges-against-former-us.

28. Russell Berman, "A Tipping Point for Automatic Voter Registration?" *Atlantic*, February 29, 2016, https://www.theatlantic.com/politics/archive/2016/02/a-tipping-point-for-automatic-voter-registration/471099/.

29. Abby Phillip and Mike DeBonis, "Without Evidence, Trump Tells Lawmakers 3 Million to 5 Million Illegal Ballots Cost Him the Popular Vote," *Washington Post*, January 23, 2017, https://www.washingtonpost.com/news/post-politics/wp/2017/01/23/at-white-house-trump-tells-congressional-leaders-3-5-million-illegal-ballots-cost-him-the-popular-vote/.

30. Adam McCann, "Most and Least Diverse States in America," WalletHub, September 9, 2020, https://wallethub.com/edu/most-least-diverse-states-in-america/38262. See also: "STUDY: Hawai'i 3rd Most Diverse State in US," *Big Island Now*, September 21, 2019, https://bigislandnow.com/2019/09/21/study-hawaii-3rd-most-diverse-state-in-us/#:~:text=Hawai%E2%80%98i%20is%20the%20third%20most%20diverse%20state%20in,U.S.%2C%20followed%20by%20the%20second%20highest%20generational%20diversity; "Quick Facts, Hawaii," Race and Hispanic Origin, United States Census Bureau, accessed August 8, 2021, https://www.census.gov/quickfacts/fact/dashboard/HI,US/PST045219.

31. "Georgia Voter Identification Requirements," Georgia Secretary of State, accessed February 16, 2021, https://sos.ga.gov/index.php/elections/georgia_voter_identification_requirements2; Michael Buettner, "Little-Known Program Offers Free Photo IDs to Vote in Virginia," VoteRiders, September 28, 2018, http://voteriders.dreamhosters.com/news_item/little-known-program-offers-free-photo-ids-to-vote-in-virginia/; "Building Confidence in U.S. Elections: Report of the Commission on Federal Election Reform," Center for Democracy and Election Management, American University, September 2005, ii, https://www.legislationline.org/download/id/1472/file/3b50795b2d0374cbef5c29766256.pdf.

32. Eitan Hersh, "How Democrats Suppress the Vote: Off-Year Elections Have Much Lower Turnout, and Democrats Prefer It That Way," FiveThirtyEight, November 3, 2015, https://fivethirtyeight.com/features/how-democrats-suppress-the-vote/.

33. Hersh, "How Democrats Suppress the Vote."

34. Hersh, "How Democrats Suppress the Vote."

35. Sarah F. Anzia, *Timing and Turnout: How Off-Cycle Elections Favor Organized Groups* (Chicago: University of Chicago Press, 2014), 90, 93.

36. Anzia, *Timing and Turnout*, 124.

37. Anzia, *Timing and Turnout*, 118. See also: Hersh, "How Democrats Suppress the Vote"; Geoff West, "Timing Is Everything: Why 'Off Year' Elections Are a Turnout Buzz Kill," The Fulcrum, August 14, 2019, https://thefulcrum.us/voting/local-election-timing-turnout.

38. Hersh, "How Democrats Suppress the Vote."

39. R. J. Reinhart, "Faith in Elections in Relatively Short Supply in U.S.," Gallup, February 13, 2020, https://news.gallup.com/poll/285608/faith-elections-relatively-short-supply.aspx.

40. Phillip and DeBonis, "Without Evidence, Trump Tells Lawmakers"; Gabriel Sherman, "Experts Urge Clinton Campaign to Challenge Election Results in 3 Swing States," *New York Magazine*, November 22, 2016, https://nymag.com/intelligencer/2016/11/activists-urge-hillary-clinton-to-challenge-election-results.html.

41. Anthony Salvanto, Jennifer De Pinto, Fred Backus, Kabir Khanna, and Elena Cox, "CBS News Poll: Most Feel Election Is 'Settled' but Trump Voters Disagree," CBSNews.com, December 13, 2020, https://www.cbsnews.com/news/cbs-news-poll-most-feel-election-is-settled-but-trump-voters-disagree/.

42. Lawrence Norden, *Voting System Failures: A Database Solution* (New York: Brennan Center for Justice, 2010), 46, https://www.brennancenter.org/sites/default/files/2019-08/Report_Voting_Machine_Failures_Database-Solution.pdf.

43. J. Alex Halderman, "Hacking Democracy," EmTech Video, September 13, 2018, Hacking Democracy - MIT Technology Review, https://events.technologyreview.com/video/watch/halderman-michigan-hacking-democracy/.

44. Lucas Ropek, "Despite Risks, Some States Still Use Paperless Voting Machines," Govtech.com, October 29, 2020, https://www.govtech.com/elections/despite-risks-some-states-still-use-paperless-voting-machines.html.

45. U.S. Congress, Senate, Select Committee on Intelligence, *On Russian Active Measures Campaigns and Interference in the 2016 U.S. Election Volume 1: Russian Efforts Against Election Infrastructure with Additional Views*, 116th Congress, 1st sess., S. Rep. 116-290, Vol. 1, 8, https://www.intelligence.senate.gov/sites/default/files/documents/Report_Volume1.pdf. Link to all 5 volumes: https://www.intelligence.senate.gov/publications/report-select-committe-intelligence-united-states-senate-russian-active-measures. See also: Colleen Long and Christina A. Cassidy, "Public, Election Officials May Be Kept in the Dark on Hacks," Associated Press, October 21, 2019, https://apnews.com/article/voting-co-state-wire-fl-state-wire-ia-state-wire-politics-fd1c7c953ff841bebe742aa27debf839.

46. Jen Schwartz, "The Vulnerabilities of Our Voting Machines: When Americans Go to the Polls, Will Hackers Unleash Chaos?" *Scientific American*, Electronics, November 1, 2018, https://www.scientificamerican.com/article/the-vulnerabilities-of-our-voting-machines/.

47. Chris Jaikaran, *SolarWinds Attack—No Easy Fix*, U.S. Library of Congress, Congressional Research Service, January 6, 2021, https://crsreports.congress.gov/product/pdf/IN/IN11559.

48. Kim Zetter, "The Crisis of Election Security," *New York Times Magazine*, September 26, 2018, https://www.nytimes.com/2018/09/26/magazine/election-security-crisis-midterms.html.

49. Geoff Hing, Sabby Robinson, Tom Scheck, and Gracie Stockton, "How Private Money Helped Save the Election," American Public Media Reports, December 7, 2020, https://www.apmreports.org/story/2020/12/07/private-grant-money-chan-zuckerberg-election. See also: "It's Time to Push Our Democracy into the 21st Century," Center for Tech and Civic Life, accessed August 21, 2021, https://www.techandciviclife.org/.

50. Richard L. Hasen, "The Untimely Death of Bush v. Gore," *Stanford Law Review* 60, no. 1 (2007): 5.

51. "Secretary of State Office Comparison," Ballotpedia, accessed February 16, 2021, https://ballotpedia.org/Secretary_of_State_office_comparison.

52. Dana Milbank and Jo Becker, "Controversy Swirls around Harris," *Washington Post*, November 14, 2000, https://www.washingtonpost.com/archive/politics/2000/11/14/controversy-swirls-around-harris/0962659a-aa23-4e2d-b3b7-5831badcd62a/.

53. "NASS Statement on Cyber Security and Election Readiness," National Association of Secretaries of State, August 5, 2016, https://www.nass.org/node/239.

54. "Building Confidence in U.S. Elections: Report of the Commission on Federal Election Reform," Center for Democracy and Election Management, American University, September 2005, iii, https://www.legislationline.org/download/id/1472/file/3b50795b2d0374cbef5c29766256.pdf.

55. "The Fight for Open Primaries," Open Primaries, accessed February 16, 2021, https://www.openprimaries.org/five_reasons_we_need_open_primaries. See also: "State by State," Open Primaries, accessed February 16, 2021, https://www.openprimaries.org/movement_by_state_updated.

56. "The Fight for Open Primaries," Open Primaries. See also: Jesse Shayne, "Five Reasons We Need Open Primaries: It's Time to Do Away with Closed Primaries," *Open Primaries* (blog), May 25, 2017, https://www.openprimaries.org/five_reasons_we_need_open_primaries.

57. Drew Desilver, "Turnout in This Year's U.S. House Primaries Rose Sharply, Especially on the Democratic Side," Pew Research Center, October 3, 2018, https://www.pewresearch.org/fact-tank/2018/10/03/turnout-in-this-years-u-s-house-primaries-rose-sharply-especially-on-the-democratic-side/.

58. Curtis Gans, "2008 Primary Turnout Falls Just Short of Record Nationally, Breaks Records in Most States," American University News, May 19, 2008, http://online.wsj.com/public/resources/documents/primaryturnoutmay2008.pdf.

59. "2020 Presidential Nomination Contest Turnout Rates," United States Election Project, accessed February 18, 2021, http://www.electproject.org/2020p.

60. Molly K. Hooper, "Fearing Primaries, Republican Members Opted to Shun Boehner's 'Plan B,'" *The Hill*, December 22, 2012, https://thehill.com/homenews/house/274407-fearing-primaries-gop-members-opted-to-shun-boehners-plan-b.

61. Adam Wollner, "Capital Eye Opener, July 3: DeMint's PAC Launches Super PAC Arm, a $3B Pharma Settlement and NY Soccer Club Backs Romney," OpenSecrets.org/ Center for Responsive Politics, July 3, 2012, https://www.opensecrets.org/news/2012/07/capital-eye-opener-july-3-de-mints-p/; Deirdre Walsh, "Rep. Ocasio-Cortez Launches Political Group to Boost Progressive Candidates," NPR, February 21, 2020, https://www.npr.org/2020/02/21/808234797/rep-ocasio-cortez-launches-political-group-to-boost-progressive-candidates.

62. U.S. Constitution, art. 2, sec. 1, cl. 2 and 3. See also: "Constitution Annotated, Article II," Congress.gov, accessed August 21, 2021, https://constitution.congress.gov/browse/article-2/.

63. "The Electoral College," National Conference of State Legislatures, accessed February 17, 2021, https://www.ncsl.org/research/elections-and-campaigns/the-electoral-college.aspx.

64. Evan Andrews, "Why Is Election Day a Tuesday in November?," History.com, updated November 2, 2020, https://www.history.com/news/why-is-election-day-a-tuesday-in -november.

65. U.S. Library of Congress, "American Memory, a Century of Lawmaking for a New Nation: U.S. Congressional Documents and Debates, 1774–1875," in *The Debates in the Several State Conventions on the Adoption of the Federal Constitution [Elliot's Debates, Volume 5] Wednesday, July 25* (1787), https://memory.loc.gov/cgi-bin/ampage?collId=lled&fileName=005/lled005.db&recNum=388&itemLink=D?hlaw:1:./temp/~ammem_49kx::%230050389&linkText=1, 367.

66. "Five Things You Need to Know about the Electoral College," National Constitution Center—Constitution Daily, October 17, 2016, https://constitutioncenter.org/interactive-constitution/blog/five-things-you-need-to-know-about-the-electoral-college.

67. Alexander Keyssar, *Why Do We Still Have the Electoral College?* (Cambridge, MA: Harvard University Press, 2020), 8–11. See also: Marina N. Bolotnikova, "Why Do We Still Have the Electoral College?" *Harvard Magazine*, July 6, 2020, https://www.harvardmagazine .com/2020/07/why-do-we-still-have-the-electoral-college.

68. Tal Kopan, "Why Two Congressional Districts Could Be Key to This Election," CNN, September 22, 2016, https://www.cnn.com/2016/09/22/politics/electoral-college-split-votes -maine-nebraska-proportional/index.html.

69. "2012 California Presidential Results," *Politico*, updated November 19, 2012, https://www.politico.com/2012-election/results/president/california/.

70. "2012 Texas Presidential Results," *Politico*, updated November 19, 2012, https://www .politico.com/2012-election/results/president/texas/.

71. "2016 Presidential Election Results," *Politico*, updated December 13, 2016, 2016 https://www.politico.com/2016-election/results/map/president/.

72. "2012 Electoral College Results," The U.S. National Archives and Records Administration, accessed February 18, 2021, https://www.archives.gov/electoral-college/2012; "2016 Electoral College Results," U.S. National Archives and Records Administration, accessed February 18, 2021, https://www.archives.gov/electoral-college/2016.

73. "2012 Electoral College Results," U.S. National Archives and Records Administration; "2016 Electoral College Results," U.S. National Archives and Records Administration.

74. Adam Morse and J. J. Gass, *More Choices, More Voices: A Primer on Fusion*, Voting Rights and Elections Series (New York: Brennan Center for Justice at NYC School of Law, 2006), 3, https://www.brennancenter.org/sites/default/files/2019-08/Report_More-Choices -More-Voices.pdf.

75. Anna Purna Kambhampaty, "New York City Voters Just Adopted Ranked-Choice Voting in Elections. Here's How It Works," Time.com, November 6, 2019, https://time.com/5718941/ranked-choice-voting/.

76. Lee Drutman, *Breaking the Two-Party Doom Loop: The Case for Multiparty Democracy in America* (New York: Oxford University Press, 2020), 181. See also: Anushe Nath, "Ranked Choice Voting: Solution to Political Dysfunction," *Berkeley Political Review*, December 18, 2019, https://bpr.berkeley.edu/2019/12/18/ranked-choice-voting-a-solution-to-political-dysfunction/.

77. David Brooks, "One Reform to Save America," *New York Times*, May 31, 2018, https://www.nytimes.com/2018/05/31/opinion/voting-reform-partisanship-congress.html.

CHAPTER 7

1. US Constitution, Preamble.

2. "Ballotpedia's Polling Index: Congressional Approval Rating," Ballotpedia, February 24, 2021, https://ballotpedia.org/Ballotpedia%27s_Polling_Index:_Congressional_approval _rating.

3. "Analyst Says US Is Most Divided Since Civil War," *The Hill*, October 3, 2018, https:// thehill.com/hilltv/what-americas-thinking/409718-analyst-says-the-us-is-the-most-divided -since-the-civl-war.

4. Christina Marcos, "Lawmakers Set Up Bipartisan Problem Solvers Caucus for New Congress," *The Hill*, February 3, 2017, http://thehill.com/blogs/floor-action/house/317764 -bipartisan-lawmakers-set-up-problem-solvers-caucus-for-new-congress.

5. "The Legislative Branch: Building Relationships Today for Results Tomorrow," Federal Managers Association, accessed February 24, 2021, https://fedmanagers.org/default .aspx?bid=94; Kimberly Amadeo, "Current US Federal Government Spending," *The Balance*, June 29, 2020, https://www.thebalance.com/current-u-s-federal-government-spending -3305763.

6. Joanne B. Freeman, *The Field of Blood: Violence in Congress and the Road to Civil War* (New York: Farrar, Straus and Giroux, 2018).

7. "A Fatal Duel between Members in 1838," US House of Representatives: History, Art & Archives, February 24, 1838, https://history.house.gov/Historical-Highlights/1800-1850/ A-fatal-duel-between-Members-in-1838/.

8. "The Caning of Senator Charles Sumner," US Senate, May 22, 1856, https://www .senate.gov/artandhistory/history/minute/The_Caning_of_Senator_Charles_Sumner.htm.

9. "The Most Infamous Floor Brawl in the History of the U.S. House of Representatives," US House of Representatives: History, Art & Archives, February 6, 1858, https://history .house.gov/Historical-Highlights/1851-1900/The-most-infamous-floor-brawl-in-the-history -of-the-U-S--House-of-Representatives/?fbclid=IwAR1TlY7rwjA-goyC2RucaPQPZ1Hdt8Fd 6ERTNYMZ-F1GjbuiHEPbNWvn3j4.

10. The thirteen budget functions are agriculture, commerce/justice/state, defense, District of Columbia, energy and water, foreign operations, interior, labor/health and human services/ education, legislative branch, military construction, transportation, treasury/postal service, and veterans' affairs/housing and urban development.

11. "US Debt Clock," USDebtClock.org, accessed February 24, 2021, https://www.us debtclock.org/.

12. U.S. Congress, Senate, Permanent Subcommittee on Investigations, Committee on Homeland Security and Governmental Affairs, *The True Cost of Government Shutdowns*, https://www.hsgac.senate.gov/imo/media/doc/2019-09-17%20PSI%20Staff%20Report%20 -%20Government%20Shutdowns.pdf, 2. See also: US Accounting Office, "Government Shutdown: Permanent Funding Lapse Legislation Needed," GAO.gov, June 1991, GAO/ GGD-91-76, https://www.gao.gov/assets/220/214395.pdf.

13. US Accounting Office, "Government Shutdown."

14. "How the Lack of Action on the Debt Limit Can Hurt the Economy," Peter G. Peterson Foundation, September 6, 2017, https://www.pgpf.org/blog/2017/09/how-the-lack-of -action-on-the-debt-limit-can-hurt-the-economy.

15. US Accounting Office, "Government Shutdown: Data on Effects of 1990 Columbus Day Weekend Funding Lapse," GAO.gov, October 1990, GAO/GGD-91-17FS, https://web .archive.org/web/20170524225012/http://www.gao.gov/products/GGD-91-17FS.

16. Specialist in National Government, "Recessions Since 1974: Review and Assessment of the Record," Congressional Research Service, May 26, 2010, https://www.everycrsreport.com/ files/20100526_RL33869_f1233c24f4c0fdc02353ca40682217f6134a2e2d.pdf.

17. Jonathan Rauch, "How American Politics Went Insane," *Atlantic*, July/August 2016, https://www.theatlantic.com/magazine/archive/2016/07/how-american-politics-went-insane/ 485570/.

18. "What Is a Continuing Resolution?," Peter G. Peterson Foundation, December 22, 2020, https://www.pgpf.org/blog/2020/12/what-is-a-continuing-resolution.

19. U.S. Congress, *The True Cost of Government Shutdowns.*

20. Danny Vinik, "Meet Your Unauthorized Federal Government," *Politico*, February 3, 2016, http://www.politico.com/agenda/story/2016/02/government-agencies-programs -unauthorized-000036-000037.

21. "Expired and Expiring Authorizations of Appropriations: Fiscal Year 2020," Congressional Budget Office, February 2020, https://www.cbo.gov/system/files/2020-02/56082 -CBO-EEAA.pdf.

22. Vinik, "Meet Your Unauthorized Federal Government."

23. Bryce Dietrich, "If a Picture Is Worth a Thousand Words, What Is a Video Worth?," *The Year in C-SPAN Archives Research* 2, article 1 (West Lafayette, IN: Purdue University, November 2015), https://docs.lib.purdue.edu/cgi/viewcontent.cgi?article=1031&context =ccse.

24. Zachary P. Neal, "A Sign of the Times? Weak and Strong Polarization in the U.S. Congress, 1973–2016," *Social Networks* 60 (2020): 103–12, https://doi.org/10.1016/j.soc net.2018.07.007.

25. Seventy former US senators, "The Senate Is Failing to Perform Its Constitutional Duties," *Washington Post*, February 25, 2020, https://www.washingtonpost.com/opinions/ former-us-senators-the-senate-is-failing-to-perform-its-constitutional-duties/2020/02/25/ b9bdd22a-5743-11ea-9000-f3cffee23036_story.html.

26. John Bresnahan, "The Demise of One of the Best Gigs in Congress," *Politico*, January 30, 2018, https://www.politico.com/story/2018/01/30/congress-republican-committee-chairs-377078; Lee Drutman, "Why So Many Members of Congress Are Retiring," *Vox*, February 1, 2018, https://www.vox.com/polyarchy/2018/2/1/16958988/congress-members -retiring-why; "Why We Left Congress, How the Legislative Branch Is Broken and What We Can Do about It," R Street / Issue One, accessed January 31, 2021, https://www.issueone .org/why-we-left/.

27. Thomas E. Mann and Norman J. Ornstein, *It's Even Worse Than It Looks: How the American Constitutional System Collided with the New Politics of Extremism* (New York: Basic Books, 2016); Robert G. Kaiser, "'It's Even Worse Than It Looks: How the American Constitutional System Collided with the New Politics of Extremism' by Thomas E. Mann and Norman J. Ornstein," *Washington Post*, April 30, 2012, https://www.washingtonpost.com/ entertainment/books/its-even-worse-than-it-looks-how-the-american-constitutional-system -collided-with-the-new-politics-of-extremism-by-thomas-e-mann-and-norman-j-ornstein/20 12/04/30/gIQA2ohKsT_story.html?utm_term=.e90b9a56358e.

28. Mark Strand and Tim Lang, "The Sausage Factory: The Hastert Rule," Congressional Institute, July 17, 2013, https://www.congressionalinstitute.org/2013/07/17/the-hastert-rule/.

29. James Wallner, "The Rules Work," Legislative Procedure, March 24, 2020, https://www.legislativeprocedure.com/blog/2020/3/24/the-rules-work.

30. Matt Flegenheimer, "Senate Republicans Deploy 'Nuclear Option' to Clear Path for Gorsuch," *New York Times*, April 6, 2017, https://www.nytimes.com/2017/04/06/us/politics/neil-gorsuch-supreme-court-senate.html.

31. "Cloture Motions," United States Senate, accessed May 11, 2021, https://www.cop.senate.gov/legislative/cloture/clotureCounts.htm.

32. Seventy former US senators, "The Senate Is Failing to Perform Its Constitutional Duties."

33. Compiled by the Joint Committee on Printing, "Tributes to Hon. Ted Stevens," Congressional Record, S. Doc. 110-4, 2007, https://www.govinfo.gov/content/pkg/CDOC-110sdoc4/pdf/CDOC-110sdoc4.pdf.

34. Jason Grumet, *City of Rivals: Restoring the Glorious Mess of American Democracy* (Guilford, CT: Globe Pequot, 2014).

35. John Hamre, from a memo to the Board of Trustees of CSIS, made available to the author by Mr. Hamre.

36. Thomas H. Kean and Lee H. Hamilton, "To Secure Homeland, Clean Up Congressional Oversight: 9/11 Commission Chairmen," *USA Today*, December 1, 2016, https://www.usatoday.com/story/opinion/2016/12/01/congress-bureaucracy-committees-911-commission-chairmen-column/94624248/.

37. Anthony L. Kimery, "Reforming Congressional Oversight of DHS Still Priority One, 9/11 Commission Members Say," Homeland Security Today, July 23, 2014, https://www.hstoday.us/kimery-report/reforming-congressional-oversight-of-dhs-still-priority-one-9-11-commission-members-say/.

38. John McCain, "Opinion: The Enduring Example of Mo Udall," *Washington Post*, December 17, 1998, https://www.washingtonpost.com/opinions/the-enduring-example-of-mo-udall/2018/08/26/3cb7c5e4-a937-11e8-a8d7-0f63ab8b1370_story.html.

39. "Legislative Lowdown—Week of December 27," The Heritage Foundation, December 27, 2004, https://www.heritage.org/political-process/commentary/legislative-lowdown-week-december-27.

40. National Commission on Terrorist Attacks upon the United States, *The 9/11 Commission Report: Final Report of the National Commission on Terrorist Attacks upon the United States* (Washington, DC: National Commission on Terrorist Attacks upon the United States, 2004), 241, http://avalon.law.yale.edu/sept11/911Report.pdf.

41. Seventy former US senators, "The Senate Is Failing to Perform Its Constitutional Duties."

42. Brady Dennis, "Most Americans Believe the Government Should Do More to Combat Climate Change, Poll Finds," *Washington Post*, June 23, 2020, https://www.washingtonpost.com/climate-environment/2020/06/23/climate-change-poll-pew/.

43. Government Accountability Office, *Opportunities to Reduce Potential Duplication in Government Programs, Save Tax Dollars, and Enhance Revenue*, Report to Congress (GAO-318SP: March 2011), https://www.gao.gov/assets/320/315920.pdf; Damian Paletta, "Billions in Bloat Uncovered in Beltway," *Wall Street Journal*, March 1, 2011, https://www.wsj.com/articles/SB10001424052748703749504576172942399165436.

44. Vera Nicholas-Gervais, Evdokia Moïse, and Akira Kawamoto, *Regulatory Reform in the United States: Enhancing Market Openness through Regulatory Reform* (Paris: Organisation

for Economic Co-operation and Development, 1999), 5, https://www.oecd.org/regreform/2756360.pdf.

45. John Laloggia, "6 Facts about U.S. Political Independents," Pew Research Center, May 15, 2019, https://www.pewresearch.org/fact-tank/2019/05/15/facts-about-us-political-independents/.

46. "Why We Left Congress: How the Legislative Branch Is Broken and What We Can Do about It," Issue One, 2018, https://www.issueone.org/why-we-left/#1545252486574-aa590bc4-c086.

47. "Why We Left Congress," Issue One.

48. Rep. Will Hurd, "Official Press Release from Office of Former Rep. Will Hurd (R-TX)," Legistorm, June 18, 2019, https://www.legistorm.com/stormfeed/view_rss/1310722/member/3048.html.

49. "Recommendations," Select Committee on the Modernization of Congress, accessed February 27, 2021, https://modernizecongress.house.gov/recommendations.

50. Jennifer E. Manning, *Membership of the 116th Congress: A Profile*, U.S. Library of Congress, Congressional Research Service, R45583 (2020), X, https://fas.org/sgp/crs/misc/R45583.pdf.

51. Roger Angell, *Season Ticket* (New York: Open Road Media, 2013).

52. "Commission on Political Reforms," Bipartisan Policy Center, 2019, https://bipartisanpolicy.org/wp-content/uploads/2019/03/5296_BPC_CPR_3Reforms_v2.pdf.

53. "Why We Left Congress," Issue One.

CHAPTER 8

1. Thomas Jefferson to John Tyler, June 28, 1804, Founders Online, https://founders.archives.gov/documents/Jefferson/01-43-02-0557.

2. Michael M. Grynbaum, "Trump Calls the News Media the 'Enemy of the American People,'" *New York Times*, February 17, 2017, https://www.nytimes.com/2017/02/17/business/trump-calls-the-news-media-the-enemy-of-the-people.html; Brett Samuels, "Trump Ramps Up Rhetoric on Media, Calls Press 'the Enemy of the People,'" *The Hill*, April 5, 2019, https://thehill.com/homenews/administration/437610-trump-calls-press-the-enemy-of-the-people.

3. Paul Farhi, "The Washington Post's New Slogan Turns Out to Be an Old Saying," *Washington Post*, https://www.washingtonpost.com/lifestyle/style/the-washington-posts-new-slogan-turns-out-to-be-an-old-saying/2017/02/23/cb199cda-fa02-11e6-be05-1a3817ac21a5_story.html.

4. "Edelman Trust Barometer 2021," Edelman, accessed April 2, 2021, https://www.edelman.com/sites/g/files/aatuss191/files/2021-01/2021%20Edelman%20Trust%20Barometer_U.S.%20Country%20Report_Clean.pdf, Slide 28.

5. Megan Brenan, "Americans Remain Distrustful of Mass Media," Gallup, September 30, 2020, https://news.gallup.com/poll/321116/americans-remain-distrustful-mass-media.aspx.

6. Amy Mitchell, Jeffrey Gottfried, Michael Barthel, and Elisa Shearer, "Trust and Accuracy," in *The Modern News Consumer: News Attitudes and Practices in the Digital Era* (Washington, DC: Pew Research Center, 2016), 8–11, http://www.journalism.org/2016/07/07/trust-and-accuracy/; "American Views 2020: Trust, Media and Democracy,"

Knight Foundation, August 4, 2020, https://knightfoundation.org/reports/american-views-2020-trust-media-and-democracy/.

7. Amanda Ripley, "Complicating the Narratives," The Center for Understanding in Conflict, accessed March 1, 2021, https://understandinginconflict.org/complicating-the-narratives/.

8. Alfred G. Hill, "The Practice of the Kansas Code of Ethics for Newspapers," *Annals of the American Academy of Political and Social Science* 101 (1922): 179–87, https://www.jstor.org/stable/pdf/1014606.pdf.

9. *An Act to Provide for the Regulation of Interstate and Foreign Communication by Wire or Radio, and for Other Purposes*, Public Law 416, *U.S. Statutes at Large* 48 (1934): 1064–105, https://www.loc.gov/law/help/statutes-at-large/73rd-congress/session-2/c73s2ch652.pdf.

10. Kathleen Ann Ruane, "Fairness Doctrine: History and Constitutional Issues," Congressional Research Service Report for Congress, July 30, 2011, https://fas.org/sgp/crs/misc/R40009.pdf.

11. United States, Federal Communications Commission, *FCC Reports*, Vol. 13, *July 1, 1948 to June 30, 1949* (Washington, DC: Government Printing Office, 1954), 1264, https://digital.library.unt.edu/ark:/67531/metadc177294/; University of North Texas Libraries, UNT Digital Library, https://digital.library.unt.edu; crediting UNT Libraries Government Documents Department. *Note:* The fairness doctrine was adopted by the FCC as a formal rule as documented in the "Report on Editorializing by Broadcast Licensees."

12. Douglas Blanks Hindman and Kenneth Wiegand, "The Big Three's Prime-Time Decline: A Technological and Social Context," *Journal of Broadcasting and Electronic Media* 52, no. 1 (2008): 119–35, https://doi.org/10.1080/08838150701820924.

13. Society of Professional Journalists, "SPJ Code of Ethics," September 6, 2014, https://www.spj.org/ethicscode.asp.

14. Federal Communications Commission, "2020 Communications Marketplace Report," FCC 20-188 (Washington, DC: Federal Communications Commission, 2020), 126, https://docs.fcc.gov/public/attachments/FCC-20-188A1.pdf.

15. Erik Wemple, "Fox News Settles Suit with Parents of Seth Rich for Promoting Heinous Conspiracy Theory," *Washington Post*, November 24, 2020, https://www.washingtonpost.com/opinions/2020/11/24/fox-news-settles-seth-rich-lawsuit-conspiracy-theory/.

16. Walter Lippmann, *Liberty and the News* (New York: Harcourt, Brace and Howe, 1920), 13, https://archive.org/details/libertynews00lippuoft/page/12/mode/2up?ref=ol&view=theater&q=shame.

17. Laura Santhanam and Joshua Barajas, "Jim Lehrer, in His Own Words," *PBS NewsHour*, January 24, 2020, https://www.pbs.org/newshour/politics/jim-lehrer-in-his-own-words.

18. Chris Cillizza, "Americans Read Headlines. And Not Much Else," *Washington Post*, March 19, 2014, https://www.washingtonpost.com/news/the-fix/wp/2014/03/19/americans-read-headlines-and-not-much-else/.

19. The Commission on Freedom of the Press, *A Free and Responsible Press—A General Report on Mass Communication: Newspapers, Radio, Motion Pictures, Magazines, and Books* (Chicago: University of Chicago Press, 1947), 55.

20. Bill Bishop, "In Politics, It's Not What They Say; It's What You Hear," *Slate*, September 22, 2008, https://slate.com/news-and-politics/2008/09/in-politics-it-s-not-what-they-say-it-s-what-you-hear.html.

21. Tom Rosentiel, "Partisanship and Cable News Audiences," Pew Research Center, October 30, 2009, https://www.pewresearch.org/2009/10/30/partisanship-and-cable-news-audiences/.

22. Andrew McGill, "The Different Ways Fox, MSNBC, and CNN Recapped Monday's Debate," *Atlantic*, September 29, 2016, https://www.theatlantic.com/politics/archive/2016/09/debate-recaps-cable-news-clinton-trump-fox-msnbc-cnn/502223/.

23. Tom Jones, "Cable News Networks Make It Feel as If We're Looking at Two Different Americas," Poynter, June 3, 2020, https://www.poynter.org/newsletters/2020/cable-news-networks-make-it-feel-as-if-were-looking-at-two-different-americas/.

24. Mark Jurkowitz, Amy Mitchell, Laura Houston Santhanam, Steve Adams, Monica Anderson, and Nancy Vogt, "The Changing TV News Landscape," Pew Research Center, Journalism & Media, March 17, 2013, https://www.journalism.org/2013/03/17/the-changing-tv-news-landscape/.

25. Robert G. Kaiser, "Bad News about the News," The Brookings Institution, The Brookings Essay, October 16, 2014, http://csweb.brookings.edu/content/research/essays/2014/bad-news.html#.

26. "Striking the Balance, Audience Interests, Business Pressures and Journalists' Values," Pew Research Center, U.S. Politics and Policy, March 30, 1999, https://www.pewresearch.org/politics/1999/03/30/section-iii-views-on-performance/.

27. Martin Gilens, Lynn Vavreck, and Martin Cohen, "The Mass Media and the Public's Assessments of Presidential Candidates, 1952–2000," *Journal of Politics* 69, no. 4 (November 2007): 1160–75, https://doi.org/10.1111/j.1468-2508.2007.00615.x; Denise-Marie Ordway, "The Consequences of 'Horse Race' Reporting: What the Research Says," *Journalist's Resource*, September 10, 2019, https://journalistsresource.org/studies/society/news-media/horse-race-reporting-election/.

28. Dan Froomkin, "Focus on Tactics over Substance Takes All the Meaning out of Politics," Press Watch, October 25, 2019, https://presswatchers.org/2019/10/horse-race-coverage-takes-all-the-meaning-out-of-political-reporting/; Thomas E. Patterson, *Out of Order* (New York: Vintage Books, 1994), 73.

29. Alan I. Abramowitz and Steven Webster, "The Only Thing We Have to Fear Is the Other Party," Sabato's Crystal Ball, June 4, 2015, http://www.centerforpolitics.org/crystalball/articles/the-only-thing-we-have-to-fear-is-the-other-party/.

30. Matthew Levendusky and Neil Malhotra, "Does Media Coverage of Partisan Polarization Affect Political Attitudes?" *Political Communication* 33, no. 2 (July 27, 2015): 283–301.

31. Chris Nolter, "TV Political Ad Spending Will Break Records in 2016, and These Broadcasters Will Cash In," TheStreet, June 8, 2016, https://www.thestreet.com/story/13594342/1/tv-political-ad-spending-will-break-records-in-2016-and-these-broadcasters-will-cash-in.html.

32. Brian Stelter, "Campaign Ad Cash Lures Buyers to Swing-State TV Stations," *New York Times*, July 7, 2013, http://www.nytimes.com/2013/07/08/business/media/with-political-ad-profits-swing-state-tv-stations-are-hot-properties.html.

33. Mary Harris and Paul Senatori, *A Media Post-Mortem on the 2016 Presidential Election* (Portland, OR: mediaQuant, Inc., 2016).

34. Brett Edkins, "Donald Trump's Election Delivers Massive Ratings for Cable News," *Forbes*, December 1, 2016, https://www.forbes.com/sites/brettedkins/2016/12/01/donald-trumps-election-delivers-massive-ratings-for-cable-news/#3d9d6a12119e.

35. Jonathan Mahler, "CNN Had a Problem. Donald Trump Solved It," *New York Times Magazine*, April 4, 2017, https://www.nytimes.com/2017/04/04/magazine/cnn-had-a-problem-donald-trump-solved-it.html?mcubz=1.

36. Benjamin Mullin, "Cable-News Viewership Falls after Trump's Exit, Ratings Races Tighten," *Wall Street Journal*, March 30, 2021, https://www.wsj.com/articles/cable-news -viewership-falls-after-trumps-exit-ratings-races-tighten-11617139081.

37. Dylan Byers, "Joe Scarborough–Donald Trump Friendship Increasing Source of Discomfort at NBC," *CNN Business*, February 12, 2016, https://money.cnn.com/2016/02/12/media/joe-scarborough-donald-trump-nbc/.

38. Erik Wemple, "An Awkward Joe Scarborough Protests That He's Not, in Fact, a 'Supporter' of Donald Trump," *Washington Post*, February 10, 2016, https://www.washingtonpost .com/blogs/erik-wemple/wp/2016/02/10/an-awkward-joe-scarborough-protests-that-hes-not -in-fact-a-supporter-of-donald-trump/.

39. Matt Gertz, "A Comprehensive Review of the Revolving Door between Fox and the Trump Administration," Media Matters for America, July 22, 2019, https://www.mediamatters .org/fox-news/comprehensive-review-revolving-door-between-fox-and-trump-administration.

40. Michael M. Grynbaum, "CNN Parts Ways with Donna Brazile, a Hillary Clinton Supporter," *New York Times*, October 31, 2016, https://www.nytimes.com/2016/11/01/us/politics/donna-brazile-wikileaks-cnn.html.

41. John G. Geer, "Fanning the Flames: The News Media's Role in the Rise of Negativity in Presidential Campaigns," Joan Shorenstein Center on the Press, Politics and Public Policy, Discussion Paper Series #D-55, February 2010, p. 5, https://shorensteincenter.org/wp-content/uploads/2012/03/d55_geer.pdf.

42. "Striking the Balance," Pew Research Center.

43. Brian Stelter, "Fox's Volley with Obama Intensifying," *New York Times*, October 11, 2009, https://www.nytimes.com/2009/10/12/business/media/12fox.html.

44. Barack Obama, "Interview with Bill O'Reilly of Fox News—Part 3 of 4," September 9, 2008, archived at the American Presidency Project, https://www.presidency.ucsb.edu/documents/interview-with-bill-oreilly-fox-news-part-3-4.

45. Grynbaum, "Trump Calls the News Media the 'Enemy of the American People'"; Samuels, "Trump Ramps Up Rhetoric on Media."

46. Fred Lucas, "Trump Blasts 'Fake News' and 'Failing' Media Outlets," The Daily Signal, February 16, 2017, http://dailysignal.com/2017/02/16/trump-blasts-fake-news-and-failing -media-outlets/.

47. Thomas E. Patterson, "News Coverage of the 2016 General Election: How the Press Failed the Voters," Harvard Kennedy School Shorenstein Center on the Press, Politics and Public Policy, December 7, 2016, https://shorensteincenter.org/news-coverage-2016-general -election/.

48. David Broder, "War on Cynicism," *Washington Post*, July 6, 1994, https://www. washingtonpost.com/archive/opinions/1994/07/06/war-on-cynicism/c815d7e9-934f -4421-a136-2936cbea1408/.

49. Danielle Kurtzleben, "From Congress to Local Health Boards, Public Officials Suffer Threats and Harassment," NPR, December 16, 2020, https://www.npr .org/2020/12/16/946818045/from-congress-to-local-health-boards-public-officials-suffer -threats-and-harassm.

50. "US: Fueled by Years of Trump's Demonization of the Media, Unprecedented Violence Breaks Out against Journalists Covering Protests," Reporters without Borders, May 31, 2020, updated June 1, 2020, https://rsf.org/en/news/us-fueled-years-trumps-demonization-media -unprecedented-violence-breaks-out-against-journalists.

51. Erin O'Donnell, "The Extinction of the Press?," *Harvard Magazine*, July–August 2020, https://harvardmagazine.com/2020/07/right-now-extinction-of-press.

52. O'Donnell, "The Extinction of the Press?"

53. Joshua Benton, "When Local Newspapers Shrink, Fewer People Bother to Run for Mayor," NiemanLab, April 9, 2019, https://www.niemanlab.org/2019/04/when-local-newspapers-shrink-fewer-people-bother-to-run-for-mayor/. See also: Lee Shaker, "Dead Newspapers and Citizens' Civic Engagement," *Political Communication* 31, no. 1 (2014): 131–48, https://doi.org/10.1080/10584609.2012.762817.

54. Swift, "Americans' Trust in Mass Media Sinks to New Low"; Jeffrey M. Jones, "Americans' Trust in Political Leaders, Public at New Lows," Gallup, September 21, 2016, http://www.gallup.com/poll/195716/americans-trust-political-leaders-public-new-lows.aspx.

55. Lippmann, *Liberty and the News*, 12–13.

56. Garrett M. Graff, "A Guide to Russia's High Tech Tool Box for Subverting US Democracy," *Wired*, August 13, 2017, https://www.wired.com/story/a-guide-to-russias-high-tech-tool-box-for-subverting-us-democracy/.

57. Commission on Freedom of the Press, *A Free and Responsible Press: A General Report on Mass Communication: Newspapers, Radio, Motion Pictures, Magazines, and Books* (Chicago: University of Chicago Press, 1947).

58. Commission on Freedom of the Press, *A Free and Responsible Press*, vi, 29.

59. Albert Camus, "Homage to an Exile," in *Resistance, Rebellion, and Death*, trans. Justin O'Brien (1960; New York: Vintage International, 1995), 102.

60. THE COMMISSION ON FREEDOM OF THE PRESS, A FREE AND RESPONSIBLE PRESS—A General Report on Mass Communication: Newspapers, Radio, Motion Pictures, Magazines, and Books (Chicago and London: The University of Chicago Press, 1947), 29. Also referred to as the Hutchins Commission.

61. Hutchins Commission, p. 36.

62. Santhanam and Barajas, "Jim Lehrer, in His Own Words."

63. *Mitigating the Negative Impact of False Information* (Palo Alto, CA: Institute for the Future, 2018), 1, 3, https://www.iftf.org/fileadmin/user_upload/images/DigIntel/3_Mitigating_Negative_impact_of_False_information_FINAL_031119.pdf.

CHAPTER 9

1. "Information and Communication Technologies (ICT)," Food and Agriculture Organization of the United Nations, accessed August 9, 2021, http://aims.fao.org/information-and-communication-technologies-ict.

2. Clay Shirky, "How Social Media Can Make History," *TED* (video), June 2009, https://www.ted.com/talks/clay_shirky_how_cellphones_twitter_facebook_can_make_history?language=en.

3. Richard Reeves, *President Kennedy: Profile of Power* (New York: Simon and Schuster, 1993), 321.

4. Bernard Marr, "How Much Data Do We Create Every Day? The Mind-Blowing Stats Everyone Should Read," *Forbes*, May 21, 2018, https://www.forbes.com/sites/bernardmarr/2018/05/21/how-much-data-do-we-create-every-day-the-mind-blowing-stats-everyone-should-read/?sh=6c3af87060ba; "Data Never Sleeps 5.0," Domo, Inc., accessed March

1, 2021, https://web-assets.domo.com/blog/wp-content/uploads/2017/07/17_domo_data -never-sleeps-5-01.png.

5. See Marshall McLuhan, *Understanding Media: The Extensions of Man* (New York: McGraw-Hill, 1964).

6. Matthew Crain and Anthony Nadler, "Political Manipulation and Internet Advertising Structure," *Journal of Information Policy* 9 (2019): 381, https://www.jstor.org/stable/ pdf/10.5325/jinfopoli.9.2019.0370.pdf?refreqid=excelsior%3A62f83c8d50d9fdf60b6b7135 6d23a2e0.

7. Richard Koman, "Inventor of Political Microtargeting Applies His Craft for Romney," ZDNet, July 5, 2007, http://www.zdnet.com/article/inventor-of-political-microtargeting -applies-his-craft-for-romney/.

8. Kathryn Montgomery and Jeff Chester, "The Digital Commercialisation of US Politics—2020 and Beyond," Center for Digital Democracy, January 16, 2020, https://www .democraticmedia.org/article/digital-commercialisation-us-politics-2020-and-beyond.

9. Tom Cheshire, "Behind the Scenes at Donald Trump's UK Digital War Room," Sky News, October 22, 2016, https://news.sky.com/story/behind-the-scenes-at-donald-trumps-uk-digital -war-room-10626155; Carole Cadwalladr, "'I Made Steve Bannon's Psychological Warfare Tool': Meet the Data War Whistleblower," *Guardian*, March 18, 2018, https://www.theguardian.com/ news/2018/mar/17/data-war-whistleblower-christopher-wylie-faceook-nix-bannon-trump.

10. "Big Five Personality Traits," MentalHelp.net, accessed March 1, 2021, https://www .mentalhelp.net/psychological-testing/big-five-personality-traits/. See also: Lewis R. Goldberg, *An Alternative "Description of Personality": The Big-Five Factor Structure* (Eugene: University of Oregon and Oregon Research Institute, 1990), https://projects.ori.org/lrg/PDFs_papers/ Goldberg.Big-Five-FactorsStructure.JPSP.1990.pdf.

11. Issie Lapowsky, "How Russian Facebook Ads Divided and Targeted US Voters before the 2016 Election," *Wired*, April 16, 1018, https://www.wired.com/story/russian-facebook -ads-targeted-us-voters-before-2016-election/; Young Mie Kim et al., "The Stealth Media? Groups and Targets behind Divisive Issue Campaigns on Facebook," *Political Communication* 35, no. 4 (2018): 515–41, https://doi.org/10.1080/10584609.2018.1476425.

12. Joseph Turow, Michael X. Delli Carpini, Nora A. Draper, and Rowan Howard-Williams, "Americans Roundly Reject Tailored Political Advertising," Annenberg School for Communication, University of Pennsylvania, 2012, 5, http://repository.upenn.edu/cgi/view content.cgi?article=1414&context=asc_papers.

13. Allison Brennan, "Microtargeting: How Campaigns Know You Better Than You Know Yourself," CNN Politics, November 5, 2012, http://www.cnn.com/2012/11/05/politics/ voters-microtargeting/index.html.

14. Terrence McCoy, "The Creepiness Factor: How Obama and Romney Are Getting to Know You," *Atlantic*, April 10, 2012, https://www.theatlantic.com/politics/archive/2012/04/ the-creepiness-factor-how-obama-and-romney-are-getting-to-know-you/255499/.

15. Tanzina Vega, "Online Data Helping Campaigns Customize Ads," *New York Times*, February 20, 2012, https://www.nytimes.com/2012/02/21/us/politics/campaigns-use-microt argeting-to-attract-supporters.html.

16. Brennan, "Microtargeting."

17. Lois Beckett, "How Microsoft and Yahoo Are Selling Politicians Access to You," ProPublica, June 11, 2012, https://www.propublica.org/article/how-microsoft-and-yahoo-are -selling-politicians-access-to-you; Brennan, "Microtargeting."

18. Brennan, "Microtargeting."

19. Brennan, "Microtargeting."

20. Antony Young, "How Data and Micro-Targeting Won the 2012 Election for Obama," MediaVillage, November 20, 2012, https://www.mediavillage.com/article/how-data-and -micro-targeting-won-the-2012-election-for-obama-antony-young-mindshare-north-america /print/.

21. Young, "How Data and Micro-Targeting Won the 2012 Election for Obama."

22. Issie Lapowsky, "Just What We Need: An Algorithm to Help Politicians Pander," *Wired*, September 30, 2015, https://www.wired.com/2015/09/just-need-algorithm-help -politicians-pander/.

23. Cade Metz, "Finally, a Machine That Can Finish Your Sentence," *New York Times*, November 18, 2018, https://www.nytimes.com/2018/11/18/technology/artificial -intelligence-language.html; Christopher Paul and Marek N. Posard, "Artificial Intelligence and the Manufacturing of Reality," *TheRandBlog*, January 20, 2020, https://www.rand.org/ blog/2020/01/artificial-intelligence-and-the-manufacturing-of-reality.html.

24. Lapowsky, "Just What We Need."

25. Chuck Todd and Carrie Dann, "How Big Data Broke American Politics," NBC News, March 14, 2017, http://www.nbcnews.com/politics/elections/how-big-data-broke-american -politics-n732901.

26. Todd and Dann, "How Big Data Broke American Politics."

27. Jason Karaian, "We Now Spend More Than Eight Hours a Day Consuming Media," *Quartz*, June 1, 2015, https://qz.com/416416/we-now-spend-more-than-eight-hours-a-day -consuming-media/.

28. Jan Zverina, "U.S. Media Consumption to Rise to 15.5 Hours a Day—Per Person—by 2015," UC San Diego News Center, November 6, 2013, http://ucsdnews.ucsd.edu/ pressrelease/u.s._media_consumption_to_rise_to_15.5_hours_a_day_per_person_by_2015.

29. Zverina, "U.S. Media Consumption," quoting James E. Short, "How Much Media? 2013 Report on American Consumers," Institute for Communication Technology Management, University of Southern California's Marshall School of Business.

30. Richard Fausset, "'It Has to Stop': Georgia Election Official Lashes Trump," *New York Times*, December 1, 2020, updated January 7, 2021, https://www.nytimes.com/2020/12/01/ us/politics/georgia-election-trump.html.

31. Craig Fehrman, "The Incredible Shrinking Soundbite," *Boston Globe*, January 2, 2011, http://archive.boston.com/bostonglobe/ideas/articles/2011/01/02/the_incredible _shrinking_sound_bite/.

32. Jessica Murphy, "Dirty, Viral Tricks: The 2016 U.S. Election Is Already Getting Ugly," *Maclean's*, April 17, 2015, http://www.macleans.ca/politics/washington/dirty-viral-tricks-the -2016-u-s-election-is-already-getting-ugly/.

33. Kate Holliday and Jordan Lieberman, "Digital Political Advertising in 2020: What We Learned," Campaigns & Elections, November 30, 2020, https://www.campaignsandelections .com/campaign-insider/digital-political-advertising-in-2020-what-we-learned; Lata Nott, "Political Advertising on Social Media Platforms," American Bar Association, June 26, 2020, https://www.americanbar.org/groups/crsj/publications/human_rights_magazine_home/ voting-in-2020/political-advertising-on-social-media-platforms/.

34. Sara Brown, "MIT Sloan Research about Social Media, Misinformation, and Elections," Ideas Made to Matter, October 5, 2020, https://mitsloan.mit.edu/ideas-made-to-matter/mit -sloan-research-about-social-media-misinformation-and-elections; the study cited is Soroush

Vosoughi, Deb Roy, and Sinan Aral, "The Spread of True and False News Online," *Science* 359, no. 6380 (2018): 1146–51, https://science.sciencemag.org/content/359/6380/1146.

35. Melinda Wenner Moyer, "Rudeness on the Internet," *Scientific American*, September–October 2012, 10, https://www.jstor.org/stable/e24942215.

36. Joel Stein, "How Trolls Are Ruining the Internet," *Time*, August 18, 2016, http://time.com/4457110/internet-trolls/. See also: Farhad Manjoo, "Troll, Reveal Thyself: Why We Need to Get Rid of Anonymous Comments," *Slate*, March 9, 2011, https://slate.com/technology/2011/03/anonymous-comments-why-we-need-to-get-rid-of-them-once-and-for-all.html.

37. Emily A. Vogels, "Millennials Stand Out for Their Technology Use, but Older Generations also Embrace Digital Life," Pew Research Center, September 9, 2019, https://www.pewresearch.org/fact-tank/2019/09/09/us-generations-technology-use/.

38. See "How Millennials Get News: Inside the Habits of America's First Digital Generation," American Press Institute, February 16, 2015, https://www.americanpressinstitute.org/publications/reports/survey-research/millennials-news/; Jeffery Gottfried and Elisa Shearer, "News Use across Social Media Platforms 2016," Pew Research Center, May 26, 2016, http://www.journalism.org/2016/05/26/news-use-across-social-media-platforms-2016/.

39. Shannon Greenwood, Andrew Perrin, and Maeve Duggan, "Social Media Update 2016," Pew Research Center, November 11, 2016, http://www.pewinternet.org/2016/11/11/social-media-update-2016/.

40. Nicholas A. Christakis and James H. Fowler, *Connected: The Surprising Power of Our Social Networks and How They Shape Our Lives* (New York: Little, Brown, 2009).

41. Douglas Guilbeault and Samuel Woolley, "How Twitter Bots Are Shaping the Election," *Atlantic*, November 1, 2016, https://www.theatlantic.com/technology/archive/2016/11/election-bots/506072/; Ana Lucia Schmidt et al., "Anatomy of News Consumption on Facebook," PNAS, January 31, 2017, https://www.pnas.org/content/pnas/114/12/3035.full.pdf; Yosh Halberstam and Brian Knight, "Homophily, Group Size, and the Diffusion of Political Information in Social Networks: Evidence from Twitter," NBER Working Paper No. 20681, National Bureau of Economic Research, November 2017, https://www.nber.org/system/files/working_papers/w20681/w20681.pdf.

42. Farhad Manjoo, "How the Internet Is Loosening Our Grip on the Truth," *New York Times*, November 2, 2016, https://www.nytimes.com/2016/11/03/technology/how-the-internet-is-loosening-our-grip-on-the-truth.html?_r=0.

43. Craig Silverman, Lauren Strapagiel, Hamza Shaban, Ellie Hall, and Jeremy Singer-Vine, "Hyperpartisan Facebook Pages Are Publishing False and Misleading Information at an Alarming Rate," *BuzzFeed News*, October 20, 2016, https://www.buzzfeed.com/craigsilverman/partisan-fb-pages-analysis?utm_term=.urbY00q21#.qmAPXXk92.

44. Alessandro Bessi and Emilio Ferrara, "Social Bots Distort the 2016 U.S. Presidential Election Online Discussion," *First Monday* 21, no. 11 (2016), https://doi.org/10.5210/fm.v21i11.7090.

45. Bessi and Ferrara, "Social Bots."

46. Guilbeault and Woolley, "How Twitter Bots Are Shaping the Election."

47. Polly Mosendz, "The Seven Types of People Who Tweet at Trump," *Bloomberg Businessweek*, April 10, 2017, https://www.bloomberg.com/features/2017-who-replies-to-trumps-tweets/.

48. Gabe O'Connor and Avie Schneider, "How Russian Twitter Bots Pumped Out Fake News during the 2016 Election," *All Things Considered*, National Public Radio,

April 3, 2017, http://www.npr.org/sections/alltechconsidered/2017/04/03/522503844/how-russian-twitter-bots-pumped-out-fake-news-during-the-2016-election.

49. David Ingram, "Facebook Says 126 Million Americans May Have Seen Russia-Linked Political Posts," Reuters, October 30, 2017, https://www.reuters.com/article/us-usa-trump-russia-socialmedia/facebook-says-126-million-americans-may-have-seen-russia-linked-political-posts.

50. William Turton, "We Posed as 100 Senators to Run Ads on Facebook: Facebook Approved All of Them," *Vice News*, October 30, 2018, https://www.vice.com/en/article/xw9n3q/we-posed-as-100-senators-to-run-ads-on-facebook-facebook-approved-all-of-them; Matthew Crain and Anthony Nadler, "Political Manipulation and Internet Advertising Infrastructure," *Journal of Information Policy* 9 (2019): 391–92, https://www.jstor.org/stable/10.5325/jinfopoli.9.2019.0370.

51. Matt Stearns, "Where Did the Web Rumors about Obama Come From?," McClatchy DC Bureau, May 8, 2008, updated June 15, 2015, http://www.mcclatchydc.com/news/politics-government/article24483037.html.

52. Janna Anderson and Lee Rainie, "Concerns about Democracy in the Digital Age," Pew Research Center, February, 21, 2020, https://www.pewresearch.org/internet/2020/02/21/concerns-about-democracy-in-the-digital-age/.

53. Shankar Vedantam, "The Power of Political Misinformation," *Washington Post*, September 15, 2008, http://www.washingtonpost.com/wp-dyn/content/article/2008/09/14/AR2008091402375_pf.html.

54. Hannah Denham, "Another Fake Video of Pelosi Goes Viral on Facebook," *Washington Post*, August 3, 2020, https://www.washingtonpost.com/technology/2020/08/03/nancy-pelosi-fake-video-facebook/.

55. Andrea Peterson, "Wikileaks Posts Nearly 20,000 Hacked DNC Emails Online," *Washington Post*, July 22, 2016, https://www.washingtonpost.com/news/the-switch/wp/2016/07/22/wikileaks-posts-nearly-20000-hacked-dnc-emails-online/; Marc L. Songini, "Republican Web Site Hit by Hacker, Taken Off-line," *Computerworld*, November 7, 2000, https://www.computerworld.com/article/2588795/republican-web-site-hit-by-hacker--taken-off-line.html.

56. David Mikkelson, "Did Schumer Delete a Tweet Criticizing Trump for Banning Air Travel from China 'Prematurely'?," Snopes Media Group, March 28, 2020, https://www.snopes.com/fact-check/schumer-tweet-china-travel/.

57. Joan Donovan, "Trolling for Truth on Social Media: What 1990s Internet Protest Movements Share with Today's Disinformation Campaigns," *Scientific American*, October 12, 2020, https://www.scientificamerican.com/article/trolling-for-truth-on-social-media/.

58. Michael Barthel, Amy Mitchell, and Jesse Holcomb, "Many Americans Believe Fake News Is Sowing Confusion," Pew Research Center, December 15, 2016, https://www.journalism.org/2016/12/15/many-americans-believe-fake-news-is-sowing-confusion/; for more recent data, see Amy Watson, "Level of Confusion Caused by Fake News about the Basic Facts of Current Issues and Events in the United States as of March 2019," Statista, October 12, 2020, https://www.statista.com/statistics/657037/fake-news-confusion-level/.

59. U.S. Department of Defense, *DoD Strategy for Operating in Cyberspace (DSOC)*, July 2011, 5, https://csrc.nist.gov/CSRC/media/Projects/ISPAB/documents/DOD-Strategy-for-Operating-in-Cyberspace.pdf.

60. Edward Wong, Matthew Rosenberg, and Julian E. Barnes, "Chinese Agents Helped Spread Messages That Sowed Virus Panic in U.S., Officials Say," *New York Times*, April 22, 2020,

updated January 5, 2021, https://www.nytimes.com/2020/04/22/us/politics/coronavirus -china-disinformation.html.

61. *To Establish an Office of Technology Assessment for the Congress as an Aid in the Identification and Consideration of Existing and Probable Impacts of Technological Application; To Amend the National Science Foundation Act of 1950; And for Other Purposes,* Public Law 92-484, *U.S. Statutes at Large* 86 (1972): 797–803.

62. Angus King and Mike Gallagher, "United States of America: Cyberspace Solarium Commission," executive summary, March 2020, https://5kb.d9b.myftpupload.com/wp -content/uploads/2020/03/CSC-Executive-Summary.pdf.

63. Yuval Noah Harari, "Why Technology Favors Tyranny," *Atlantic,* October 2018, https://www.theatlantic.com/magazine/archive/2018/10/yuval-noah-harari-technology -tyranny/568330/. "Editor's Note: This article is part of a series that attempts to answer the question: Is democracy dying?"

64. Brown, "MIT Sloan Research about Social Media, Misinformation, and Elections"; the study is Lesley Chiou and Catherine Tucker, "Fake News and Advertising on Social Media: A Study of the Anti-vaccination Movement," NBER Working Paper 25223, National Bureau of Economic Research, November 2018, https://www.nber.org/system/files/working_papers/ w25223/w25223.pdf.

65. Audrey Conklin, "Mark Zuckerberg Loses $7 Billion as Companies Drop Ads," *Fox Business,* June 27, 2020, https://www.foxbusiness.com/money/mark-zuckerberg-loses-7-billion -as-advertisers-drop.

CHAPTER 10

1. James Madison, "The Federalist Number 10, [22 November] 1787," National Archives, Founders Online, November 22, 1787, https://founders.archives.gov/documents/ Madison/01-10-02-0178.

2. Joseph de Maistre, "Letter 76 on the Topic of Russia's New Constitutional Laws, August 27, 1811," Famous Sayings and Their Authors: A Collection of Historical Sayings in English, French, German, https://archive.org/details/famoussayingsan00lathgoog/page/n200/ mode/2up?q=Maistre, 201.

3. Christopher Muther, "Instant Gratification Is Making Us Perpetually Impatient," *Boston Globe,* November 2, 2016, https://www.bostonglobe.com/lifestyle/style/2013/02/01/ the-growing-culture-impatience-where-instant-gratification-makes-crave-more-instant-grati- fication/q8tWDNGeJB2mm45fQxtTQP/story.html.

4. Jean-Claude Juncker, "Profile: EU's Jean-Claude Juncker," *BBC News,* July 15, 2014, https://www.bbc.com/news/world-europe-27679170.

5. Thomas B. Edsall, "Democracy, Disrupted," *New York Times,* March 2, 2017, https://www.nytimes.com/2017/03/02/opinion/how-the-internet-threatens-democracy .html?smprod=nytcore-iphone&smid=nytcore-iphone-share&_r=0.

6. Paul Roberts, "Instant Gratification," American Scholar, September 8, 2014, https:// theamericanscholar.org/instant-gratification/#.

7. Ron Fournier, "Eric Cantor and the Curse of 'Short-Termism' in Politics and Business," *Atlantic,* June 15, 2015, https://www.theatlantic.com/politics/archive/2015/06/ eric-cantor-and-the-curse-of-short-termism-in-politics-and-business/460512/.

8. Larry D. Rosen, L. Mark Carrier, and Nancy A. Cheever, "Facebook and Texting Made Me Do It: Media-Induced Task-Switching while Studying," *Computers in Human Behavior* 29, no. 3 (May 2013), https://doi.org/10.1016/j.chb.2012.12.001.

9. Cited in Ronald Aslop, "Instant Gratification and Its Dark Side," Bucknell University News, July 17, 2014, https://www.bucknell.edu/news/instant-gratification-its-dark-side.

10. Barry Glassner, *The Culture of Fear: Why Americans Are Afraid of the Wrong Things* (New York: Basic Books, 1999).

11. John Aloysius Farrell, "Christie, Nixon and the Case for Revenge Politics: Chris Christie, Richard Nixon and the Case for Retribution in Politics," *Politico*, January 10, 2014, https://www.politico.com/magazine/story/2014/01/chris-christie-was-right-102045/.

12. "Public Trust in Government: 1958-2021," Pew Research Center, U.S. Politics & Policy, May 17, 2021, https://www.pewresearch.org/politics/2021/05/17/public-trust-in-government-1958-2021/.

13. Ben Shapiro, "Yes, Politics Is Dirty. But That's Not an Excuse for Making It Dirtier," *DailyWire*, July 19, 2017, http://www.dailywire.com/news/yes-politics-dirty-thats-not-excuse-making-it-ben-shapiro.

14. Andrea Salcedo, "Trump Suggests He'll Fire Fauci 'a Little Bit after the Election'," *Washington Post*, November 2, 2020, https://www.washingtonpost.com/nation/2020/11/02/trump-fauci-suggests-firing-election/.

15. Jean M. Twenge, W. K. Campbell, and Nathan T. Carter, "Declines in Trust in Others and Confidence in Institutions among American Adults and Late Adolescents, 1972–2012," *Psychological Science*, September 9, 2014, https://doi.org/10.1177%2F0956797614545133.

16. David Grusky and Eric Rice, "Generation X Not So Special: Malaise—Cynicism on the Rise for All Age Groups," Stanford News Service, August 24, 2000, https://news.stanford.edu/pr/98/980821genx.html.

17. Maya Angelou, "Facing Evil," Moyers on Democracy, March 28, 1988, https://billmoyers.com/content/facing-evil/.

18. Saumya Dixit, "What Is QAnon? Here's How the Pro-Trump Conspiracy Theory Caught Fire and Spread through Social Media," Meaww, updated January 15, 2021, https://meaww.com/what-is-q-anon-theory-pro-donald-trump-conspiracy-cabal-child-sex-racket-social-media-q.

19. Aidan Quigley, "Who Is Alex Jones? His Top Five Conspiracy Theories Ahead of NBC's Megyn Kelly Interview," *Newsweek*, June 16, 2017, https://www.newsweek.com/who-alex-jones-his-top-five-conspiracy-theories-ahead-nbc-megyn-kelly-626633.

20. Jesse Singal, "The North Dakota Crash Was an Inside Job: It's Scary How Easy It Is to Get People to Believe in Conspiracy Theories a Little," The Cut.com (Vox Media Network), October 27, 2016, https://www.thecut.com/2016/10/its-easy-to-get-people-to-sorta-believe-conspiracy-theories.html.

21. Amber Day, "Can Jon Stewart and Stephen Colbert Influence the Outcome of the Midterms?" *Washington Post*, November 4, 2014, https://www.washingtonpost.com/posteverything/wp/2014/11/04/can-jon-stewart-and-steven-colbert-influence-the-outcome-of-the-midterms/.

22. "American Trends Panel (Wave 1)," Pew Research Center, survey conducted March 19–April 29, 2014. Q22. Based on Web Respondents, https://www.journalism.org/dataset/american-trends-panel-wave-1/.

23. Erik Black, "One Intriguing Argument Why Potential Voters Aren't Going to the Polls," MinnPost, October 8, 2014, https://www.minnpost.com/eric-black-ink/2014/10/one-intriguing-argument-why-potential-voters-aren-t-going-polls/.

24. "Voter Turnout," FairVote, updated August 6, 2019, https://www.fairvote.org/voter_turnout#voter_turnout_101.

25. Barry Popik, ed., "Bad politicians are elected by good citizens who don't vote," The Big Apple (Blog), December 2, 2010, https://www.barrypopik.com/index.php/new_york_city/entry/bad_politicians_are_elected_by_good_citizens_who_dont_vote.

26. Asma Khalid, Don Gonyea, and Leila Fadel, "On the Sidelines of Democracy: Exploring Why So Many Americans Don't Vote," NPR, September 10, 2018, https://www.npr.org/2018/09/10/645223716/on-the-sidelines-of-democracy-exploring-why-so-many-americans-dont-vote. *Note:* Presentation of data credited to Miles Watkins based on NPR analysis of L2 registered voter data.

27. "Is the System Broken? The Right of Citizens of the United States, Who Are Eighteen Years or Older, to Vote Shall Not Be Denied or Abridged—26th Amendment to the Constitution, 1971," PBS.org NewsHour Extra, July–December 2000, https://www.pbs.org/newshour/spc/extra/features/july-dec00/brokensystem.html.

28. Peter L. Berger and Richard John Neuhaus, "Mediating Structures and the Dilemmas of the Welfare State," in *To Empower People: From State to Civil Society*, ed. Michael Novak, 2nd ed. (Washington, DC: AEI, 1996), 158.

29. "Is the System Broken?," PBS.Org NewsHour Extra.

30. Kei Kawashima Ginsberg and Abby Kiesa, "Getting Young People to Vote: Seven Tips for the Classroom," *National Council for the Social Studies: Social Education* 83, no. 4 (2019): 194–99, https://www.socialstudies.org/system/files/publications/articles/se_8304194_0.pdf.

31. Jonathan R. Cole, "Ignorance Does Not Lead to Election Bliss," *Atlantic*, November 8, 2016, https://www.theatlantic.com/education/archive/2016/11/ignorance-does-not-lead-to-election-bliss/506894/.

32. William Gonch et al., "A Crisis in Civic Education," American Council of Trustees and Alumni, January 2016, https://www.goacta.org/wp-content/uploads/ee/download/A_Crisis_in_Civic_Education.pdf.

33. "Amid Pandemic and Protests, Civics Survey Finds Americans Know More of Their Rights," Annenberg Public Policy Center at the University of Pennsylvania, September 14, 2020, https://www.annenbergpublicpolicycenter.org/pandemic-protests-2020-civics-survey-americans-know-much-more-about-their-rights/.

34. Michael A. Wolfe, "From the Three Stooges to the Three Branches—It's Back to School," Missouri Courts, August 28, 2006, https://www.courts.mo.gov/page.jsp?id=3232. As noted in this source: These are the "reflections of then-Missouri Chief Justice Michael A. Wolff" and appeared in his "Law Matters" column the same month and year.

35. "How Did U.S. Students Perform on the Most Recent Assessments?" The Nation's Report Card, accessed September 25, 2020, https://www.nationsreportcard.gov.

36. Patrick Riccards, "National Survey Finds Just 1 in 3 Americans Would Pass Citizenship Test," The Woodrow Wilson National Fellowship Foundation, October 3, 2018, https://woodrow.org/news/national-survey-finds-just-1-in-3-americans-would-pass-citizenship-test/.

37. Zachary Keyser, "Millennials, Gen Z Don't Know about Holocaust," *International Fellowship of Christians and Jews* (blog), September 17, 2020, https://www.ifcj.org/news/fellowship-blog/millennials-gen-z-dont-know-about-holocaust/; *US Attitudes toward Socialism, Communism, and Collectivism* (Washington, DC: Victims of Communism Memorial Foundation, October 2019), 13, https://victimsofcommunism.org/wp-content/uploads/2019/12/VOC-YG_US-Attitudes-Socialism-Communism-and-Collectivism-2019.pdf.

38. Franklin D. Roosevelt, "Fireside Chat," American Presidency Project: UC Santa Barbara, April 14, 1938, https://www.presidency.ucsb.edu/documents/fireside-chat-15.

39. Tom Jacobs, "Here's How We Can Stop Exaggerating Our Political Differences," *Pacific Standard*, July 28, 2015, https://psmag.com/news/lets-stop-exaggerating-our-political-differences-heres-how.

40. "How Do Clinton's and Trump's Tax Plans Compare?" Tax Foundation, October 2016, https://files.taxfoundation.org/legacy/docs/Presidential%20Tax%20Comparison%20-%20Oct%202016.pdf.

41. Janna Anderson and Lee Rainie, "3. Concerns about Democracy in the Digital Age," Pew Research Center, February 21, 2020, https://www.pewresearch.org/internet/2020/02/21/concerns-about-democracy-in-the-digital-age/.

42. "[Notes for an Oration at Braintree, Spring 1772.]," National Archives Founders Online, February–May 1772, https://founders.archives.gov/documents/Adams/01-02-02-0002-0002-0001#DJA02d067n1. Original source: The Adams Papers, *Diary and Autobiography of John Adams*, Vol. 2, *1771–1781*, ed. L. H. Butterfield (Cambridge, MA: Harvard University Press, 1961), 56–61.

43. Stephen Sawchuck, "How 3 States Are Digging In on Civics Education," *Education Week*, July 17, 2019, https://www.edweek.org/teaching-learning/how-3-states-are-digging-in-on-civics-education.

44. Sawchuck, "How 3 States Are Digging In."

45. "Service-Learning and Community Service in K–12 Public Schools: Definitions," National Center for Education Statistics, September 28, 1999, https://nces.ed.gov/surveys/frss/publications/1999043/index.asp?sectionid=2.

46. "H.R.6415—Inspire to Serve Act of 2020: 116th Congress," Congress.gov, March 27, 2020, https://www.congress.gov/bill/116th-congress/house-bill/6415/text?q=%7B%22search%22%3A%5B%22Inspire+to+Serve+act+of+2020%22%5D%7D&r=7&s=6.

47. Inspired to Serve—The Final Report of the National Commission on Military, National, and Public Service (Arlington, VA: National Commission on Military, National, and Public Service, March 2020), https://inspire2serve.gov/sites/default/files/final-report/Final%20Report.pdf, 2, 6.

48. Lawrence A. Cremin, ed., *The Republic and the School: Horace Mann on the Education of Free Men* (New York: Teachers College Press, 1957), 92.

CHAPTER 11

1. Gleb Tsipursky, "How to Address the Epidemic of Lies in Politics," *Scientific American*, June 15, 2017, https://blogs.scientificamerican.com/observations/how-to-address-the-epidemic-of-lies-in-politics/.

2. Jonathan Swift, "Upon the Art of Political Lying," *The Examiner*, no. 15, November 9, 1710, https://ia803203.us.archive.org/8/items/sim_examiner_november-2-november-9-1710_1_15/sim_examiner_november-2-november-9-1710_1_15.pdf.

3. Olivia Solon, "Facebook's Failure: Did Fake News and Polarized Politics Get Trump Elected?," *Guardian*, November 10, 2016, https://www.theguardian.com/technology/2016/nov/10/facebook-fake-news-election-conspiracy-theories?CMP=oth_b-aplnews_d-1.

4. "In Presidential Contest, Voters Say 'Basic Facts,' Not Just Policies, Are in Dispute," Pew Research Center, October 14, 2016, https://www.pewresearch.org/politics/2016/10/14/in-presidential-contest-voters-say-basic-facts-not-just-policies-are-in-dispute/?utm_source=adaptivemailer&utm_medium=email&utm_campaign=16-10-14%20panel%20election%20report&org=982&lvl=100&ite=413&lea=66827.

5. Craig Kafura and Bettina Hammer, "Republicans and Democrats in Different Worlds on Immigration," The Chicago Council on Global Affairs, October 8, 2019, https://www.thechicagocouncil.org/research/public-opinion-survey/republicans-and-democrats-different-worlds-immigration.

6. Abby Budiman, "Key Findings about U.S. Immigrants," Pew Research Center, Fact Tank News in the Numbers, August 20, 2020, https://www.pewresearch.org/fact-tank/2020/08/20/key-findings-about-u-s-immigrants/.

7. U.S. Department of State, *Reports on Terrorism 2018*, October 2019, https://www.state.gov/wp-content/uploads/2019/11/Country-Reports-on-Terrorism-2018-FINAL.pdf, 198.

8. Jerry Haar, "Immigrants Are an Economic Boon to America," *The Hill*, January 7, 2020, https://thehill.com/opinion/immigration/477154-immigrants-are-an-economic-plus-for-the-nation. *Note:* "A myriad of economic studies finds that immigrants are a net economic benefit to the country."

9. U.S. Department of Homeland Security, *The Perils of Illegal Border Crossing*, July 19, 2018, https://www.dhs.gov/news/2018/07/19/perils-illegal-border-crossing.

10. "Most Dangerous Journey: What Central American Migrants Face When They Try to Cross the Border," Amnesty International, February 20, 2014, https://www.amnestyusa.org/most-dangerous-journey-what-central-american-migrants-face-when-they-try-to-cross-the-border/.

11. "Undocumented Immigrants' State & Local Tax Contributions," Institute on Taxation and Economic Policy, March 1, 2017, https://itep.org/undocumented-immigrants-state-local-tax-contributions-2017/; *Note:* Source for 50 percent data point is Niall McCarthy, "How Much Tax Do America's Undocumented Immigrants Actually Pay? [Infographic]," *Forbes*, October 6, 2016, https://www.forbes.com/sites/niallmccarthy/2016/10/06/how-much-tax-do-americas-undocumented-immigrants-actually-pay-infographic/?sh=58f5c2a31de0.

12. "Ronald Reagan on Border Security," Reagan.com, June 18, 2019, https://www.reagan.com/ronald-reagan-on-border-security.

13. Aaron Sharockman, "Truth Check: Clinton and Trump on the Truth-O-Meter," Politifact, November 1, 2016, https://www.politifact.com/article/2016/nov/01/truth-check-clinton-and-trump-truth-o-meter-1-week/.

14. Kevin Roose, "We Asked for Examples of Election Misinformation. You Delivered," *New York Times*, November 4, 2018, https://www.nytimes.com/2018/11/04/us/politics/election-misinformation-facebook.html.

15. Andrew Young and Kabir Sehgal, *Walk in My Shoes: Conversations between a Civil Rights Legend and His Godson on the Journey Ahead* (New York: Palgrave Macmillan, 2010).

16. "Federalist Papers: Primary Documents in American History, Federalist No. 5 The Same Subject Continued: Concerning Dangers from Foreign Force and Influence," Library of Congress, accessed January 28, 2021, https://guides.loc.gov/federalist-papers/text-1-10.

17. Paul J. Zak, "The Neuroscience of Trust Management Behaviors That Foster Employee Engagement," *Harvard Business Review*, January–February 2017, https://hbr.org/2017/01/the-neuroscience-of-trust#:~:text=Employees%20in%20high%2Dtrust%20organizations,working%20at%20low%2Dtrust%20companies.

18. Aristos Georgiou, "Climate Scientists Slam Rick Santorum's 'Conspiracy Theory' That They're in It for the Money," *Newsweek*, November 26, 2018, https://www.newsweek.com/rick-santorum-slammed-conspiracy-theory-climate-scientists-are-it-money-1230584.

19. Jessica McDonald, "How Much Will the 'Green New Deal' Cost?," FactCheck.org, A Project of The Annenberg Public Policy Center, March 14, 2019, https://www.factcheck.org/2019/03/how-much-will-the-green-new-deal-cost/.

20. Varshini Prakash and John Podesta, "Donald Trump Wants a Fight on the Green New Deal. So Do We," *The Nation*, July 24, 2020, https://www.thenation.com/article/environment/climate-action-podesta-prakash/.

21. Sidney Hook, *Sidney Hook on Pragmatism, Democracy, and Freedom: The Essential Essays*, ed. Robert B. Talisse and Robert Tempio (Amherst, NY: Prometheus Books, 2002), 16.

22. "Americans' Confidence in Government, Each Other Are Not Seen as Top-Tier Problems," Pew Research Center, U.S. Politics and Policy, Trust and Distrust in America, July 18, 2019, https://www.pewresearch.org/politics/2019/07/22/trust-and-distrust-in-america/prc_2019-07-22_trust-distrust-in-america_0-07/.

23. Julia Azari, "Every President Claims to Have a Mandate. Does Trump Actually Have One?" *Vox*, November 17, 2016, https://www.vox.com/platform/amp/the-big-idea/2016/11/17/13658374/trump-mandate-history-presidential-politics. Other source of interest: Julia R. Azari, *Delivering the People's Message: The Changing Politics of the Presidential Mandate* (Ithaca, NY: Cornell University Press, 2014).

24. Justine Coleman, "70 Former Senators Propose Bipartisan Caucus for Incumbents," *The Hill*, February 25, 2020, https://thehill.com/homenews/senate/484556-70-former-senators-propose-bipartisan-caucus-of-incumbent-members.

25. Katherine M. Gehl and Michael E. Porter, *Why Competition in the Politics Industry Is Failing America—A Strategy for Reinvigorating Our Democracy* (Cambridge, MA: Harvard Business School, 2017), https://gehlporter.com/wp-content/uploads/2018/11/why-competition-in-the-politics-industry-is-failing-america.pdf.

26. Azari, "Every President Claims to Have a Mandate."

27. David E. Rosenbaum, "The 1992 Campaign: Democrats; Tsongas Economic Plan Suggests Few Sacrifices," *New York Times*, February 24, 1992, https://www.nytimes.com/1992/02/24/us/the-1992-campaign-democrats-tsongas-economic-plan-suggests-few-sacrifices.html.

28. Al From, *The New Democrats and the Return to Power* (New York: Palgrave Macmillan, 2013), 39.

29. "Robert H. Michel," The Dirksen Congressional Center, accessed January 30, 2021, http://www.dirksencenter.org/research-collections/robert-h-michel. *Note:* Digital availability pending for "Change, Politics, and the Future of Congress of Tomorrow," presented during Congressional Institute Trip to Houston, Texas, March 24–26, 1988.

30. Mark A. Uhlig, "Jesse Unruh, a California Political Power, Dies," *New York Times*, August 6, 1987, http://www.nytimes.com/1987/08/06/obituaries/jesse-unruh-a-california-political-power-dies.html?mcubz=1.

31. Jeffrey M. Jones, "In U.S., New Record 43% Are Political Independents," Gallup, January 7, 2015, http://news.gallup.com/poll/180440/new-record-political-independents.aspx.

32. Compiled using state-by-state data from the following source: Primary Elections State-by-State, Independent Voter Project, https://independentvoterproject.org/map.

33. Jonathan Rauch, "How American Politics Went Insane," *Atlantic*, July/August 2016, https://www.theatlantic.com/magazine/archive/2016/07/how-american-politics-went-insane/485570/.

34. Eli Skogerbø and Gunn Sara Enli, "Personalized Campaigns in Party-Centered Politics," *Social Media and Election Campaigns* 16, no. 5 (2013): 131–33, https://doi.org/10.1080/1369118X.2013.782330.

35. Brian L. Ott, "The Age of Twitter: Donald J. Trump and the Politics of Debasement," *Critical Studies in Media Communication* 34, no. 1 (2017): 59–68, http://dx.doi.org/10.1080/15295036.2016.1266686.

36. Ott, "The Age of Twitter."

37. Drew Desilver, "A Productivity Scorecard for the 115th Congress: More Laws than Before, but Not More Substance," Pew Research Center, January 25, 2019, https://www.pewresearch.org/fact-tank/2019/01/25/a-productivity-scorecard-for-115th-congress/.

38. Edward-Isaac Dovere, "The Democratic Debates Aren't Pleasing Anyone," *Atlantic*, September 19, 2019, https://www.theatlantic.com/politics/archive/2019/09/2020-democratic-debates-arent-pleasing-anyone/598306/.

39. Dovere, "The Democratic Debates Aren't Pleasing Anyone."

40. Dovere, "The Democratic Debates Aren't Pleasing Anyone."

41. Avik Roy, "How Obamacare Dramatically Increases the Cost of Insurance for Young Workers," *The Apothecary—Forbes Blog*, March 22, 2012, https://www.forbes.com/sites/theapothecary/2012/03/22/how-obamacare-dramatically-increases-the-cost-of-insurance-for-young-workers/?sh=7fdecf7f7e46.

42. Congressional Budget Office, "Who Went without Health Insurance in 2019, and Why?," September 2020, https://www.cbo.gov/publication/56658.

43. Molly K. Hooper, "'You Lie': Rep. Wilson Apologizes for Yell," *The Hill*, September 10, 2009, https://thehill.com/homenews/house/58035-you-lie-mccain-calls-on-wilson-to-apologize.

44. Dr. Eric Ostermeier, "That Time Barack Obama Spoke about 'Treason,'" Smart Politics, February 7, 2018, https://smartpolitics.lib.umn.edu/2018/02/07/that-time-barack-obama-spoke-of-treason/.

45. J. D. Tuccille, "In Today's America, Everybody Who Disagrees with You Is a Traitor," *Reason*, October 1, 2019, https://reason.com/2019/10/01/in-todays-america-everybody-who-disagrees-with-you-is-a-traitor/.

46. Aaron Blake, "How Many Americans Truly Hate the Other Political Party? About 1 in 4," *Washington Post*, June 19, 2017, https://www.washingtonpost.com/news/the-fix/wp/2017/06/19/how-many-americans-truly-hate-the-other-political-party-only-about-78-million/.

47. "Quote of the Day," Good News Network, December 19, 2020, https://www.goodnewsnetwork.org/barry-goldwater-quote-about-disagreement/#:~:text=Quote%20of%20the%20Day%20%E2%80%9CTo%20disagree,%20one%20does,not%20have%20to%20be%20disagreeable.%E2%80%9D%20%E2%80%93%20Barry%20Goldwater.

48. Thomas B. Langhorne, "Congress Doesn't Live Here Anymore | Secrets of the Hill," *Courier & Press*, updated October 14, 2018, https://www.courierpress.com/story/news/2018/10/14/congress-doesnt-live-here-anymore-secrets-hill/1265733002/.

49. Andrea Shalal, "Federal Watchdog Probing Trump Campaign's Use of White House—Lawmaker," Reuters, November 5, 2020, https://www.reuters.com/article/usa-election-trump-investigation-idINKBN27M0EF.

50. Nahal Toosi, "State Department Memo Warned Senate-Approved Officials Against Appearing at Partisan Events," *Politico*, August 24, 2020, https://www.politico.com/news/2020/08/24/state-department-memo-pompeo-rnc-400897.

51. U.S. Congress, Senate, *Arthur H. Vandenberg—Biography of Arthur H. Vandenberg*, accessed January 31, 2021, https://www.senate.gov/artandhistory/art/artifact/Painting_32_00042.htm.

52. Olivier Knox, "Obama to Romney: 'We Have One President at a Time,'" abcnews.go.com, June 19, 2012, https://abcnews.go.com/amp/Politics/OTUS/obama-romney-president-time/story?id=16607446.

53. Kevin Liptak, "Obama Takes Harsh Political Rhetoric Abroad," CNN, November 18, 2015, https://www.cnn.com/2015/11/18/politics/obama-criticizes-republicans-while-abroad/index.html.

54. Matt Arco, "Christie Calls Obama an Ineffective Negotiator during European Trade Mission," NJ.com, updated March 29, 2019, https://www.nj.com/politics/2015/02/christie_blasts_obama_as_ineffective_negotiator_du.html.

55. John Fritze, "Trump's Japan Trip: President Blasts Biden, Democrats, Mueller while Bringing Politics to World Stage," *USA Today*, updated May 27, 2019, https://www.usatoday.com/story/news/politics/2019/05/27/donald-trump-japan-dismisses-north-korea-missiles-blasts-joe-biden/1249202001/.

56. David M. Herszenhorn and Emmarie Huetteman, "Democrats End Sit-In after 25 Hours, Drawing Attention to Gun Control," *New York Times*, June 23, 2016, https://www.nytimes.com/2016/06/24/us/politics/senate-gun-control.html; Josh Keller, Iaryna Mykhyalyshyn, Adam Pearce, and Derek Watkins, "Why the Orlando Shooting Was So Deadly," nyt.com, June 12, 2016, https://www.nytimes.com/interactive/2016/06/12/us/why-the-orlando-shooting-was-so-deadly.html.

57. David Rutz, "Ryan Slams Democratic Sit-In as 'Political Stunt,' Calls Out Their Fundraising Off It," *Washington Free Beacon*, June 23, 2016, https://freebeacon.com/issues/ryan-slams-democratic-sit-in-as-political-stunt-calls-out-their-fundraising-off-it/; "A Sit-In on the House Floor Over Gun Control," *Atlantic*, June 22, 2016, https://www.theatlantic.com/liveblogs/2016/06/house-democrats-gun-control-sit-in/488264/.

58. Evelyn Rupert, "Democrats Fundraise Off Sit-In," *The Hill*, June 23, 2016, https://thehill.com/blogs/floor-action/senate/284564-dems-fundraise-off-of-sit-in.

59. Adam Clymer, "Jesse Jackson Tells Receptive G.O.P. It Can Pick Up Votes of Blacks," *New York Times*, January 21, 2017, http://www.nytimes.com/1978/01/21/archives/jesse-jackson-tells-receptive-gop-it-can-pick-up-votes-of-blacks.html?mcubz=0.

60. Lee Hamilton, "Lee Hamilton: Without Civility, Our System Won't Work," Howey Politics Indiana, February 20, 2020, https://howeypolitics.com/Content/Columns/Lee-Hamilton/Article/Lee-Hamilton-Without-civility-our-system-won-t-work/10/300/23127.

61. U.S. Congress, House, *Patient Protection and Affordable Care Act*, H.R. 3590, 111th Cong., 2nd sess., introduced in House September 17, 2009, https://www.govinfo.gov/content/pkg/BILLS-111hr3590enr/pdf/BILLS-111hr3590enr.pdf.

62. "Chris Cuomo under Fire for Saying Nothing about His Brother's COVID Deaths Coverup Scandal," TheWashingtonTime.com, February 13, 2021, https://www.thewashingtontime.com/chris-cuomo-under-fire-for-saying-nothing-about-his-brothers-covid-deaths-coverup-scandal/.

63. Daniel Kaufmann and Aart Kraay, "Worldwide Governance Indicators," World Bank, accessed March 7, 2021, https://info.worldbank.org/governance/wgi/. See also: Daniel

Kaufmann, Aart Kraay, and Massimo Mastruzzi, *The Worldwide Governance Indicators Methodology and Analytical Issues* (Washington, DC: The World Bank, Development Research Group, 2010), http://info.worldbank.org/governance/wgi/pdf/WGI.pdf.

64. Jeffrey D. Sachs, *The Price of Civilization: Reawakening American Virtue and Prosperity* (New York: Random House, 2011).

65. Amy Chua and Jed Rubenfeld, "The Threat of Tribalism," *Atlantic*, October 2018, https://sherielabedis.com/2018/12/18/the-threat-of-tribalism-by-amy-chua-and-jed-rubenfeld/.

66. Russell Razzaque, "The Politics of Paranoia / Paranoia and Politics Is a Toxic Mix," *Psychology Today*, July 19, 2012, https://www.psychologytoday.com/us/blog/political-intelligence/201207/the-politics-paranoia.

67. Kathy Frankovic, "Voters Favored Divided Government, Even Though They Didn't Vote That Way," YouGovAmerica, November 16, 2020, https://today.yougov.com/topics/politics/articles-reports/2020/11/16/divided-united-government-voters-poll. See also: "The Economist/YouGov Poll November 8-10, 2020 - 1500 U.S. Registered Voters," YouGov, accessed August 8, 2021, https://docs.cdn.yougov.com/q2rwpojo39/econToplines.pdf, 7.

68. John Stuart Mill, *On Liberty* (London: John W. Parker and Son, 1859), 85–86.

69. Henry Adams, "The Session, 1869–1870," in *Historical Essays* (New York: Charles Scribner's Sons, 1891), 374.

70. Sam Rayburn's phrase "any jackass can kick a barn door down, but it takes a carpenter to build one" originally appeared in a 1953 edition of Drew Pearson's syndicated column entitled the 45 "Washington Merry-Go-Round." Please see barrypopik.com for additional details: Texas, The Lone Star State: "Any jackass can kick a barn down, but it took a carpenter to build it" (Sam Rayburn) (barrypopik.com). Barry Popik, ed., "'Any jackass can kick a barn down, but it took a carpenter to build it' (Sam Rayburn)," The Big Apple (Blog), January 4, 2007, https://www.barrypopik.com/index.php/texas/entry/any_jackass_can_kick_a_barn_down_but_it_took_a_carpenter_to_build_it_sam_ra/.

CHAPTER 12

1. Sandra Day O'Connor, "Text of Sandra Day O'Connor's Commencement Address (2004)," Palo Alto, California, June 13, 2004, https://news.stanford.edu/news/2004/june16/oconnor-text-616.html.

2. Jessie Kratz, "The National Archives' larger-than-life statues," Pieces of History, National Archives, May 22, 2018, https://prologue.blogs.archives.gov/2018/05/22/the-national-archives-larger-than-life-statues/.

3. [Sherman Anti-Trust Act]: Act of July 2, 1890 (Sherman Anti-Trust Act), July 2, 1890; Enrolled Acts and Resolutions of Congress, 1789–1992; General Records of the United States Government; Record Group 11; National Archives, Our Documents, https://www.archives.gov/historical-docs/todays-doc/index.html?dod-date=702&_ga=2.197980079.182085447.1628350073-1699404848.1627513984. [Clayton Anti-Trust Act]: "Clayton Antitrust Act—An Antitrust Legislation that Sought to Further Strengthen the Sherman Antitrust Act," Corporate Finance Institute, accessed August 7, 2021, https://corporatefinanceinstitute.com/resources/knowledge/finance/clayton-antitrust-act/; [Federal Trade Commission Act]: "15 U.S. Code Subchapter I—Federal Trade Commission, Cornell Law School / Legal Information Institute, accessed August 7, 2021, https://www.law.cornell.edu/uscode/text/15/chapter-2/subchapter-I. See also: "Antitrust Laws and You,"

United States Department of Justice, accessed August 7, 2021, https://www.justice.gov/atr/antitrust-laws-and-you.

4. "H.R.3622—Goldwater-Nichols Department of Defense Reorganization Act of 1986," Congress.gov, accessed August 7, 2021, https://www.congress.gov/bill/99th-congress/house-bill/3622.

5. Inspired to Serve—The Final Report of the National Commission on Military, National, and Public Service (Arlington, VA: National Commission on Military, National, and Public Service, March 2020), https://inspire2serve.gov/sites/default/files/final-report/Final%20Report.pdf, 2, 6.

6. *Inspired to Serve—The Final Report of the National Commission on Military, National, and Public Service* (Arlington, VA: National Commission on Military, National, and Public Service, March 25, 2020), https://inspire2serve.gov/reports/final-report.

7. Doris Kearns Goodwin, *Team of Rivals: The Political Genius of Abraham Lincoln* (New York: Simon & Schuster, 2005), 367. See also: Abraham Lincoln, "'July 4, 1861: July 4th Message to Congress' / Transcript—Presidential Speeches, Abraham Lincoln Presidency," University of Virginia, Miller Center, https://millercenter.org/the-presidency/presidential-speeches/july-4-1861-july-4th-message-congress.

8. Jean Edward Smith, *FDR* (New York: Random House, 2007), 538.

9. William Gray, "New poll: Voters want to reduce the influence of big money in politics," Issue One, November 9, 2018, https://www.issueone.org/new-poll-voters-want-to-reduce-the-influence-of-big-money-in-politics-should-be-a-top-priority-in-next-congress/.

10. "National Park Service Museum Collections—Rising Sun Armchair and Detail," Independence National Historical Park, accessed August 7, 2021, https://www.nps.gov/museum/exhibits/revwar/image_gal/indeimg/armchair.html.

11. "Rising Sun Armchair and Detail," Independence National Historical Park.

12. "Text of Eisenhower's Speech Ending Campaign with Appeal for National Unity," *New York Times*, November 4, 1952, https://timesmachine.nytimes.com/timesmachine/1952/11/04/issue.html.

13. John Adams, "From John Adams to James Warren, 22 April 1776," National Archives / Founders Online, accessed August 7, 2021, https://founders.archives.gov/documents/Adams/06-04-02-0052.

Index

AAPOR. *See* American Association for Public Opinion Research

AARP. *See* American Association of Retired Persons

Abramowitz, Alan, 36, 116

ACTA. *See* American Council of Trustees and Alumni

Adams, John, 15–16, 175, 185; on preservation of liberty, 154; on public business, 27

Adams, John Quincy, 86; presidential election of 1828, 31

Ailes, Roger, 117

al-Assad, Bashar, 34

Ambrose, Stephen E.: on American citizen soldiers, 13

America First Action, 53

American Association for Public Opinion Research (AAPOR): on push polls, 40

American Association of Retired Persons (AARP), 21–23

American Council of Trustees and Alumni (ACTA), 152

American Leadership, xiv, xv, 9; retreat of, 6

American National Election Studies (ANES), 28, 147

Amnesty International, 158

Anderson, John, 70

ANES. *See* American National Election Studies

Angell, Roger, 104

Angelou, Maya, 148

Annenberg Public Policy Center (University of Pennsylvania), 41–42, 72

Annenberg School for Communication and Journalism (University of Pennsylvania), 129

Anzia, Sarah, 81

AOC. *See* Ocasio-Cortez, Alexandria

artificial intelligence, xv, 105, 139; and deep fake videos, 136; and microtargeting, 130–31; use of, 84

ATF. *See* Bureau of Alcohol, Tobacco, and Firearms

The Atlantic, 55, 80, 135, 152, 168

attention deficit, 145

autocracy, xiv, xv, 6, 12–13, 142, 176

Automatic Voter Registration (AVR), 78

Azari, Julia, 161

Bannon, Steve, 37

Barksdale, William, 92

Barnett, Randy, 67

Bell, Jennifer, 24–25

Bessi, Alessandro, 134–35

Biden, Joe, 3, 32–33, 35, 38, 40, 53, 66, 72, 80, 82, 103, 117, 148, 162, 167–68

Big Tent Project, 54–55

Bipartisan Campaign Reform Act (also known as McCain-Feingold), 47

Bipartisan Policy Center (BPC), 105

Bishop, Bill, 112

Boehner, John, 85, 96

Bono (Paul David Hewson): speech at Georgetown University, 9

Boogaloo Bois, 40

Boxell, Levi, 39

BPC. *See* Bipartisan Policy Center

Brandeis, Louis: famous saying, 100

Brazile, Donna: infamous role in townhall debate, 118

Brennan Center for Justice (New York University Law School), 63, 79, 82

Broder, David, 119

Brookings Institution, 20, 42, 64, 114

Brooks, Preston, 92

Buckley v. Valeo, 52, 56–57

Bureau of Alcohol, Tobacco, and Firearms (ATF), 94

Bush, George H. W., 29, 32, 37, 45, 50, 70; Clean Air Act, 170, 184

Bush, George W., 50, 77, 84, 86, 112, 137, 161–62

Bush v. Gore, 79

Butler, Andrew, 92

Cambridge Analytica, 128–29

campaign finance, 54–55, 57, 61, 157, 163; campaign contributions, 21-22, 45, 50–51, 57-58, 116; "dark money," 54–55; donors, 10–11, 23, 25, 28, 46–48, 51–56, 58, 128, 130, 163–64, 168; Internal Revenue Code sections, 21–22, 54–55, 58; law, 25–26; "Money Bomb," 56; political fundraising, xii, 19–20, 24–25, 32, 38, 42–43, 48–52, 54, 56–59, 103, 115, 130, 145, 163–64, 168, 179; "primary purpose test," 54; public finance, 58; reform of, 47, 56

CampaignGrid, 130

Campaign Legal Center (CLC), 54, 56

Cantor, Eric: on short-termism, 144

Carter, Jimmy, 33, 47, 70, 80, 84, 95, 161–62, 170

Castle, Mike, 66

CATO Institute: on the Motor Voter Act, 78

CBO. *See* Congressional Budget Office

celebrity, 73, 119, 130; national obsession with, 149–50

Census, US, 62

Center for Computer Security and Society (C2S2), 82

Center for Digital Democracy, 128

Center for Public Integrity, 24, 50

Center for Responsive Politics (now OpenSecrets), 55

Center for Strategic and International Studies (CSIS), 101

Chang, Priscilla, 83

checks and balances, 101, 107, 143, 162

Chester, Jeff, 128

China, 6, 12, 38, 137–38, 184; authoritarianism, 174; cybersystems, use of, 141; exploiting digital tools and social media networks, 8; Jinping, Xi, 38

Christakis, Nicholas, 134

Chua, Amy, 171

Cilley, John, 92

citizenship, 78, 119, 141, 151–52, 154–56, 178, 180–82

Citizens United, 116, 179; desired reversal of, 57; and super PACs, 24, 53; unlimited and undisclosed political donations, role in, 56, 116; *v. Federal Election Commission*, 53, 56

civic literacy, 153, 155, 181

civility, 4, 119, 148, 164–69,

civil rights, 76, 159, 169, 176, 181–84

CivXNow, 155

Clayton Antitrust Act, 178

CLC. *See* Campaign Legal Center

Cleaver, Emanuel, II, 167

Clemenceau, Georges, 152

CLF. *See* Congressional Leadership Fund

climate change (and atmospheric warming), 5, 37, 103, 144, 148, 160–61, 184

Clinton, Hillary Rodham, 35, 40, 110, 113, 118, 137, 148, 170; presidential election of 2016, 2, 29, 80, 82, 86, 88, 117, 159

Clinton, William J., 29, 45, 50, 70, 78, 112, 158, 162–63, 170, 184; on never-ending presidential elections, 34

CNN, 113–14, 117–18, 160, 170; aiding Donald Trump's prospects as a presidential candidate, 116–17; Democrats' patronizing of, 112; on microtargerting, 130; portion of programming devoted to opinion, 114; on presidential debates, 71, 112–13

Coalition for Free and Open Elections (COFOE): on ballot requirements for minor party

candidates, 67

Coffman, Mike, 85

COFOE. *See* Coalition for Free and Open Elections

Cold War, 6–7, 12, 28, 151, 176, 183

Cole, Jonathan, 152

Commission on Freedom of the Press (aka Hutchins Commission), 112

Commission on Presidential Debates (CPD), 70

Committee for the Study of the American Electorate, 152

"Committee of Eleven on Postponed Matters," 87

Common Sense Media, 145

communism, 5–6, 12, 152

community press, 120

congressional bills: appropriation bills, 94, 98, 169; authorizations, 93–94, 100, 102, 105, 169, 180; budget bills, 93

Congressional Budget and Impoundment Control Act: and fiscal cliff, 94

Congressional Budget Office (CBO), 94-95

congressional districting, 62–65, 75, 88, 128, 161; gerrymandering, 62–65, 87–88, 139; Permanent Apportionment Act, 62

Congressional Leadership Fund (CLF), 54

Congressional Record, 51, 91, 138

conspiracy theory, 7, 137, 149

Constitutional Convention, 75–76, 87, 88, 91, 184

consumer price index, 47

Continental Congress, 175

controlled chaos, 6–9

Conway, Kellyanne, 113

Cook Political Report, 63

Cooper, Roy, 65

cost of running for office, xii

COVID-19, 3, 4, 35, 38, 105, 132, 138, 144, 170, 183

CPD. *See* Commission on Presidential Debates

CPI. *See* Consumer Price Index

Cronkite, Walter, 114, 170

Crossroads GPS, 54–55

CSC. *See* Cyberspace Solarium Commission

CSIS. *See* Center for Strategic and International Studies

C-SPAN, 34, 95, 100

C2S2. *See* Center for Computer Security and Society

Cuomo, Andrew, 170

Cuomo, Chris, 113, 170

cybersecurity, 5, 83–84, 78, 102, 126, 139; bot attacks, 7; Cyberspace Solarium Commission (CSC), 5, 139; hackers, 40, 82–83, 136, 146; Internet bots (Web robots or bots), 7, 134–35, 138–39, 180; "putinbots," 7; Russian hackers, 40, 83

cynicism, ix, 39, 56, 86, 119, 147–48, 159–61

Dann, Carrie, 131

DARPA. *See* Defense Advanced Research Projects Agency

Daschle, Tom, 36, 100

DCCC. *See* Democratic Party, Democratic Congressional Campaign Committee

D-Day, 1, 6, 13

DEA. *See* Drug Enforcement Administration

debates, xii, 2, 42, 68–73, 113, 134–35, 165–66, 172, 180; democratic primary debates, 165; presidential debate reform, 72; presidential debates, 68–73; republican primary debate, 165

debt-to-GDP ratio, 94

Defense Advanced Research Projects Agency (DARPA), 139

Delaney, John, 33
Delay, Tom, 160
Deming, W. Edwards, 16
DeMint, Jim, 85
democracy, ix, xi, xii, xiii, xiv, xv, 3–16,
    19–21, 27, 29–30, 38, 42, 44, 46, 53,
    56–57, 61, 65, 68, 72–73, 75–76, 79,
    81, 83–84, 88–89, 90, 94, 102, 104–5,
    107–8, 110, 112, 119–21, 125–26,
    128–29, 135–36, 138–41, 143–44,
    151–52, 154–57, 159, 161–63, 170–71,
    173, 175–78, 180–85
Democratic Party, xiii, 3, 16–17, 32, 39,
    46, 64, 81, 147, 163; and Commission
    on Presidential Debates, 70; and
    Democratic Congressional Campaign
    Committee (DCCC), 48, 168; and
    Democratic National Committee
    (DNC), 15, 19, 26, 45–46, 70, 110,
    118, 137, 147–48; and Democratic
    National Convention, 32; and
    Democratic Senatorial Campaign
    Committee (DSCC), 48; Donna Brazile
    and Chair of, 118; and solicitation of
    Roger Tamraz, 45–46, 53
Democratic-Republican Party, 16, 31, 62
Dent, Charlie, 97
Department of Energy, 46
Department of Homeland Security (DHS),
    83–84, 101–2
Dewey, Thomas, 69
DHS. *See* Department of Homeland
    Security
Diamond, Larry, 89
digital political ads, 56
disinformation, 7, 25, 111, 121–22, 126,
    132, 136, 138, 141, 159, 180
distrust, 7, 11, 37–39, 57, 78, 80–81, 86–
    87, 95, 100, 110–11, 120, 128, 147–49,
    159–61, 177
DNC. *See* Democratic Party, Democratic
    National Committee
DOE. *See* Department of Energy
Dole, Bob, 70
Donovan, Joan, 135
Drug Enforcement Administration (DEA),
    94

Drutman, Lee, 39, 63
DSCC. *See* Democratic Party, Democratic
    Senatorial Campaign Committee
DSPolitical, 130
Dukakis, Michael S., 37, 70
Duncan, Arne S., 5
duopoly, xii, xv, 10, 12, 16–18, 25, 58–59,
    72–73, 178, 183; control on general
    ballot access, 66; financing political
    combat, 116; grip on power, 12, 16, 61,
    89, 104, 115
Duty & Honor, 54–55

EAC. *See* Election Assistance Center
earmarks: appropriations, 98
Edsall, Thomas B., 39–40; on weakening of
    political parties, 25–26
education, 4, 5, 79, 121, 141, 152, 155–56,
    165, 179, 180–81
E-Government, 126
Eisenhower, Dwight D., 32, 69, 185; order
    transmitted on D-Day, 13; on US
    Communist Party, 166; warning in 1961
    Farewell Address to the nation, 18
Election Assistance Commission (EAC), 78,
    82, 84
election industry, xi, xii, xiii, xiv, 10, 15,
    32, 128
elections: administration of, 77–78, 82–84;
    campaign contributions. *See* campaign
    finance, campaign contributions;
    congressional elections, 34, 41, 63–64;
    election rigging, 3; integrity of, 44,
    58, 76–78, 80–82, 84, 135; midterm
    elections, 2, 36, 41, 52, 85, 134, 150;
    "off-cycle" and, 80–81; popular vote
    and, 33, 80, 86–88, 162; presidential
    elections, 3, 24, 31, 34, 36, 47, 55, 58,
    76–77, 82, 85, 88–89, 115, 118, 134,
    137, 150, 153, 158, 162; primaries,
    3, 25, 26, 29, 33–34, 40, 58, 63–69,
    72, 76, 80, 85-86, 152, 161, 164, 179;
    plurality winning and, 20, 29, 68, 89,
    99, 162
Electoral College, 31–32, 86–88, 161;
    versus proportional system, 88; and
    "winner takes all," xiii, 87–88, 179

Employment Act of 1947, 183
entitlement programs, 4, 22–23, 41, 163, 151
executive branch, xiv, 21, 28, 50, 61, 93, 98, 101–3, 139, 169; rulemaking and congressional oversight of, 103
executive orders, 102–3, 162
extreme poverty, 13, 176

Face the Nation, 69, 149
FactCheck.org, 135
Fairness Doctrine, 70; withdrawing the rule, 109, 121
fake news, 107–8, 110, 116, 123, 134, 140, 148, 180; post-truth politics and, 159
Fauci, Anthony Stephen, 3, 148
FBI. *See* Federal Bureau of Investigation
FCC. *See* Federal Communications Commission
FDA. *See* Food and Drug Administration
FEC. *See* Federal Election Commission
federal budget, 4, 163; budget bills, 93
Federal Bureau of Investigation (FBI), 7, 40, 135, 148–49; operating on expired authorization, 94
Federal Communications Commission (FCC), 121; "equal time," 70, 109
federal debt, 4, 94, 144, 176
Federal Election Campaign Act of 1974, 58
Federal Election Commission (FEC), 23–24, 43, 47, 53–54, 56, 58, 140
Federalists, 16, 31, 62
Federal spending, 93–94, 170
Federal Trade Commission (FTC), 94
Federal Trade Commission Act, 178
Ferrara, Emilio, 134–35
First Amendment, 123
FlackCheck.org: on deceptive practices common in political ads, 41, 43
Flake, Jeff, 104
Flinders, Matt, 38
Floyd, George, 113, 119
Food and Drug Administration (FDA), 180
45 Committee, 54–55
founders (framers), ix, x, xiii, 15, 26, 48, 52, 61–62, 64, 109, 175; bicameral legislative branch, opting for, 61–62;

coequal branch of government, design of, 97; legislative branch, design of, 91; nation's chief magistrate, on choosing, 87; on self-government, 161
Fournier, Ron, 2
Fowler, James, 134
FOX News, 71, 110–14, 117–18, 149
Frank, Barney, 48–49
Franklin, Benjamin, 75–76, 175, 184
freedom, x, xii, xiv, 5–7, 11–13, 56, 68, 75–76, 89, 101, 107–9, 112, 119, 121–22, 138, 140, 142, 151, 168, 171–73, 175–76, 181–82, 184–85
Freedom Caucus, 28, 96
Freedom House, 5–6
Freeman, Joanne, 92
From, Al, 163
Fruman, Igor, 54
FTC. *See* Federal Trade Commission
fundraising. *See* campaign finance, political fundraising
fusion voting, 88–89, 179

Gage, Alexander, 128
Gans, Curtis, 152
Gastil, John, 73
Gazette of the United States, 108
Gehl, Katherine, 17–18
generation types: Baby Boomer (Boomers), 133, 146, 151; Generation X (Gen X), 133; Generation Z (Gen Z), 145; Millennials (Gen Y), 5, 12, 133, 145, 151–52
Gentzkow, Matthew, 39
Georgetown Center for the Constitution (Georgetown University), 67
Gerasimov, Valery Vasilyevich, 6–9, 11
Gerry, Elbridge, 62, 87
Gertz, Matt, 117
Gianoli, Gerard J., 23
Gingrich revolution, 95–96
Glassner, Barry, 146
Global Energy Producers, 53–54
golden mean, 161
Goldwater, Barry M., 37, 166
Goldwater-Nichols Department of Defense Reorganization Act of 1986, 179

Google AdWords, 130
Gore, Albert Arnold Jr., 29, 65, 77, 79, 82, 86, 137
GOTV [Get Out the Vote], 133
government, x, xi, xii, xiv, xv, 1, 4–5, 8–9, 12–16, 18, 21, 25–27, 31, 34, 39, 46–48, 50, 52–53, 56–58, 61–62, 72, 75, 77–79, 87, 89, 90–97, 103–5, 107–8, 113, 115, 120–22, 126, 128, 139, 140–41, 143–44, 146–52, 154–58, 160–63, 167, 169–73, 177, 180–82, 185
government shutdowns, 93–94, 180
Graff, Garrett, 121
Graham, Lindsey, 34
Grand Canyon National Park, 23
Graves, William, 92
Greatest Generation, 185
Great Seal of the United States, 175, 185
Greene, Sam, 144
Green New Deal, 160
Green Party, 29, 70
Guiliani, Rudy, 53
"gun-show loophole," 22

Halderman, J. Alex, 82
Hamilton, Lee, 169
Hamre, John, 101
Harrari, Yuval Noah, 139–40
Harrison, Benjamin, 86
Harris, Vincent, 132–33
Harwood, Richard, 20
Hastert, Dennis, 97
HAVA. *See* Help America Vote Act
Hayes, Rutherford B., 86
health care, 4, 23, 38, 170, 176; Affordable Care Act (ACA) (Obamacare), 22, 115, 145, 165, 169; costs of, 23, 38, 176; insurance, 22–23, 165, 170
Help America Vote Act (HAVA), 82
Helsinki Accords, 68
The Heritage Foundation, 79, 101
Hersh, Eitan, 80–81
Heslin, Shiela, 46
Hogan, Larry, 65
Holman, Craig, 52
Holmes, Steven A., 67
Hook, Janet, 39

Hook, Sidney, 161
Horton, Willie, 37
House Majority Fund, 54
human rights, xii, xiv, xv, 6, 9, 12, 75, 158, 175, 185; danger to, 30
Humphrey, Hubert, 33
Hurd, Will, 104
hybrid warfare, 6, 7, 138

Icivics, 155
immigration, 5, 38, 104, 158; border wall, 158–59
Independence National Historical Park, 184
Independent Commission on the Security Forces of Iraq, 237
Independents, 17, 64, 66, 85, 104, 164, 179, 182
Information Sciences Institute (ISI), 134
International Space Station (ISS), 13
Internet, 11, 20, 24, 25–26, 37, 42–43, 56, 71–72, 78, 82–83, 109–10, 119–20, 125–27, 132–38, 140–42, 144–46, 148, 151, 164, 184
Internet Research Agency (IRA), 129
Iowa, 33, 46; poll takers disclosure requirement, 43
IRA. *See* Internet Research Agency
Iran, 8, 40
Iraq, xi, 102, 145
ISI. *See* Information Sciences Institute
Israel, Steve, 49
ISS. *See* International Space Station
Issacharoff, Samuel, 5; on weakening of political parties, 26
Issue One, 2, 19, 48, 55, 58, 104
Iyengar, Shanto, 37; on animosity towards opposing party, 27

Jackson, Andrew, 16, 31, 161
Jackson, Brooks, 135
Jackson, Jesse, 169
Jacobs, Tom, 153
Jamieson, Kathleen Hall, 42–43
Jay, John, 160
Jefferson, Thomas, 175; Democratic-Republican Party, 16; importance of free of the press, 107

Jenkins, Lynn, 104
Jim Crow Laws, 76–77
Johnson, Gary, 70–71
Johnson, Lyndon B., 37, 77, 169–70, 184;
    Voting Rights Act proposed by, 76
Johnson, Sam, 106
Jolly, David, 49
Jones, Alex, 148–49
Jones, James L., USMC (Ret.), xi, 4
Jones, Jim, 49
Jones, Tom, 113
journalism: "yellow journalism," 108, 112
journalism and news: broadcast networks,
    126; distrust of, 8, 111–23, 128, 177;
    media, 11–12, 19, 20, 25–26, 29, 31–
    32, 38–39, 68, 71–73, 106–23, 131–32,
    147, 157, 177, 180, 183; MSNBC, 71,
    112–14, 116–17; network television,
    109; "News deserts," 120; Newsmax,
    112; *New York Times*, 23, 25, 27–28,
    32, 51, 67, 89–90, 129–30, 159; One
    America News, 112; PBS NewsHour,
    36–37, 111, 151; press, bias of, 11,
    108–10, 118, 141
Journalist's Resource, 116

Kagame, Paul, 6
Kaiser, Robert: on lack of accuracy and
    fairness in reporting, 114
Kamarck, Elaine C., 42
Kaptur, Marcie, 48
Kawashima-Ginsberg, Kei, 152
Keith, Damon J., 108
Kelly, Walt, 9
Kennedy, John F., 9, 69
Kennedy School of Government (Harvard
    University), 115, 118
Kennedy, Ted, 49
Keyssar, Alexander: on the inability to
    change with Electoral College, 87
Khrushchev, Nikita Sergeyevich, 28
King, Angus, 53
King, Martin Luther, Jr., 13, 177
Kissinger, Henry: on how national
    leadership has changed, xiii
Koch brothers, 26, 56
Krupenkin, Masha, 27, 37

Lamont, Ned, 65
League of Women Voters (LWV), 70
Lehrer, Jim, 111, 122
Levine, Peter: on the Koch brothers'
    political network, 26
Lewis, Charles, 50
Lewis, John, 168
Libertarian Party, 70
Lieberman, Joe, 65
Lincoln-Douglas Debates (also known as
    The Great Debates of 1858), 71
Lippmann, Walter, x, 111, 121
lobbying, 21, 57, 71; and the NRA, 22;
    poor public reputation, 50
LoBiondo, Frank, 104
Los Angeles Times, 39
Luce, Henry, 121
LWV. *See* League of Women Voters

Mackenzie, Scott B., 24
Madison, James, 16, 62, 143
Maistre, Joseph de, 143
Majority Forward, 54–55
Mann, Horace, 156
Mann, Thomas, 97
Mansfield, Mike, 76, 100
Martin, Joe, 182
Massie, Thomas H., 19
Mayersohn, Andrew, 36
McCain-Feingold, 47
McCain, John S., xii, xiii, 21, 58; American
    exceptionalism, 172; on benefiting
    candidates and super PAC contributors,
    53; 2000 presidential primaries, 40
McCarthy, Eugene, 33
McConnell, Mitch, 92
McCutheon v. FEC, 56
McGill, Andrew, 113, 168
McGovern-Fraser Commission, 33
McLuhan, Marshall, 127, 177
McNair, Denise, 76
Michel, Bob, 163
microtargeting, 128–31, 140
Mill, John Stuart, 174
misinformation, 24–25, 111, 126–27, 133,
    137, 140–41
Mondale, Walter, 70

money in politics, 57, 183. *See also* campaign finance

Moniz, Ernie, 160

Montesquieu: *Spirit of the Laws*, 61

Montgomery, Kathryn: on commercial digital media and marketing ecosystem, 128

Moonves, Les, 116

Motor Voter Act (MVA), 78

Mueller, Robert, 168

MVA. *See* Motor Voter Act

Nader, Ralph, 29

NASS. *See* National Association of Secretaries of State

Nathan, George Jean, 150

National Association of Secretaries of State (NASS), 84

National Commission on Military, National, and Public Service (NCMNPS), 155, 181

National Commission on Terrorist Attacks Upon the United States (9/11 Commission), 11, 102, 148

National Defense Authorization Act, 93, 169

National Endowment for Democracy (NED), 163

National Gazette, 108

National Rifle Association (NRA), 21–22

national security, xi, 16, 30, 73, 93, 138, 158, 160, 179; National Security Act of 1947, 183;

National Security Council (NSC), 45–46; National Security Strategy (NSS), xiv

national service, 155

National Weather Service (NWS), 94

NATO. *See* North American Treaty Organization

NCMNPS. *See* National Commission on Military, National, and Public Service

NED. *See* National Endowment for Democracy

New America Foundation, 63

9/11 Commission. *See* National Commission on Terrorist Attacks Upon the United States

Nixon-Kennedy debates, 69–70, 71

Nixon, Richard M., 32, 69–71, 87, 146, 161–62, 184; and antipathy toward government, 95; 1960 presidential election, 36, 77; specific legislative proposals, 170

Nolter, Chris, 116

North Atlantic Treaty Organization (NATO), 3-4, 6; Dwight Eisenhower commander of, 32; and Vladimir Putin, 6

"North Dakota Crash," 149

North Korea, 8, 13, 167–68

NRA. *See* National Rifle Association

NRCC. *See* Republican Party, National Republican Congressional Committee

NSC. *See* National Security Council

NSS. *See* National Security Strategy

Nutrition Labeling and Education Act, 180

NVRA. *See* Motor Voter Act

NWS. *See* National Weather Service

Obama, Barack, 2, 4, 32–33, 50, 58, 66, 70, 78, 88, 96, 98, 102, 103, 115, 117–18, 129, 136, 148–49, 153, 158–62, 165–67; on gerrymandering, 64; 2012 presidential campaign and microtargeting, 130

Ocasio-Cortez, Alexandria (AOC), 85, 96

O'Connor, Sandra Day, 177

O'Donnell, Christine, 66

OECD. *See* Organisation for Economic Co-operation and Development

Office of Technology Assessment (OTA), 139

Older Americans Act of 1965, 151

One Nation, 54–55

Open Debate Coalition, 72

OPIC. *See* Overseas Project Investment Corporation

Organisation for Economic Co-operation and Development (OECD), 103–4; on burdens on US regulatory system, 171

Ornstein, Norm: on the characteristics of modern congress, 97

O'Rourke, James S., IV: on democracy in the digital age, 154

OTA. *See* Office of Technology Assessment

Ott, Brian: on Twitter and public discourse, 164

Overseas Project Investment Corporation (OPIC), 46

PACs. *See* Political Action Committees

Palin, Sarah, 136

Parker, Sarah Jessica, 130

parliamentary maneuver: "filling up the tree," 97

parliamentary procedure, 167; "closed rules," 97; cloture, 99; cloture petition, 98; filibuster, 98–99; "nuclear option," 98–99; as partisan weaponry, 99; regular order, 96–97, 105, 179

Parnas, Lev, 53

partisan gridlock, 84, 94, 102

partisanship, 10–11, 25–27, 34, 91, 95, 98, 104, 159, 161, 181, 183; bipartisanship, 95, 171, 176–77; hyper, 95–96, 100–101, 110, 114, 159, 161; and media, 118–19; negative, 2, 9, 25–27, 36–39, 42, 55, 101

party duopoly, xii, xv, 10, 12, 16, 61, 104, 178

Patriot Majority, 54–55

Patterson, Thomas: on rise of horse-race journalism, 115

Pelosi, Nancy, 9, 92, 137, 168–69

Perot, Henry Ross, 29; barred from debate, 70; as third-party candidate, 67

Perry, Oliver Hazard (Admiral), 9

Pizzagate, 148

Podesta, John D, Jr., 40; Republican Party approach to climate crisis, 160

Political Action Committees (PACs), 20–21, 23–24, 154; outside expenditure-only groups, 43; Super. *See* Super PACs

political advertising, 56, 69–70, 116, 129, 140; "issue ads," 47; negativity, 35–36, 118; spending, 56, 116, 133

political and public polling: congressional approval rating, 63; Congress's resistance to passing anti-push polling legislation, 43; Gallup, 2, 22, 81, 108; Harris poll, 64; push polling, among

dishonest campaign tactics, 41; trust in government, 1–2, 9, 58, 147, 154

political campaigns, xii, 2, 25, 34, 42, 44, 68, 91, 115, 117–18, 126, 129–30, 154, 157; campaign cost, 58; campaign financing. *See* campaign finance; campaign spending, 47, 58–59

political consultants, xii, 19–20, 23–24, 27–28, 35

political culture, xii, xiii, xiv, xv, 2–5, 11–12, 32, 35, 39, 42, 55, 59, 61, 71, 82, 104, 110, 117–18, 120, 149, 151–53, 163–64, 168, 172, 176–78, 183

political division, xii, xv, 12, 89–90, 110

political polarization, 1–2, 27–28, 39, 95–96, 105–6, 161

PolitiFact, 43, 159

Pompeo, Mike, 53

popular vote, 33, 80, 86–88, 162; direct popular vote, 87; presidents losing the popular vote but winning the electoral college, 86–87

Port, Jack, 1, 6, 13

Porter, Michael, 17, 162

Potter, John "Bowie Knife," 92

Powell, Colin L., 36

Poynter Institute for Media Studies, 113

Prakash, Varshini, 160

Prall, Kyle Gerald, 24

Presidential Election Campaign Fund, 58

presidential elections. *See* elections

press, 24, 33, 38, 43, 68, 72, 85, 100, 105, 107–10, 112, 114–15, 117–22, 126, 131, 143, 145–46, 149, 159–60, 164, 169–70. *See also* journalism and news, press, bias of

Primaries. *See* elections

primary elections. *See* elections

The Princeton Review, 71

Problem Solvers Caucus, 64, 92

proportional system, 88

Proud Boys, 40

Public Citizen, 52

Putnam, Robert, 151

QAnon, 148–49

Quartz Media, 131

Radel, Henry "Trey," 19
Ranked-Choice Voting (RCV), 88–90, 179; reforms such as, 29–30
Rauch, Jonathan, 55; on gerrymandered congressional districts, 64
Rayburn, Sam, 174
RCV. *See* Ranked-Choice Voting
Reagan, Ronald Wilson, 32, 41, 45, 47, 50, 70, 95, 184; description of America, 9; on gerrymandering, 64; opposing border fences, 158–59; and pro-federalism proposals, 170
Reid, Harry: and the "nuclear option," 98–99
Reporters without Borders (RSF), 119
Republican Party, 17, 26, 39, 45, 64, 89, 147, 168; National Republican Congressional Committee (NRCC), 19, 48; Republican National Committee (RNC), 19, 20–21, 26, 33, 38, 45, 71, 169; Republican National Convention, 20, 32, 38, 167; Republican Senatorial Campaign Committee (RSCC), 48
Rice, Condoleezza, 76
Rich, Seth, 110, 147–48
Ripley, Amanda, 108
RNC. *See* Republican Party, Republican National Committee
Roberts, Paul, 144
Robinson, James Harvey, 34
Roller, Emma, 32
Romney, Mitt, 70, 88, 129–30, 153–54, 167; on money and influence, 49
Roosevelt, Eleanor, 69
Roosevelt, Franklin Delano, 14
Roosevelt, Theodore, 58
RSCC. *See* Republican Party, Republican Senatorial Campaign Committee
RSF. *See* Reporters without Borders
R Street Institute, 19
Rubenfeld, Jed: on diversity as one of America's great assets and defining characteristics, 172
Russia, 6–9, 142, 168; blitzing of foreign cyberspace, 7; disinformation campaign against the U.S., 121; probing hackers, 83; public-information campaigns to disgrace democracy, 72; and Trump

campaign, 159; use of bots to spread false news, 135
Ryan, Paul, 96, 168; contributions from outside congressional district, 52

Sabato, Larry J., 41
San Diego Supercomputer Center (SDSC) (University of California, San Diego), 131
Sandy Hook, 22
Santorum, Rick, 160
Scam PACs, 24
Schattschneider, E. E.: on modern democracy without parties, 29
Schoolhouse Rock, 96
Schumer, Chuck, 137; on the advent of Super PACs, 53
Schweitzer, Peter, 48
SCL Group, 129
SDSC. *See* San Diego Supercomputer Center
Select Committee on the Modernization of Congress: on partisan hunger to make congress more effective, 104–5
self-funded candidates, 52, 164
Senate Intelligence Committee, 135; on foreign interference in the 2016 election, 83
Senate Leadership Fund, 54
Senate Majority PAC, 54
separation of powers, 105
service learning, 155, 181
Sessions, Pete, 53
Shapiro, Ben: on politicians maintaining power and position, 147–48
Shapiro, Jesse, 39
Shays, Chris, 19
Sherman Antitrust Act, 178
Sheingate, Adam, 20
Shirky, Clay, 126
Shorenstein Center on the Press, Politics, and Public Policy (Harvard Kennedy School): on false news and propaganda, 137; on the increase in negative advertising, 118–19; the nature of online platforms, 135
slavery, 69, 87, 92; the evil of, 13; GOP platform opposing, 16

Smith, Margaret Chase, 69
social media, 8, 39, 73, 96, 105, 115, 119–20, 127–30, 133–40, 142, 145–46, 148, 158–59, 164; advertising bought on, 129; analysis on, 134; BuzzFeed, documents obtained by, 48; Facebook, 73, 129, 130, 133–37, 139–40, 142; Facebooker, 145; Instagram, 134, 140, 142; and Internet culture, 142; millennials and, 133, 145; misrepresentation of identities, 135; online disinhibition effect, 133; and Russian operatives, 135; Snapchat, 127, 132, 134, 139; sponsor of electronic town halls, 73; targeting of groups by demographic preferences, 129–30; weeding out and labeling deceptive content, 140; YouTube, 73, 127, 130, 136–37, 139, 142
social security, 41, 151; future insolvency of, 4
Society of Professional Journalists (SPJ), 122
Solar Winds, 83
"sore loser" laws, 66–68
Soros, George, 56; on funding political causes and enterprises, 26
South Korea, 13
Soviet Union, 28; collapse of, 45; and US nuclear missiles imbalance with, 37
spending bills, 93, 169; "continuing resolutions," 94, 180
SPJ. *See* Society of Professional Journalists
Stanford's Center on Democracy, Development, and the Rule of Law, 89
Stassen, Harold, 69
State Department, 8, 94, 158
Stein, Jill, 29, 70–71
Stelter, Brian, 118
Stevens, Ted, 100
Stevenson, Adlai, 69
Sumner, Charles, 92
Super PACs, 20, 22, 24, 26, 36, 38, 50, 52–55, 57, 85, 116, 136, 179; Independent expenditure-only political committees, 53
Supreme Court, 24, 57, 95, 98–99, 152; *Buckley v. Valeo* (1976), 52, 56–57; *Bush v. Gore*, 77, 79; *Citizens United v. FEC*, 24, 53, 56–57, 116; *McCutcheon v. FEC*, 56; on partisan districting, 64
Swift, Jonathan, 158

Tamaz, Roger, 45–46, 53
Taplin, Jonathan, 136
Tea Party, 28, 66, 96
technology, 6, 12, 56, 81, 104, 109, 121, 123, 125–26, 128, 131, 137–39, 141–42, 145–46, 151, 157–58, 165, 176, 180, 183; information and communications technologies (ICT), 125–27, 141–42, 138–39
Tenet, George J., 11
The Federalist (commonly known as the *Federalist Papers*), 62, 160; *Federalist No. 10*, 143;
Federalist No. 56, 62
third-party, 17, 42–43, 67–68, 70–71
tobacco industry: 1998 tobacco legislation, xiii
Tocqueville, Alexis de: *Democracy in America*, 9
Todd, Chuck: microtargeting and widening of the partisan divide, 131
trias politica, 87, 143; doctrine of, 61; American version of, 61
Trump-Biden Presidential Debate, 3
Trump, Donald J., 1–2, 9, 20, 27, 32, 37–38, 50, 63, 76, 86, 96, 99, 107–8, 110, 113, 116–19, 135, 137, 147–48, 153–54, 158–59, 165, 167–68; executive orders, 102–3, 161–62; presidential impeachments, 53–54, 76, 167–68; Super PACs, 26, 53–54; 2020 presidential elections, 3, 7, 24, 33, 35, 40, 72, 76, 80–82, 88
Tsongas, Niki, 19
Tsongas, Paul, 162–63
Tuccille, J. D.: on the delegitimization of political opponents, 166
tweeting, 115, 134, 137

UDHR. *See* Universal Declaration of Human Rights
Ukraine, 53–54
UnitedHealth Group, 23

Universal Declaration of Human Rights (UDHR), 75

unlimited contributions, 36

US Capitol, 2, 19, 21, 42, 48, 51, 92, 96, 100, 146, 165, 167; siege on, xi, 3, 83, 132

US Congress: approval rating of, 49, 63; districting, 62–65, 75, 88, 161; dysfunction of, xiii, xiv, xv, 2, 7, 12, 29–30, 99, 100, 178, 183; oversight of, 100–3, 140–41, 162, 169, 179; parliamentary procedure. *See* parliamentary procedure

US Constitution, 16, 61–62, 64-67, 157, 172–73, 175, 177, 181–82; amendment of, 88; Electoral College, 86–88; reference to the press, 107

US House of Representatives: congressional committees in, 100–102, 105, 139, 179; congressional debates, xii, 5, 42, 68–69, 72, 75, 91, 94, 165–66, 135, 138, 172, 180; congressional subcommittees in, 101–2; House Committee on Rules, 97; House Government Affairs Committee, 93; Select Committee on the Modernization of Congress, 104–5

US Senate, xi, xii, xiii, 8, 16, 19, 22–23, 41–42, 45–46, 48, 52, 56, 62–63, 65, 69, 76, 85, 87–88, 91–92, 95–99, 100–2, 138, 148, 162, 170, 179–80; "advice and consent," 93; Senate Committee on Commerce, Science, and Transportation, xiii, 138, 165; Senate Foreign Relations Committee, 167; Senate Intelligence Committee, 83, 135; Senate Select Committee on Intelligence, 7

Van Buren, Martin, 16, 32

Vandenberg, Arthur, 167

virtues, casualty of, 157; balance, 4, 11, 161–63, 65–66, 81, 96, 102, 107, 143, 171–74; civility and respect, 164–69; duty, x, xv, 4, 8, 70, 93, 140, 169–71, 180, 182, 185; honor, xi, xii, 1, 8, 83, 120, 157, 182; inclusion, 128, 163–64; substance, 164–66; trust, 159–69; truth and facts, 157–59

voting: Voluntary Voting System Guidelines (VVSG), 78; vote counting, 81–83; voter fraud, 3, 77, 79–80; voter identification (Voter ID); 79–80; voter participation, 77, 81–82, 85, 150; voter registration, 78, 83; voter suppression, 77, 79, 81, 88; voter turnout, 35, 66, 78, 80–81, 150, 164

Voting Rights Act (VRA), 63, 76

VVSG. *See* Volunteer Voting System Guidelines

Walters, Riley, 101

Walt, Stephen, 33–34

Wamp, Zach, 48

Washburn, Cadwallader, 92

Washington, George, 8, 10, 184; on factions and parties, 15

Washington Post, 114, 117; "Democracy Dies in Darkness," 107

Wasserman, David, 63

Watts, Clint: on Putin's disruption campaign, 7; on Russian bots, 135

weapons of mass destruction, 12

Webster, Steven, 36, 42, 116

White House, 3, 33, 103, 118, 167; campaign dollars and access to, 45–46

Whitehouse, Sheldon, 55

Wikileaks, 110, 118, 137

Woodrow Wilson National Fellowship Foundation, 152

World Bank: Worldwide Governance Indicators, 171

World War II (WWII), x, 14, 75, 109, 121, 167, 176, 183

World Wide Web (WWW), 7

Wyman, Kim, 80

Young, Andrew: on importance of truth, 159

Yovanovitch, Marie, 53

Zahn, Harry, 36–37

Zuckerberg, Mark, 83

About the Author

John Raidt has served as a professional staff member of three national commissions—the National Commission on Terrorist Attacks Upon the United States (9/11 Commission), the Commission on the National Guard and Reserves, and the Independent Commission on the Security Forces of Iraq—and as deputy to General James L. Jones, USMC (Ret.) Special Envoy for Middle East Regional Security. As a senior staff member in the US Senate, his roles included service as legislative director for US senator John McCain and chief of staff for the US Senate Committee on Commerce, Science and Transportation. Raidt holds a bachelor of arts in journalism from Arizona State University and a master of public administration from Harvard University's Kennedy School of Government. He is a nonresident senior fellow at the Atlantic Council and editorial contributor to *The Hill* newspaper in Washington, DC.

CPSIA information can be obtained
at www.ICGtesting.com
Printed in the USA
BVHW060621080122
625012BV00002B/6

9 781538 151259